TO BE
DISPOSED
BY
AUTHORITY

The Decline
and Rise of
British Industry

The Decline
and Rise of
British Industry

David Clutterbuck
and
Stuart Crainer

MERCURY BOOKS
Published by WH Allen & Co. Plc

Copyright © 1988 David Clutterbuck and Stuart Crainer

All rights reserved. No part of this publication may be
reproduced, stored in a retrieval system, or transmitted
in any form or by any means, electronic, mechanical,
photocopying, recording, or otherwise without the prior
permission of the publishers.

First published in 1988
by the Mercury Books Division of
WH Allen & Co. Plc
44 Hill Street, London W1X 8LB

Set in Meridien and Helvetica by
Phoenix Photosetting, Chatham, Kent
Printed and bound in Great Britain by
Mackays of Chatham PLC, Chatham, Kent

British Library Cataloguing in Publication Data

Clutterbuck, David, *1947–*
   The decline and rise of British industry.
   1. Great Britain. Manufacturing industries,
   1870–1986
   I. Title   II. Crainer, Stuart
   338.4'767'0941

   ISBN 1–85251–030–7

Foreword

Over the past hundred years there has probably been an average of one book or major report each year on the theme of 'Where did British industry go wrong?' There has always been room for theory-bashing and analysis of our failure to compete in specific sectors or across the board of industry. Self-flagellation, it seems, is a long-lasting national preoccupation.

Take the following quote from a government commission, speaking about German industrial competitors, who were 'in knowledge of markets, desire to meet the tastes of customers, determination and tenacity gaining ground on British business'. Or a quote from *The Times*, which shortly after wondered why we were 'constantly being told that they are supplanting us in everything'. Familiar sentiments? Yet those comments, collected in *Issues* magazine by an American academic, Professor Robert Hayes of Harvard Business School, are from a hundred years ago. Even at that time, informed observers were complaining that British industry simply didn't have its act together.

Faced with increasing competition from 'upstarts' such as Germany and the United States, British companies' primary competitive response was to ignore them in the hope they would go away. A naive assumption that customers would always recognise the superiority of the British product assured that even the thought of competitive response was unseemly. Hayes explains some of the events that led to loss of competitiveness in this way:

> Britain's Consul-General in Hamburg warned in 1888 that Britain's 'merchants and manufacturers must not despise small beginnings; if they allow their competitors to outdo them in small markets the total results may prove more disastrous than they could ever think possible'. But British manufacturers continued to concentrate on large existing markets and, worse, large orders. This allowed German industry gradually to build up its experience and scale to the point where a dozen years later it was competing head-to-head with Britain in the large markets as well.

He quotes a writer in 1933, who complained:

in England . . . industrial plant, at one time the 'workshop of the world', was growing antiquated in comparison with Germany's, whose 'businessmen were less given to putting the profits of industry into deer forests and hunting lodges . . . How could a people (who were) tenaciously individualistic, wedded to outworn ways of doing things, their manufacturing leadership passing, continue to even hold their own against another people of superior genius for methodical exactness and laborious energy, of better education, of higher talents in collective organisation of national economic life?

To stress that this is not a particularly British problem, Hayes uses the illustration of the watch industry, where arrogance and complacency has seen world market domination lost successively by the Germans, the French, the British and Swiss over five centuries. In each case, the very fact of dominance has bred a refusal to accept or implement new ideas, or to admit the threat from younger, more aggressive competitors.

If the topic of British industrial decline has been aired so often, then what more is there to say? Surely the arguments have all been heard before? In fairness, they have, in the most part. Just about everybody involved has managed to blame everyone else. The sole exception is the National Economic Development Council, which is not allowed (officially) to blame anybody, but is a convenient whipping boy for the frequent occasions when things go wrong.

In this book we set out to do something which has, to the best of our knowledge, not been done before. Almost everything useful that has been published is either fact and academic analysis, or opinion and anecdote based on perceptions of individuals or pressure groups. A great deal that is not very useful combines the two in an undifferentiated manner, particularly in party political treatises. So, in our study of British industry's past and future, we determined to differentiate as much as possible between perception and demonstrable fact. There are times when this becomes difficult (one man's statistic is another man's lie), but by and large we believe we have been successful. Our research method was as follows.

● *To establish perceptions* we wrote to the chief executives or chairmen of some 200 *Times* 1000 companies, asking them to detail what they considered to be the principal causes of Britain's industrial decline and what they considered should be done to stimulate its renaissance. About 25 per cent replied, many of them also sending copies of relevant speeches or articles they had written. We also interviewed in person the relevant spokesmen of the three major political parties, representatives of the major employers' organisations, trades union leaders and other industrial observers. A massive literature survey provided additional material, as did specific surveys of personnel managers on the themes of leadership and incentives.

● *To establish what was known in a quantifiable manner* we sought data from a wide spectrum of agencies and research institutions. Wherever possible, we tried to obtain statistical comparisons over several decades and/or with major competitor countries.

The resulting mass of information provided us with a number of recurrent themes – problems that were clearly perceived by some or all of the people we questioned as contributing to the decline of British industry. The data allowed us to make comparisons between these varying perceptions and between those perceptions and the facts available. Each chapter therefore deals with a theme or group of themes arising from the interviews, firstly by considering whether and how they contributed to the decline and secondly by looking both at what has been accomplished to overcome the problem (if indeed it was a problem) and at what still needs to be done.

We have tried – successfully we hope – not to impose our own opinions and perceptions beyond the minimum necessary to create a coherent structure. Even where a perception is regarded as accurate by all shades of opinion in our research, we have tried to avoid accepting it as such unless there is supporting evidence. Inevitably, many perceptions are not capable of *quantifiable* proof either way. How, for example, do you prove a decline in the quality of leadership without some form of personal testing duplicated exactly across the years? We are aware of only one instance of this happening, and that was not in the UK. In such cases, we are forced back upon anecdotal data and an admission that, while the perception is almost certainly correct, historians a few decades on may take a different view. For this reason, we believe, it is the consideration of what needs to be done in the future that counts, rather than the accuracy of our perception of the past.

Lord Young, when still Secretary of State for Employment, put forward the theory that our recent economic history has run in hundred-year cycles, each stimulated by a dramatic event. It took the loss of an empire – the rich American Colonies – in 1776 to generate the commercial impetus and strength of innovation that started the Industrial Revolution. Then, in 1876, Disraeli made Queen Victoria the Empress of India, setting in motion a swing of British society away from entrepreneurism towards administration. In 1976, as Young expresses it, 'We became a Third World country when we called in the International Monetary Fund.' The shock, like that of the loss of the colonies, has taken a number of years to make its impact felt in a resurgence of the entrepreneurial spirit.

It might be possible to project the theory further back. Certainly the golden years of the first Queen Elizabeth were noted for the emergence of the great merchant adventurers. They were followed by the less economically dynamic era of colonial consolidation, described in *A New History of England* by L C B Seaman in the following terms:

> Eighteenth-century imperialism was ruthless and deliberately fostered by government. It was pursued, not to spread civilisation, nor to convert the heathen; such considerations intruded into Victorian imperialism, rendering it self-conscious and hesitant. It was pursued as part of an expansionist commercial policy committed to denying foreigners (and colonists) as much of the world's trade as possible, so that England should have as large and exclusive a trading empire as could be obtained: an empire protected by trade discrimination against foreigners and colonists and by restrictions on their right to ship goods to and from England and its possessions. Policy, whether in war or peace, was directed to the crude accumulation of wealth. The balance of trade must always be in England's favour.

The essential *lack* of entrepreneurial spirit during this time was disguised in large part by British success in battle on both land and sea. The result of these wars was a constant expanding of empire. Yet at home, where the spoils of war could be seen in extravagant wealth among both aristocrats and traders, initiative and innovation were becoming less and less valued. As Seaman expresses it:

> Those who set the tone of eighteenth-century thinking were men for whom religion had been purged of enthusiasm, and whose universe, no longer magic and mysterious, was an ordered mechanism governed by unchanging laws fashioned by Newton and a Supreme Being . . . If to this were added the perfection of the English constitution and the success of its warfare and commerce, it is not surprising that it was fashionable to believe, either with grave piety or smug complacency, that everything was right, that nothing ought to be changed and that, indeed, nothing could be changed.

It was hardly surprising, then, that those seeking adventure or with ambition to make their fortune aimed to do so in the colonies, rather than at home.

The idea of economic cycles is not new, at least for the global economy and for specific mature trade sectors. The Russian economist Kondratieff put forward the theory in the 1920s that the economy of capitalist countries went through major long-term cycles of growth, each about forty-five years long. The first half of that period tended to have longer periods of boom than recession; the second half just the opposite. If Kondratieff is to be believed, then from about 1973 we have been in a global economic downswing, not due to end until the mid-1990s. The theory – like every other in economics – has its critics, but it has held up remarkably well so far. In effect, it gives Britain only a few years to get its act together in readiness to seize the expanded opportunities of the early twenty-first century.

If Lord Young is right, then maybe – just maybe – we are entering an era where we can concentrate on the future strongly enough to use the past for practical lessons rather than for recriminations. If that is indeed so, then the possibilities are substantial for British industry to create a new empire, based this time not on territories held by military might but upon markets gained and expanded through ingenuity, quality of product and service, and sheer determination to win. In the past thirty years the world economy has changed out of all recognition. In the next thirty, it is likely to change at least as much, perhaps more. As the newly industrialised countries, particularly China, assert their economic independence and muscle; as Europe (we hope) moves closer towards a real common market; as the United States either stages a dramatic comeback or continues its steady decline to the point where it is no longer the economic pivot of the world; as all these and other, unpredictable, changes occur, the opportunities for British industry at least equal the threats. If the UK can maintain its share of world trade at 10 per cent, in a greatly expanded world economy this would represent a significant but achievable goal. Indeed, it is our contention, from analysing all the hundreds of interviews, articles and reports that went into the writing of this book, that the most useful thing any government, of whatever political shade, could do right now is to begin preparations for just such an objective, involving all sides of industry in the assessment of what needs to be done and how it should be achieved. Planning thirty years ahead may seem ambitious, but our Japanese competitors do it routinely. The decision is at base remarkably simple: are we to be driven by tomorrow's global economy or are we going to be one of the countries driving it?

DAVID CLUTTERBUCK
STUART CRAINER

Nothing, least of all the business world, stands still. Change is fast and furious. Some aspects of industry covered in this book have been overtaken by recent developments. Training and education initiatives, for example, have been springing up with remarkable regularity. The unions are divided on the question of single union and no-strike agreements.

Success in the future, to a large extent, demands that companies in all sectors are as receptive to change as possible. Only then will the elements of the rise in British industry become long-term factors.

Contents

1

An Overview of Decline

'The low rate of investment led to a low rate of productivity in a world where our competitors were reinvesting or emerging nations were investing from scratch. A lot of our industries are still competing with depreciated technology.'
Malcolm Bruce MP, Social and Liberal Democrats Industry spokesman, 1987

'Higher inflation followed by higher unemployment. That is the history of the past twenty years.'
James Callaghan, then Prime Minister, at the Labour Party Conference, 1976

'The empire created the illusion that we didn't need other forms of activity. Though we were rentiers, we were not very successful at it. We ended up being exploited by the empire, which everyone assumed was a source of wealth. A lot of our talent went out there. Getting cocoa back was not a good exchange.'
Sir John Hoskyns, director general of the Institute of Directors, 1987

'Britain's relative decline has been underway since the 1860s or 1870s. In large part it was unavoidable and to be expected.'
Peter Jenkins in The Rebirth of Britain, *1982*

DECLINE BY STANDING STILL?

Decline is a relative term. In the 1930s, Gandhi was invited to visit Blackburn to see for himself the deprivation and misery caused by Indian textile tariffs.Gandhi concluded that the poverty and distress was indeed obvious, but in India, he pointed out, it was far worse. In the fifty years since then Britain has, in the eyes of some, continued to pay the price for its initial industrial success. The world's first industrial power has suffered a relative decline in industrial performance. The decline has not been restricted to industry, but it is perhaps in industry that the decline has had the most far-reaching social, economic and political effects.

Despite the decline in Britain's importance as an industrial nation, much of the period since the end of the Second World War has seen unparalleled prosperity. Between 1954 and 1977 British gross domestic product grew by the impressive figure of 75 per cent. In his book *The Politics of Recession*, published in 1985, R W Johnson postulated that there was a break-off point in Britain's industrial life: 'The post-war period ended in 1973 and a new era began. For all the difficulties of those times, the period from 1945 to 1973 is likely to be remembered as something of a golden age.'

The post-war era began with a mood of irrepressible optimism. After giving so much for Britain, people began to demand something in return. Their ideas on what the nation should provide for them became clarified, perhaps for the first time. The onus was on the nation to produce the fruits of victory.

Hope and victory made an intoxicating cocktail. Hopeful messages of a better world to come were consumed with relish. The Beveridge Plan sold over 800,000 copies and there was a flurry of optimistic projections for full employment – *Work for All, After the Blitz, The Plan for London* and Beveridge's *Full Employment in a Free Society*, published in November 1944. Ideas of what could and needed to be done flourished, among them, Keynes' managed capitalism, Abercrombie's regional and national planning and Butler's education for all. It was no longer a question of the limitations of what could be done, but how quickly it could be achieved. No one foresaw that full employment would lead to problems of its own.

In the years immediately following the war, the optimism seemed well-founded. Britain still had an empire and was the recipient of the largest slice of Marshall Aid (around £700 million). Full employment was never achieved, though at times it was amazingly close. Britain's gross domestic product easily outstripped those of France, West Germany and Japan. Amidst a pleasant home counties garden party in 1957 Harold Macmillan could assert that Britain had never had it so good. For a time this was true. It was too good to last.

Looking back from the late 1980s, this mood of optimism seems woefully naive. Britain's complacent air of invincibility has been blown away during the intervening years. The British Empire has disappeared and Britain's share of world trade has steadily declined. The defeated powers in the war, Japan and Germany, have emerged to cast Britain into the shade. West Germany now accounts for twice as much world trade, and Japan three times as much, as Britain. In the last twenty-five years, GDP has grown nearly twice as fast in West Germany as in Britain and four times as fast in Japan.

British business finance has been dragged along with the trend. According to the Bank of England's own figures, Japanese banks in London now hold nearly a quarter of all banking assets in Britain. Seven out of ten of the world's top banks are Japanese. Only two are American. None are British. From the optimistic note of the years immediately after 1945, commentators in the 1960s and 1970s voiced entirely different perspectives. In 1966 one painted a particularly bleak picture of post-war Britain:

> The present crisis is a general malady of the whole society, infrastructure and superstructure – not a sudden breakdown, but a slow, sickening entropy . . . The world-conquering entrepreneurs of the mid-nineteenth century had become flaccid administrators in the mid-twentieth century.

Britain's apparent industrial decline was assiduously charted and predicted by commentators of all political persuasions. In 1973, Lord Rothschild, head of the government think-tank, warned that by 1985 Britain would have half the GNP of West Germany and France and be on a par with Italy.

3

He was officially reprimanded. By 1974 the right-wing pressure group, Aims of Industry, maintained that the 'crisis' was there for all to see:

> Nobody who lives in Britain can have failed to notice that life seems to get nastier each year . . . Each winter brings the nightmare that industry will grind to a halt, homes will be blacked out and old people will freeze because coal is not being mined or electricity is not being generated.

With the pamphlet entitled *Reds Under the Bed?* it was clear where Aims of Industry apportioned blame. Others enthusiastically muscled in on identifying the causes and nature of decline. The contributory factors were diverse and complex. The debate continues today.

THE RELICS OF EMPIRE

The Churchillian bulldog spirit, Britain standing indomitably against its foes with an empire and a democratic tradition, is still revered today. British sympathies seem naturally to lie with the bullied underdog. The Falklands War was enthusiastically supported on these grounds. Mrs Thatcher, portrayed in popular cartoons as a new Churchill complete with cigar, encourages the continuation of this largely anachronistic image. The Conservative Party's 1987 election campaign made much of the Battle of Britain and used a bulldog as its mascot. The empire is long dead, but the relics of empire continue.

The persistence of this belief in Britain's prowess was revealed by a University of Loughborough survey in July 1987. It demonstrated that the British faith in the virtue of being British continues. The survey of forty-five international companies showed that British companies were increasingly aiming down market and that the major advantages they saw themselves as possessing were low prices, a 'traditional brand name' and 'being British'. A sales director commented typically: 'There is still a strong buy-British attitude in this country. Our customers know that we are an established British company – British-made is the benefit we are offering them.' Significantly, British companies see themselves as weaker on research and development capabilities, design, large-scale manufacturing, process development and cost reduction – many of the most important aspects of being internationally competitive.

4

In fact, for many years, the empire provided a shelter for many of the inadequacies of British industry. In the recession of the 1930s, Britain, Belgium, Holland, Portugal and France were able to fall back onto their colonial trading systems as the world economy buckled. For those without colonies the recession hit hard – in the United States unemployment hit 25 per cent and there were six million unemployed in Germany when Hitler took power. Even after the Second World War there was some American concern that Britain, with its troops in Germany, Greece, Persia, India, Egypt, Palestine and the Far East, was set on rebuilding its empire. This was not to be and with the gradual dismantling of the empire and the reductions in tariff barriers after the end of the war, Britain was exposed to international competition for the first time since the late nineteenth century.

AMATEUR ADMINISTRATORS

The recollections and views of most of our interviewees, and of many authors, can be summarised as follows. The vestiges of empire were disparate and often negative in their effect on industry. There was a sophisticated administrative system and a huge number of intelligent and highly trained people who had been reared to serve. Innovation and management were not major requirements for administering the outer reaches of Britain's domains.

It also left a tradition of amateurism, of muddling by secure in the knowledge of British superiority. The British Empire was a money-making venture, but it did not take commercial expertise to make money from it. As a result, industry, in the years after the war, was the haven of engineers, inventors and inspired amateurs. Even in the 1950s, the British car industry was dominated by gentlemen and pre-war autocrats like the Rootes family, Sir William Lyons at Jaguar and BMC's Leonard Lord. The aerospace industry was managed by engineers like Richard Fairey, Frederick Handley Page, Thomas Sopwith and Robert Blackburn, whose skills were not necessarily managerial.

The aims of industry seemed as much to be scientific advancement as wealth creation. 'It was no longer proper to create wealth; it was only proper to possess wealth,' says Peter Holmes of Shell. Making money from

5

industry was most readily identified with the textile barons of the north – chaps who liked to get their hands dirty and then allow their sons to inherit the family fortune. John Egan, chief executive of Jaguar, has reflected on the British attitude to wealth in *The New Elite*: 'I don't think working for a living has ever been highly regarded in this country. We have always preferred to inherit money or to have some strange knack like playing snooker. Even the Great Train Robbers got a grudging respect. To say that you have earned large sums of money has always brought a great deal of criticism.'

Lord Young, Secretary of State for Trade and Industry, believes there has been a distrust, even a contempt, for industrially-generated wealth. 'The prime reason for decline, no question about it, has been the anti-industry bias of the past hundred years,' he says.

The Institute of Directors is damning of the treatment of business leaders in its *A New Agenda for Business*. It believes that they were unnecessarily isolated:

> For most of the post-war period British business leaders were virtually second-class citizens. They made little contribution to public debate, and lacked the confidence needed to comment on government perform-ance. Locked into a declining economy by exchange controls, facing union demands they could afford neither to resist in the short-term nor concede in the long, buffeted by stop-go economic policies, they lived from year to year, increasingly concerned with risk avoidance and short-term liquidity.

Progress away from the imperial mentality has been slow. The empire left a range of intimidating structures and systems which applied to every aspect of life. The structures of empire, and enthusiastic adherence to them, have limited and slowed progress. The liking for structure and strict organisation persists. Says Sir Adrian Cadbury: 'As a country we suffer from structural arthritis. Our institutions are rigid and it requires a great deal of energy or substantial external shocks to bring about change.' The politician, Shirley Williams, has described the development of her own distaste for the institutions weaned on the free milk of the empire in her book *Politics Is For People*: 'I began to feel that Britain's problems were largely institutional, and that her institutions have bred attitudes, especi-ally class attitudes, that militate against a common effort to resolve her problems. The institutions, most of them intended to improve the quality of human life, have become bastions for particular interests against those of society as a whole.'

These institutional structures stretch throughout industry as well as British culture. Professor Tom Cannon of Stirling University has reflected on the commercial effects of rigidity through a study of the failure of the British munitions industry to adapt to change during the past 200 years. Why, he asks, did none of the cannon-makers of the Napoleonic era survive? The answer appears to be the strength of the network of relationships built up by the manufacturers and their customers, the military. The stronger the networks, the more stable the relationships. Because outsiders were excluded, there was 'no grit in the middle to stimulate change'. Change was eventually forced upon the military by new suppliers outside the network.

Tom Cannon has found strong parallels in other industries, such as railways, where relationships simply became too cosy. 'The British are very good at making and maintaining networks,' he says. 'Perhaps too good.' The liking for such structures and the ability to maintain them has been one of the elements in the 'structural arthritis' which Sir Adrian Cadbury complains of.

WE SHALL NOT BE MOVED

The structures of empire, in the opinion of many of our respondents, bred complacency. Says Sir John Hoskyns of the Institute of Directors: 'We started to take trade and commerce for granted rather than develop a distaste for them. Business is the most intellect and character testing activity you can engage in.' Yet, industry remained for many years an almost disreputable occupation. Even today, says the CBI's John Banham, 'Only 10 per cent of Oxford graduates go into business, compared with 20 per cent who go into accountancy.'

The view that the empire bred complacency perhaps originates from industries such as textiles where Britain's dominance has been broken. The ready-made market provided by the Commonwealth and the fact that Britain invented the business in the first place, produced seemingly blind confidence in the future. People were boundlessly confident. One economic sage commented: 'We've been making all the world's cotton cloth that matters for more years than I can tell, and we always shall.'

Initially there was ground for confidence. At the end of the war

Blackburn was still one of the world's largest loom exporters. But warnings were energetically ignored and during the following decades, confidence in the commercial power of the empire meant that the British textile industry failed to move with the times. It refined and improved a range of conventional shuttle machines rather than pursue new techniques from the continent. As the Swiss and others developed air jet, water jet and shuttleless looms, Britain was left behind. Between 1959 and 1967 the number of firms involved in textiles fell by 36 per cent. Whereas textiles accounted for a quarter of manufacturing employment in 1907, by 1970 their contribution had collapsed to less than a third of that amount. Worse was to follow.

LAME DUCKS

For many industries the fail-safe mechanism lay in the bottomless coffers of government. Some believe that reliance on governmental support was a contributory factor to the demise of some companies, even industries. 'In Britain, the industries which declined or died were primarily those that believed that they could operate with indifference to world competition and that their own attempted suicide would always be prevented, or at least delayed, by government action,' says I. G. Butler, chairman of the Cookson Group.

The by-product of this belief was that public funds could not be channelled into developing new business opportunities. This continues today. Says Simon Hornby, chairman of W H Smith and the Design Council: 'We continue to prop up declining industries rather than letting them go and investing in new industries much more quickly.'

The refusal to channel investment effectively or, in some cases, the decision not to invest at all meant that in many industries Britain set the early pace, only to be overhauled when fresh innovation and investment were required. 'Our mistake was to invest in booms,' says Merrick Taylor, managing director of Motor Panels.

Investing mainly in established successes often meant not investing in the future. W B Walker in *Technical Innovation and British Economic Performance*, published in 1980, surveys the historical background to British industrial decline and sadly concludes: 'The post-war decline of Britain as

8

a major trading nation no longer seems surprising. Low investment and productivity, the burden of public spending, rising imports are but symptoms of a more general failure to adjust to a new international order and to the emergence of more efficient business practices, or rather to adjust fast enough to keep pace with rapid changes occurring elsewhere in the world economy.'

There are many examples. In the early 1900s Dunlop was the first to manufacture rubber tyres in Japan. But in the 1970s Dunlop failed to move with the times and was eventually taken over by Sumitomo Rubber, which promptly worked out a strategy for improving manufacturing capability and performance. Now the company is back on the way to profitability, but Avon is now the sole British-owned tyre producer.

Similar stories of success followed by innovative lethargy can be found in many of Britain's industries. It was in 1952 that Nissan began to make the Austin A40 under licence. Thirty-four years later, the wheel had come full circle and Nissan was encouraged by the British government to begin production of its Bluebird model at a plant in northeast England. The Hillman Minx, another famous model of car, was also made under licence in Japan in the 1950s. Its originator, Rootes, no longer exists.

What happened in the British car industry can be seen as symptomatic of what happened in industry as a whole. From a position of preeminence, a combination of foreign competition, short-sighted management and disastrous industrial relations brought the industry to its knees. In 1950 Britain was the world's largest car exporter and at the forefront of design and innovation. By 1985 British car production was 14 per cent of Japan's and 25 per cent of West Germany's. The table on page 10 demonstrates the level of decline experienced by the British car industry in comparison with our European competitors.

THE DECLINE OF STEEL

The decline, and virtual demise, of the British steel industry was equally eye-catching. At one time an acerbic critic commented, 'The British industry turns out steel as a by-product, its main product being self-pity.' Calls to halt the 'decline' began many years before Ian MacGregor's massive rationalisation programme in the early 1980s. As early as 1920

Percentage shares of European car production, 1960–1982

	1960	1982
West Germany	35.2	38.5
France	22.8	28.5
Italy	11.6	13.3
Belgium	3.8	9.7
UK	26.2	9.1
Netherlands	0.4	0.9

(Source: P Dicken, *Global Shift*, 1986)

The Times was calling for replanning and restructuring of the industry. Even so, later schemes to improve the performance of the industry were short-term, involving the imposition of tariffs and the patching up of old works rather than the construction of new ones.

This trend was not limited to the steel industry. 'The immediate post-war period in the late 1940s and early 1950s was one of pent-up demand and a need for production that often forced companies to postpone introducing processes that reduced costs,' say industrialists Robert Malpas and Duncan Davies (*Link Up*, September 1986).

In fact, in the early 1960s, the steel industry was still profitable. Paradoxically, it was too profitable for its own good. Money was not reinvested in the industry and overmanning was accepted – the company could afford a few extra men and who knew when extra capacity might be demanded. Union issues were blissfully avoided as improvements in equipment led to little or no increase in productivity. The 296,000 British steelworkers in 1950 rose to 326,000 in 1960. In an industry of low wages, the number of workers seemed unimportant.

The introduction of the Llanwern and Ravenscraig strip mills in the early 1960s was the crucial development in the industry. It came just at a time when the problem of overproduction was being aired. Top management examined steel plants in Japan and their working practices, but the new mills had traditional demarcation lines. Overcapacity and constant overmanning gradually became too pressing to ignore. As late as 1973 the British Steel Corporation was optimistic and presented a ten-year development plan for the British steel industry. This involved spending £3,000 million to reshape the industry. The 1974 OPEC oil crisis killed the idea. Radical restructuring and decreases in manpower were inevitable – the 255,000 steelworkers of 1970 became 166,000 in 1980 and by 1983 this number had been more than halved to 70,000. Some of Britain's most famous steel mills, for example Ebbw Vale and Corby, were closed for good.

Decline was equally dramatic in other traditional areas of industrial strength. In machine tools Britain slumped from being the world's number three exporter in 1960 to holding a small 5 per cent slice of the market. The country's biggest producer, Alfred Herbert, was simply broken up. In textile machinery the decline was also rapid – between 1970 and the early 1980s, exports fell by 50 per cent. The British are now consigned to niche markets (very successfully in the case of companies like Mackie), lacking the size to make an impact as global competitive forces.

MANAGEMENT FLAWS

Amongst our interviewees, at least, the ritualistic laying of blame upon trade unions has been tempered by an admission that managers were at least as culpable. There is surprising agreement on all sides that managers in industries such as steel were simply not allowed to manage. Brian Budd, chairman of Monsanto, believes that laissez faire and amateur management, resulting from Britain's industrial dominance in the early part of the century, led companies to pay insufficient attention to product design and technical development. Limited skills in selling and marketing were further weakened by the ready market of the empire. The overall effect was to remove incentives to reduce costs through manufacturing efficiency.

In his *The Changing Anatomy of Britain*, Anthony Sampson comes to the conclusion: 'For two decades after the Second World War British companies were sitting ducks for the predators – sitting on valuable assets, with weak managers and passive shareholders.' This view is supported by a number of senior British businessmen. Simon Hornby of W H Smith comments: 'There was a complacency and apathy in many companies' owners or major shareholders.'

11

In the past decade, British post-war managers have been variously accused of lack of commitment, imagination and foresight. Sir Alex Jarratt, chairman of Smiths Industries, believes that the responsibility for overmanning is as much managers' as unions': 'Too much of our business has been bureaucratised. We have too often been over-managed and under-managed,' he says.

Criticism of the role played by managers also comes from Lewis Robertson, rescue chairman in a number of companies and chairman of Borthwicks. He argues, 'The prime cause has been bad management, bad selection of management, weak supervision of management by the board and indifference by investors to the composition of the board.'

THE VACUUM OF RESPONSIBILITY

A side effect of management's deficiencies is seen as the assumption by the unions of more power than was traditional or good for sound management. The failure of management allowed unions to exercise their industrial muscles. 'A large part of the reason for Britain's industrial decline has been a lack of commitment by management,' says Michael Peacock of Nurdin and Peacock, the wholesale grocers. 'This same lack of commitment has I believe in the past left a vacuum which was filled by troublemakers so that in more recent days even good management has had to struggle hard to restore good relationships with workforces.'

In some industries poor industrial relations certainly went hand in hand with decline. By the 1970s, the car industry was in a state of disarray faced with the twin problems of appalling industrial relations and chronic over-capacity. Strikes had become increasingly common. The 1956 strike at Austin Morris after 6,000 workers were laid off was followed by strikes in the 1960s against piece work. Ironically, the end of piece work in 1971 slowed down production. In 1970 Ford's British operation had 166 strikes. In West Germany, Ford lost a single day through a token strike. The glut of strikes combined with a lack of investment and many other factors meant that, by the end of the 1970s, all of the big British car makers (except for Ford) were losing money. In 1980 alone, British Leyland lost £536 million.

In the 1970s union power was at its peak. A writer in *The Director* observed in 1972: 'Britain is in the hands of the trade union bosses . . . who appear to have lost all sense of economic reality.' In his famous valediction to Britain in 1979 featured in *The Economist*, the diplomat Nicholas Henderson reflected on the advantages of French industrial relations over the British system: 'No French manager thinks twice about changing people's duties or their timetables . . . nor does he hesitate to install new machinery and instruct people that from Monday onwards they will be working at x instead of y.' It should be noted that the largest French union is Communist controlled. Henderson went on to bemoan the state of British society in general. 'How poor and unproud the British have become . . . It shows in the look of our towns . . . and in local amenities; it is painfully apparent in much of our railway system . . .'

THE BREAK-OFF POINT

Henderson was, in some ways, speaking in the middle of a storm. Britain remained inadequately prepared to cope with world recession. In *The Politics of Recession* R W Johnson reflected: 'Very little that we learnt about the world of 1945–73 has prepared us for an era of world recession, high inflation, mass unemployment, the chaos over currency and gold which has followed the collapse of Bretton Woods, the growing divide between Europe and the USA, the resurgence of the Cold War, the oil crisis, the world debt crisis and the rise of new economic power in the world.'

It was inflation that most irritated the public. Government controls were seen to be entirely inadequate. Shirley Williams, as Minister for Prices and Consumer Protection, led one of the most unsuccessful ministries of all time. Between January 1974 and December 1976, prices rose by 68 per cent.

Britain's inertia, caused by colonial and managerial shortsightedness as well as a catalogue of industrial relations troubles, was heightened by the oil crises of the 1970s. The problem was an international one. 'Over the past decade European economies have slipped from an era of sustained growth into near stagnation. The two oil shocks and the consequent decline in world trade showed up inherent structural weaknesses and pushed the continent into conditions of rising unemployment, loss of international market share, overcapacity and declining corporate profitability,' said John

13

Stopford and Charles Baden-Fuller of the London Business School in 1986.

Yet oil-dependent Japan survived higher energy costs, slower growth and the world trade crisis. It became more competitive as its companies altered their strategies. In Britain, blessed, perhaps saved, by North Sea oil, decline accelerated. In 1966 Britain had twelve of the world's 100 largest companies outside the United States. By 1986 this had been reduced to six: the Royal Dutch/Shell Group, BP, Unilever, ICI, British American Tobacco and Esso UK.

The gloomy predictions continued. In his *The Break Up of Britain*, published in 1977, Tom Nairn predicted 'rapidly accelerating backwardness, economic stagnation, social decay and cultural despair'. In many ways he was to be proved right. Reflecting on the previous ten years, Sir David Nickson, chairman of the CBI, observed in 1987, 'Though it now seems aeons ago, few managers who have survived those years will forget the circumstances: double-figured inflation, crippling industrial disputes, incessant bureaucratic interference with business, deep recession, high taxation, the stifling of enterprise and initiative. These were the factors which so demoralised us then.'

By 1983 industrial production was below the 1970 figure and when Margaret Thatcher came to power in 1979 she inherited a lower level of manufacturing output than Harold Wilson had done in 1974. Inflation was at 10 per cent, but it was to get far worse before any improvement could be sighted.

THE DECLINE IN COMPETITIVENESS

The cumulative effects of this cycle, and the many other factors involved, were a decrease in Britain's industrial competitiveness. In November 1983 the former director general of NEDC, Geoffrey Chandler, told *Management Today*, 'The immediate cause of decline can be simply stated: it is lack of competitiveness. The contributory factors have been underlined repeatedly by the NEDC and its offshoots. Poverty of design, quality and marketing, inadequate and inappropriate investment, restrictive or outdated work practices, sharp fluctuations in government policy towards industry – the list clearly illustrates the joint nature of the responsibility.'

Writing in the days before business gurus, Ovid noted in *The Art of Love*, 'A horse never runs so fast as when he has other horses to catch up and outpace.' Somehow, however, British industry proved reluctant to leave the starting gate. Competitiveness was, in many cases, sacrificed for corporate might. Size, it was thought, would insulate companies from the coldest economic chill. If Ovid had been around he might have recorded that Britain concentrated on increasing its stable rather than breeding thoroughbreds.

The competitiveness expert Michael Porter observed in *Competitive Advantage* in 1985, 'After several decades of vigorous expansion and prosperity, many firms lost sight of competitive advantage in their scramble for growth and pursuit of diversification. Today the importance of competitive advantage could hardly be greater.' In practice, competitiveness did not even figure in board level discussions in many companies. Where it was discussed, it was often only in terms of current domestic markets, rather than future global markets. It was a severe failing, stresses Alistair Graham, director of The Industrial Society. 'The link between competitiveness and employment should be a regular item on every boardroom agenda and in every collective bargaining session.'

Britain's technological competitiveness has also increasingly been doubted. Since the 1960s, Britain's technological prominence has waned – this is especially true in the electronics and chemical industries and is discussed further in the chapters on Education and on Research and Development.

ACCELERATING BACKWARDNESS

The effects of being uncompetitive have been felt like an icy wind throughout British industry. Britain's share of world manufacturing trade has slumped from around 15 per cent in 1964 to under 8 per cent in 1986. In November 1982, the Treasury reported a dismal situation:

> Over the past five years or so, and partly reflecting the poor level of competitiveness, UK industry has lost share in both overseas and domestic markets. Between 1977 and the first half of 1982, the volume of world trade rose by a total of about 18 per cent, while UK exports of

15

manufactures were unchanged. In the domestic economy over the same period, the demand for manufactures changed very little; but import volumes rose 40 per cent, while output of the UK manufacturing sector fell 14 per cent.

Import penetration had been rising for decades beforehand, but it was not until mid-1982 that Britain became a net importer of manufactures. The economic equation is apparently simple: oil exports financed increased manufacturing imports. In 1986 Britain's deficit in manufactures was £8 billion. In 1970 British imports of manufactures were 62 per cent of manufactured exports. Now, the import-export ratio is over 115 per cent. The demand for imported goods is huge – a third of British clothing, two thirds of consumer electronics and two thirds of toys are foreign made. The decline in manufacturing jobs has been immense. The Scottish TUC estimates that Scotland has lost a third of its manufacturing jobs since 1979. Even as late as 1986, Britain was losing 14,000 manufacturing jobs each month.

Decline of manufacturing jobs, 1979–1986

Manufacturing jobs	per cent
UK	−28
Japan	+4.9
United States	−2
Canada	−1.4
West Germany	−8.5
Italy	−9.4

(Source: Department of Employment)

No other country has met with such a massive decrease in manufacturing employment. The gains in service industries have not compensated.

The arguments over the merits of service industries centre around the inability to regenerate the jobs lost from manufacturing. John Smith, the

The employed labour force (number of employed in thousands)

	June 1979	June 1986	Percentage change
Manufacturing	7,127	5,162	−28
Services	13,205	14,074	+6.6
Other	2,237	1,819	−18.7
Total	22,639	21,055	−7
Self-employed	1,824	2,664	+46
Armed Forces	314	323	+2.9
Employed labour force	24,777	24,042	−3

(Source: Department of Employment)

Labour Party's economic affairs spokesman, sees a strong, growing manufacturing industry as essential. 'Services are less internationally tradeable than manufactured goods by five to one, according to the House of Lords Select Committee on Overseas Trade. You have to have a strong manufacturing base if you are to maintain a positive balance of payments. Our industrial competitors are not abandoning manufacturing capacity,' he says. Smith believes that the real decline in manufacturing has been disguised. 'The decline of British manufacturing is best shown by the decline of the balance of trade in manufactured goods. In 1979, there was a surplus of nearly £5 billion. In 1986, there was a deficit of £8 billion. It has been masked in trade balance terms by North Sea oil. Instead of being used to re-equip and modernise industry it has been used to pay for unemployment.'

Sir Adrian Cadbury also draws attention to the link between North Sea oil and manufacturing decline: 'What has happened in reality is that employment in manufacturing industry in Britain has declined rapidly, while our more aggressive competitors have maintained or increased employment in manufacturing. I accept, of course, the basic swing from manufacturing to service industries in all advanced economies and also the degree to which we were overmanned in this country. The argument, which does not stand up, is that manufacturing must shrink, because of oil.'

17

Alistair Graham of The Industrial Society is equally pessimistic about the capacity of service industries to create enough jobs. 'We have not yet won the argument between manufacturing and services. Services still account for only 12 per cent of world trade. All the evidence suggests that the service sector won't provide the jobs we need for the future.'

As we write, manufacturing output is still below 1973 levels. Nevertheless, the Conservative Party continues to have faith in the ability of service industries to generate wealth. It sees the move from manufacturing to service industries as a revolution. Says Lord Young: 'The argument over manufacturing versus services is futile. I suspect there was an equal amount of argument when we moved off the land 200 years ago. The important thing is to create more wealth – from whatever sector.'

Whilst the creation of wealth will remain the priority, the problem of unemployment will not disappear. Throughout this period, the dream of full employment has finally been put to rest. Indeed, high levels of unemployment are anticipated for the future. Unemployment levels which would not long ago have brought talk of revolution are now almost acceptable (though few would admit to this). In 1972 unemployment breached a million; it reached two million in 1981 and three million in 1982. The then Chancellor, Dennis Healey, was already warning in 1975 of the perils ahead. 'We must reverse the process of de-industrialisation – of a steady loss of jobs and factory capacity year after year.' The process continued, only slightly improved by new methods of calculating the numbers unemployed.

Unemployment

	Official monthly averages		Official monthly averages
1979	1,295,700	1984	3,159,800
1980	1,664,900	1985	3,271,000
1981	2,250,400	1986	3,289,100
1982	2,916,900	1987	2,953,350
1983	3,104,700		

(Source: Department of Employment)

While the overall level of unemployment appears to have stabilised in 1987, appears to be dropping back in 1988, and will be helped considerably in the next decade by demographic factors, the decline in manufacturing jobs does not appear to have been halted.

The social, economic and psychological effects of long-term unemployment are impossible to gauge. It has probably contributed to social unrest, but its effects on industrial skills may be of even greater importance. The financial cost has been immense. In 1986–7 alone the government estimated that £5.6 billion would be paid out in unemployment and supplementary benefits.

In the opinion of some, Britain has been irrefutably altered since 1945, its industrial dominance diminishing decade by decade. Martin Wiener, in his *English Culture and the Decline of the Industrial Spirit 1850–1980*, provides a startling image of post-war Britain. 'Having steered clear of the rocks of political turmoil or military defeat, the British found themselves becalmed in an economic Sargasso Sea.'

American academic, Dean Henry Rosovsky of Harvard Business School has dated the start of Britain's decline to 1880, but believes that it wasn't appreciated until after 1918. Said Rosovsky, writing in 1980 in *Atlantic Monthly*, 'Most economic historians agree that Britain's climacteric occurred about a hundred years ago, but this fact did not really become a matter of public concern until after World War One . . . In my opinion, the principal factors were internal and human, and therefore avoidable. British entrepreneurship had become flabby; growth industries and new technology were not pursued with sufficient vigour; technical education and science were lagging; the government–business relationship was not one of mutual support.'

By 1982, Ralf Dahrendorf, former director of the London School of Economics, painted an even gloomier picture.

It must be said in all brutality: there is no indication whatsoever of unemployment being reduced significantly, inflation abating seriously, and above all of the economy of Britain returning to the growth trail. Britain not only shares the condition of the rest of the OECD world, which is one of considerable difficulties in the face of economic decline, but it has eroded its own potential for improvement to a frightening extent. There is little or no chance of Britain being significantly better off at the end of the century than it was in the 1960s, and a good chance that the country as a whole, and many individuals in it, will be worse off.

19

CONCLUSION

The picture emerges of a nation declining in manufacturing terms from a variety of causes ranging from simple indifference to lack of investment and a loss of the will to win. John Smith identifies a simpler reason: 'If there is an English disease it is too great a preoccupation with history. The causes of our decline are less important than what we can learn from our competitors now.' There is much to be said for this view. However, we believe that the lessons of recent decades can be used to identify where we most urgently need to learn from our competitors and to innovate beyond their current performance. In the following chapters we will attempt to look at some of these factors and the lessons that can and are being learnt elsewhere.

2

The Decline of Industrial Relations

'With the timidity and incompetence of management growing . . . union decisions became regarded by the non-active union member with almost the sanctity of law. Unions were blamed for exercising power they never really possessed and which has been quickly lost as soon as it received any real challenge.'
Lord Chapple, 1987

'Our problem was that we went in for unofficial wildcat strikes as a means of preventing improvements in productivity. This made management very wary of going in for radical changes.'
Michael Ivens of Aims of Industry, 1987

'Trade unions had no regard to the economic realities and the changes that were going on in the world; restrictive practices abounded and strikes proliferated.'
R W Adam, chairman of London and Scottish Marine Oil, 1987

'The involvement of all employees in the innovation process not only smooths that process but enhances it. Innovative ideas are not the prerogative of management.'
CBI Vision 2010 Group, 1986

THE ROAD TO DISCONTENT

Before venturing too deeply into the opinions of our various commentators, it is worthwhile making a short historical review of the industrial relations climate and the role of trade unions in the past forty years, and particularly in the past twenty years, when the chickens came home to roost. The 1970s were the apotheosis of the trade union movement. Vested with power and industrial clout it brought down Edward Heath's government and dictated the terms for the Labour governments of Harold Wilson and James Callaghan. 'Industrial managers and unionists concentrated on civil warfare. It was like arguing about deckchair arrangements on the *Titanic*!' says one of the executives in our survey. Strikes, extremists, walk-outs, sit-ins, militant shop stewards, free collective bargaining and incomes policy; this was the vocabulary of the time, or at least of the media of the time. The faces of Jimmy Reid on Clydeside or Derek Robinson at British Leyland became famous. Their hectoring politics briefly elevated them from the soap box to the position of power brokers.

For many, the trade unions represented industrial anarchy with demands and beliefs which flatly contradicted commercial rationale or even common sense. A TUC spokesman admits, 'In the 1970s we were not equipped to take on the responsibility.' It was clear that union leaders like Jack Jones and Hugh Scanlon were intent on avenging the injustices and inequality of the 1920s and 1930s. With burgeoning membership (unions usually benefit from periods of inflation as they offer an element of security to employees) the effects were dramatic. Dennis Barnes and Eileen Reid in their book published in 1980, *Government and Trade Unions*, observed, 'In the last ten years three successive prime ministers have been prevented by the industrial and political power of the unions from pursuing policies they declared essential to the national interest. All lost the elections which followed the defeat of their policies.'

Many industrialists believe the unions were misdirecting their energy. Said BP chairman Sir Peter Walters in a June 1984 lecture, 'If the trade unions concentrate more upon the role of representing their members, and less upon policy formulation for the corridors of power, I am sure that relations between management and unions would enter a more productive phase.'

Among our survey respondents, criticism of industrial relations was widespread. One executive commented, 'The practice of over-employing and the general industrial relations climate prevented organisations from being lean and effective.' Another defends the role of management: 'I do not believe British companies have ever lacked a supply of executives who could display creativity or who were dedicated and hard working. The industrial relations climate in the UK offered such a barrier to the implementation of good ideas that it seemed that Britain lacked these things.'

The unions had, to some extent, outgrown their traditional roles of fighting for higher wages and improving working conditions. The social historians Sidney and Beatrice Webb's definition of a trade union describes its traditional function: 'A trade union, as we understand the term, is a continuous association of wage earners for the purpose of maintaining or improving the conditions of their working lives.' In the 1960s and 1970s the unions attempted, and succeeded in many cases, in broadening their activities and increasing their powers.

Symptomatic of this was the Winter of Discontent, the stream of wage strikes in the winter of 1978–9 which undermined the already tenuous hold of the Callaghan government. Nevertheless, Prime Minister Callaghan found time to goad the opposition leader, Margaret Thatcher, on the perils of over-reaction. 'You don't want to believe all those things you read in the newspapers about crisis and upheavals and the end of civilisation as we know it. Dearie me, not at all.' As the winter drew on, jocularity was less in evidence.

STRIKES AND PRODUCTIVITY

Strikes and industrial discontent, once known as the 'British disease', are probably the most trumpeted of the reasons people ascribe to Britain's industrial decline. Sir John Hoskyns of the Institute of Directors doesn't mince his words on the issue. 'There was a lot of syndicalist power play, pol-itically motivated wrecking or sheer ignorance,' he says. 'It has a lot to do with a deeply ingrained lack of understanding of the economic process.' A survey respondent adds, 'Productivity became a dirty word and change of any sort became an opportunity for disagreement.'

Leading unionists are prepared, in hindsight, to take some of the blame. John Lyons, general secretary of the Engineers' and Managers' Associa-tion, now observes, 'The decline of the 1970s was down to the unions.' The effect of union power, in the opinion of many we talked to, was to undermine the role of management. Managers, cowed by union demands, found themselves with no escape from the pressure of strike threats and pay demands. Union power hit first at management; then, however, it swung against the unions themselves.

But what were the root causes of the so-called British disease and what was its extent and its effect on industry? Comparing days lost through industrial disputes with those lost in France and West Germany demon-strates its disastrous growth in Britain.

Days lost in industrial disputes (in thousands)

	1957	1977
Britain	6,012	10,142
France	3,506	2,434
West Germany	69	86

(Source: Nicholas Henderson, *Channels and Tunnels*, 1987)

The Institute of Directors has identified the British attitude to pay increases as a crucial factor in the creation of the British disease. In *A New Agenda for Business* the Institute says, 'The appalling post-war record of industrial relations in British business with all its consequences in low productivity and a rigid labour market stemmed from a single assumption, unquestioned by both management and unions: that the price paid for work should, unlike other prices, be fixed on a collective basis.'

The principle that pay increases had to be earned all but disappeared in the 1970s as people became accustomed to earning more each year. Dr

David Grieves, personnel and social policy managing director at British Steel, worked in an industry particularly afflicted by ever rising labour costs. 'During the periods of successive government incomes policy and the growing inflation of the late 1960s and early 1970s, British unions developed an expectation that nationally negotiated wage increases would flow automatically year by year.' In the steel industry this led to labour costs forming a huge 30 per cent of total costs.

The tendency towards national negotiations over pay in some of Britain's largest industries meant that huge numbers of variables were quibbled over. 'The outstanding characteristics of the national pay structure is the rigidity of its relationships,' says G G C Routh in his *Occupation and Pay 1906–60*. This rigidity meant that different unions anxiously argued the case for their members whilst management found itself increasingly bound to accept that wage rises were inevitable.

The issue of whether people doing the same job in different companies under differing circumstances should earn the same amount of money is complex and probably irresolvable. Making fair comparisons between similar jobs within the same firm has proved difficult enough, if the effects of recent 'equal value' legislation are an indication. In practice, it was a recipe for chaos with complicated wage negotiations and perpetual calls for parity. Increasing inflation made the scenario even more demanding for managers.

The effects of the resulting industrial action were disastrous. Relative productivity sank miserably as that of other countries improved. In the car industry the effects were dramatic. At Ford's Halewood plant, productivity was 50 per cent lower than West German factories producing the same product. Similarly, in 1980 Peugeot Talbot's Ryton plant near Coventry was 30 per cent less efficient than similar French plants. Only 85

Output per person employed: average annual percentage increase

	1960–68	1968–73	1973–79
Britain	2.7	3.0	1.3
France	4.9	4.7	2.8
West Germany	4.2	4.1	2.9

(Source: Nicholas Henderson, *Channels and Tunnels*, 1987)

per cent of the plant's scheduled production was achieved. A 1973 report by a government think tank showed that the American car industry was three times as productive as the British.

Productivity levels in British manufacturing industry have remained internationally uncompetitive. Productivity did increase, but at a slower rate than for our competitors. (The rate of increase decreased in most countries, of course, as a result of the post-1973 depression.)

By 1986, Britain's productivity and labour costs compared unfavourably with all its major competitors. Taking Britain as a base the table below demonstrates the difference:

Labour productivity and labour costs in manufacturing in 1986

	labour productivity	labour costs
Belgium	154	97
France	184	66
West Germany	178	97
Italy	155	82
Japan	176	73
Netherlands	205	76
Britain	100	100
United States	267	60

(Source: G F Ray 'Labour Costs in Manufacturing', *National Institute Economic Review*, May 1987. Provisional estimates)

It should not be assumed, however, that the reasons for falling productivity are solely, or even primarily, a matter of poor industrial relations. Our commentators on all sides of industry agree that other factors, such as failure to invest in state-of-the-art equipment, were equal or greater contributing factors.

Not mentioned by any of the people we surveyed, yet we feel worth investigating in passing, is the impact that poor industrial relations had upon willingness to experiment. The concept of semi-autonomous work groups – where operators learn each other's skills and work as a team, with the supervisor acting more as a guide and counsellor than a boss, originated in the UK, at the Tavistock Institute. Takers in Britain were few and far between. Our Scandinavian competitors, however, seized and developed the idea rapidly. Employers' organisations in those countries believe that the flexibility of operation and the improvement in shop-floor-management relations that resulted have been significant in maintaining productivity advances. Another country that took close note was Japan. It is sad that the quality circles concept so many companies are importing from Japan owes its origins in part to ideas developed in the UK which we were unable to apply because of failures in our own industrial relations climate.

THE DECLINE OF TRADE UNIONS

Most of our commentators agree that the public's growing disapproval of mass strike action (that's not to say that managers were too happy either) and unemployment coupled with a growing realisation of its effects on industry has played a part in the decline in trade union membership. In 1979, trade union membership in Britain stood at just over 12 million. By 1988 it had been reduced to a little over 9 million. For the first time since the Second World War less than half of the working population belongs to a union. The years following the Winter of Discontent have seen the unions decline in importance as a political issue and, perhaps, as a political force. The public's interest has waned – in 1979, prior to the election, it was reported that 73 per cent of the electorate saw trade union power as the most important problem facing the government; at the 1987 election only 1 per cent thought this was the case. The fall in public interest is not simply a whim, but an international phenomenon.

The decline in union power and importance is certainly not restricted to Britain (in the same way as the strikes and disquiet of the 1970s were not). In America, only 18 per cent of the workforce now belongs to a union. In France, union officials have found themselves increasingly out of step with their conservative members and less than 10 per cent of the workforce is now unionised. Australian unions are small, splintered and underfunded, while West German unions admit they have lost some members as a result of unemployment and worker disillusionment. Franz

Membership of the ten largest unions

	1986	1985	change	percentage
TGWU	1,377,944	1,434,005	−56,061	−3.9
AUEW	857,559	974,904	−117,345	−12
GMBU	814,084	839,920	−25,836	−3.1
NALGO	750,430	752,131	−1,701	−0.2
NUPE	657,633	663,776	−6,143	−0.9
ASTMS	390,000	390,000	—	—
USDAW	381,984	385,455	−3,471	−1
EETPU	336,155	347,635	−11,480	−3.3
UCATT	249,485	248,693	+792	+0.3
TASS	241,000	251,254	−10,254	−4.1

(Source: TUC)

Steinkuehler, leader of the West German metalworkers' union, sums up the German situation, though his comments have international application: 'In the 1980s unions have been on the defensive, ideologically, politically and socially.' In fact, only in West Germany and Sweden has union membership remained relatively stable in recent years. In Japan, membership is generally restricted to male workers in large corporations – women and part-time workers are largely ignored. The company-orientated unions in Japan are inextricably linked with company performance – any downturn in the Japanese economy will soon be reflected in union membership.

Many of these problems have also been experienced in Britain. Publicly, however, the blame for the fall in membership has been attributed chiefly to increased unemployment. Whilst unemployment has undoubtedly cost many members, the potential membership of the unions has, in fact, increased in size since 1979 as the working population grew by more than one million in 1985 and 1986 alone to reach 28 million.

The failure of trade unions to take advantage of the growth in their potential markets has meant that they are increasingly seen – and not only by our industrialists – as the Aunt Sally of British politics: large, bumbling and old-fashioned. Attempts at instigating change have been conspicuously unsuccessful. The *In Place of Strife* plans submitted to the 1974 Labour Government and the Bullock Commission's attempts to bring the unions into the boardroom both collapsed. Now, the director of The Industrial Society, Alistair Graham, has caustically noted that the unions are 'having to run very fast to decline gracefully'.

TRADITIONAL ROLES

Unions appear to enjoy tradition and history, the concept of the working class struggle, bosses against workers. Without this framework the unions have found it difficult to assert a new identity. Traditional union leaders like Jimmy Knapp of the National Union of Railwaymen and Arthur Scargill of the National Union of Mineworkers remain important and influential figures in the trade union movement. But they are the old voices of unionism, staunch left-wingers from the industrial heartlands. Their position of power, heavy industry, is no longer the bedrock of union membership nor, indeed, of the economy. Both the NUR and NUM have conspicuously failed to prevent huge redundancies in their industries: in consequence, NUM membership has fallen from a massive 700,000 in 1945 to less than 100,000 in 1987. Shipbuilding, steel, coalmining and the railway industry have all been turned from industrial monsters with strong influential unions into relatively tame victims of rationalisation. Working practices within heavy industry were also once a cornerstone of union power. In recent years, however, demarcation and restrictive working practices within these industries have become regarded as increasingly anachronistic.

The bias within the unions towards activism rather than representation can be exaggerated. Nevertheless, union officials were traditionally selected on political criteria rather than their ability to provide effective representation. The call of the 1980s, however, is not for class awareness, but for economic reality, not for craftsmen or specialists, but for flexible multi-skilled workers in service rather than manufacturing industries. Union attachment to the past still continues according to some observers. Says Peter Wild of the Association of Independent Businesses: 'Few trade unions are sufficiently forward thinking to embrace ideas of democracy,

29

or to come to terms with the need for more radical reform and change of direction to meet the needs of the future.' An executive in our survey adds, 'With few exceptions, trade union leaders have failed to find a constructive alternative to the policy of opposing all change.'

In his *The European Executive* in 1962, David Granick observed the malaise affecting British unions: 'It is more important to have union officials who truly belong to the working class, in every possible fashion, than those who might be more effective in handling grievances and wage claims . . . Morality takes precedent above expediency.'

There has been a tremendous growth in non-unionised companies, particularly in the high technology fields. A survey of Scottish companies revealed that employment grew by 90 per cent in non-unionised companies in the electronics industry (1983–7) whilst only by 30 per cent in unionised plants. People no longer seem to find unions essential. This development may, to some extent, be a result of the elimination of many of the traditional class barriers. There is now a far larger affluent middle class than ever before. Increased wealth has eroded the traditional centres of union membership in the same way as it has affected the popularity of the Labour Party. Some 40 per cent of Britons are now regarded as middle class, yet many unions have failed to abandon their working class, cloth cap image. For the first time the number of shareholders, over 8 million, now rivals the number of union members.

As a by-product of this affluence there has been a growth in the numbers of women and part-time workers. Together with the young, these big sectors of working society have been largely isolated from the union movement. The idea of unions as craft-orientated groups whose membership should be greatly valued – and therefore restricted – continues inside many of the unions, if not outside them.

DETACHED FROM MEMBERS

Clearly reflected in many of the views we gathered was that the unions had grown detached from their members and society. 'Trade union leaders have become rather arrogant and proud,' Lord Murray, the former TUC general secretary, has observed. 'We haven't listened carefully enough to what our members were trying to tell us.'

John Lyons, general secretary of the Engineers' and Managers' Association, believes that the unions developed 'an attitude of near invincibility born out of overconfidence and an associated failure to examine what the economic and political facts of life really were towards the end of the 1970s. Eventually this developed into arrogance.'

The scenes of the 1970s where union leaders juggled with millions of votes at Labour Party conferences drew attention to the inadequacies of union democracy. One union leader recalls the time he was going to be introduced to Harold Wilson only to be told to wait because 'Harold's talking to two million votes'. The Healey-Benn contest for the Labour Party deputy leadership was perhaps the finest example of such farces. Constitutional change was, in many respects, inevitable.

One chief executive commented, 'Union leaders should never forget that unions are there to protect their members. They had become too politicised and forgot their raison d'etre.' Even so, the increased isolation of unions from the mainstream of popular demands has meant that their opposition to Conservative Party legislation since 1979 has been impotent. The 1980 and 1982 Employment Acts and the 1984 Trade Union Act have reduced union powers. The next stage in the government's legislation is also unlikely to be stopped, though in this case opposition comes from the CBI and Institute of Directors as well as the TUC. Norman Fowler, the Employment Secretary, has said that the Employment Acts were intended to 'adjust the balance of power'. Other policies such as lower taxes, wider home ownership and privatisation have also eroded union support. Members have come to realise how little the unions, despite their power, have been able to achieve.

Faced with such problems, the conventional role of the unions is being reassessed. But 'getting out of the tramlines of tradition is not easy', as Bill Jordan of the AUEW has said.

In the opinion of some of our respondents the 'them and us' attitude persists. Observers on all sides see the unions as having failed to tackle the hierarchical organisation of industry and their own internal workings. They have, instead, reinforced many of the prejudices. Management's and employees' pay packages are still dealt with separately and attempts at tackling the complexities of status have been entirely unsuccessful. Harmonisation expert, Dr Alan Arthurs of Bath University says, 'The difficulties and costs of changing an existing stratified workplace to single status have daunted most British companies who have given it serious consideration.'

The dream of worker participation has, for the most part, remained a

31

dream. Indeed the Bullock Report's recommendations for increased worker participation in some ways caught the unions on the hop. As a result of long-held prejudices both on the part of many union stalwarts, who feared that their authority could be undermined and who were in any case opposed to 'doing management's job for them', and on the part of managers fearful of loss of what little control they believed they still had, the Bullock Report was generally ignored. According to Arthurs, the prime cause is the continuation of hierarchies and what he calls 'the strong self-image of the British working class', which has contributed greatly to the lack of fair or innovative schemes to improve participation during the last few decades.

The threat of statutory employee participation raised by the EEC Fifth Directive did prompt more companies to take an interest. But the idea has progressed only as far as the 1982 Employment Act which stipulated that all companies with more than 250 employees include a statement on employee involvement in their annual report.

In all the discussion and debate on these issues, it is easy to forget that industrial relations is a two-sided affair. Even within the most strike-ridden industries, there were during the 1950s, 1960s and 1970s companies with enviable industrial relations records. In shipbuilding, for example, Bristol Channel Ship Repairers was an oasis of calm in a maelstrom of decline and conflict. Management and unions worked together to secure orders, to resolve operating problems and educate the employees in the realities of business survival. At one stage, management and unions met for the annual wage negotiations to discover that only a few pence a week separated their calculations of a fair increase. The amount was split in two. End of negotiations. Sadly, BCSR was swallowed up in a late rationalisation of the British shipbuilding industry. As we shall see in the chapter on leadership, senior managers over the past forty years by and large received the unions they deserved. As Sir Peter Walters of BP said in 1984, 'Many managers have all but ignored their personal responsibility to involve the workforce.'

The lack of opportunity for employees to become actively involved in their own companies may well have been a contributory factor to poor industrial relations in some industries. Even now, British commitment to participation is half-hearted in the eyes of some. Dr Greg Bamber of Durham University Business School claimed in his 1987 report *International and Comparative Industrial Relations*, 'Britain stands out as a country which provides its workers with very few chances of participating in helping to run their company.'

The fundamental nature of the problem and its repercussions were forcibly put by a leading Japanese industrialist in *International Management*:

You European entrepreneurs are going to lose out to us. You will lose because defeat is already in your minds. You are thoroughly convinced that competitive companies are made up of people on top who think, and people below who carry out instructions. Even those of you who sometimes say the opposite believe this. But we Japanese . . . are now convinced that in a world of greater uncertainty, turbulence, aggressiveness, a company's chances of survival are so tenuous that all its resources must be used, down to the most modest contributor . . . To you, management is the art of conveying management's ideas down to the workers. Our approach is to engage the intelligence of all employees in the service of a specific mission. In short, the reverse of your method.

3

The Rise of Industrial Relations

'British trade unions have an absolutely crucial role to play in our country's affairs as far ahead as one can see. Whether we are ignored by governments or courted by them is largely in our own hands. If we play our part in seeking to unite this country instead of dividing it, governments will certainly want to listen to us again, because we shall be speaking with the authority of widespread support, not only among our own members, but in Britain at large.'
John Lyons, general secretary of the Engineers' and Managers' Association, 1987

'We believe in tomorrow and our employees being part of it. Involvement is in the best interests of everyone.'
Brian Nelson, chief executive of H P Bulmer, 1987

'Anyone who ignores the ability of the whole workforce to contribute to prosperity by adopting high-handed and inflexible attitudes, is bound in the long term to succumb to those competitors who are already anticipating the changes.'
Bryan Stevens, director, Industrial Participation Association, 1987

'The media projection of the union-employer relationship is a travesty of the truth.'
Gavin Laird, general secretary, AUEW, 1986

TALKING SHOP

One of the results of our survey that gave us most pleasure was the clear opinion among most observers on all sides – industrialists, union leaders and politicians – that the days of confrontational industrial relations, if not completely over, were clearly numbered. In particular, they saw a 'new realism' among both unions and management. This has been somewhat dented by the wrangles early in the 1980s over single-union deals, but there appears to be a continuing confidence that the underlying trend is away from the traditional class warfare style of industrial relations.

The traditional them-and-us attitude of unions has always precluded too close an involvement with management. For many unionists, however, the new role of the unions will involve more direct contact with management and its decisions. Many have begun a new kind of campaign – Gavin Laird of the Amalgamated Union of Engineering Workers suggests that 'workers are brought into the decision-making process'. The initial calls have been for managers to supply their employees with far greater information. Ignorance, it is argued, breeds discontent and creates a poorly motivated workforce. And the call is not entirely falling on deaf ears. Management too is beginning to believe in the merits of improved communications. Whereas in the past, new procedures or equipment have been usually introduced without union agreement or consultation, the future may well involve unions taking a part in the selection of new equipment as well as helping in its introduction.

Changing attitudes are perhaps summed up by an Austin Rover shop steward, Colin Brownhill. On winning £10,000 for the best suggestion made by an Austin Rover employee as part of its 'bright ideas' scheme, he commented, 'When I started here everything was very haphazard. It was the shop steward and not the management who gave us all the information.' Brownhill went on to say, 'Quality is going to sell cars now. We have to be better than the opposition because of our past reputation. This place has seen big changes in the time I have been here – not just because of all the robots and modern equipment installed by the management. The attitude of the workforce has changed completely. Everyone wants this place to make a profit.'

Changing perceptions were revealed in a MORI poll in August 1987 which showed that 48 per cent of union leaders agreed with the statement that 'the main responsibility of companies is to perform competitively, even if this means reducing the number of people they employ'. Such a proposition would have been quickly dismissed in the past and, indeed, it formed the chief objection to Coal Board philosophy during the miners' strike.

The new outlook is supported by Tony Mitchard, chief executive of Avon Rubber, who comments, 'The unions needed to be convinced that their members are helped by the company's competitiveness.' Sir Ronald Dearing, the Post Office chairman, calls for an aggressive, positive approach from the trade union leadership. 'Instead of defending the past, it should be challenging management for any want of drive, vision and courage to make the change industry needs and within that framework, ensure that society affords sufficient protection for those who are displaced by change, and ensure that its members who remain in employment are competitively rewarded in relation to the value of what they do.' Few industrialists can foresee a union-free business environment. One we interviewed thought it 'would be difficult to run a big company without the involvement of unions'.

The new 'business unionism' may well mark increased union interest in having a role in industrial power through the work place rather than by way of politics. The belief that the days of shop-steward militancy are past and that the political profile of the unions is being re-thought is widespread among our survey contributors.

The vanguard of left-wing leaders is slowly being replaced by moderate pragmatists such as Gavin Laird, Eric Hammond of the electricians' union, the EETPU, and John Lyons of the Engineers' and Managers' Association. On the shop floor, stewards are now much younger (with an average age of thirty), their constituencies larger and the facilities available to them smaller. It is unlikely unions will ever be apolitical, but some increasingly give that impression.

On management's side, the realities of maintaining an increasingly skilled and flexible workforce appear to be pushing in the same direction.

Dominated neither by appeasement nor aggression in their attitude towards industrial relations, the majority of our industrial leaders seem concerned to build bridges of confidence with their employees – unionised or not – on the grounds that they need active support at all levels if they are to achieve their strategic objectives.

WORK AND HARMONY

'There are dissenting voices, but the need to break down status barriers in British industry can be said to have become part of the conventional wisdom of good employee relations,' says Alan Arthurs of Bath University. The organisations backing such changes are impressively diverse. The CBI has pressed management to 'encourage a steady movement towards harmonisation of status and conditions between staff and shop floor'. ACAS has similarly observed that there has been a trend towards harmonisation, though it hedges its bets by finding such changes 'somewhat intangible'. Bodies such as the Institute of Personnel Management and the National Economic Development Council have also called for the 'breaking down of artificial divisions' between managers and workers.

There has been a commitment to change on the part of management too. At a basic level this commitment may simply involve an acceptance of the importance of the role of the workers. As Bryan Upton, managing director of Richardsons of Sheffield commented: 'We have to be fair to our workers. A business without workers doesn't run.' The equation that low pay creates low morale may well be gaining widespread acceptance. 'We do not actually want a low-paid work force,' says an ICI manager. 'What we want is a high pay, high productivity situation.'

As workforces shrink and core skills become increasingly scarce and valuable, most companies in our survey recognise that they must genuinely treat their human assets as assets, investing in training and motivation, providing opportunities for personal fulfilment through work, if they wish to encourage loyalty, productivity and creative input. The means they use vary from extensive communications to incentive schemes and profit-related pay.

SINGLE STATUS

At the outer extreme of harmonious industrial relations is the ideal of a single-status workforce where white and blue collar workers have equivalent status. The concept of single status overturns virtually all traditional practices on pay and working conditions – the reserved parking space, the separate entrances for blue collar employees, the widely differing rates of pay, benefits and working hours. 'When I first became a manager at this company,' says one senior executive, 'there were eight separate dining rooms.' These largely artificial divisions have become increasingly impractical to maintain. One reason is that, while much blue collar work has become increasingly skilled, much white collar work has been de-skilled. Whereas once the white collar worker would most likely be better qualified than his blue collar colleague, now the opposite is true. UK subsidiaries of Japanese companies provide influential examples. At Toshiba, for example, clerical workers are expected to perform the tasks of machine operatives and vice versa. The narrowing of status differences and the lessening of inhibitions about communications provide benefits which companies increasingly appreciate. After all, breaking down barriers brings savings – the costs of administration, and catering, can be greatly reduced by narrowing the gulf in working practices between workers and managers.

For unions, single status remains a controversial issue, however. Bill Jordan, president of the Amalgamated Engineering Union, is hoping it can be achieved more widely. 'Single status has to come,' he says. 'I am determined to see single status introduced in every factory where we have members.' Clearly the barriers to single status will not be easily eliminated. The attitudes and habits of decades cannot be expected simply to disappear. It was in the nineteenth century that John Stuart Mill observed, 'All human exertion is compounded of some mental and some bodily elements. The stupidest hodman, who repeats from day to day the mechanical act of climbing a ladder, performs a function partly intellectual. On the other hand, there is some bodily ingredient in the labour most purely mental, when it generates an external result.'

COMMUNICATING THE MESSAGE

Jean Paul Getty, in an interview in 1974, observed the importance of keeping people in touch with what was going on in a company. 'I think obviously a man wants to feel he is participating in what he is doing, that he is doing valuable work and that his work is appreciated. I think he should have full information about the job he's doing, what his objectives are, what his problems are.'

Avon Rubber attributes some of its success in turning losses into profits to improved communications at all levels in the company. Its success is such that large-scale redundancies and radical changes in working practices were able to be introduced with the full co-operation of the workforce. Unions were kept fully informed of the decision to make over 500 people redundant while the company called on the remaining workforce to keep to the same production levels. As a result, production rose by 60 per cent at one plant and 40 per cent at another. Avon's chief executive, Tony Mitchard, claims to have developed his approach from the Japanese model. 'They elevated human relations in the working environment. We have to do our own version,' he says. Mitchard willingly shares information concerning sensitive issues such as share prices with union officials. Avon's profits rose by 35 per cent in 1986 and most of the jobs lost have now been replaced. Mitchard believes that success naturally brings rewards and that employees increasingly realise this is the case. 'I feel strongly that if the company is making good profits and the shareholders are satisfied, the employees get a good deal.'

Better communications have also accompanied success at Coloroll, the Lancashire home furnishings group which has grown steadily from a turnover of £6 million and profits of £500,000 in 1978 to a predicted turnover of £250 million by 1990. Coloroll has an information system which keeps everyone up to date with the company's progress. 'How are we doing?' boards on the shop floor give production targets as well as output and efficiency figures, and an extensive system of reporting problems, grievances and questions has been installed. This is supported by monthly team briefings of every member of staff, an ideas programme, save as you earn and share option schemes, profit-related bonuses, children's trusts for gifted and disabled children and sponsorship of the Red Devils parachute team which gives all employees the chance to try parachuting.

Staff involvement need not cost the earth and can undoubtedly provide great benefits. The once dowdy high street chain, Woolworths, provides a notable example. In 1985 it conducted an attitude survey among its employees. It discovered they thought that management was failing to communicate with them. As a result, Woolworths spent £5 million in management training. Each manager was despatched on a three-day course every year for three years. On the shop floor, new communication channels were introduced with a training programme which, if successfully completed, brings employees a £150 bonus. Employees also designed the company's new uniforms. The development of trust and security helped breed confidence in the company's future.

STRIKES AND PRODUCTIVITY

New attitudes of both unions and management may have already proved significant in Britain's increased productivity and the fall of strikes to a fifty-year low. In fact, the issue of strikes was subject to a great deal of media exaggeration even at their height. For the most part, industrial action involved contracting industries with reputations for poor management.

The signs are that strikes are now being used more realistically and sparingly as a last means of bargaining. The miners' strike may well go down in history as the last throw of the unions in conviction or power politics, though unofficial strikes have continued to cause problems in the industry. British Coal's complaint at the end of 1987 brings back memories of the 1970s. Hit by wildcat strikes, it observed, 'We just can't go on having situations where a trivial local dispute involving a handful of men is allowed to spread to bring 14,000 men out and cost millions of pounds in lost production. It is madness.'

Clive Jenkins, leader of the ASTMS, emphasises how seriously his union takes strike action: 'We are not in favour of strikes. The executive authorises about forty a year but hardly any of them happen because employers know that, having taken that step, the union is serious. Greater size may mean more authority but it also means greater responsibility.'

Britain is now a little above middle rank in terms of international comparisons of industrial stoppages, according to the Department of Employment. Since the 1970s the number of days lost through strikes has been drastically reduced, as the table below demonstrates.

The only major blot has been the 1984 miners' strike which alone cost 22.5 million days.

41

Millions of working days lost through strikes

1977	10.1
1978	9.4
1979	29.5
1980	12.0
1981	4.3
1982	5.3
1983	3.8
1984	27.1
1985	6.4
1986	1.9

(Source: Department of Employment)

The improvements have been particularly marked in the car industry. Whereas in 1970 the British car industry employed 500,000 people and lost 57 days per employee through strikes every year, in 1986 its 300,000 employees lost a mere half day through strikes per person. Peugeot Talbot's UK plants are now virtually on a par with its European ones – it hasn't had a major dispute since 1979. At Austin Rover the changes are equally impressive with productivity up by 125 per cent on 1979 figures. Nissan has been so impressed by its British workforce that it has embarked on a major new investment programme.

The sudden rash of strike calls in early 1988 – particularly at Ford and Land Rover – gives rise to concern that a backlash may be occurring. Certainly some of the Ford manual workers saw their dispute as a chance to reassert union power. Nonetheless, the affair was unusual in that national officials were far more moderate in their demands than their members.

Ironically, the new legislation requiring ballots before strike action seems to have strengthened the position of the unions, because management now knows that union officials are not bluffing. The conciliation service, ACAS, has observed that, 'Ballots have been used by trade unions to demonstrate the strength of feeling among their members in ways which some managements have found difficult to counter.' Indeed, some unionists claim managers are more likely to oppose ballots than the unions themselves. The ballots are a testing ground, not necessarily leading to immediate action. In many cases it seems both unions and management use the results of ballots to reassess or confirm their stances.

NO-STRIKE AND ONE-UNION DEALS

Though they are denounced by some unionists as 'surrendering principle to the requirements of the company' and as 'the economics of the quick buck', no-strike and one-union agreements look like becoming increasingly commonplace. The first of these was the electricians' union's agreement with Toshiba in Plymouth. These deals could be said to amount to the union becoming a kind of industrial relations consultant for a particular company. More positively, they may be said to represent a new method of management-union co-operation. Even so, no-strike deals, despite large-scale media coverage, only cover about 10,000 workers, a minute 0.5 per cent of the working population.

Such agreements are championed by the electricians' union, EETPU, much to the annoyance of many other unionists. The EETPU's pragmatic approach is gaining ground and has already had some measure of success in negotiations with Yuasa, the Japanese battery maker, and Hitachi in South Wales. 'The days of confrontation are over and won't be revived,' says one of the EETPU's national officers. Frank Chapple has jokingly commented that strikes are permissible if 'they affect no one, are for lower wages, occur in a lunch hour under a Liberal government and on a day when workers in every rival country are also on strike'. Says Peter Wickens, personnel director at Nissan UK, 'There is no such thing as a no-strike agreement.'

No-strike and one-union deals are a direct response to the lack of union representation in much of the high technology sector. Companies like IBM, National SemiConductor and Nippon are non-union and there is a tendency for new high technology companies to be non-union from their inception. The TUC General Secretary, Norman Willis, identifies this as a disturbing trend and says that there are 'worrying signs that it is fashionable in management circles to marginalise or exclude trade unions'. Willis, critical of 'business unionism', sees it as highlighting self-interest rather than the caring and practical sides of union membership. 'Of course, the self-interest element is there, but if that is the sum total of trade unionism then the British trade union movement would have withered and perished long ago,' he said in a recent 'State of the Nation' speech.

On the other hand, new towns and green field sites have sought to attract companies precisely because of the lack of union organisation in those areas. Basingstoke and Bracknell are notable examples. In Milton

43

Keynes, a typical non-union new town, there have been attempts to reverse this trend and the local trades council organised a trade union week to increase local union awareness.

The chief problem so far with one-union deals, say their critics, is that they create toothless unions, which fail to provide the traditional benefits of union membership. At one Nissan plant, the AEU found that only one in six of the workforce had joined the union after a year – it was simply not regarded as powerful enough. A MORI union poll demonstrates how far 'business unionism' has to go before it becomes generally acceptable to unionists – only 8 per cent of union leaders approved of no-strike deals.

On the plus side, one-union, no-strike deals achieve what has been the primary goal of the union movement since its inception – job security and high rates of pay. This is all very well in growth sectors, but the principle has not been well tested in declining sectors, where job security is much harder to guarantee and where pay settlements may be depressed.

THE ASCENDENCY OF MANAGEMENT

Many in our survey sample believed that with the backing of legislation and the apparent tide against unionism, managers have been given the chance once more to manage. The controversial strikes of the miners and the printworkers may well have upset this position had they succeeded; in the event, the managers were victorious.

The emergence of the entrepreneur as a hero of the age means that, in the eyes of many unionists, managers can ride roughshod over their employees. When an ICI subsidiary removed pay bargaining rights from its workers, a union official said, 'It is clear evidence that employers now feel so confident and macho that they do not even have to deal with trade unions, that they can strip unions of bargaining rights.' A National Union of Railwaymen spokesman has claimed: 'Immediate financial considerations override long-term social, economic and environmental issues.'

Recent research at the London School of Economics has shown that senior managers are increasingly taking sole responsibility for non-pay issues and restricting union involvement to direct pay negotiations. Even so, very few managers could imagine life without the unions.

The new openness in company communications has not always allayed union suspicions. One executive commented: 'The real problem for shop stewards is not that they are threatened by improved management communications; it is that for the first time we are actually listening to employees and acting on what they say. Shop stewards see this as treading on their patch.'

Suspicion stretches to attempts at worker participation, which unions often see as cosmetic gestures. Says John Edmonds, general secretary of the General Municipal and Boilermakers' Union, 'People have talked about designing common objectives, but what I think they actually mean is securing worker, middle management and junior management support for objectives which are set at a senior management level.' Such difficulties may well continue to exist. Edmonds, for one, is realistic. 'The company is not designed as a primary objective to produce security, it is designed to produce profits.' Managers will continue to manage. Whether they listen to unions is another matter, but unions will not simply disappear.

NEW ROLES FOR UNIONS

'Trade unions are working under a new and difficult era and a harsher environment,' says Dr John Burton of Leeds Polytechnic. In the face of a decline in membership and Britain's changing social and economic climate, trade unions are beginning to respond. Almost all now accept the need for change, whether it be to attract new members or in attitudes towards new technology. The TUC General Secretary, Norman Willis, has called on the unions 'to concentrate on consolidating and rebuilding'. He exhorts unions to: 'provide a service that is comprehensive and relevant. And that doesn't mean bickering with one another. It means reaching out to the majority of workers who are not members.'

Further stark realism is provided by a National Union of Railwaymen spokesman: 'Leadership has to reflect the needs of the day. The general social and economic situation must influence its effectiveness.'

Nissan's Peter Wickens in his recent book *The Road to Nissan* has this to say on the future of unions:

45

Trade unionism will not disappear; it will remain relevant but its role will change. How well it is able to recognise the need for and accommodate such change will significantly affect its continuing influence and role in our industrial society. The fact that this question is now at the top of the TUC agenda and is being vigorously debated augurs well for trade unionism . . . If, however, the debate is not concluded and the trade union movement drifts without a clear idea of the direction in which it is sailing, there can be little doubt that its relevance will be increasingly questioned by those people who really matter – the actual and potential membership.

Attracting new members is now an important issue. Whereas in the past unions had and exercised the power of exclusion, now their attention is focused on inclusion. Inter-union disagreements over who should be in each union are increasingly common. Unions like the Transport and General Workers' Union are making energetic attempts to spread their membership to new fields. The TGWU's 'Link-Up' campaign aims to attract part-time and casual workers. Nevertheless, one of its officials admitted that the union is 'permanently recruiting simply to decline'. In general, the more militant unions have greatest difficulty recruiting. Some moderate unions, however, are steadily growing. MATSA, the 79,000-strong white collar section of the GMB, has grown by 19 per cent since 1979. Yet, while all trade unions admit the importance of recruitment, their officials spend a mere 10 per cent of their time trying to recruit new members, according to a London School of Economics Survey in October 1987.

The question is: in which role can unions work most effectively to the benefit of their members in the late 1980s and beyond? Shorn of many of their traditional welfare responsibilities, unions are increasingly broadening their facilities. The AUEW offers advice on a wide range of issues including care and house insurance, mortgages and life assurance. The idea of a union credit card, already used in America, is even being mooted. The TUC is also examining the more co-ordinated and sophisticated approach to union services seen in Sweden and West Germany. The TUC committee considering these issues explains that such services 'may be particularly important in attracting members in industries and locations, and from specific groups of workers, with no strong tradition of trade union organisation'.

Conservative legislation has, ironically, pushed the unions towards a more professional and outward-going stance. The GMB has particularly championed more effective communications with members and the use of public relations. It uses consultants to prepare its publications and has tried to remove clichés, jargon and the old-fashioned hectoring union style from its public pronouncements. It has a new logo and a clearly defined image with pastel colours and conciliatory rather than confrontational words. With the need for regular ballots, unions are more likely to have and to use computerised membership lists. These can be used for communicating with members more regularly and intimately than ever before.

One of the most significant developments for the union movement as a whole has been the expansion of the trade union financial institution, Unity Trust. Unity Trust is owned jointly by over sixty unions and the Co-op Bank. It was started in 1984 with the aim of making 'prudent and profitable investments' in the British economy. Eventually, it is intended to turn Unity Trust into a people's bank in competition with the major clearing banks. With profits rising to £350,000 in the first half of 1987, the trust is already planning a move into the City as well as becoming involved with local councils and employees' share ownership programmes, such as that already set up at Roadchef (discussed later in this chapter). It now offers a wide range of services – pensions, insurance, investment management, balloting and communications consultancy are all now part of Unity Trust's work. Most of these activities are accepted components of the union role for many of our most successful competitors, such as West Germany, and have long been so.

While union services must always compete in normal markets against specialist companies (and the troubles of the West German trade union bank are an example of what can happen when it fails to do so), the provision of a broad range of commercially and socially useful services can be a major reason for membership.

TRAINING

The same pattern of development of new union-backed services is seen elsewhere in increased union provision for training in the workplace. The argument goes that improving the skills of the union's members provides management with a more effective workforce and, therefore, gives unions a greater chance of influencing management decisions.

The need for greater training within industry is acknowledged by both management and unions. Graham Day, chief executive of Rover, has observed, 'The nation's pool of skills must be renewed, enhanced and expanded.' But for Day it is clear where the onus for improvement lies. 'Unless they [management] take a positive initiative, nothing will happen.' Nonetheless, the unions now see training as an area of increasing influence. The TGWU has an extensive education programme, costing over £1 million and servicing 16–17,000 members every year. The training is wide-ranging, and is intended to teach members how to make the most of the union's facilities and to be more aware of their working environment.

The EETPU is another notable example of a union adopting training as a strategic weapon. Its training programme was set up in 1983 and now involves mobile courses as well as those at the union's Cudham Hall training centre with its purpose-built laboratories. The EETPU's courses were launched as a direct replacement for company-run apprenticeship schemes which had been virtually abolished during the recession of the early 1980s; 25,000 craft and technician apprentices were recruited in 1978–9; 7,000 in 1986–7.

Despite its high reputation, the apprenticeship system was rejected by many employers as too expensive and by young people as too long. The Youth Training Scheme, though frequently derided for its low pay and failure to provide sufficiently rigorous qualifications, is accepted by many unions as a necessary evil of high unemployment. A TUC spokesman sees it as 'having a lot of potential for improving the initial training of young people'.

The EETPU's general secretary, Eric Hammond, recognises the gravity of the training problem. 'Training remains under-rated and unresourced.' He calls for a more aggressive approach: 'Staff need to be adaptable and responsive to change, in particular to adopt new skills as new opportunities arise.'

TECHNOLOGY

There is evidence to show there has been a radical change in the attitude of unions towards new technology. The distrust of technology because it has brought job losses has, it seems, been cast aside. Union talk of preparing for the leisure society (most famously documented in Clive Jenkins' and Barrie Sherman's *The Leisure Shock*) where machines do all the work and union members cultivate suntans is a thing of the past. No longer is technology regarded as a threat to the survival of unions. A TUC spokesman says that unions are 'looking for a constructive role within new technology'.

The past slowness in coming to terms with new technology is attributed, by John Lyons of the Engineers' and Managers' Association, to what he sees as the basic nature of unions: 'It is very difficult to initiate proposals for technological change which will lead to loss of their members' employment.'

Roy Grantham of the Association of Professional and Executive Staff, (APEX), recollects, 'In 1979, my union wrote a book on new technology. We said we shouldn't fight it, but we should make sure it was not being introduced just to cut jobs, but to create wealth. In the UK, workers are more co-operative on new technology than employees on the Continent, but managers are less co-operative than their European counterparts.'

The AUEW's Gavin Laird, however, is unequivocal about his union's stance on technology: 'We have accepted and indeed encouraged the implementation of new technology. In my experience, our members are constantly pressing management to replace outdated machinery with modern equipment.'

Organisations such as ACAS, the Policy Studies Institute, the Economic and Social Research Council and the Department of Employment have backed union claims that they actively encourage technological advances. Indeed, a joint TUC-CBI agreement on new technology has been talked about for some time. As technological change has already affected over one third of the British workforce, such a change in attitude is perhaps inevitable. It has also to be noted that changes are frequently introduced without consultation or agreement and often lack the necessary supportive training. By pushing for an increased role in management and in furthering training programmes, unions are increasing their direct influence on employment conditions.

Indeed, in one survey 61 per cent of managers regarded union attitudes to technological change as positive. Research also points to stable rather than declining union powers. 'There is little evidence ... of union influence declining,' reported a recent book, *New Technology and the Process of Labour Regulation*.

ATTRACTING NEW MEMBERS

Many unions are already trying to broaden their appeal, particularly to women and part-time workers. A mere 33 per cent of women who work part-time and 50 per cent of those who work full-time are union members, according to a Low Pay Unit report of October 1987. So the General, Municipal and Boilermakers' Union is pushing women's issues to the forefront of its policies. Its traditional negotiating priorities have been drastically rethought to bring new emphasis on female issues such as cancer screening or pregnancy testing rather than on conventional issues such as shift or bonus pay. The GMBU (where women make up 31 per cent of the members) has launched a workplace scheme, which involves women in discussion groups and, according to the union, gives them 'a chance to relax, talk, laugh and learn with colleagues'. This is backed up by the appointment of an equality officer at each of the union's branches. The union has also discussed whether women should be allocated a certain number of positions on its executive. Norman Willis has supported such developments and has stated his vision of the unions' involvement with women: 'In the future, our role must be to act as the most articulate, most persuasive, most dynamic voice of women in Britain.'

BIGGER AND BETTER

Less visibly aggressive attitudes towards technology and fewer calls for strike action are accompanied by the trend of unions to amalgamate into larger, more powerful organisations. In the past ten years TUC affiliation has fallen from 113 to 88 as a result of union mergers. Gavin Laird predicts a mere 20 affiliates by 2000 (in 1961 it was 189) whilst Eric Hammond has been talking of the TUC evolving into a single union. Whereas the traditional union divisions previously prevented the slightest murmur of merger, white and blue collar unions now talk of amalgamating.

The trend to amalgamation is particularly strong in high technology industries. The enormous innovations of the last twenty years have, in many cases, blurred the boundaries between jobs and occasionally eliminated them entirely. Amalgamations of unions like ASTMS and TASS give the unions a great deal more power as well as saving them substantial amounts of money. The ASTMS/TASS amalgamation has a prospective membership of 700,000. The print unions are also slipping inexorably towards merger. The trend to merge means that negotiations with management can be conducted from a far stronger and more stable position. The days of one industry, one union (as in West Germany) may not be far away.

THE FUTURE FOR THE UNIONS

In many ways the unions have shown durability and adaptability in the recent years of declining membership and of new legislation, which they initially found so difficult to stomach. The financial implications of reduced membership have not been as serious as was initially expected. Indeed, the first study of union finances since 1970, by two academics in 1987, revealed that the unions are in 'remarkable' financial health. Even large traditional unions, like the Iron and Steel Trades Confederation, have stabilised their finances, despite loss of members. Nevertheless, the choice for the unions is stark: continuing decline in membership and power or basic changes in attitude, role and structure. The latter alternative increasingly seems the more likely.

There seems to be a high degree of consensus among many industrialists and union leaders that the unions' new role will involve far greater consultation with management on subjects as diverse as manpower, investment, productivity, marketing, new forms of work organisation and technology as well as discussions on job opportunities and job security, re-skilling and training.

The Industrial Society has already called for unions and management to identify common objectives which include;

- Providing employment and creating new jobs

- Producing a surplus which will ensure future investment

- Creating the exports vital to a trading nation's economy

- Treating people with justice at work.

Firm statements of joint objectives could well eliminate the balancing act between what are seen variously as dictatorial management and irrational unions. Even so, the cliché that managers get the unions they deserve may continue to apply.

Given increased co-operation between management and unions as a likely development, many of the means by which unions have exercised their power may have to be altered. Former union leader, Lord Chapple, has proposed a code of conduct which eliminates many of the controversial aspects of union activity. He calls for:

- Total repudiation of violence in industrial disputes

- A pledge not to strike before agreements expire

- Commitment to use strike action only as a last resort

- A disavowal of strikes for political purposes

- The right of workers not to join a union (with the simultaneous acceptance that they shouldn't receive union benefits).

Legislation may well press unions into accepting aspects of this code in other forms. The TUC and individual unionists are increasingly aware that they have to develop their own role for the future or have it developed for them. TUC leader Norman Willis is pragmatic about the future, though he has to bear in mind the political considerations raised by the growth of 'business unionism'. Norman Fowler, Secretary for Employment, also attempted to map out his vision of the unions in years to come at the Institute of Economic Affairs Conference in October 1987:

> Trade unions – responsible and democratic trade unions – can make a substantial contribution to this country's future prosperity. But there is no place for the old-style, bully-boy, parochial and short-sighted trade unionism of yesterday. If they are to make their most positive contribution trade unions – or at least some trade unions – have to move away from their old traditions of confrontation and conflict. They have to recognise – as so many of their members have already done – that the interests of employees and employers can only be served by co-operation.

The proposed Employment Act, the next step in the Conservative government's union legislation, will offer a severe test. Its contents, particularly the option for those who don't vote for strike action to ignore a majority vote for striking, have been criticised by the TUC, the CBI and the Institute of Directors. The government promises that the legislation 'will bring about changes which not only add to individual freedom, but can help rid our economy of outdated practices and attitudes which have handicapped us in the past'.

With this legislation to face, the TUC itself takes a dourly realistic view of its future. In a series of internal papers it has predicted continuing struggles. Its labour market prognosis is bleak and concludes, 'It is hard to avoid the conclusion that the growth areas in the economy will be in industries, regions and districts and among groups of workers where trade union organisation has traditionally been weak.'

Loss of union members in Britain has been internationally un-paralleled. Whilst the number of employees has grown, union member-ship has continued to fall. Both our industrialists and many of our trade union commentators accept that it is a spiral which will only be stopped by enlightened, commercially minded unions.

SHARING THE SPOILS

The 1978 Finance Act opened the way for a large increase in profit-sharing schemes. Union involvement in them may well offer a practical way forward. The enthusiasm for them has extended beyond the large high-performance companies like BTR, who were first attracted to them in the 1970s. Now organisations like British Home Stores, Marks and Spencer, Midland Bank, Commercial Union, MK Electric, Legal and General, ICI, and the National Westminster Bank have all followed suit. As the profit-sharing trend increases in popularity, more ways are being found of providing incentives. Large cash sums at Christmas time are increasingly being replaced by rewards in the forms of shares and more complex systems of profit-sharing.

The trend towards profit-sharing in Britain has its origins in America. Since the early 1980s, profit-sharing has gained a strong foothold in the American business world. American unions now see profit-sharing as an essential benefit on top of salaries. The United Automobile Workers Union has concession agreements with both General Motors and Ford which include profit-sharing. Steel, lumber and telecommunications all now have some measure of profit-sharing in America and, by 1985, 18 per cent of all employees in medium and large American companies were reported to be included in profit-sharing deals. Profit-sharing, in theory, gives management flexible labour costs. From the union point of view, it brings some justice to the distribution of company profits. American unions are concerned, however, by the tendency to accept wage cuts against promises of a share in the profits.

There is growing evidence that profit-sharing can help a company's performance. A 1987 study of profit-sharing by Wallace Bell, former director of the Industrial Participation Association, and Dr Charles Hanson of Newcastle University, concluded that: 'The economic performance of profit-sharing companies, taken as a group, was superior by a significant degree to that of non-profit-sharers.' Their survey of 414 company performances between 1975 and 1985 showed that profit-sharing companies had 52.8 per cent greater profit growth over this period and a 50 per cent higher return on sales. The most startling statistic produced by the survey was that profit-sharing companies recorded a 78 per cent increase in share dividends over the ten-year period; companies without profit-sharing recorded a 43 per cent rise. Bell and Hanson are enthusiastic about the future role of profit-sharing. 'We believe that profit-sharing, properly adapted to each company, can enable most well-managed companies to operate even more successfully.'

P D Richard, personnel manager at the Bank of Scotland, thinks profit-sharing creates a greater commercial awareness among employees. 'I believe that profit-sharing and share ownership schemes have been worthwhile and although it cannot be argued that they are great incentives, they do create an awareness of the need for all staff to be conscious of company profitability.'

Among companies which have recently introduced profit-sharing schemes is Heinz. Its scheme gives its 3,750 employees a choice between a taxable cash payment and an allocation of company shares. Heinz refers to it as 'prosperity sharing' and managing director John Hinch says that it is about 'motivation, enthusiasm and communication. It gives us all the incentive to help ourselves by helping the company. The more prosperous the company, the greater the pay out'. In return Heinz gets greater worker flexibility and, it hopes, increased productivity. Hewlett Packard's British operation followed the example of its American counterpart by sharing out around £2 million every year in profit bonuses with 12 per cent of pre-tax profits being distributed to employees of greater than six months' standing.

A more surprising area where profit-sharing is beginning to find a place is the car industry. Once bedevilled by industrial relations problems, companies are now seeking to create trimmed-down, highly motivated workforces. Lada Cars at Bridlington already has a profit-sharing bonus scheme in operation. It has provided industrial bonuses of up to £10,000 with the minimum payment being around £2,500. The scheme's opening year cost Lada an estimated £800,000. The results, however, were a 30 per cent increase in UK sales from 1985 figures.

Everyone at the recently privatised Jaguar company who has been with the firm for over a year is also now a shareholder. This has been one of the building blocks in turning Jaguar into a profitable company once more. Arnold Bolton, manager of corporate affairs at Jaguar, believes employees now 'feel they are part of Jaguar and they have a responsibility to the company'.

One of the most innovative schemes has been introduced by the car repair company Kwik-Fit. Its profit-sharing scheme started in 1984. It splits the proceeds of each month's sales between the company and the individual depot. Out of its 50 per cent share, the depot pays for all controllable costs like heat, light, stock discrepancies and bounced cheques. The depot manager then gets 5 per cent of what's left to add to his monthly salary, which is typically double the industry norm. As one by-product of the scheme, the company's electricity bill was cut by £200,000 in the first winter of its operation. Profit-sharing schemes do not always work, however. The full motivating impact can clearly only be felt within a climate where employees already have positive attitudes.

EMPLOYEE SHARE-OWNERSHIP PROGRAMMES

One of the most well known incentive schemes is that of H P Bulmer, the Hereford cider producers. It established an Employee Council in 1977 and now has a profit-sharing scheme which divides out shares rather than hard cash. As a result, employees now own around 3 per cent of the company's shares. The scheme is resoundingly popular with 92 per cent of the workforce in favour and 74 per cent agreeing it has helped to create a better atmosphere at the company. Bulmer's managing director, Brian Nelson, sees the side effects of the share scheme as open communications, free debate and closer, more honest examination of problems, allied to a more decisive and energetic attitude to change. Commitment to the future of the company is felt at every level. Union officials are heavily involved in the Employee Council, which deals with all the human relations issues at the company. 'Employees are investing their lives in the company,' points out John Allday, union convenor. And Eddi McMenamin, a senior union official, confirms that, 'The trade unions and management at Bulmer are both equally committed to employee participation.'

The incentives at Bulmer have broken down many traditional barriers. 'There has been a change in how people perceive the company,' says personnel director Mike Pearce. 'There's a great advantage in talking to people as shareholders, not workers.' The Employee Council at Bulmer gives the people in the company a voice which is, following a period of initial suspicion, now being used. The Employee Council makes recommendations to the main board, which are usually accepted. It has produced a whole range of improvements in health care and pension schemes at Bulmer. It was even given the responsibility for setting up a code of practice when the company required redundancies. As a result 340 people were offered a redundancy package created by the Employee Council – only twelve were compulsory redundancies and only one ex-employee didn't find another job.

With nearly 20 per cent of the adult population of Britain now shareholders, it is increasingly accepted that workers who own shares in their own company have a vested interest in its success. The Bulmer example is being followed. Indeed 1.5 million people already own shares in the company they work for. It is increasingly fashionable for companies to reward their workforces with company shares.

Of course, employee share ownership on its own is no guarantee of good industrial relations. British Telecom has a large proportion of shareowners in its workforce. Ironically in BT's case, when the employees decided to strike they justified their action as the best thing for the company in which 96 per cent of them owned shares. The ignominy of shareholders striking has already also been felt by Jaguar and Thames TV.

Employee share schemes are less common than management-only schemes, although the latter tend to be seen as having a more direct effect as an incentive. Among the most innovative of recent schemes is that introduced by the Burton Group in January 1987. The Burton scheme is progressive in its linking of performance to access to shares, its setting of higher limits than is usual on the number of options which can be granted and the use of an independent remuneration committee to oversee the scheme's implementation. The ambitious nature of the Burton scheme is shown by the fact that the maximum volume of options can be the equivalent of eight times a manager's salary. Potentially 10 per cent of Burton's capital could be involved under the executive share-option scheme.

With three different types of share-option scheme now approved by the Inland Revenue as qualifying for tax concessions, it is likely that the use of share options will expand greatly. A large number of the companies covered in our survey were already instigating such schemes. Most of our industrialists felt that the pros outweighed the cons – rising share prices bring profits, while if the share price falls workers can still take their savings plus the tax free bonus. Interestingly, Bulmer, with a rapidly increasing share value, has found that over half of its employees retain their shares, though with a wary eye on the share price.

THE AMERICAN EXAMPLE

The major problem with many of the British share schemes, according to Unity Trust, is that employees do not tend to be loyal shareholders. As a result, they do not build up a significant stake in the company. Unity Trust has carefully researched into the possible ways of providing employee share-ownership programmes of benefit to all parties. It found the solution in America. There, ESOPs have blossomed in the last decade. From fewer than 300 in 1974, the number has increased to over 9,000. Louis Kelso, an ESOP guru, has estimated that ten million Americans are now involved in buying all or part of the companies they work for – this accounts for 8 per cent of the workforce. The American tax incentives are such that they cost the government an estimated $13.3 billion between 1977 and 1983.

There is, of course, the suspicion that ESOPs do not necessarily boost a company's prospects. Indeed, in America, companies can create an ESOP as much to take advantage of the tax incentives as to benefit the workforce. There has also been the suggestion that the companies are spreading risk in case of business failure and giving employees shares which are not of the same value as those publicly available.

However, Louisiana senator Russell Long (son of the populist Huey Long who championed the phrase 'Every man is a King') has claimed that only 2 per cent of American ESOPs have run into trouble. A 1984 study from the National Center for Employee Ownership in the USA has pointed to a relationship between employee ownership and corporate performance. The study of 347 companies found that over a ten-year period companies with employee share-ownership plans generated 46 per cent more jobs and 40 per cent greater sales growth than those without employee ownership.

Unity Trust's research examined international experiences of ESOPs from central government programmes in Sweden to trade union companies buying shares in Holland and trade union equity investment in West Germany. Its ESOP model is based on the American example, though it is tailored to fit British laws and financial requirements.

Under the American ESOP scheme, a bank advances money to a trust which in turn buys new shares in the company for the employees. This generates finance for the company in the form of new shares and gives employees a holding in the company. The first British ESOP, using the Unity Trust model, was installed by RoadChef early in 1987. The Gloucester-based organisation, the largest privately owned motorway service company in Britain, felt the ESOP offered a means of encouraging greater motivation in its workforce by making them feel part of the company. RoadChef's managing director, Tim Ingram-Hill, calls it 'an ideal plan'. 'It allows us to make use of pre-tax profits to offer a potentially tax-free gift to our employees,' he says.

The impetus for the Unity Trust ESOP came from the Hotel and Catering Workers' Union (part of the giant General Municipal and Boilermakers' Union) which covers the RoadChef staff. The union suggested a meeting with Unity Trust, and RoadChef found itself, for the first time, listening to plans for an ESOP which was both practical and beneficial to all concerned. Unity Trust's Mike Marsden, who is developing the involvement in ESOPs, realised that RoadChef provided an ideal starting point for the ESOP model. 'RoadChef has a forward thinking, communicative management team,' he says. Unity Trust's close working relationship with trade unions also allowed some of the traditional obstacles and suspicions to be overcome easily.

Under the RoadChef ESOP, its 700 employees are eligible for a free issue of shares when they have been with the company for three years. To operate this the company set up a £650,000 trust fund, which allocates the shares and buys them back tax-free when workers leave or retire. Unity Trust itself provided £350,000 of the trust fund and sees it as a means of providing shares for employees in perpetuity. The self-generating nature of the scheme means that the trust fund does not have to be replenished every few years but will naturally fill up as people leave the company and sell their shares.

Tim Ingram-Hill sees it as a means by which employees can save money without effort: 'In a way, we're running a savings account for each eligible member of staff,' he says. 'It's like a savings account from which they cannot be tempted to withdraw money when they think they could use it. And it provides them with a very nice nest-egg when they retire.' RoadChef expresses its philosophy simply: 'We believe that employees who have a tangible financial stake in the business have an even stronger incentive to help their company grow.' A third of the RoadChef workforce, at its nine motorway service areas, qualified for the scheme immediately and by January 1988 around half of the company's employees were involved. For those not yet eligible, there is the attractive prospect of becoming future beneficiaries.

The RoadChef ESOP heavily involves the local unions. June Latham, a senior shop steward of the Hotel and Catering Workers' Union, is on the Board of Trustees. Both unions and management are clear, however, that the ESOP is not part of the wages or other benefits employees receive. It has to be treated as a separate entity.

Unity Trust's Mike Marsden draws attention to the fact that ESOPs can be particularly useful in buy-outs where the existing management attempt to buy a company from a controlling firm. RoadChef was bought out from Lindley Catering Investments in 1983, but Marsden thinks that ESOPs can fulfil a vital role in buy-out negotiations. The bait of having an ESOP can unite a workforce behind a buy-out team. In the often delicate negotiations involved in a buy-out, the support of the workforce can be of great influence. The RoadChef ESOP has been instituted at the Provincial Bus Company following another buy-out, and Unity Trust's ESOP portfolio is quickly expanding. An employee buy-out is part of the privatisation programme for the National Bus Company – controversial territory for a trade union backed organisation like Unity Trust. The ESOP at Provincial involves a trust which owns 80 per cent of the company shares and which was paid for with an open-ended loan from Unity Trust, though Barclays Bank was also involved in the scheme's financing. The remaining 20 per cent of the equity is owned directly by employees. The aim of the seven-person trust is to act 'for the benefit of all employees, past and present'.

Another recent ESOP backed by Unity Trust is also in a company which has been bought out – Doncaster Wagon Works, a former British Rail Engineering subsidiary. As well as preserving 643 jobs, the ESOP will give employees 13 per cent of the ordinary share capital, fully financed by future profits. In many ways, the Doncaster Wagon Works scheme is a test case for ESOPs. It is Unity Trust's first ESOP in a large-scale traditional engineering company and brings to the forefront the question of union attitudes to privatisation. It involves ESOPs being used as one weapon in arresting the decline of a traditional industry.

Mike Marsden affirms, 'ESOPs are really going to take off. They will have a positive role in the future of trade unions.' Many union traditionalists remain to be convinced. To assure the future success of ESOPs such attitudes need to be altered radically. Nevertheless, without advertising its product, Unity Trust has found demand to be accelerating rapidly. It has now concluded an ESOP with Armstrong Engineering in Coventry and plans to establish one at Llanelli Radiator, a Rover Group component plant and the subject of a buy-out, are well advanced. Despite the small number of ESOPs in existence at the moment, Unity Trust is very optimistic and envisages at least ten million British employees in ESOP-type schemes by the end of the century.

The whole concept of employee share ownership has also received a boost from the main postal union, the Union of Communication Workers, which sees it as a more viable option to nationalisation in the late 20th century. It argues for government policies which would increase the spread of shares among employees of all companies above a certain size, and which would 'collectivise shareholders' power to make employees' views heard at general meetings and at board level'. It backs its arguments by pointing out that up to 4 million trade unionists now hold shares.

PROFIT-RELATED PAY

The participation scheme with perhaps the most enthusiastic government backing is profit-related pay (PRP). It is estimated that up to 1.5 million employees were covered by PRP schemes by March 1988. To date, PRP schemes cover more than 70,000 people. This estimate may well be outstripped if tax relief for PRP continues to expand – almost half of all PRP payments in the private sector are now tax-free.

The scheme has provoked a mixed reception. At the centre of the concern of trade unions is that if profits fall, wages fall. Norman Lamont, when he was Financial Secretary to the Treasury, saw this as the lesser of two ills: 'For the employee this means a temporary reduction in pay. No one will be overjoyed about that but it has to be compared with the alternative if pay schemes are inflexible. One word describes it – redundancy.' Another worry is that, under PRP, workers will be less enthusiastic about increases in staffing. More people means a reduced share of the profits. Moreover, whilst the structures to enable an expansion of PRP are being introduced, there is the fear that the link between performance and profit may be lessened by calculating PRP from net rather than operating profit. Another likely problem is that PRP may become an accepted part of a person's salary rather than a valuable bonus – if this becomes so, much of the motivational effect will be lost. In fact, the impetus to introduce PRP seems more usually to be equated with greater pay flexibility than any real desire for a more equitable sharing of finances. Its chief enthusiast, Martin Weitzman, makes much of PRP's role in declining businesses, where it can cut down the wage bill when money is short.

The Industrial Participation Association is suspicious of the likely developments in PRP. Says Bryan Stevens, the IPA director, 'PRP is primarily about controlling wages and not about motivating employees. It only motivates when the company is doing well.' The chief difficulty may well be in communicating what PRP involves. An IPA survey, in October 1987, pointed out this problem and reflected, 'It is hard to discern any great enthusiasm for the PRP package.' The IPA report calls into question the basic raison d'etre of PRP as it now stands. 'Strong doubts were expressed about whether PRP would achieve one of its objects of reducing pay when profits fell. There was an underlying feeling that the probable industrial upheaval if pay were reduced would make the scheme unlikely to work.' In the case of PRP, government enthusiasm and money may well not be enough.

FUTURE PROFIT PARTICIPATION

Profit participation still has a long way to go. A survey by Coopers & Lybrand of Britain's top 1,000 companies, published in conjunction with Monks Partnership early in 1987, showed that only 16 per cent of the companies had profit-sharing schemes and only 33 per cent had SAYE share option schemes. The report was optimistic that these figures would grow but pointed to the low percentages of people taking up share option schemes. Britain only has around 1,500 Inland Revenue approved all-employee share schemes. Profit-sharing remains, for the most part, the domain of executives.

ESOPs provide a way round some of these problems in that they can give employees shares without them having to pay or having to get involved in the complexities of normal share ownership. The benefits can be broad ranging for management, unions and employees. Unity Trust identifies the chief advantages as providing companies with capital for expansion at modest costs, creating a substantial and permanent employee shareholding in the company, and giving employees, whether they are on the shop floor or white collar staff, a long-term capital stake in the company's future. The problem for Unity Trust, and organisations like it, lies in persuading the various parties that ESOPs can benefit them all.

Many remain to be convinced. The Centre for Alternative Industrial and Technological Systems has found 'no intrinsic advantages' for workers in ESOPs and concluded that over a three-year period in Britain's biggest companies, workers in a contributory scheme could just as easily lose by up to £590 as gain by up to £770. 'In many instances, a straight-forward (and quite modest) pay award would be preferable to an ESOP or profit-related pay,' they say, and argue that ESOPs and PRP are being used to ease unions out of wage fixing. 'The very high degree of managerial control over the design and operation of ESOPs/PRP schemes makes it very difficult for unions to enter meaningful negotiations in this area,' they conclude.

In more general terms, the popular demand for worker participation remains strong. *British Social Attitudes 1987* revealed that 80 per cent of people thought that workers should be given a greater say in running their workplace (against 68 per cent in 1984 and 54 per cent in 1974). Whether this demand will be translated into action depends on a change in man-agement attitudes and further easing of legislation to make it easier to offer some form of employee participation.

Managers may well fear that profit-sharing, PRP and such schemes will undermine their capacity to manage. It is true that PRP, for example, means that employees have far greater access to accounts. Involvement and participation demand openness and often radical restructuring and training. Bryan Stevens of the IPA is enthusiastic about the possibilities, but does not underestimate the changes required. 'Relatively few companies understand that they have to work in a different way to fully tap the resources of their employees. In the future, competition will not be product and quality orientated, but be about how motivated and involved employees are.' Stevens believes that leadership requires employee involvement at all levels. Without involvement and suitable rewards and incentives, the cost may be a return to the industrial relations problems of the past.

Michael Peacock of Nurdin and Peacock makes a similar call for greater involvement of employees. 'I believe more commitment is required of management and also a more genuine interest in their workforce. Otherwise, if and when we return to full employment, we will pay the price.'

Just how far we still have to go is illustrated by the Institute of Personnel Management's regular study of company annual reports. While more companies are taking deliberate steps to increase employee involvement, the IPM finds what it calls 'a depressing lack of commitment' in a high proportion of employers. More than half of its sample of 300 companies meet their legal obligations to report employee involvement activities with no more than a standard paragraph in the annual report. Says the IPM, referring to the Employment Act 1983: 'The voluntarist approach inherent in Section 1 has been taken advantage of by a large number of companies to say (and apparently do?) as little as possible on the subject.'

It would in our opinion be foolishly optimistic to conclude that all of Britain's industrial relations problems have been resolved. Neither militant unionism nor militant management has disappeared. Moreover, as unions change their roles, they may open up new areas of potential conflict. The rapid division of the workforce into full-time core workers (the traditional mainstay of union membership) and temporary or part-time peripheral employees (the new target areas of recruitment) may provide a whole new spectrum of divisiveness. The sudden flurry of strike threats and token strikes at the beginning of 1988 indicates how precarious the balance can be.

The key to the future lies in the capability of both unions and management to create trust and to focus attention on mutual objectives. More has been accomplished than either side would have imagined ten years ago. But much remains to be done.

4

The Decline of Education and Training

'Education is the worst product we produce in this country . . . Korea is putting more effort into education than Britain.'
Roy Grantham, general secretary, APEX, 1987

'There is urgent need in the interests of the industrial and commercial prosperity of the country to secure an improved system of technical and commercial training.'
Government Green Paper, 1941

'We have not put development of managers as our number one national goal.'
Alistair Graham, director, The Industrial Society, 1987

'For a long time only one in three of our school-leavers received any systematic vocational education or training once they left school. Only a minority of employers invested in the basic training of young people apart from apprentices. The apprentices were the lucky few. For adults the position has been, if anything, worse. Few have been able to find opportunities to retrain in mid-career or any encouragement and reward for investing their time and effort in learning. Even now, only a minority of employers encourage their employees – including their managers – to train and retrain.'
Norman Fowler, Secretary of State for Employment, The Times, 17 February, 1988

'[Business school teachers] are afraid of getting their minds grubby, let alone their hands.'
Sir Douglas Hague, former head, Prime Minister's Economic and Social Research Policy Unit, The Times, 5 February, 1988

EDUCATING FOR INDUSTRY

Of all the perceived contributory causes of industrial decline mentioned in the responses to our survey of industrialists, by far the most common was education and training. The school and university system came in for extensive criticism for failure to provide industry with recruits of the kind it needs. There is a strong perception among leading businessmen that school teachers are biased against industrial careers and are opposed to producing 'industrial cannon fodder'. At the same time, there is a refreshing candour among the businessmen about the failure of business itself to invest sufficiently in training. What appears to have happened, in many cases, is that both sides have left the responsibility to the other.

How accurate are these perceptions? There has been ferocious debate over vocational education in recent years and a certain amount of data has been produced among all the opinions. This data includes the following:

- According to a report by the Department of Employment, 25 per cent of the long-term unemployed cannot read or write, or carry out simple sums.

- The 1986 annual report of HM Inspector of Schools found that a minimum of 20 per cent of lessons in state schools were substandard. For thirteen-year-olds, the proportion of unsatisfactory lessons rose to 33 per cent. In the 1987 report HMI claimed that one third of teachers were not up to the job. Shortage of teachers was causing subjects such as Latin, French, design and technology to be dropped from the curriculum in many schools.

- Japanese children attend school 240 days a year; British children in state education only 196.

- In spite of 3.5 million unemployed (or 2.5 million, depending on which set of statistics you use) there are still vast skills shortages in

Britain. A study of 1,164 companies by the Confederation of British Industry and the Manpower Services Commission in 1987 found that one in five companies expected their output to be affected by skills shortages. The survey identified more than 250 occupations where workers were in short supply, ranging from electronic engineers to mechanics and welders.

● Data on the participation of eighteen-year-olds in higher education is complex and often fudged. Comparisons made by the OECD in the early 1980s, using data from 1976, provided the information that, in terms of entry into higher level education, Britain lies fifteenth, behind Austria and West Germany. The Department of Education and Science disputed this figure and provided instead statistics that put Britain in second place, with 40 per cent against the United States' 42.8 per cent. The then Under-secretary of State said he thought the real figure was somewhere in between.

● By the age of seventeen only 17 per cent of Britons are still at school. The comparative figures for seventeen-year-olds in the United States and Japan are 82 per cent and 92 per cent respectively.

● Spending on education in Britain was 5.3 per cent of gross domestic product in 1978–9. By 1985–6, it had fallen to 4.7 per cent.

● In 1986 there were 40,000 apprentices in Britain, compared with 700,000 in West Germany. The collapse of the apprenticeship system was a gradual affair until the early 1980s. Whereas 25,000 craft and technician apprentices were recruited in 1978–9, a mere 7,000 were recruited in 1986–7.

● The number of full-time students in Britain rose by 85,000 between 1978–9 and 1986–7. Another 50,000 full-time student enrolments are predicted by 1990.

● An assessment of the MSC's Adult Training Strategy by the National Audit Office in 1987 found that the MSC simply didn't have enough information about skills gaps to know whether the money it was spending was being used effectively or not. As a result, some skills gaps were growing while in other areas surpluses were being swollen.

● A survey of management training carried out by Bath University for the Economic and Social Research Council found that even large companies in Britain spent relatively little time or money on training managers. Twenty per cent of large companies (those employing 1,000 people or more) do not send managers on courses at all. Among small firms employing 20–49 people, 75 per cent did no management training at all.

● According to the Manpower Services Commission, British companies on average spend only 0.15 per cent of turnover on training. By comparison, French employers have a compulsory levy of 1.6 per cent of employment costs; Germans spend 2 per cent of turnover and Japanese 3 per cent. In cash terms, West German companies spent £7 billion on training in 1980; the UK, with a similar population size, spent £2.5 billion.

- A recent study by the National Economic Development Council (NEDC) looked at the making of top managers in Britain, the United States, France, West Germany and Japan. It found that there were very clearly defined routes to the top in all of the countries except Britain. In the United States, the route is via business school; in Japan via well mapped out career paths within companies; in France, through the *grandes ecoles*; in West Germany, through advanced university courses, frequently leading to doctorates. In the UK, the nearest clear route to the top was via the narrow functional specialisation of accountancy. Most top managers made it via relatively haphazard routes in which any special training they acquired was incidental and fortuitous. (Britain has twenty times as many accountants as Japan; thirty times as many as West Germany. One main reason for the disparity, concludes the report, is the lack of any other relevant form of professional qualification.) Intriguingly, only the UK does not seem to be particularly worried about top management training, although it has most to be worried about.

- Production foremen in Britain are primarily promoted from the shop floor without gaining formal qualifications. West German foremen have to pass examinations as craftsmen or mastercraftsmen.

- Approximately 25 per cent of all US undergraduates take some form of business studies course; in the UK less than 2 per cent. The United States, with a population of 250 million, has an annual output of between 60,000 and 70,000 MBAs; the UK, with 50 million people, produces approximately 1,200.

So what does all this add up to? Once again, assigning unique responsibility to any one sector of education or of industrial training would be both dangerous and unjustified. Indeed, the blame, if blame there is, appears to be fairly evenly spread among all parties. And, refreshingly, it seems that all – or almost all – parties are prepared to accept that they have got it wrong.

Carrie Lapham, head of Caerlon Comprehensive School, near Newport, clashes frequently with other headteachers who see his efforts to create greater liaison between his school and local industry as providing 'industrial fodder'. He points to a lamentable lack of knowledge of what industry is like among the teaching profession, recalling that: 'In my first grammar school, the careers master was the head of classics. A young lad said he wanted to be a metallurgist. "It's a rather heavy sort of thing to be," he was told, "and you'll get awfully hot and be stripped to the waist all the time."'

It's not just ignorance of industry which pervades teaching. Indeed, the general competence of teachers has increasingly been questioned. The 1987 annual HMI's report concluded that a third of all primary and secondary teachers in England were not up to the job.

At the polytechnics, spokesmen such as Keith Alan-Smith, head of Oxford Polytechnic's School of Business, admit freely that academic qualifications in management 'inspire little confidence among those who appoint managers, since they merely certify academic success. They confirm nothing about the holder's ability actually to manage anything'. Michael Powell of the Committee of Vice-Chancellors and Principals declares, 'We are simply not producing enough industrialists.' He points the finger at the secondary school system, where students specialise too early, abandoning sciences and other valuable subjects, and he argues for a much broader curriculum all the way up the secondary school and on into the first year of university. This is effectively what happens among our key competitors, the United States and Japan, where first degrees are far less academically specialised.

THE SCHOOLS

One of the clearest indicators of the failure of our education system is the proportion of illiterates and innumerates in the available workforce. The range of employment options open to people who lack literacy or numeracy (or both) is limited and becoming increasingly so. A worker who cannot understand warning signs, or who is unable to perform simple calculations, is a liability. The fact that 60 per cent of children still leave school without formal qualifications indicates that the problem is far from resolved. As long ago as the mid-1970s, the Centre for Policy Studies, a Conservative think tank, asserted in a pamphlet entitled *English our English*, 'When children leave English schools today, few are able to speak and write English correctly; even fewer have a familiarity with the literary heritage of the language.'

The UK is not alone in having a literacy problem. The United States has 25 million illiterate adults. Between 50 and 75 per cent of its long-term unemployed fall into this category. In Britain, the government's Adult Literacy and Basic Skills Unit now estimates that six million adults have basic problems with reading, writing, spelling or simple arithmetic. Of these, 300,000 cannot read or write in practical terms. In a time when unskilled work is declining the figures are disturbing (even more so when some claim the estimates to be conservative).

There are similar worries voiced by the National Foundation for Education Research. Its research into mathematical ability shows that the performance of British children has deteriorated over the last twenty years. In 1964, half the fourteen-year-olds in England and Wales could find the average of 1.5, 2.4 and 3.75. In 1981, only one in three could do so. Its study of 2,500 pupils confirms the traditionalist viewpoint that educational standards have fallen. International comparisons reflect the deficiencies – in all five areas tested, the Japanese came top, while the Dutch were always in the top four.

A more recent study, by the International Association for the Evaluation of Educational Achievement, gave a standard test in physics, chemistry and biology to 10-year-old children in 15 countries and to 14-year-olds in 17 countries. The British 10-year-olds ranked 11th; the 14-year-olds ranked 10th, behind such countries as Poland and South Korea.

To Correlli Barnett, author of the perceptive study of post-war Britain *The Audit of War*, the failure of education is a long-standing sore. He sees the problem both in terms of the quantity and the quality of education. In 1937–8, he points out, only one in five British children had any kind of further full-time education after the age of fourteen and less than a quarter of these stayed on to obtain leaving certificates at eighteen. Of the 80 per cent who didn't go on into further education at fourteen, only 4 per cent were receiving even part-time education. Barnett compares the 20,000 children attending day-continuation schools in Britain with the 1,800,000 children attending comparable sandwich courses in West Germany. He quotes a memorandum from the English Board of Education that demonstrated that while many industries in Britain provided vocational training for 10 per cent or less of entrants, their German counterparts made such training compulsory for *every* entrant. He concludes, 'While most young Germans were learning a trade as well as continuing their education, most young Britons had been dumped out of school to look for work in obsolete, failing industries situated in decrepit "depressed areas".'

The eventual reaction to this educational scandal was to raise the school leaving age, first to fifteen, then to sixteen. The result was that, while students had more academic education pumped into them, they were still launched unprepared into the workforce. Only now, with the Youth Training Scheme and similar initiatives, is this failure to link educational and vocational training being tackled.

In terms of the quality of education, Barnett argues that the rot set in with Dr Thomas Arnold, headmaster of Rugby during 1827–41, and his fellow

Victorian educational crusaders. Says Barnett: 'The public schools and, thereafter, Victorian Oxbridge, set out to produce Christian gentlemen, like knights in Burne-Jones stained glass, to govern the empire, join the church or the law or the public service: not to produce hard-driving technologically aware leaders of an industrial nation in a tough, competitive world.' Other educational philosophers, such as Cardinal Newman, carried on the theme, dividing the world of education into the philosophical and the mechanical. The former was an activity fit for a gentleman, in that it was the essence of a liberal education, giving him 'a cultivated intellect, a delicate taste, a candid, equitable, dispassionate mind, a noble and courteous bearing in the conduct of life'. The latter was the role of ruder minds, of people with lesser social ambitions.

Peter Holmes, chairman of Shell, states:

> During the second quarter of the nineteenth century there was a dramatic change of direction. A need had arisen to educate a large number of middle class sons for service in the colonies. To meet this need a large number of secondary public schools were created in the middle years of the nineteenth century. The ethos of the teaching of these schools was essentially that the supreme aim in life should be to serve. These schools admirably suited their purpose and created many thousands of fine district officers for the empire, but they totally stifled the impetus for wealth creation.

This approach may well have served the economy well when the primary need was for administrators of an expanding empire. In a world where what Newman described as 'the particular and practical . . . the useful or mechanical arts' are the key competitive weapons between economies, liberal education has become a ball and chain of gigantic proportions. Part of the problem is that the liberal education has turned out to be largely a quark. Without an empire to rule, with the church in decline over the past decades and certainly no longer a passport to gentlemanly status; with public service increasingly less desirable as an occupation, the openings for liberally educated gentlemen are fewer and fewer. Only the City and a handful of bureaucratic large companies that administer their own remnants of empire hold out as havens for those with a good education in nothing in particular. And even there, as we shall see in later chapters, the citadel is rapidly falling.

As long ago as 1869, Herbert Spencer was lamenting:

> That which our schools' courses leave almost entirely out, we thus find to be what most nearly concerns the business of life. Our industries would cease were it not for the information which men acquire, as best they may,

71

after their education is said to have finished. The vital knowledge – that by which we have grown as a nation to what we are and which now underlies our whole existence – is a knowledge that has got itself taught in nooks and corners, while the ordained agencies for teaching have been mumbling little else but dead formulae.

P L F Crowson, economic adviser to Rio Tinto Zinc, sums it up in this way:

Britain's problems seem to lie in its adversarial political system, and in educational and governmental systems whose prime object for over a century was to turn out good administrators. This meant that technical and business skills were not as highly regarded as they may have been in mainland Europe and Japan. When the educational system is combined with an extremely efficient financial system which has always been designed for servicing trade rather than industry, the mixture becomes fairly predictable.

There is little doubt in the minds of our industrialists that many teachers still regard education as an end for its own sake. If we were educating people for unemployment there might be some justification for such an approach. But the economic realities suggest that those who are going to work for their living should receive an education that at least partially prepares them for their chosen vocations. Given that industry is still a major employer, there should, logically, be some focus on the particular and practical. Moreover, the liberal education system has failed in one important respect. It has not – with some exceptions at higher education level – taught people to learn. Having escaped from the classroom, few people willingly venture back unless they have a strong motivation. Those that do often find it hard, because the process and techniques of learning are a subject rarely taught in schools.

Nick Georgiades, director of human resources at British Airways, sees the historical legacy in this way:

We made an error when we chose to put national resources into a number of infrastructure activities, such as the nationalisation of the coal industries, railways and so on. All of these were right, but we forgot to do the most important thing possible – build and invest in the manpower of this country.

In the United States, they realised their soldiers had been deprived of tertiary education and gave them opportunities to return to school, which they did, in droves. It is only now that we are beginning to understand how that failure to educate shaped the culture of British industry. If you never had the opportunity for tertiary education, do you value it?

No, you don't. You got where you are today in spite of the fact that you didn't have a university education . . . As a result, we have built into the British culture a negative view of the value of education, both for our managers and our workforce.

We have enough competence in this country to lead an educational renaissance, if we chose to do it, and if those who manage our educational institutions recognised their national responsibility. But I don't think they do. They are concerned with the traditional elitist views of what university education is about, and while they persist in this view of the world, they will act as a block to the needs of management education.

In the realms of management, lack of education has, in the opinion of some observers, had significant ramifications. Says Sir John Hoskyns, director general of the Institute of Directors, 'I don't think there has been enough awareness that we were amateurs as managers, that there was a body of knowledge effective managers needed to have. Our business schools will say that the financial ignorance of the managers who come on courses is frightening. Managers are embarrassed at admitting their ignorance.'

To Alistair Graham, head of The Industrial Society, the opportunity, when a consensus on the quality and the objectives of education could have been achieved, was missed. He explains, 'We didn't develop a consensus across society on raising the quality of education, because education became a political issue – should schools be selective or non-selective? The changes were made at a time when education was in ferment.' This politicisation of the schools continues. Even now he points out, 'Governing bodies of schools don't have industrial managers, but political appointees instead.'

The quality of education is revealed in other ways, too. Take the teaching of science and mathematics. Today the shortage of teachers in these subjects is widely blamed on poor salaries. Yet in 1949, when salaries were relatively higher in the teaching profession, the same shortages were apparent. In 1961, the Minister for Education, Sir David Eccles, complained, 'The schools and industry are both short of mathematicians. The fact of the shortage and its gravity have been recognised in the educational world for some time.'

The Guardian reported in February 1987 that it was twice as difficult to fill a vacancy for a physics teacher as for posts in any other discipline. More than half the teachers of maths and physics in secondary schools did not take those subjects as their main degrees. Said the newspaper, 'Nearly one physics lesson in five is taught by someone who has no more than an A level in the subject, if that. In maths, the proportion is only slightly lower . . . At present, one secondary school in five offers no physics after the second year. In other words, pupils have to give it up at twelve or thirteen.'

The 1986 House of Lords Select Committee on Science and Technology recorded a variety of complaints about the lack of support for physics in particular and science in general in our schools. ICI told the committee, 'Unless something is done very soon the research funding problem will solve itself in a disastrous way – there will be so few good young scientists coming forward that even with the limited funding, we shall be able to support them all.' The Institute of Physics also expressed 'grave and growing concern about the state of physics education in our schools and institutions of higher education' and noted that 'physics is fundamental to the nation's wealth-producing industries'. This was further supported by Manchester University's Professor Irvine who reflected, 'A higher percentage of pupils in English schools give up the study of mathematics and physics at an earlier age than in any comparable industrial nation. A contributory factor must be that more than 80 per cent of our school pupils will never be exposed to a graduate physics teacher.'

Even information technology, recognised by all sides as an essential area of knowledge for most jobs in the coming decades, receives far less classroom attention than industry says it needs. Resources and suitable teaching experience are both extremely limited. In 1986 the Department of Education revealed that there was only one microcomputer for every 100 pupils in primary schools. About a third of teachers had not been given even introductory training in classroom use of information technology.

But it is not only lack of resources and trained staff which hinders education in Britain. The degree of specialisation at an early age has also been much criticised. Says Sir George Porter, president of the Royal Society, 'Most Britons leave science for ever at the age of about fifteen and have had precious little of it before that.' Our competitor nations, by comparison, specialise much later. Whilst most sixth formers in the UK study only three subjects, their counterparts in the United States study six and, in Japan, eight.

The need for less specialisation and broader, more commercially useful skills was put by Peter Benton, director general of the British Institute of Management, in *The Sunday Times* in January 1988: 'Few now believe that a narrow specialist skill acquired in youth is sufficient. As technology permeates, and every aspect of commercial or public work changes, the individual needs broad skills to swim through.' The tragedy is less that such a situation could come about – that can perhaps be excused by our

74

educational legacy – but that we have been so complacent about rectifying it.

The trouble with quality comparisons in education is that they perforce focus primarily on the relative importance given to particular subjects. There is very little data that compares standards. What we do know in quality terms is that our fiercest competitors, the Japanese, have set and consistently achieve significantly higher educational standards in a wider range of subjects than any other country. This educational disparity is growing and is making a major contribution to Japanese industrial advancement, because the raw recruits Japanese companies have to work with are of a higher calibre in educational terms. As long ago as 1970 Japanese ten- and fourteen-year-olds came top of the developed countries in their knowledge of biology, earth sciences, chemistry and physics. Comparisons of examination scores of Japanese and US high school students indicate that a 98 per cent pass in the United States is the equivalent to a 50 per cent pass in Japan. While ahead of the US, British students are still way behind their Japanese equivalents in these basic subjects.

A more recent survey of experts in six countries by *US News* compared the performance of schools in Britain, the United States, Japan, West Germany, France and the Soviet Union. Britain and the United States scored lowest in maths and science and, remarkably, in the knowledge and use of their own language. Britain also came a resounding bottom of the pack in foreign language abilities. Only in social sciences was the UK ranked highly.

The Schools Inspectorate, itself under constant sniping over the way in which it assesses schools and teachers, visited West Germany in 1986 to compare educational systems and achievements. Its report stresses the lack of focus in the UK on what the goals of education in schools should be. It maintains that the German schools are more successful at 'providing young people with attainable goals to work towards. Because there is understanding of, and broad agreement about, what education is seeking to achieve in respect of pupils' needs, parental aspirations, employers' general requirements and the nation's social and economic intentions, the standing of education, of its teachers and its institutions is relatively high.'

The generally lower status accorded to teachers in Britain compared to their counterparts in other countries has not helped the situation. As Alistair Graham recalls, 'Teacher training is a disaster area. Teaching used to be a natural fallback if you failed to get into university.'

HIGHER EDUCATION

One of the more pungent commentaries on higher education and industry comes from the Council for Industry and Higher Education, chaired by GEC chairman James Prior and made up of twenty-two heads of companies and ten senior dons. The Council recently called for opening up colleges and polytechnics to 'far more people from a wider range of backgrounds for a bigger choice of courses more relevant to the information society in which they work.' It describes the typical conduct of discussions with academia as 'sprawling meetings and voluminous paperwork lacking crisp decisions' and argues that if industry received a product more to its liking, it would automatically invest more in universities and polytechnics. If industry is to pay more of the costs of maintaining a higher education system, it argues, then it must be able to exercise the same kind of control that it expects its own customers to insist on. The typical graduate output, it maintains, is 'expensive racehorses for everything' rather than horses for courses.

Britain has, in fact, conspicuously lagged behind her competitors in many crucial areas. The 1947 Urwick Report on management education noted, 'There is in Great Britain a serious lack of men and women competent to instruct in management subjects.' Britain's first colleges of advanced technology opened in 1963, 120 years after Germany's; Britain's first two business schools opened in 1965, 66 years after Harvard. The demand for management and business courses now far outstrips available places. In 1986–7 only 27 per cent of those applying could find places on undergraduate management or business courses. This is the lowest rate in any of the ten most popular degree subjects. As a result, INSEAD, the European Business School of Fontainebleau, takes more MBA students from Britain than from any other country. Again, the demand is immense – it receives around 2,000 applications for 300 places.

VOCATIONAL TRAINING

A Coopers & Lybrand study in 1985 of British companies' attitudes towards training demonstrated that the vast majority of companies did not consider it to be an important component of their strategy. David Hussey, managing director of Harbridge Consulting Group, draws a number of conclusions from this report and from a British Institute of Management survey published the year before.

In most companies, management training is seen as an act of faith: something which is desirable, but not immediately translatable into economic performance in the marketplace. It is thus seen as postponable cost.

Benefits from management training have seldom been demonstrated. This is partly because the low status of those in the training function limits their ability to provide appropriate training, and partly because few companies attempt to evaluate the results of training. Many believe (a) that evaluation is difficult, and (b) that money allocated to evaluation cannot be spent on training. The result is that little hard evidence can be shown to senior management to demonstrate that management training is more than an act of faith.

Budgetary approaches vary between companies, but few are conducive to good training decisions. Many companies control the out-of-pocket expenses of training rigidly (e.g. hotels, lecturers' fees, development of courses), but rarely consider the opportunity or salary costs of those undergoing training. As a result, very few companies know what they are spending on management training.

There was a marked bias to the running of personnel and behavioural type courses, which often reflect the skills and interests of company trainers and only occasionally meet training needs.

Training initiatives tend to originate from appraisals at the individual level. It is hard to find a top down initiative.

This uninterest on the part of top management, says Hussey, ignores the problems that lack of training causes in the implementation of the strategies which they spend so much time formulating. The top six problems of strategy implementation have been found to be 'took more time than expected', 'unexpected major problem surfaced', 'co-ordination of implementation activities inadequate', 'management attention distracted', 'inadequate capabilities of personnel', and 'inadequate training of lower level employees'. All of these could have been eased or resolved with properly applied training.

Part of the problem may be the lack of competence of many board members. Bryan Nicholson, chairman of the Manpower Services Commission, reportedly described Britain's boardrooms as 'blighted by amateurs because no one had prepared them for it'. Also, part of the problem, laments Graham Day, chief executive of the Rover Group, is that while top management has an intellectual appreciation of the need for constant training, it all too often lacks the will to translate this into action plans. But, says Day, the time is past when acquiring new or top-up skills can be regarded as a one-off exercise. 'For the most part,' he declares, 'skills enhancement will become an ongoing process in the normal course of employment. For many vocations, this is already a reality. Consider the military technician, the aircraft pilot and the surgeon . . . However, unless management takes a positive initiative, nothing will happen.'

The scale of the problem is illustrated by a study from the Science Policy Research Unit (SPRU) at the University of Sussex. It looked at the impact of new technology on skills levels of factory operators in Britain, the United States, West Germany, Japan and Norway. It found two very divergent attitudes between the British and US companies on the one hand, and the German, Japanese and Norwegian firms on the other. The British and US companies saw automation as a useful means of deskilling tasks; the other countries as a means of increasing the skills of the workforce. At one British firm singled out as typifying the prevalent attitude, the operators were considered too inexperienced in materials and cutting technology to be allowed to program their own computer numerical control machines. The company had even locked the controls to prevent tampering. At two similar German companies, operators were trained in programming and encouraged to take control of their machines. Making use of their intelligence, stressed managers in these companies, speeded up the flow of work, reduced breakdowns and bottlenecks and led to better quality. One of the firms had even paid the operators overtime to write programs at home.

The SPRU report pointed out that if British companies are to make effective use of industrial robots they will have to adopt the German attitude towards operator skills. To maintain and repair these expensive machines, for example, requires a combination of electrical, electronic, hydraulic and programming skills. Such multifunctional people are rare on British shop floors, increasingly common on our competitors'.

The problem goes back some time. For example, in the shipbuilding industry of the 1940s, Britain built 50 per cent of the world's shipping; by the 1960s Japan did. Part of the reason behind this was that in Japan, virtually all managers were qualified engineers and the workforce was constantly trained and retrained.

The International Labour Organisation has shown that 20 per cent of British firms believe that the current shortage of employees trained in information technology is greatly detrimental to industry. An ILO report claimed that European (not just British) education and training objectives are still 'anchored in yesterday's world' and 'by and large they are conservative and inflexible, lacking aggressiveness and fine tuning to the present labour market'.

Britain's laggardly approach to developing scientific and technological skills has also been picked up by Sir Kenneth Durham, president of the British Association for the Advancement of Science. Durham, chairman of Woolworths and deputy chairman of British Aerospace, identifies the problems under four headings:

Society's apathy

An educational system which cultivates this apathy

Industry's lack of success in using new technology

Governments with unclear visions of educational aims and needs

Durham has criticised 'the cult of Oxbridge' and expressed distaste for a culture where more prestige is carried by someone studying classics at Oxbridge and going into banking than someone reading engineering at Salford and going into manufacturing.

But it is not only in highly technological or newly technological industries that Britain lags behind. Comparative qualification levels in basic industries, such as brickwork and carpentry or plastering and plumbing, demonstrate Britain's lack of educational competitiveness. Britain produced 240 plumbers and plasterers with advanced certificates in 1983, according to *The Sunday Times*. The equivalent figures for Germany were 6,070 and for France 4,565. We produced just over 2,000 people with advanced qualifications in carpentry; Germany produced more than 25,000, France 10,400. Even taking into account people gaining lower qualifications in these trades the number of newly qualified plumbers and plasterers in the UK rises to only 1,840 and newly qualified carpenters to less than 8,000.

The most obvious effect of this is skills shortages. Despite large-scale unemployment, some industries are still suffering acute shortages of suitably qualified manpower. The Association of Independent Businesses, for example, observes that small businesses' sales were affected by skill shortages. Companies are experiencing difficulties in recruiting engineers, particularly electronic engineers.

According to a review in November 1987 of the economic effects of the Youth Training Scheme by Cambridge University, the scheme does little to redress these shortages. Indeed, many trainees are learning skills which are not in short supply. Retailing accounts for 25 per cent of YTS trainees, hotels 7 per cent, hairdressing 6 per cent and clerical work 10 per cent. The Cambridge University research team also asked managers if they could detect an increase in the number of skilled workers which could be attributed to the YTS. Only nineteen said the scheme had had a generally positive effect with 217 reporting no noticeable change.

The same deficiencies are evident when it comes to office skills. For the same year nearly twenty times as many people received qualifications as personal assistant in France than in England, and more than ten times in what newspapers describe as 'intermediate secretarial/clerical'.

Even apparently well trained people often require extensive retraining before beginning work. The Federation of Recruitment and Employment Services has claimed that most companies who employ computer studies graduates have to completely retrain them. It points out that a typical company recruiting fifty computer science graduates every year will have to give them a three-month business induction course and an additional nine months' specific systems training before they can begin to work.

At the managerial level the deficiencies have been easier to disguise, but are becoming increasingly less so. Professor Charles Handy's *The Making of Managers* (1987) draws highly unfavourable comparisons with foreign competitors. Handy found that more than 33 per cent of British managers had had no management training since starting work and only 20 per cent of managers had degrees or professional qualifications of any sort. In comparison, 63 per cent of West German and 85 per cent of American managers had such qualifications.

A study by Professor Alan Mumford and colleagues at the International Management Centre at Buckingham found that 'most directors . . . have learned through a mixture of relatively accidental and unstructured experiences'. The study, which involved interviews with 144 directors in 41 companies, also concluded that the formal management development processes available didn't provide the continuous education necessary for senior level jobs.

Concern has also been expressed at the lack of management teachers being produced. The Foundation for Management Education has surveyed the years 1981–6 and found that a mere 263 doctoral students had qualified in business and management studies. At best, it calculates that this provides 53 potential new management teachers every year. To put this into perspective, British business needed 90,000 new managers each of those years but produced only 5,000 graduates with first degrees in business studies each year and only 2,200 with MBAs.

Not surprisingly, managers without qualifications can cause problems. The difficulties begin when people take their first steps up the management ladder. Summarising the opinions of Dr Robb Wilmot, former chairman of ICL and now co-chairman of European Silicon Structures, *The Director* recently commented:

> Robb Wilmot has no time for people who blame the uncompetitiveness of British industry on government, the unions, the Japanese or any other external factors. The blame lies squarely with managers, he says. If managers in the UK were as good as their counterparts in more successful countries, they would be able to overcome such problems. So why are managers in the UK so much less effective than in other countries? One reason is that they are not provided with the intellectual tools to do the job. Many people become managers because they are good at something else, and are promoted. When that happens they rarely undergo any sort of training or preparation for their new jobs, being expected to pick it up as they go along. And after they have done the job for some years, they receive little encouragement to update or refresh their skills, to cope with the rapidly changing conditions in world markets.
>
> Particularly at senior levels, argues Wilmot, managers need to spend much of their time reorienting themselves and their organisation to changes in their business environment. If managers are to be able to operate in a business environment that is already extremely complex, is changing rapidly and is influenced by unfamiliar issues such as new techniques, widely varying commodity prices, terrorism and very low interest rates in competitor countries (notably Japan) they need to resensitise themselves, to recalibrate, regularly.

Other managers echo the problem. An executive at John Laing recalls, 'I came from a nationalised industry. There was no formalised career structure. The company declared it spotted high flyers and trained them. But you were slotted into a particular position, where you might stay for forty years.'

THE NEED FOR CHANGE

Training at all levels remains problematical. Part of the trouble is that training's benefits are often intangible. Resulting improvements in productivity, for example, can easily be ascribed to new investment rather than improved

81

training. For this reason, statistics on training are unreliable. Yet a survey of 500 leading companies carried out by IFF Research in 1985 showed that 69 per cent of employees in Britain had not received any training at all in the previous year. The average time spent on off-the-job training was a meagre 1.9 days a year – about a quarter of the average in West Germany.

Distressingly poor educational and training standards are consistently revealed by statistics. The major problem is who should take the initiative? At the moment the government bears the brunt. It, for example, spends £1 billion a year on the YTS whereas in West Germany such schemes are funded by industry. Though the government may be in the driving seat, change demands the co-operation of educationalists and industrialists at all levels.

5

The Rise of Education and Training

'We must capitalise on the growing doubt about the ability of the British education and training system to develop British talent and skill.'
Sir Douglas Hague, Chairman, Economic and Social Research Council, 1987

'It is hard to resist the impression that it took the shock of recession on the one hand and the shock of reduced university funding on the other to bring together, in more widespread and practical ways, the vast amount of talent that was waiting to be tapped in these previously separated worlds.'
Sir Alex Jarratt, Chairman, Smiths Industries, 1987

'If we want to create more jobs, then improving the quality of education is vital.'
Basil de Ferranti, 1985

'It is essential that employers realise that they are going to have to train and retrain people already in employment. What we need to remember is that seven out of ten of the people who will be in the workforce in the year 2000 are in the workforce already. Most of them left school at the minimum leaving age and most of them have never had any systematic education and training since then.
   Adult training now needs to be given a new priority.'
Norman Fowler, Secretary of State for Employment, in The Times, *17 February, 1988*

'We are in a new industrial revolution which requires management trainees to develop "action learning" from real experience within business and industry, rather than get tied up with theory and academia.'
Sir Douglas Hague, former head, Prime Minister's Economic and Social Research Policy Unit, The Times, *5 February, 1988*

REALISTIC PROGRESS?

Are the education and training systems pulling themselves together suffi-ciently to provide people capable of fuelling an industrial revival? Most of the industrialists and trade unionists we interviewed remain distinctly pessimistic. There was a general sense that, while the signs of realism in the education system are patchy, they do exist and they are widespread. In this chapter we shall look at some of the examples of educational institu-tions and companies which have got their act together and are over-coming skills shortages and, by making people more employable, are helping to reduce unemployment. We would like to have based this chapter on data that showed trends across the country and allowed for comparisons with overseas competitors. Sadly, most of the data that does exist is primarily based on example or anecdote.

Earlier we looked at perceptions of education's role in industrial decline through the three categories of school, university and vocational training. It is helpful to take those same categories to look to the future through the eyes of our survey sample and other observers.

SCHOOLS

Carrie Lapham, head of Caerlon Comprehensive School, has an enviable record of placing sixteen-year-old school-leavers into jobs in an area where the unemployment rate is 15 per cent. Only 2 per cent or less of his 200-plus school-leavers each year have no job to go to. Declaring, 'I am not interested in educating people for the dole queue,' he has established, with several other local schools, an extensive net of contacts, consisting of parents, governors, ex-pupils and their friends, which the headteachers can tap to find jobs for youngsters. Careers evenings at Caerlon involve advisers from nearly fifty different professions and the careers and sits vac noticeboard is as long as a cricket pitch. Eight local schools participate in the East Gwent Schools' and Employers' Consortium, chaired by Lapham's deputy, where employers and teachers exchange information on employment needs, new examinations and other areas of mutual interest.

The significance of this example is not that the approach has been so successful, but that it is regarded as remarkable. It would be an exaggeration to say that the majority of employers and educational establishments have now become committed to the educational changes necessary for industrial survival. To summarise the industrialists' view, the schools, in particular, find it difficult because they are still structured for one overriding purpose – pushing as many children as possible through educational qualifications. If anything, this pressure is likely to increase. Providing lesser examinations for lesser brains merely exacerbates the problem. Moreover, there is always likely to be a shortage of public funds for experiments aimed at meeting industry's vocational needs.

In practice, the initiative to resolve industry's problems with the educational system must come directly from industry itself. In every other area of business, companies are starting to pay increasing attention to the quality of their suppliers. They know that 'garbage in' is no longer acceptable in manufacturing, service or any other business activity, because it results either in 'garbage out' – defective products that the customer is not satisfied with – or expensive corrective action. At present, most companies are merely checking and correcting the human resources goods inward. Given that unemployment now allows them, by and large, to select the best of the available labour, many are now asking how they would be able to cope with re-educating people for work as declining unemployment forces them to draw upon the less well educated.

Once the education system is viewed as another supplier, with problems of its own, then recriminations become less important than practical help. It is now common practice for large companies to invest time and counsel in helping suppliers reach and maintain an acceptable quality of output. The same principle should apply to the education system. Some practical steps have already been taken by companies, schools and the government, both individually and in collaboration.

Involvement in curricula

The range of initiatives by companies in collaboration with local and national government in recent years is quite wide, even if the total impact is still very limited. At the Polytechnic of North London, for example, is the Primary Schools Industry Centre, which produces teaching materials on industrial topics. The Industrial Society has a series of publications on the subject and so does the Schools Curriculum Industry Project.

Other initiatives include Project Trident, London Compact, Understanding British Industry, the Schools' Council Industry Project and British Schools Technology. The London Compact scheme, based on an American idea, makes a direct link between school work and securing a job on leaving school. The scheme guarantees jobs for school leavers who reach required targets of attendance, punctuality, skills and academic ability. Already twenty-five London companies are taking part with the hope of expanding the numbers to over fifty, securing jobs for about 300 school leavers.

Of more specialist intent is British Schools Technology (BST), initially funded by government, which aims to improve the teaching of technology. Under the chairmanship of Sir Henry Chilvers, vice-chancellor of Cranfield Institute of Technology, thousands of teachers have been retrained in the basics of advanced telecommunications, factory automation and robotics, modern computing and computer-aided design. Because most schools cannot afford to buy the necessary equipment for teaching these subjects, BST fitted out a number of buses, which tour as mobile laboratories in these specialist areas.

Kenneth Baker's city technology colleges scheme may help this process along. The first of twenty semi-independent colleges opened in September 1988 in Birmingham with 180 places. Alternatively, according to its critics, the scheme may simply suck away the limited resources for teaching these subjects into a small number of élite centres, while reducing the quality of the technological education available to those attending normal schools. Against this, it has to be said that the first college has stressed that its intake will not simply be from the most academically gifted. The major criteria for entry will be interest and motivation (of children and parents) to pursue the course of general studies which emphasises mathematics, science, technology and business studies. It has to be noted that the push for science orientation in schools did not prevent the numbers of A level science candidates falling by 10 per cent between 1985 and 1987.

A number of other initiatives are under way to encourage technology and science education. The Engineering and Technology Programme was introduced in 1985 with the aim of adding 5,000 more student places in high quality courses in engineering and information technology disciplines by 1990.

The debate, like many of the initiatives, we suspect, is only just beginning. Certainly, the issue of relative pay – should we pay teachers of these subjects more than their colleagues in arts subjects to attract more highly-qualified people into the role? – will figure in it. The only point of agreement on all sides is that there is a need for more, better-trained teachers in these subjects.

Baker's other major reform, the introduction of a national curriculum and national standards, may be of benefit to employers in that they will presumably be better able to assess one candidate's qualifications against another's. In practice, however, the differential in standards between examination boards below degree level is not so great that it often makes a material difference in recruitment. Employers tend to make hiring decisions on a number of factors, not least personality and aptitude demonstrated in extracurricular ways; the certificate of education merely provides a rough guide to intelligence level. The national curriculum could work against employers, however, if it limited the subjects covered, or ignored regional variations in skills needs, or prevented local employers having an input into curricula. It has also been criticised for stultifying creativity – an attribute companies are increasingly learning to value.

Some impact may also be felt from Baker's decisions to require all schools with co-opted governors to ensure that the local business community is represented on the governing board, and to encourage all teachers to spend time working in industry during the school holidays 'at least once every ten years'. Typical of the reaction of our industrialists might be 'Why has it taken so long?'

There are experiments at primary level, too. At Warlingham School, for example, which caters for children between the ages of three and twelve, the teaching of technology starts in the kindergarten and permeates all subjects. In geography, for example, explained one of the teachers in a newspaper interview, 'They can study harbours, lifting devices and cranes. Children are naturally inventive. We're trying to make sure they stay creative.'

Finally, after great huffing and puffing, examination courses in industrial topics are emerging. Business studies, engineering science, design and technology all appear on the curriculum. But they are far from universally available.

Nor do we yet have school courses specifically oriented towards youngsters who want to work in a particular industry. But there is potential, for example, for including practical modules in sixth-form courses, designed specifically to give a grounding in, say, electrical, mechanical or civil engineering. While pupils would follow a basic course in physics, they could select a career-orientated module to form one-third or more of the whole. Part of the module could include a short vacation spell working in the relevant industry.

Such an initiative would have to come at industry federation level, or perhaps higher. Easier to arrange would be closer ties between teachers and the training departments of individual companies. A great many of the skills taught by companies are behavioural. Indeed, the trend in training expenditure is quite clearly away from basic skills of machine operation (which can be learnt fairly quickly in most cases) towards techniques and personal relations. Increasingly, the fortunes of companies are seen to rest upon how well its people can work as a team, can provide initiative, and can resolve problems at the lowest possible level.

It is therefore a paradox that the areas where companies are having to expend the most training effort are those which education professionals, most opposed to the concept of more industrial orientation, consider most important – the production of well-rounded, well-adjusted individuals, capable of further learning. Some of the commonplace courses now carried out inside firms and virtually unheard of in schools and universities include the following:

Listening   Listening is a skill that most people need to learn. There is ample evidence to suggest that people untrained in listening skills absorb less than 20 per cent of the information given them in a normal conversation. Moreover, they are less able to structure conversations to ensure they have correct understanding or full information. Listening skills are fairly easily acquired and develop rapidly with practice after a short course of two days or less.

Time management   The ability to manage time is critical in any supervisory or managerial job. Unless people can organise their time effectively, they will find it difficult to organise other people. Industry uses well-tried techniques of teaching time management, which have scarcely penetrated the school system at all. (Many teachers would benefit from them, let alone their pupils.)

Effective communications   Understanding how people communicate is an essential part of working life, particularly in management or professional jobs. Even machine operators need to write the occasional clear concise memo. Schools and universities teach primarily essay style – exactly the opposite of what is needed in business, where a two-page memo is usually excessively long.

In terms of interpersonal behaviour, like teamwork, there is a good case for teaching at an early stage of secondary education the skills developed in recent years to interpret communications styles. It is now practical to train most people to recognise the posture and language clues that indicate whether others are on the same wavelength of understanding, whether they are in agreement and so on. It is also practical to train people to make use of the strengths and weaknesses that other people bring to a team. Some of these techniques have been developed for business; others have their origins in psychiatric therapy. What they have in common is that they help both individuals and teams to be more effective, more sensitive to the feelings of people they deal with. In addition, some of these techniques, such as the inaptly named 'neurolinguistic programming', teach people to structure the way they communicate, so that the risks of misunderstanding are minimised.

Very few schoolteachers, it appears, are aware that these techniques exist. Fewer still appreciate the impact they might have upon pupils' ability to learn. Yet amidst all of the attributes that make up the well-rounded individual of the liberal tradition, being able to communicate must surely score highly.

All of these are basic skills that we currently teach only in business, often when a person reaches a fairly senior level and can no longer manage without them. At this stage, it is invariably much harder to change habits, even though the capacity to understand what is required on an intellectual basis probably increases. The time to teach such skills is in the schools. Companies can do so by detailing their own trainers to train teachers and by lending training materials. The payback lies in improvements in the ability of new recruits to contribute rapidly to corporate goals beyond the mechanistic routine of their first job.

Exposing children to the realities of industry

One of the best ways to give youngsters a taste of industry and commerce is to allow them access to the workplace. A variety of schemes, of varying degrees of success, are now available, from 'shadowing' (where youngsters spend a period of time with managers as they go about their business) to direct work experience. Illustrative of the latter is a scheme, financed by Shell and involving several enterprise agencies and Durham Business School, in which 110 students are working in small, high technology businesses for their summer holidays. The school-industry link is one assiduously cultivated by government. Schools Industry Liaison officers are now used by 70 per cent of the local education authorities in England and Wales.

Young Enterprise has been in business for twenty-five years, giving fifth- and sixth-form students the opportunity to learn about business by running their own companies. In 1987 it involved 1,100 companies and 21,000 young people. The students elect their own board, make their own decisions on what to manufacture or what service they intend to provide and appoint their own managers to handle production, marketing, finance, personnel and so on. The companies, which are usually wound up at the end of the school year, usually have a mentor in the shape of a manager from a local firm who advises them on how to tackle the multiple problems that arise, such as bad debts, the failure of a supplier, or quality problems in production. Most companies raise capital from friends and relatives, which they invest in the business. Whether they make or lose money, the experience gives the students an insight into how business works.

The problems with Young Enterprise companies are threefold. Firstly, the vast majority of secondary schools do not take part. Secondly, the calibre of the company's mentor is important. If he or she cannot make the mental switch from working in a big company where there are departments to do everything, then advice given will not be very realistic. It is better to have mentors from small companies, but these are the people most difficult to reach and involve. Thirdly, the commitment and industrial awareness of the teachers is critical. If the teacher is uninterested, or doesn't have a clue how a business works, the students will gain proportionately less from the experience. Durham Business School, which has helped set up similar schemes to Young Enterprise in the northeast, has tackled this latter problem by training teachers to run enterprises of this kind. A pilot scheme with 50 schools in 1986 was extended to 400 schools in the region in 1987. Dr Allan Gibb, director of the Business School, maintains that 'in terms of developing enterprise learning systematically across the school curriculum, Britain is probably in the lead'.

Another helpful initiative is Understanding Industry, funded by the investment group 3i, which describes its role as: 'To attract a far greater proportion of high calibre entrepreneurial recruits with the ambitions to make a success out of manufacturing. To . . . encourage an awareness and an appreciation of industry's importance at an early age, so as to establish industry as a worthwhile career option.' Understanding Industry's reach is small, however. In 1987 it was only reaching 2.5 per cent of schools with sixth forms. By 1990 it aims to reach 7 per cent of sixth forms, with 28,000 children studying industrial subjects in class time.

Work experience for teachers

The need for teachers to have intimate practical knowledge of industry has been accepted by the Department of Education and Science. Its 1987 report *Partnership: Working with Education* states: 'Teachers' understanding of industry will influence their attitudes towards it, and the attitudes of their students. This understanding needs to be informed, up-to-date and backed by first-hand experience, not based on hearsay or second-hand impressions.'

Teachers in Industry (TII), a CBI initiative, has been one of the more successful schemes. Under TII, companies such as Courtaulds and BAT provide summer vacation jobs for teachers. The jobs are usually real jobs, in the sense that they have a clear output, but they are intended to give the teacher as broad as possible an experience of what makes industry tick. BAT (UK) Exports, for example, gave a Hampshire English teacher the task of reviewing its computer documentation and suggesting improvements. Said the teacher, Jill Dewar:

> Because teachers and management are on the whole mutually ignorant of each other's systems and work, teachers tend to steer the more able students towards the 'professions', as they are unaware of the professionalism that exists within industry and its challenging and demanding nature.
>
> As my secondment progressed, the differences between education and industry were increasingly revealed. I learned that there is an emphasis in industry on getting things done – achievement of objectives is all important and excuses are irrelevant: 'We have a problem. What are we going to do about it?' It is no use moaning about the circumstances – you have to look at the resources available and use them to your advantage.

91

The TII initiative has now come under the umbrella of Understanding British Industry. UBI involves 4000 educationalists and nearly 600 business people every year. Its schemes include teacher placements in industry and industrialist placements in education. UBI has now set up a joint programme with Rank Xerox to provide management training for senior teachers and a National Centre for Industrial Secondments for teachers funded by the Goldsmiths' Company and British Telecom. Even so, UBI chairman Sir James Cleminson has complained, 'I am disappointed that despite tremendous effort and generous support from many firms, UBI is still not adequately funded . . . we still need cash to support the action necessary in the field.'

Sir Alan Dalton, chairman of English China Clays, believes that support for UBI is far too low and that it is in need of greater industrial backing and organisation.

> The education system is not producing the skills needed by industry and leaving the liaison between the two to the meagre and essentially voluntary resources of bodies like UBI is absurd. Industry can and should do more in its own interests, but is frustrated by incessant fiddling by bureaucrats and examiners which is leading to lower and lower standards being regarded as acceptable in order, apparently, not to be unkind to the low performers. School-industry liaison is too important to be left to the muddling of the multiplicity of bodies involved in that field.

INDUSTRIAL TWINNING

Even so, an increasing amount of industrial twinning now goes on, though the Centre for Industrial Studies at The King's School, Grantham, points out some of the difficulties: lack of continuity in liaison; largely one-way traffic of the liaison; and the generally fragmented nature of the contact, which makes it difficult to influence overall policy within both the schools and the companies. King's has experimented successfully with the concept of a resident industrialist, an experienced businessman whose responsibilities include identifying areas in the curriculum where industrial or vocational elements can be included and designing case studies, exercises and teaching materials to fill those gaps. The industrialist, being able to talk to companies in their own language, is able to establish a continuous rapport and sell the concept of involvement in school activities more easily than a teacher. He or she can draw upon resources in friendly firms for aid in teaching working skills, such as report writing. King's also runs a student company, much along the lines of Young Enterprise, but with the difference that it is a going concern, with only the employees and directors changing from year to year.

HIGHER EDUCATION

In both Japan and the United States large companies have set up their own universities which award degrees relevant to the business, or have persuaded existing universities to adapt degree courses to the company's specific needs. In the latter case, it is increasingly common in the United States for the teaching to take place on the company's premises, rather than in the university. One benefit of this arrangement is that the lecturer can see for himself just how relevant what he is teaching really is.

In Japan, the flurry of technology-oriented colleges established by companies was sparked off in 1981 by Toyota, which spent well over $200 million on the Toyota Technological Institute. Mitsubishi, Nissan and Matsushita are among the other large companies that have followed suit. Traditionally, these companies have had excellent relationships with universities, cultivating relationships with professors and relying on their recommendations when recruiting. But the companies have found that they are often ahead of the university curricula in the technology they want to apply in the factories, so they are still constantly training and retraining engineers. Moreover, the universities find it difficult to offer the multidisciplinary courses which the firms now need.

Students at these Japanese company colleges may be practising engineers or school-leavers working on the factory floor. Either way, they combine their job with their studies. Courses tend to include both company-specific material and the diploma studies that would usually be offered at ordinary technical colleges.

Both of these approaches are open only to firms with thousands of

93

employees, but the principle is now beginning to draw favour in Britain. Jaguar has set up its own school, at a cost of £38 million, to train the engineers the formal education system can't. W H Smith, the newsagent chain, for example, has come to an agreement with Oxford Polytechnic to provide a tailor-made series of courses for its 2,000 managers. The managers may earn a certificate or a diploma in management studies, or, at the top of the learning tree, an MBA. Completion of in-house training courses earns academic credits, but the managers also have to undertake separate studies and project work.

W H Smith instituted the scheme because it was aware that in-house training, particularly at the management level, was frequently in danger of becoming insular. Maintaining standards was also a constant battle. At the same time, the normal polytechnic or university management course was not designed with company needs in mind. The in-house degree resolves both problems. Other companies following the same route include the Burton Group, IBM UK and the Woolwich Equitable Building Society.

At the same time, the necessity for universities to make up falls in income resulting from reduced grant allocations has stimulated many of them to take a very different stance in their relationships with industry. Instead of competing with industry for research funds, technology-oriented universities are now openly courting companies. Inevitably, this has meant that they have had to offer something industry is willing to buy.

Leading the field in this pragmatic approach to research and funding are Warwick and Salford Universities. Warwick doubled its research income from industry between 1982 and 1987. For example, its manufacturing systems engineering group, led by professor Kumar Bhattacharyya, earns over £1 million each year, simply by giving industry what it wants. At Salford, fully 12 per cent of the university's total income comes from industry. Academic staff are actively encouraged to act as consultants.

Not everyone is happy with this blatantly commercial approach. Apart from those who attack it on ideological grounds – that it limits choice of research subjects and diverts attention from basic research towards developmental research – there are many observers who fear that a combination of financial stringency and compliance with industrial imperatives will lead to a decline in arts and minority interest subjects. Warwick's vice-chancellor, Dr Clark Brundin, claimed in an interview that arts subjects have not suffered at all in his university 'because we have no hesitation in moving resources around the system to back up areas which cannot earn income outside'. However, Warwick is relatively well-funded, both from its own fundraising activities and from its 'most favoured' status with the University Grants Committee (on the principle of to those that hath shall be given). For other universities, the problem of underfunded arts courses may well be very real. Also of concern is how much capacity there is to earn money from handling research for industry. Brundin admits that 'we are getting near to the limit of what we can earn from those departments which can earn money'.

Comments from the industrialists and other observers in our survey indicate the following:

- Liaison between universities and companies on the technology and engineering side is making rapid strides, but there are still vast opportunities unexplored. The main problem appears to be that many university departments either still do not want to become involved in industrial projects, or, more frequently, do not know what they have to offer, or how to present themselves in a way that industry will value. There is a strong case for training university staff in negotiation and selling techniques and for creating far wider opportunities for interchange of staff between universities and companies. The exchanges should not be simply from laboratory to laboratory, but also between university departments and the production floor, marketing and other departments. The relative disparities in rates of pay and the organisational rigidity of most universities are among the most serious barriers to such interchanges.

- Liaison between other areas of university activity, with a few exceptions such as business studies and finance, have been primarily on a basis of charity.

- There is a case for including some form of business studies within the majority of degree courses. Those students who go on to finance or business careers would find it valuable in that it would give them more realistic career expectations. Those who continue in teaching should have an obligation to be industrially aware, for their students' sake.

- A general course for the first year of degree studies would provide students with a much broader education before they specialise than they receive at present. If evidence from the United States is relevant, a broader education may be generally beneficial. A survey by the University of Illinois questioned students who had graduated ten, twenty and thirty years earlier about what they had done with their degrees. Four out of five had followed careers which made little or no direct use of their college majors.

Michael Powell, of the Committee of Vice-Chancellors and Principals, believes that all universities and polytechnics should seek to establish close working relationships with industry. Among the obvious things they can do, he suggests, is invite industrialists to sit on academic advisory committees and create short 'top-up' courses for industrialists on important business issues.

A development towards greater mutual understanding may be provided by the seven new technology centres planned by the government. They are intended to act as centres where higher education and industry can collaborate with the aim of identifying training expertise and needs. The first such centre, at Cardiff, involved funding from Pickup (Professional, Industrial and Commercial Updating Programme). Pickup, financed by the MSC, involves colleges, polytechnics and universities in adult training.

Another significant step forward is the new MBA course introduced by City University Business School in 1987. Designed and managed by a consortium of companies and academics, it has no fixed duration of studies and no fixed abode. Most of the course takes place in the student's own workplace. The student agrees with his course tutor and his employer what he needs to learn and the course is constructed individually for him as a mixture of tuition and 'action learning' – learning by undertaking projects where he has to put the new skills and knowledge into practice. The formal tuition does not have to be solely that offered by the Business School – both sides recognise that some specific needs will best be met elsewhere. At the end of the course, students are assessed not by examination but by their performance.

VOCATIONAL TRAINING

The National Council for Vocational Qualifications (NCVQ) was set up in 1986 with the dual aims of improving vocational qualifications by basing them on the standards of competence required in employment and establishing a framework of National Vocational Qualifications. The NCVQ aims to do this by 1991 in order to respond to the urgent need for greater organisation in vocational training. It estimates that only 40 per cent of the British workforce holds any sort of qualifications that relate directly to their employment. In contrast, in Germany 66 per cent of workers have relevant qualifications.

What is clear from commentators on both sides of industry is that there is a need for some kind of organised body to co-ordinate training needs between scattered companies. The need arises particularly at the small company level, where identifying training needs is difficult enough, but constructing training programmes is simply too expensive and too time-consuming.

The Youth Training Scheme (YTS), started in 1979, has, to a large degree, supplanted the apprenticeship. Now a two-year programme, the YTS guarantees training to all sixteen- and seventeen-year-olds. Recent follow-up surveys of trainees show that around 22 per cent return to unemployment on completing the scheme with 30 per cent staying in a full-time job with the company they were attached to and 28 per cent finding work with other companies. The scheme also appears to have had some success in creating training awareness. Cambridge University research in 1987 for the MSC showed that 42 per cent of the companies featured said that the scheme had encouraged them to improve the training they offered young people.

National Training Awards, presented for the first time in 1987, may provide some means of focus. The first year's awards attracted 1,200 entries, virtually all from the private sector. Amongst the winners was British Steel, which gained recognition for a training scheme at the general steel plant in Scunthorpe. As a result of the training exercise, British Steel has calculated that £330,000 has been saved on the plant's monthly operating costs. The new National Council for Vocational Quali-fications may also cut away some of the confusion created by having 600 bodies awarding 6,000 qualifications.

Experience suggests, however, that neither exhortations by the chan-cellor and other politicians, nor the multitude of reports on the necessity of greater investment in training, will be of much help in persuading small companies to allocate significantly more resources to training. A recent EEC-funded study of training needs of small businesses in the Thames Valley found that almost all of the companies surveyed assumed they could poach people with the skills they needed from elsewhere. This myopia had led some of them into situations where they had little choice but to pay under-the-counter inducements when employing people with particularly scarce skills. While the demand for those skills grows, the supply remains relatively constant.

TASS, the manufacturing union, believes strongly that the industry training boards should be revitalised. It maintains, 'The acute shortage of technicians can be traced (at least in part) to the refusal by employers to

97

commit adequate funds to this vital area of training. To alleviate the situation, employers should be levied specifically to train a large number of technicians.'

By the time this book appears, we expect the debate over statutory versus voluntary training to have heated up considerably. A House of Commons' paper in mid-1987, entitled *Manpower Services Commission – Adult Training Strategy* has added fuel to the discussion. Noting that a large proportion of employers is content to let someone else do their training, the Committee of Public Accounts concludes that any deterioration in the economic climate would result in a further decline in training activity by these firms. The Committee suggests that the MSC's review of its adult training strategy in 1988 would be a good time 'to consider alternative arrangements, including the option of a more formalised structure, aimed at ensuring employers actually carry out the training role that is vital to the economy'.

On the other hand, it is clear that industry's expenditure on training *is* rising in general. The most comprehensive exploration of industry's expenditure on training, carried out by Deloitte, Haskins and Sells for the MSC in 1987, showed that about £5 billion was spent on training in 1986. This exceeds the MSC's 1984 estimate by a third (though the 1984 figures were questioned by a number of industrialists for excluding the training expenses of central and local government as well as nationalised industries).

Even so, France still trains nearly three times as many mechanical and electrical craftsmen and technicians as Britain, according to the National Institute of Social and Economic Research in January 1988. It observed, 'the fact that France has increased the numbers attaining craft qualifications during the past decade of industrial recession, instead of the decline observed in Britain, means that France is moving towards a situation comparable to Germany's, where the typical industrial worker is vocationally qualified to craft level.'

There are, however, signs that collaboration between industry and academia in vocational training is at last taking off. A national scheme of local collaborative projects set up in 1984 had involved more than 1,100 companies and 286 projects within its first two years. Under the scheme, small groups of employers discuss with local polytechnics and universities what kind of training and updating of skills they need. Where required, a specific study of training needs is undertaken. Then the academic institution and the companies design the training programmes together. Typical of the kind of project is one where three firms in the export trade have teamed up with Aston University and two colleges of further education to produce briefing packs on international trade. The question mark over this sort of activity is how well it would survive without government cash – more than half the money has come from public funds.

The rise of new training methods, such as distance learning and self-development, also makes it easier for employees at all levels to learn. Self-development, as the name implies, pushes the onus of responsibility for developing skills and knowledge back onto the shoulders of the individual. Distance learning describes the means of delivery and frequently combines several different media.

A good illustration of how a self-development scheme can work is at Texaco, which has created a central resource of hundreds of books, packaged courses and other learning resources. Employees can borrow from the library at will and a computer monitoring system automatically highlights items in high demand, so extra copies can be ordered. People are expected to do most of their studying at home, but some use of company time is permitted. Two methods are used to identify what people should study. Firstly, the employee can make use of self-assessment questionnaires that help him pinpoint major strengths and weaknesses. Secondly, the formal employee appraisal scheme has been adapted to point people towards training materials relevant to their weak areas. Every manager and professional employee has a catalogue of the contents of the library, categorised by subject and periodically updated.

The best illustration of the spread of distance learning is the Open University (OU), whose business school has some 7,000 students, either taking a professional diploma or courses in specific elements of management, such as marketing or managing people. The OU's new School of Management offers MBAs as well. Many of these students are sponsored by their employers. According to the OU Business School chairman, Dr Roy Close, '60 per cent take the courses to improve their performance and prospects or to update their skills and knowledge. The range of managerial levels that are attracted to these methods of learning is wide. One half of them are middle and senior managers, one half junior.'

Among the spate of recent reports on the state of management training, two in particular stand out. Published simultaneously, they come to very similar conclusions. Professor Charles Handy's *The Making of Managers* and Constable and McCormick's *The Making of British Managers* suggest a move to a two-part qualification scheme on the model of professional associations and institutes. Handy advocates that periods of early study followed by a preliminary examination should lead to a full qualification. John

Constable's report for the BIM and the CBI suggests increases in management training that would cost an estimated £138 million extra per year by the late 1990s. Under Constable's recommendations, the bill would be met by £28 million from central government, £6 million from local authorities and £104 million from companies and individuals. A good proportion of these recommendations throw the ball into the government's court. But what role should government play in ensuring that industry gets and continually upgrades the skilled workforce it needs?

The Social and Liberal Democrats Party spokesman on Trade and Industry, Malcolm Bruce, believes that the present government has it entirely wrong and that its job is not to create personnel for industry. Says Bruce, 'I'm wholly against this government's education and training policy. It seems to despise academic education. That goes against 2000 years of progress. Targeting down a vocational course at an early age will make education drab and boring and will decrease the quality of output. The government's job is not to create people for industry, which can only take 15–20 per cent of them anyway. Industry is not going to be the main direct employer for the future.' Bruce believes that flexibility between sectors is all-important. 'I'd like to see more interchangeability between industry, finance and the civil service.'

Some answers to the questions raised by the recent reports were given by Michael Beck, head of management policy at the MSC. Speaking at Ashridge Management College, he outlined four key roles for the government to play in a renaissance of industrial training and education. The first is as *leader*, setting goals that supersede all the different and sometimes conflicting interests of the various government departments working in this area. The second role is as a *catalyst*, initiating experiments and then publicising those that succeed. The third role is as the *establisher of infrastructure and systems* – large-scale innovations such as the Open College, which would be unlikely to happen without some form of governmental intervention. The last role is as *regulator of standards*, to give employers viable measures of managerial competence that will be consistent nationwide. While Beck was speaking in a personal capacity, his comments can be taken as a useful indication of the way government is thinking.

Other encouraging signs come from the various employers' bodies and institutions. The CBI and the Institute of Directors have both begun to take a strong interest in encouraging senior managers to continue learning and in providing infrastructures and materials for them to do so. The

IoD explains its interest as resulting from a number of factors. For a start, the pressure on companies and boards 'to perform more effectively if they are to survive at all' is growing. The pressure isn't just competitive; it also comes from financial intermediaries and politicians. Then there is pressure from recent legislation on the responsibility of the director. Negligence and incompetence can now be legal cause for disqualification and perhaps bankruptcy. (In the United States, a similar pressure arises from disgruntled shareholders, who are apt to sue directors personally if they do not like the way in which the company has been managed.) Another pressure comes from senior managers themselves, who recognise, for example, that they are often outclassed in international negotiations. And lastly, the presence of new methods of delivery, such as distance learning, have woken them up to the possibilities of using long journeys more profitably.

Among the IoD's ideas for meeting the need for director training are: a method of measuring directors' knowledge and competence, specially constructed training packages, and a scheme of accreditation for institutions offering director training.

The Government's Policy Unit, the CBI and the British Institute of Management are collaborating to formulate a management education policy based on a code of best practice. It now has a task force (the Charter Initiative) studying the adequacy of industry's approach to education. Companies joining the Initiative will commit themselves to integrating learning and work in a continuous development programme, using career planning and performance appraisal, and co-operating with the local education system. A second objective of according professional status to management (the chartered manager) and providing better means of measuring management capabilities has met with much less enthusiasm from industry.

The issue of management competence is interesting in that it could not have been discussed meaningfully as little as ten years ago. There simply weren't effective ways of measuring it. After all, most of the theories about what made a good manager have had to undergo radical revision in the light of experience, as the exceptions proved more numerous than the rules. The breakthrough came via the American Management Associations, which commissioned studies of 1,800 managers rated by their superiors as 'average' or 'superior'. One of the main differences between the two groups was, as might be expected, technical knowledge and skills. Some skills related only to specific jobs or specific companies. But the study found that there were four other major abilities that made the difference. These were:

- Entrepreneurial ability: a continuing interest in doing things better and in initiating action. They were proactive rather than reactive.

- Intellectual ability: being able to think logically, to play with new concepts and to extrapolate scattered items of information into a meaningful picture.

- Socio-economic ability: being objective in evaluating arguments, making accurate assessments of situations and people (including themselves), having good self-control.

- Interpersonal ability: the ability to work with and through other people. Effective managers have self-confidence in their ability as a leader; they enjoy developing other people's skills; they are concerned about the impact of what they and their team do; and they are good at communicating, particularly orally.

The key abilities of directors may well be different. But the knowledge that the role can be broken down in this way is a spur to developing training approaches that will measure competence and remedy weaknesses.

The study by Mumford and his colleagues referred to earlier also makes the point that 'the skills and experience required in order to be an effective director have not been fully identified and used in developing schemes . . . but could be'. Mumford advises training based not on abstract courses, but on developing skills around problems and opportunities that arise within the executives' jobs.

The one institution that should logically have taken a lead in management training many years ago is the British Institute of Management. However, its contribution to management training and education has been at best half-hearted and marginal. Like the cautious man who waits so long to dip his toe in the water that his bath turns cold, the BIM has been so tardy that it has an enormous credibility problem in educational terms. It has allowed its role to be usurped by other bodies and will have to struggle hard to regain it.

The issue remains just how seriously all parties – government, industry, trade unions and the education system – are going to take the question of how to provide the super-educated workforce the 1990s will demand. No one appears to question the need for targeted training and education as an essential prerequisite of sustained industrial renaissance. Everyone is prepared to tinker a little, but no one, it appears, is prepared to shoulder the responsibility and say, 'We must provide the resources required to create a highly-educated, adaptable, constantly learning workforce.' One of the most perceptive and positive analyses of the training and education problem to appear in recent years is contained in a report for the Public Policy Centre, by David Sainsbury and Christopher Smallwood. It makes four key recommendations:

1.   'The government needs to set clear standards for the education system.' Clearly, Kenneth Baker's concept of a national curriculum is a step in this direction, but a much clearer definition is still required of what the education system is supposed to be producing. The present situation is a bit like building a factory and making the employees start work without telling them what they are expected to make.

2.   'We need to make the education system much less specialised.' Sainsbury and Smallwood point out that: 'In 1960, Germany changed its system and allowed children in what we call the sixth form to specialise in any two subjects of their choice. They found, however, that this resulted in a shortage of students coming forward to study science and engineering. They therefore abandoned the experiment.'

3.   'YTS ... needs to be incorporated into an effective national training scheme. The authors recommend that this scheme should be funded by a remissible tax system.'

4.   'A national programme to raise the level of skills of British managers must be part of any attempt to revive the British economy.'

Another contribution to the debate is the CBI 'Young Turks' project Vision 2000, which aims to examine the key components of economic renaissance. Its conclusions regarding the way forward for education amount to the following:

1.   A broad national curriculum.

2.   Schools must generate in their students an appreciation of the role of wealth creation in society and a recognition that the provision of all social services is dependent upon it.

3.   Priority must be given to the acquisition of the skills of evaluation and assessment over those of record and recall.

4.   Teachers' pay must be related to performance.

5.   Business must give clear signals to institutions and students alike of the skills it requires from post-compulsory education.

103

6.   The funding of higher and further education must be changed so that institutions are more responsive to customer choice.

7.   The standard pattern of three terms and three holidays per year should be changed to fit working patterns.

8.   Companies must encourage and reward continuous self-development.

9.   Redundancy payments should be in the form of non-exchangeable retraining grants.

10.   Management should be recognised as a skill for which training is essential.

To implement the changes suggested by the Constable and Handy reports, Philip Sadler, principal of Ashridge Management College, has called for a new co-ordinating agency. Sadler believes that, amidst the plethora of government education bodies, management development is neglected. Says Sadler, 'Management education is a relatively peripheral issue for each one of them. No one agency or department is accepted by the others as the appropriate one to take the lead and co-ordinate national action.' He goes on to call for increased funding from industry for management education.

Some important recommendations of the Constable report are already underway – by 1990, Britain will probably be producing 5,000 MBAs per year, compared to 2,200 in 1987. Many commentators lace criticism of the present state and status of education and training with an element of optimism. John Banham of the CBI has written in *Manpower Policy and Practice*, 'The key to business success lies with ourselves: in the quality of our management. We are fortunate in the UK to have some of the best-managed companies in the world. We need more of them and we need to promulgate the message that it is the first prizes, not the second, for which we should aim.' Alistair Graham of The Industrial Society believes that the capacity for change exists, and that the question is merely how fast it can be acted upon. Says Graham, 'The question is: are we moving fast enough to take the advice offered ? It's not going to happen automatically.'

A national human resource development initiative, embracing all schools, all employers, all local authorities and trade unions, is perhaps the required means of pulling together the host of individual, scattered initiatives that are currently merely scratching the surface of the problem.

Says R W Adam, chairman of London and Scottish Marine Oil, 'There is a crying need for an improvement in educational standards and this improvement must be a joint operation between government, unions and parents.'

Unfortunately, history offers little encouragement. The 1902 Education Act provoked a debate as effusive as that held today. The aims, even then, were similar – the Conservative government wished to develop science and technology rather than classics and religion. There was an increase in science graduates and even Eton eventually installed laboratories – in 1957. One third of the graduates, however, became primary school teachers and the chance to increase scientific expertise in industry was missed.

In our view, this failure on all sides to grasp the nettle of the education and training gap is probably the greatest debilitator of our future economic growth. It is at the very heart of all other problems, for increasing the calibre of the people taking decisions and carrying out operations at all levels of an organisation automatically overcomes the barriers to effective innovation, the organisational rigidity, and the other evils of our industrial past. The solution must be an admission of responsibility, a commitment of resources and a sharing of the tasks needed to be done to ensure effective lifelong vocational learning. All of the elements are there, albeit in many cases only in embryo.

Now the primary task of any educational initiative is to reach a consensus on what resources truly are needed in the education and training of the workforce to remain internationally competitive; consensus on how to ensure that the vast majority of individuals and companies use those resources effectively; and consensus on how the resources will be found. Other countries have, to a greater or lesser extent, achieved this consensus. Our survival as an industrial nation depends heavily on whether we can do so, too.

105

6

The Decline of Leadership

'Management lost the will to manage.'
Sir John Hoskyns, director-general, Institute of Directors, 1987

'The post-war belief that the world owed us a living and the rapid advance of welfarism led too early to the conclusion that exertion in the nation's interests was a thing of the past. In the laissez-faire environment of that era power was handed over to trade unions in a vacuum created by industrial management, the divide became deeper; suspicion about means and motives reached corrosive and destructive levels. Leadership lost its followership as standards evaporated and there was too much evidence of self-interest.'
Sir Alan Dalton, chairman, English China Clays, 1987

'The prime reasons for Britain's industrial decline generally lie with management. I have entered businesses in engineering, in iron founding, in steel manufacture, in meat and food manufacture and in construction, and in all cases their troubles have been attributable in the first level to weak management.'
Lewis Robertson, chairman, Borthwicks, 1987

'In Britain we have had thirty years of management not meaning what it says; of government intervening in major strikes, and so undermining the management of public sector companies; of militant stewards justifying a harsh and aggressive line by pointing to a history of last-minute concessions by weak and indecisive management.'
Sir Michael Edwardes, Back from the Brink, 1983

FAILING TO MANAGE?

It became very clear early on in our research that 'the decline of leadership' had both a narrow and a broad interpretation. To some (the majority, particularly among industrialists), it meant the failure of managers to manage – the abandonment of responsibility. To others, it was a much broader issue, encompassing industry, government and trade unions equally. In all three institutions, it was felt people at the top had shown themselves to be pusillanimous, egocentric, narrow-minded and smug. In this chapter, we will confine ourselves to discussion of managerial leadership, if only because the leadership qualities of government and trade unions belong elsewhere in the book.

To even begin to test whether there really has been a decline in leadership and what impact, if any, that might have had on industrial performance, we first need to define what leadership is. Definitions of the nature of leadership abound, from the complex and obscure to the blunt comparison of US academic Warren Bennis: 'Managers do things right; leaders do the right things.' In practice, however, the basic definition of a leader is simply a person others will follow. The key traits that make people follow leaders, even though they may not entirely agree with where they are going, are:

- A recognition that they really do know what they are doing and where they want to go
- A recognition that they care about the organisation and the people in it, even though they may have to take ruthless actions
- An acceptance that they have integrity and courage.

These are the qualities needed to gain and keep a following. They define a leader, but not necessarily an *effective* leader, i.e. someone who takes their organisation in the right direction and is able to adapt to circumstances.

The impact of a presence or absence of leadership at the top is documented by a massive research study carried out some years ago in the United States. Richard Ruch, author of *Image at the Top – the Critical Role of the CEO*, analysed data on 3,500 hourly-paid employees of General Motors in the United States. The survey questionnaire was 13 pages long and had 128 questions. His most significant conclusion was that the employees' view of top management, from the plant manager right up through GM Central Office executives and the chairman himself, had the greatest single impact on worker job attitudes of all the factories studied. In many cases, the workers did not even know the names and faces of these top executives, yet their view of them was the major ingredient in having a positive (or negative) work attitude. The employees' major concerns were whether top management seemed to know what it was doing and whether it cared about the workforce.

The *only* way for would-be business leaders to achieve recognition and acceptance is to communicate their message constantly, using every medium available but particularly face-to-face discussion. To be truly effective *in the long term*, they also have to have the complementary skill of being good listeners and also be good teambuilders. These secondary characteristics are frequently absent in politicians, for example.

Of course, there are many other ways of looking at leadership. These tend to examine the way leaders behave, or the way they think, or combine the two. Among the most interesting theories are those of industrial psychologist Mort Feinberg, academic Harold Leavitt and political scientist James McGregor Burns – all from the United States. Feinberg presents a list of essential qualities he claims are found in all effective leaders. Among them are the following:

- Drive and energy. Effective managers can do several different things at once (and enjoy it).

- Dedication. Not just working late – that can simply be a sign of incompetence – but willingness to make sacrifices for the job, e.g. to make a last-minute change to domestic plans in order to catch a plane to sort out a customer's urgent problem.

- Competitiveness. Says Feinberg: 'Effective managers are interested in winning. It is not their sole concern – they are also interested in fairness and self-growth – but it is a high priority. They are constantly evaluating their own performance in light of the competition and striving to do better at each opportunity.'

109

- Honesty. Not only must they be trustworthy, but they must also be honest with themselves. Says Feinberg: 'Are they aware of some of their own limitations? How honest are they with you? How consistently do they produce the results that they said they would produce? Are their levels of aspiration out of touch with reality or are their goals close to what they can reasonably achieve?

Leavitt, on the other hand, divides managers into three types: implementers (people who get things done, who are good at persuasion, commanding and manipulation); problem-solvers (logical analysts with a passion for finding the right answers); and pathfinders (impractical, stubborn rule-breakers who often act impulsively, yet inspire others with their vision of what could be achieved and whose passion is to determine the right questions). It is from the ranks of the latter that most leaders emerge; but the most effective leaders will be people who can apply all three behaviours and thinking patterns as required.

James McGregor Burns was the first to identify the difference between what he called transactional and transformational leadership. Transactional leadership concerns the necessary day-to-day activities that ensure an organisation functions and survives. It is like the captain of the ship maintaining course. Transformational leadership 'creates institutional purpose'. It changes the direction and destination of the organisation and in doing so often changes the culture, too. In essence, this is another way of describing the pathfinder.

In Britain, the doyen of leadership studies is Professor John Adair, who sees the leader's role in terms of enabling. The effective leader, he maintains, focuses on the task to be achieved, builds and supports the team he needs to achieve it, and counsels, coaches and motivates the individuals so that they give their best to the team effort.

It was Adair who pointed out the fallacy of many previous approaches to leadership, particularly what he calls situational approaches. These assume that people take on leadership roles by virtue of their status (for example, their job title), their personality (the 'natural' ability to take command), or their technical knowledge. While it is true that we naturally defer to others in all of these situations – who but a real expert would dare to argue car mechanics with a garage technician, for example – the potential for being *mis*led is high. The ability to dominate does not necessarily imply that the individual has any other characteristics of good leadership and, indeed, as other research has shown, may indicate exactly the opposite. Moreover, an individual's status and technical knowledge are only valid within specific situations – we would not normally defer to

110

the garage hand on how to run a business. The problems arise particularly when we allow deference in an appropriate situation to spread into other, inappropriate situations.

Finally, our own research into the perceptions of people at all levels in successful and unsuccessful British companies, published in *The Winning Streak* and its sequels, indicates that effective industrial leaders:

- Are highly visible
- Have a clear vision of the company's future
- Set clear objectives for all managers/sub-leaders
- Provide opportunities for others to practise and gain leadership skills
- Set high standards, both for themselves and everyone else, and expect to meet or exceed them
- Have high integrity
- Care passionately about winning.

Before attempting to measure the calibre of leadership in British industry against these criteria, it is prudent to document the evolution of management styles during the past forty years. The historical development of modern management stems from the Victorian entrepreneurs, who, to generalise, combined a ruthless pursuit of profit with high moral aims. Significantly, those companies from that era which are still household names tend to be those whose moral aims were genuine, not feigned. Their survival is, to a large extent, a reflection of the strength of the vision that those entrepreneurs had for the future of their companies.

It should also be remembered that British management capabilities have been questioned for over one hundred years. Historian Alfred Marshall noted of the 1870s, 'Many of the sons of manufacturers were content to follow mechanically the lead given by their fathers. They worked shorter hours; and they exerted themselves less to obtain new practical ideas.' (*Industry and Trade*, 1919).

In the years after the First World War, the military model of management came increasingly to the fore. Managers were there to command. They had a *right* to manage and exercised it. The job held substantial status, both in terms of monetary reward and perks such as separate dining rooms (canteens were for lower orders) and, later, private spaces in the car park. On their own patches, managers ruled supreme and peers were actively discouraged from interfering in any manner.

This autocratic view of the managerial role gradually gave way in the

111

1960s to the concept that no manager was an island and that people at all levels in the organisation needed to work together. Autocratic responsibility was therefore shared out horizontally and, to some extent, diffused among a group of managers.

By the late 1960s, workers' participation was becoming increasingly popular. While British companies, trade unions and successive governments all actively resisted the kind of workplace democracy the Allies had imposed upon West Germany – experiments with worker directors in a handful of organisations such as British Steel were simply used to show that 'it couldn't work here' – the idea that people below might have something useful to say about how the job should be done gradually took root. Often resisted by trade unions as much as managers on the grounds that they saw no reason to do management's job, participative management grew rapidly. Managers were taught to communicate downwards through briefing groups and, in some cases, to listen to the messages coming from below. While some companies experimented with semi-autonomous workgroups and similar schemes, most were content to limit participation to providing information about what was going on.

For some companies, however, the advent of participation meant the effective abdication of middle management. Strong shop floor trade unions negotiating directly with top management or all-powerful personnel directors bypassed the senior line managers on all-important issues. It was scarcely surprising that, in these companies, managers retreated to the safety of bureaucracy. Bereft of real authority, they had nothing else to fall back upon.

Says Sir Alex Jarratt, chairman of Smiths Industries, 'In the earlier post-war years we allowed shop floor control to pass from first-line supervision to the shop stewards and as time went on and the going remained good, we burdened top management with the weight of top-heavy superstructures.' Such companies were, however, atypical. The majority of British companies either dealt with relatively weak unions or negotiated locally on local issues.

The global industrial recession of the late 1970s brought companies to crisis point. Michael Pitman of the Institute of Personnel Management identifies the characteristics of the decline of leadership as 'management sloth, low productivity and effectiveness of managers, and lack of respect for managers'. One of our survey respondents simply states of the post-war years, 'There was a lack of strong, sound leadership.' Another adds, 'There was a loss of control by management. Instead, people looked to trade unions for leadership.' Richard Giordano, chairman of BOC, has caustically observed of management in the 1970s, 'A fellow came to work in the morning. He could not fire anybody. He did not set the wages. He did not set prices. His own pay was probably frozen. He was hardly managing the business.'

In company after company the next step was to replace transactional leaders with transformational leaders whose task was to stem losses, trim back unprofitable operations and restore the health and direction of the organisation. Suddenly, managers who had been unable or unwilling to manage found themselves obliged to do so if they wished to save their own jobs. Many failed to adapt and either retired or became consultants. Inevitably, there was a certain backlash. 'Macho management' allowed repressed managerial Rambos to reassert their autocratic authority while the time of crisis demanded ruthless action.

In the late 1980s, a more balanced role has emerged. There is no excuse for autocratic management and there is a recognition in most companies that it is likely to be counterproductive in the present environment. Instead of a right to manage, companies now stress the *responsibility* to manage. The fashionable management style is a mixture of benevolent autocracy and participation, in which the manager consults and listens but takes the final decision.

To some commentators, this new style of management is a reflection of more responsible attitudes among trade unions and certainly it is true that the vestiges of macho management are most observable in industries, such as coal and newspapers, where industrial relations are most confrontational. But, equally, it can be said that 'responsible' trade unions have emerged in sectors which have best adopted the new management style.

This description of the evolution of management styles is necessarily a broad generalisation. But it does seem to accord with the perceptions of hundreds of managers. The significance of this evolution to a balanced management style is that it has taken us so long to get there, by comparison with our major international competitors, such as Japan, West Germany and Scandinavia. It is often assumed that participative management was natural to the Japanese, but this is not so. Japan's industry, like that of West Germany, was also organised on the military, autocratic model in the pre-war years. Both countries had to learn to achieve workplace consensus through new styles of management. The British simply carried on as before. On the trade union side, there are still many leaders who doubt whether we have got there yet and who perceive

113

management's mood as merely a reflection of confidence because it holds the balance of power.

So, how does this background of confused development of management identity relate to the key qualities of leadership?

COURAGE

In large part, the story of both the car industry and Fleet Street between the 1950s and the 1970s is a story of management which lacked the courage of its convictions. 'A lot of the heads of big business are not really businessmen, but bureaucrats. They've never really risked anything themselves,' says Sir John Hoskyns.

In some cases, the failure to take what top management knew was the right course of action to preserve the health and competitiveness of the company was no doubt motivated by humanitarian considerations. But this is an excuse that can be applied only rarely. European business schools use a case study of the *Financial Times*' foray into Europe to demonstrate this issue. The official reasons advanced by top management for launching a European edition were plausible, even if the venture did not come good until much later than predicted. But in reality, top management was trying to restore the company's fortunes by looking to greener fields elsewhere.

DEDICATION

There is no doubt that the rash of mergers in the 1950s and 1960s created monolithic companies with which people had great difficulty in identifying. Part of the process involved the wiping out of proud company names and with them the commitment of the managers in those organisations. Of the monolithic British Motor Corporation, Roy Grantham comments: 'The fate of BMC was decided by bad management. It had superb designers and engineers but appalling management'. Two examples quoted in *The Winning Streak* are worth repeating here:

- One of the first steps Peter Harper of Hanson Trust took on taking over the UDS group was to give the stores back their traditional name of Allders. Restoring the name went a long way towards restoring the staff's self-confidence and general image of the company, he believes.

- At Jaguar, John Egan was the sixth chief executive in eight years. He describes what happened at the company: 'In 1975 an attempt was made to subjugate Jaguar, along with other marques such as Rover, Land-Rover, Triumph, Austin-Morris, MG and so on, under the ill-fated Leyland Cars umbrella.

  At one stage Jaguar flags at the entrance to the factory were torn down. Only Leyland flags were allowed to be flown on the premises and telephonists were threatened with disciplinary action if they answered callers with, 'Good morning. Jaguar Cars.' Instead they were supposed to say, 'Good morning. Leyland Cars,' and if any further address was needed, 'Large assembly plant number one.' Worse still, the then two constituent factories of Jaguar were put into two quite separate organisational units within Leyland – the Power and Transmission Division and the Body and Assembly Division – hardly an appropriate fate for one of the most famous marques in the world motoring industry.

  Sir Michael Edwardes' . . . genius was to recognise immediately that no progress was possible unless famous marque names were recreated as a focus for group and individual loyalty.'

There is ample evidence that people identify more readily with a small organisation than a large one. However, there are also many examples of large companies which have retained a high degree of identification with their employees and are highly successful over the long term. There is no conclusive evidence one way or the other as to whether managers have grown more or less committed to their jobs over the past forty years. Talk of a decline in the work ethic in general is misleading. It is doubtful that the work ethic – the idea that hard work is good for its own sake – was ever a significant factor in working attitudes and behaviours at any time since the beginning of the industrial revolution. More significant, perhaps, is American research that suggests that people have grown less and less willing over the past twenty-five years to make personal sacrifices for their employer. Instead, the most able managers seek to balance the demands of home and career. The research, carried out at American Telephone and Telegraph during 1956–60 and 1977–9, found that newer recruits 'just aren't as interested in advancing up the corporate ladder'. Unfortunately, comparable research for Britain is not available, although much the same conclusions could perhaps be expected.

If this is indeed what has been happening, it may have made an impact on our industrial performance relative to those countries which had to rebuild their economies after the Second World War. Most managers are familiar with the hierarchy of needs theory of Abraham Maslow. Maslow maintained that there are five levels of needs that people are compelled to fulfill. The first level of need is physiological, relating to hunger, thirst and sleep. The second relates to safety; the need for shelter and security. Then come sociological needs such as belonging and friendship, followed by self-esteem needs such as status, recognition and self-respect. Finally, once all of these needs have been satisfied, come 'self-actualisation' needs such as personal growth and satisfaction in a job well done. People in the shattered economies of Japan and West Germany in the post-war decades had their attention focused on the essential physiological and safety needs, followed gradually by sociological needs – hence their ability to build a new management style from scratch. This was the level at which Britain and the United States were starting. In the post-war boom people were motivated by self-esteem. There simply wasn't the pressure to focus back on the basics.

One quantifiable measure is the numbers of hours people work. In common with every other developed country these have been on the decline in Britain since the turn of the century. As the table opposite shows, working hours in Britain have dropped below those in many of our competitor countries.

However, it is clear by comparison with the socialist countries that length of working week does not equate closely with industrial perform-ance. Moreover, the figures relate only to the *average* working week. Since the mid-1950s, the trend line for a group we can call committed profes-sionals – managers, doctors and others whose jobs require a professional commitment – has diverged rapidly. Senior managers, it has been found, worked an average of fifty-three hours a week in 1986 and the trend line is upwards. Given the shortage of managerial talent, the likely working week for committed professionals may reach sixty hours by the end of the century (the same as for all workers at the beginning of it), while the average working week will fall to between twenty-five and twenty-eight hours.

The implications of this for companies are severe. How can they moti-vate people to provide that level of commitment? Certainly they will have to consider changing the reward patterns, both to provide greater material

Working weeks in various countries

	Average hours		Average hours
Switzerland	43–44	Italy	39 or less
Japan	40 or more	Belgium	38
US	40 or less	Rumania	46
		East Germany	43.75
West Germany	39–40	Czechoslovakia	42.5
France	39 legal maximum	Hungary, Poland	42
UK	39 or less	USSR	41

and status incentives, but also to restructure jobs so that managers will find increased self-fulfilment in their work.

The fact that managers are working these long hours (to what purpose and how effectively is another matter) indicates that lack of dedication among British managers is probably not a serious contributory cause of industrial decline. Indeed, the achievement of more balanced lives is probably a plus point rather than a minus.

INTEGRITY

In the wake of so many recent City scandals, it is tempting to talk of a decline of business morality. This may well be the case, but we have been unable to track it, nor to establish any relationship between moral turpitude and general industrial decline. However, in our researches for *The Winning Streak*, we found many examples of companies where integrity towards employees, customers and suppliers was an essential ingredient in their success. These companies worked hard to ensure that they did always operate with integrity. We also found that less successful companies typically paid much less attention to ensuring that integrity was a core value in their operations. This is not to say that they set out to be dishonest – far from it – but that they did not work hard enough to create an

117

atmosphere of mutual trust between the company and its various contacts. Inevitably, the only people who could create that atmosphere were
the chief executives and chairmen. There is a reasonable argument that
the predominance of 'bean-counters' at the helm of large companies in
the 1950s to 1970s focused top management attention on numbers rather
than people and that this was readily interpreted by employees and
customers alike as a lack of integrity.

If we are to believe the export promotional agencies, a large part of the
decline of the market for British manufactured goods appears to be due to
perceptions, both at home and abroad, that products are unreliable and
overpriced – in essence, that companies were not giving the customer fair
value for money. In the customer's mind, that is tantamount to saying
that the company is not dealing with integrity. Although the reasons that
these goods were uncompetitive were multiple and in many cases outside
the control of the company itself, the marketplace reality is built upon
such perceptions. Where the reasons were within the control of companies, customers had good cause to assume that they were not dealing
with integrity. They had clearly forgotten their moral responsibility to
provide customers with a product that met their needs at a reasonable
price. Again, the only place the blame can lie for such a situation must be
at top management's door.

HIGH VISIBILITY

Time and again in our researches of successful and unsuccessful companies, we have observed that managers – and particularly top managers
– in successful organisations constantly make their presence felt. They
take time out to visit the operations, talk to people at all levels, hear for
themselves and react to what they hear. They have the common touch
sufficiently to, for example, say thank you, by telephone or in person,
to people at the lowest levels for an exceptional piece of customer
service. They spend a great deal of time showing people in the organisation that they care about it and are interested in *everything* that happens in it.

The one thing that struck us most in talking to these executives was that
they are not the norm; indeed, they are so unusual that their behaviour

has been often regarded by their peers as at best peculiar, at worst a dangerous anachronism. The concept that the chief executive's role is to keep away from the coalface because he will only make the workers uneasy runs deep in British management lore. It runs counter, of course, to the best of military practice – the most brilliant generals almost all had the common touch – but that just goes to show how it is possible to extract and apply only the worst elements of a good example.

For forty years and more, Britain's chief executives have built concrete and mortar barriers between themselves and their workforces. Frequently physically removed from the sites where the productive work was done, they erected ever larger and more imposing corporate headquarters. The more remote they became, the less real control they were able to exercise over the business, and the more bureaucrats they needed to filter and select information on which decisions could be made. The only information on which they could rely, not being third, fourth or nth hand, was financial and even that became increasingly questionable as unit managers learned to play the system to do the things that needed to be done but were proscribed by the rules.

And rules there were, by the ton. As the headquarters' bureaucracy grew, the inhabitants had continuously to invent new rules to justify their existence. Most, inevitably, told unit managers what they could not do, rather than helping to expand the scope of what they could do. The more centralised decision-making became, the less initiative could be taken by the units themselves. The organisation's competitive responses became slower, and unit managers were less willing to stick their necks out for what they knew was right.

We are convinced by observation of successful companies in many countries that rules are a poor substitute for a strong culture (in the sense of a set of shared values and 'right' behaviour), led by a strong top management. Setting a clear example of the kind of behaviour and thinking patterns required removes the need for most rules – people in general are smart enough to be able to work out for themselves how old and new issues should be tackled once they understand the values that underlie 'the way things are done here'.

Nonetheless, remote management and heavy bureaucracy were not symptoms solely of the UK at this time. The same was equally true of large slices of industry in the United States, West Germany, France and Japan – and it still is.

A CLEAR SENSE OF MISSION

Many Japanese companies have planning horizons of thirty years or more. The typical UK firm may plan five years ahead, at best. Certainly, the industrial regeneration of both Japan and West Germany owed much to far-sighted visions by senior figures in both industry and government.

In the post-war years the family firm, which had been slowly declining, became obsolete as mergers and takeovers brought the professional manager to the fore. The old-fashioned entrepreneur did not fit easily into the new managerial environment. With him disappeared some of the core values that had sustained the Victorian company. In particular, the rise of the professional manager meant a shortening of horizons. Unlike the family entrepreneurs, who would typically be concerned with the nature of the company they would hand on to their grandsons, the professional manager typically reached the top in his late fifties and retired within five to seven years. The span of his commitment rarely extended beyond that date, if only for the pragmatic reason that the new CEO would want to do things differently and would impose his own concept of the future of the organisation. This lack of long-term planning led in many cases to absurd switches in direction every few years – for example, between centralisation and decentralisation – as successive CEOs attempted to make their mark. In the resulting confusion, continuity of culture and values was an early victim. Ironically, throughout much of this period industry was complaining vociferously about the damaging effects of swings of government between left and right. Few of the complaining executives stopped to consider the beam in their own eyes.

Again, however, it seems that the UK was not alone in this development. The United States is perhaps farther along this route and certainly most Western countries have seen the same decline in family companies and growth of professional management. One possible variable is the quality of training of the professional managers in each country, which is broadly seen as lower here than in our competitors. It may also be true that other countries have means of overcoming the problems of shorter horizons and lack of continuity in professionally managed firms. In Japan, for example, consensus management (overestimated as it so often is – there are few more autocratic chief executives than the top dogs at some Japanese companies) ensures that values and long-term objectives are hammered out at many levels of the organisation. Those who rise to the top jobs have contributed to the setting of long-term goals and are strongly committed to them. Radical changes of direction are therefore difficult to make and extremely time-consuming. In both the United States and Japan, the position of president is often used to allow former CEOs to continue to contribute to the planning of overall strategy, while not interfering in the day-to-day running of the company. This useful device is not often used in British companies, where the new CEO usually cannot wait to see his predecessor put out to grass.

Sir John Hoskyns suggests that the process of constant change at the top of major British companies may have been accelerated by the bureaucratic culture. 'The top job is a position of status. It carries a knighthood. So it's not fair for someone to hang on to it too long,' he explains.

CLEAR OBJECTIVES

Clear understanding of the overall corporate mission is essential if people at middle and junior management levels are to be able to put their tasks into perspective. If they cannot see how what they do contributes to the whole picture, then their commitment will inevitably be lower. So companies without a strong, well-understood mission are unlikely to have managers focused on clear objectives.

Trying to compare objective-setting in the UK and its competitor countries is not easy. There simply isn't an effective measure. The best we can rely on is anecdotal evidence, which suggests that many managers, particularly in the middle levels of companies, felt dangerously adrift in the period 1950 to 1980. This feeling found expression particularly in their unwillingness to take risks on their own initiative. Not knowing for sure whether a new venture or a new way of doing things fitted the overall direction of company strategy, many managers chose the safe option of sticking to the rules. In doing so, they reinforced the corporate bureaucracy. (If they did take a risk and it went wrong, they strengthened the hand of the bureaucracy even more.)

121

PROVIDING OPPORTUNITIES FOR OTHERS TO LEAD

Our international researches into excellence show clearly that successful companies tend to provide people with broad management responsibilities as early as possible. Less successful organisations promote people through the ranks of one function, such as sales or accounting, then expect them to acquire general management skills when they reach a senior position in their forties or fifties – by which time their capacity to learn behavioural skills is diminished.

The growth of bureaucracy undoubtedly limited the opportunity for young managers to broaden their experience. The cross-functional tasks that, in an autonomous unit, would be assigned to younger managers, were largely absorbed by people at head office. The system became self-perpetuating. Where the only internal candidates of suitable rank for the top job were functional professionals who had not had broad exposure to the whole range of management skills needed to run a modern company, they compensated for their own inadequacies by reinforcing the bureaucracy in a (largely vain) attempt to control, even if they couldn't understand. While the Japanese in particular were deliberately cycling high-flyers through numerous departments to expand their managerial know-how, British firms (with a few notable and very successful exceptions) saw only the problems of such an approach. Every time a new and functionally inexperienced manager came in to head a department, they explained, efficiency would be reduced while he came up to par and then, as soon as he was performing well, he would be moved on. To a certain extent, that was and is true. But the British firms were making the fatal error of confusing functional expertise with management expertise. While a good leader-manager needs to have sufficient technical expertise to earn the respect of his subordinates and to make basic decisions, his primary skill lies in the completeness of his understanding of the management function. The higher up the organisation he goes, the more he needs to cast off functional specialisations and to master the strategic elements of a wide range of disciplines, including finance, marketing, human resources, applied technology and communications.

To the extent that our competitors recognised this more than we did, they were at an advantage. However, quantifying that advantage, or indeed documenting it in detail, is not possible. What we can catalogue is numerous cases where the one-discipline background of top management has been a significant factor in corporate decline or collapse. Perhaps the best documented example is Rolls-Royce, where an overwhelming engineering orientation at top level meant that marketing and financial considerations were given short shrift until it was too late.

SETTING HIGH STANDARDS

To a large extent this relates to the issue of mission. Companies that have a clear, well-understood mission tend to have high ambitions. Then they set high standards of performance to achieve them. They find, on the whole, that the higher the standards you set (within reason) the higher the standards people achieve. The trick is to aim slightly above what people know they can do, and keep raising the pole each time they learn that they can do it.

Almost every highly successful company we have examined, inside or outside the UK, has the common characteristic that the key managers care passionately about winning. Many of our observers feel that this was not the case with British industry in the immediate post-war decades. Correlli Barnett's argument that, having won the war, we forgot about winning the peace, is backed up by forceful arguments, which need not be repeated here. It would be interesting to conduct a study to relate the language and tone of annual reports in different countries with what was happening in their respective industries. We expect that such a study would show that the language of the 'aggressor' nations in the peacetime trade was more positive, more ambitious, more buoyant, stressing opportunities rather than problems. The comparative UK annual reports, we expect, would be characterised by cautiousness of language, and talk of problems rather than opportunities.

Certainly, the history of the decline of the major manufacturing sectors is one of waning ambitions. None of these industries collapsed under one sudden attack. In all cases, decline was a gradual affair, a long series of debilitating skirmishes. Call it marketing myopia, if you will, or any other metaphor that fits, but the unarguable fact is that, instead of regarding each lost skirmish as an affront to be revenged, British car, engineering, electronics companies, and many others, simply retreated. The will to win, the ambition to become major global players, was replaced by an acceptance

123

that decline was inevitable. All that remained was the will merely to survive, and even that disappeared in all too many cases.

Some observers, such as R W Adam of London and Scottish Marine Oil, are kinder in their analysis: 'In the post-war period the UK still had access to substantial traditional markets – the old empire. It took a number of years before other countries, due to war damage or lack of skills, were able to penetrate these markets. This bred a certain amount of complacency in the minds of British management who were slow to adapt to changing circumstances.'

7

The Rise of Leadership

'Industrial regeneration can only be led by managers and the responsibility lies clearly with them to energise their enterprises, bringing their unions with them, change the attitudes of society towards the key role of management and win the support of local and national Government.'
Sir Ronald Dearing, chairman, The Post Office, 1987

'Leadership is a priceless gift that you earn from the people who work with you and you have continuously to earn that right.'
Sir John Harvey-Jones, former chairman, ICI, 1987

'Management is out of date now. We're talking about leadership. We've had too much management in this country and not enough leadership . . . The climate was created in the 1980s for these people to emerge. They wouldn't have got jobs during the corporatist era of the 1960s and 1970s.'
Walter Goldsmith, chairman, Food for Britain, 1987

MANAGERS ARE MANAGING

The consensus of industrialists and politicians of the right and centre is that the captains of British industry have finally begun to learn how to lead rather than to manage. Said an executive in our survey, 'The whole notion of leadership has taken on increased legitimacy. There is an increasing recognition of the personal need to take charge, to take initiatives, and organisational structures are responding to that.' Another observed, 'In some areas more than others, leading companies have caught the spirit of excellence. The connection has been made in some areas between creative management and bottom-line performance.' On the left there remains some scepticism (if not outright disbelief), based on an assessment that few fundamentals have changed in terms of management's capability, and that the only real change has been in the balance of power.

Whatever the truth, everyone seems agreed on two basics:

- The quality of leadership has been exceedingly strained in recent decades and this has been the cause of much industrial indecision and strife.

- The situation is capable of remedy; more and better leaders can be developed.

The vestiges of poor management standards and practices cannot be removed overnight. Their effects will continue to be felt, a situation mourned by Social and Liberal Democrat Malcolm Bruce: 'Bad managers allowed bad management practices. When good managers came in they were hampered in what they could do by entrenched attitudes and ways of doing things.' Labour's John Smith believes there is a long way to go:

'Industrial management is weak in this country. It needs to be strengthened,' he says.

Many executives also realise that the orientation of the past takes time to change. Says one manager in our survey, 'Today's leaders are the product of the 1960s and 1970s. They still conform to their role models of that period. Short-term profits are still all important, inhibiting long-term or risk investment.'

There also seems to be a considerable level of agreement on the *kind* of leaders required. Few union leaders would dispute the following definitions from Shell's Bob Reid, who declares the qualities the new leaders will require are:

- Perceptiveness – an understanding of human relations.
- Communication – an ability to present and articulate a problem to others and to hear, interpret and evaluate their reactions.
- Judgement – the ability to take a position which has a logical and ethical integrity.
- Positive self-analysis – a capability to analyse yourself objectively, your personal strengths and weaknesses and then to go and do something about it.

Comments by other industrialists focus on the creation of an environment where managers can learn to lead. It is no coincidence that one of the meanings of the word 'manage' is 'to get by'. This seems to have been for many managers the primary interpretation of their role. Simply redefining their role as leaders can do a great deal in restoring their confidence, pride and sense of direction.

In many industries, and for many managers, the eighties have proved a lesson in commercial survival. Basic Darwinian logic still persists in business. E J Hughes, personnel manager of Cornhill Insurance, observes that 'The bitter lessons of recession coupled with high unemployment appear to have been learned and implemented. Survival as the first requirement of industry is no longer seen as text book or remote – it has been shown to be a reality.'

Some survey respondents cite the inspiration of others. One observes, 'The revival of leadership is down to personalities such as Colin Marshall, John Harvey-Jones of ICI and Christopher Hogg of Courtaulds, who have considerably changed ailing companies.'

Sir Alex Jarratt is adamant that the recession of the late seventies, severe as it was in its impact on middle management levels, had a positive effect in making managers' responsibilities clearer and in obliging them to accept responsibility. Whereas it had been possible previously to spread responsibility within the bureaucracy, now individual managers have to carry the can for the performance of the operations under their control. Says Jarratt, 'One of the beneficial aspects of recession is that it has caused most of us to look critically and act promptly on our overheads – and it is sad to say that because again it sounds like a reaction rather than an initiative. In particular it has encouraged us to seek slimmer, more decentralised, more personally accountable management structures than we had previously.'

To create this kind of leadership mentality, says Jarratt, company boards must set an example through:

- Preparedness to think and plan long-term, in terms of the markets to be served, the products to serve them, and the changing competitive and technological environment in which this will take place. I daresay that a good pilot should always be able to fly by the seat of his pants if the emergency is such as to demand it, but it is no way to fly a 747 across the Atlantic.

- Putting in place the organisational structures that will make these things happen. In particular, creating units that will be market-driven and profit-oriented, led by management who are held to be, and feel, personally responsible and accountable for the outcome, and are rewarded accordingly. I am very much in favour of the importance that is now generally attached to the development of smaller companies in · this country, particularly in those product areas where the people inputs are greater than those of any other factor of production. But we still have a heavy concentration of large companies.

- Proportionally more so than most of our competitors, we need to instil, wherever we can, the small company mentality into the constituent parts of large ones. I have found few things more pleasing than hearing the management of a subsidiary talking about their company as if they owned it. We must not allow size to blunt the spirit of enterprise.
  This will not happen by accident. It will have to be planned for, and implemented, as a continuous commitment over a long period of time. It requires changes in organisation to provide:
  Fewer layers of management.
  Clearer lines of command.

- Placing responsibility for producing short-term and long-term plans, for the resources to be employed in them, and the profit to be secured from them as far down the line – and as near the served market – as possible.

●   Clear guidelines on the freedoms and constraints to be placed on such managers.

Colin Southgate, managing director of Thorn-EMI, is in the process of creating a leadership environment of this kind. As he explains it, the company he took over:

> . . . grew from mainly acquisition [culminating in the Thorn-EMI merger] to a group of diversified, semi-independent companies ranging from manufacturing bomb fuses to hiring music artists, from semi-conductors to TV rental, with very little synergy whatsoever. In short, it was an unwieldy conglomerate, too diversified to manage, bureaucratic and with a rigid hierarchy, decentralised with no central direction or management information system, and made up of fiefdoms. Its products (often of high quality) were not wanted or were too late for an increasingly global marketplace; it had outmoded plants and the majority of its managers had a UK or at best a UK-exporter mentality. It was, in other words, a traditional British company.

Southgate sees the creation of a leadership environment in terms of a small number of fundamentals, among them team-building, managing change and effective communications. He explains:

> Commitment, not control, produces results. The best and the brightest will gravitate towards those corporations that foster personal growth. The manager's new role is that of coach, teacher and mentor. In addition to the traditional three Rs we hope they've learned at school, we must teach them how to learn, create and think the Rs of the new information society. If all you have is a hammer, your problem is bound to be a nail. The best people want a sense of ownership. Authoritarian management is being replaced by networking, requiring an approach of greater consensus and diplomacy. Team building must be undertaken on a cross-functional as well as functional basis. Intuition and creativity are challenging the quantitative numbers approach, though not substituting for it.
>
> Once a vision is created and articulated, it is about attracting and motivating people. This process is alignment, which transforms a leader's vision into a shared corporate one . . .
>
> Managing change is something you learn in new start-ups and the high-tech industry, whereas it's not a habit acquired in the businesses of the smokestack era. In the information-based economy it is vital to so shorten lines of communication that you speed up the response; that

you balance planning with action, to build up a sufficient push-pull between R & D and the market place, and have sufficient information on the external environment and the competition on which to base decisions.

On the question of cultures, we are trying to build into our external identity those shared values which reflect our underlying personality and go to make up our corporate market positioning. In other words, the excellent leader doesn't rely solely on what the outside world thinks or says to find his unique territory in the market place. It's just part of the equation . . .

The vacuum created by an absence of communication will soon be filled with rumour, drivel and poison. The excellent leader realises that the company has an image whether it wants it or not and the priority must be informing, commenting, persuading, convincing.

Leaders create energy by instilling purpose in others. It's about belief and single-mindedness. The optimum mix for leadership is a delicate blend between financial resources and human creativity if a leader is to add value and grow those around him.

It makes the difference between success and failure, best illustrated by differentiating between managers who just ask, 'Why?' and leaders who delve deeply enough into their imaginations to ask, 'Why not?'

This welcome preoccupation with the importance and style of leadership is unprecedented in British business. One reason that it has come to the fore may be that so much has been accomplished in recent years by senior managers who were not afraid to assume their leadership role. The example quoted most often by our industrial observers is Michael Edwardes.

One of the principal lessons of Edwardes' approach is that he recognised that an effective business leader has to carry the entire workforce with him. It is much the same message as that provided by Richard Ruch's research that we examined in the chapter on leadership decline. Sir John Hoskyns recalls a conversation with Edwardes shortly after the fever of British Leyland's industrial relations malaise had broken.

Edwardes told me that he had been patted on the back for throwing Red Robbo out. He went down to the shop floor to find out what people thought. He told all the shop stewards he would meet them in the canteen at one o'clock, but went to the shop floor first. People there said it was the best thing that could have happened. The stewards didn't have a leg to stand on.

Although Edwardes, Egan, McGregor and other gutsy chief executives received most of the congratulations (and the brickbats, when things turned sour), there were hundreds of other people in similar but less public positions who were doing much the same job of transforming ailing companies into healthy ones, or reasonably fit companies into fighting fit ones. These transformational leaders knew exactly what they wanted to achieve and why they wanted to do it. Their methods were not always applauded, but they carried other people along with them because they had the courage of their convictions. These leaders should not be confused with the bean-counters who simply cut costs (particularly people) when the recession first began to bite. Rather, they emerged as a response to the failure of the bean-counters to provide a stable base for the future. The distinction between the two is fundamental: the transformational leaders had a strong vision of what they wanted to build in the medium to long term, once the leaks in the ship had been plugged; the bean-counters' vision was limited primarily to short-term survival.

The fact that there are two types of turnaround executive – both frequently successful in their own terms – needs to be absorbed thoroughly by boards of directors. The cost-cutting game can typically only be played once. Unless the company embarks immediately after-wards upon consolidation and growth, the next crisis will probably kill it. The debate over whether we are truly out of the recessionary wood will be resolved only historically. If crisis returns, the company needs to be sure that the turnaround leader has the vision to regenerate rather than just amputate.

Of course, leaders like this are in relatively short supply. Many com-panies will no doubt continue to appoint chief executives who, while not caretakers, are competent administrators, capable of maintaining steady, often highly respectable rates of growth within the vision already estab-lished. These leaders should not be underrated. After a period of instability and radical change, the corporation, like the human body, needs rest, recuperation and consolidation. Key functions continue; new initiatives are taken. But the radical searching – asking the right questions, rather than seeking the right answers – is deferred. The mistake is to appoint a succession of such leaders, or to allow a transactional leader to continue in his role for too long. After a long period of not being stretched, stimulated or challenged, the organisation experiences a different kind of stress. The stress of lack of vision and purpose, of failure to appreciate and embrace change, leads to symptoms such as the loss of frustrated key talent, while the lesser talents stay; the growth of internecine corporate politics; the

131

displacement of innovation as a key top management commitment; and, perhaps most damaging of all, the loss of the aggressive spirit of determination to win and the acceptance of less than challenging standards. It must also be said that managers who have vision only, or who have faulty vision, can be equally disastrous. The ability to balance continuity with the past and drive for the future will be one of the key attributes companies need to seek in their top management.

Many of these points were reiterated in our survey of personnel professionals. The leadership characteristics examined in Chapter 6 were again brought up. 'I believe the courage of Mrs Thatcher has done much to set an example in terms of strong positive leadership at the top,' one executive observed, and her formidable image does seem to have impressed many in business.

The essentials of strong leadership – dedication, integrity, visibility, sense of mission, clarity of objectives, high standards, and providing opportunities for others – were generally seen in our survey to have been reborn. The scale of this renaissance in leadership qualities is, inevitably, unquantifiable. A number of our survey respondents, however, pointed out that successful leaders are not all high-profile media figures. Said one, 'Leadership gets confused with high City profiles. The best-managed companies are not necessarily the darlings of the City and vice versa. There are a lot of unsung heroes.'

'The changed economic reality, internationalisation of markets and of competition are providing new challenges to business performance and leadership,' said one executive. It was frequently argued that the opportunity to lead allows managers to develop long-dormant skills. Said one manager, 'The business environment has improved, allowing good leaders to display leadership qualities. This has a knock-on effect of developing leadership qualities.'

Sir John Hoskyns is similarly optimistic: 'More, bigger businesses are being driven by younger, numerate people who have spent their formative years in a reasonable, tolerant tax regime. These people are increasingly international in outlook. They are beginning to work on the assumption that new ventures will probably succeed.'

So how do we go about creating more and better leaders? There is a role for all partners in industry – companies themselves, government, unions and the business schools. Companies need to spell out what kind of leaders they want and make available the resources and opportunities for executives to learn leadership skills as early as possible. Alistair Graham of The Industrial Society is concerned about the latter trend. Says Graham,

'Companies are not good at giving people major responsibility in their early years to stretch them.' Business schools, which turn out knowledgeable strategists and analysers of accounts, need to concentrate at least some of their MBA coursework on developing the leadership capabilities of students, something that is severely lacking now. Greater involvement with companies, to provide learning opportunities where MBA students are forced to exercise leadership skills, perhaps during a one-year practical, would be of some help.

For the unions, there is the interesting possibility of following Japanese practice, where interchange of personnel between company management and union management is accepted as a natural path of advancement. It is not unusual for the chief executive to have been a senior union official at some stage in his career and, indeed, it is looked upon as a beneficial experience. While UK and Japanese unions are not directly comparable, the potential for mutual benefit is high in businesses where both the company and the trade union structures are led by competent managers, who understand both sides of the people-finance equation.

Government's role in encouraging the growth of leadership is to stimulate the business environment in such a way that it becomes attractive to lead. This is partly a matter of tax and incentives, but equally one of creating and reinforcing public perception that to win in business is a respectable, admirable activity. A basic requirement for the latter, however, is that politicians should share that belief passionately themselves. Even among the Conservative party, regarded by many as the party of big business, this is probably true of only a minority of MPs.

8

The Decline of Flexibility

'Many declining organisations experience the phenomenon that the most mobile people quit first, leaving their less mobile colleagues behind. If those who are mobile include some of the best people, then, unless remedial action is taken, the decline of the organisation may be irreversible, as the good people leave the less able behind.'
Charles Baden-Fuller, London Business School, 1987

'People are reluctant to move, even a comparatively small distance, to take new jobs. This is a natural reaction. What woman welcomes the turmoil of moving house? Who wants to separate herself from old friends and neighbours, to set about finding new schools for the children and discovering by experiment who is the best local butcher? . . . There must be some mobility of labour. If people are not willing to move as their fathers did, the economy cannot thrive.'
Margaret Thatcher, Prime Minister, The Times, 21 July, 1980

'Too many British managers have their heads buried in the sand, are too resistant to change, and see innovation as suspect.'
Bruce Scott, vice chairman, CBI, Northwest Region, 1986

'There are still many examples of poor and out-of-date management in British industry; and many of the older industries are still too fragmented, with companies, and factories, which are too small by present-day international standards. In such industries there is clearly a need for restructuring and rationalisation. And even in newer industries British companies are much smaller than their international competitors.'
Tony Crosland, Socialism Now, 1974

THE INFLEXIBLE ORGANISATION

Most of our survey sample recognised that inability to respond to change – let alone pre-empt it – was a major cause of industrial decline. Inflexibility was seen in many forms: in the way organisations are structured; in production processes and use of technology; in management systems; in the division of labour; and in terms of employees' geographical mobility.

Each of these is, in its way, a separate issue. Yet, according to several of our commentators, most are linked by one underlying root cause – the unswerving pursuit of size at the expense of responsiveness. The one group that scarcely mentioned this as a cause at all were the industrialists. There still seems to be a naive belief in the virtues of the massive organisation that is not supported by the evidence from either side of the Atlantic.

BIGGER IS BETTER

'Institutions are created for the purpose of resisting change. That's their main function and they preserve all kinds of things that one doesn't want. But how to get rid of them I do not know,' said the historian A J P Taylor. The enthusiasm for corporate size, rather than quality or flexibility, has highlighted the inherent conservatism of business organisations. The trend was identified at an early stage, but was generally ignored. 'The main current of legislative opinion from the beginning of the twentieth century has run vehemently toward collectivism,' observed A V Dicey in 1914 in his book *Law and Public Opinion in England*.

'Smaller business units were virtually forgotten in the 1940s and 1950s with the big is beautiful mentality,' says Brendan Donnellan of the Association of Independent Businesses. The case was influentially backed by J K Galbraith in his book *The New Industrial Estate*, 1967, which argued that the modern industrial world demands the large-scale efficiency of massive companies.

The international prevalence of mergers in the 1950s and 1960s began a trend which has never really been halted. People, particularly managers, are impressed by size. The American motor industry came to be dominated by the big three of General Motors, Ford and Chrysler while in Britain the 1960s saw a succession of mergers which brought the big four banks into dominance, and created the giants GEC and AEI as well as transforming the motor industry. In food and drink there was the Cadbury Schweppes merger in 1969 and, in insurance, a rapid series of combinations and expansions. The Rank cinema chain joined with Xerox; Beechams absorbed Lucozade and Badedas, while Booker moved from its base of sugar, rum and African trading into engineering, as well as other sectors of the drink and food industry. The question which follows is: did these newly-merged companies manage to capitalise on their size to become international forces?

The benefits of size have been much discussed. Governments have announced their disapproval of monopolies but have done little to prevent them. They can only comment on the effects of mergers. The 1978 Labour government report on mergers policy concluded, 'The evidence suggests that in something like half of the merger cases studied, profitability was reduced – or at any rate was not increased.' Government monitoring has taken on a variety of guises. The Monopolies Commission, established in 1948, was later followed by the Office of Fair Trading (1973) and the Department of Prices and Consumer Protection (1974–9). This has done little to stem the flow and the trend for mergers has continued with Thorn-EMI, Racal-Decca and GEC-Avery to add to the list in recent years. There were, in fact, nearly 11,000 mergers of industrial, financial and commercial companies in the UK between 1965 and 1978. Of these a mere forty-three were referred to the Monopolies and Mergers Commission. Thirteen were found to be against the public interest.

The belief in acquisition as a route to success continues and in 1986 an estimated £13,047 million was spent on a total of 694 acquisitions, against £1,080 million spent in 1970.

Company acquisitions (excluding mergers) of industrial and commercial companies, 1970–1986

	Number of acquisitions	Expenditure on acquisitions (£ million)	FT index of industrial ordinary shares (1935=100)
1970	787	1,080	361.0
1972	1,203	2,523	503.8
1974	503	500	251.2
1976	352	448	368.0
1978	564	1,090	479.4
1980	469	1,475	464.5
1982	460	2,177	574.5
1984	566	5,373	854.9
1986 (prov)	694	13,047	1,287.1

(Source: *Britain in the 1980s: Enterprise Reborn*, 3i, 1987)

This frenzy of activity has to be set against the low level of takeover activity in some of Britain's competitors. West Germany and Japan were particularly notable for the relative stability of their large organisations during the period of Britain's decline. The belief in growth by acquisition is one of the fundamental differences between Japanese and British firms. One of the most frequent comments we have heard in British executive offices when discussing corporate strategy is that 'organic growth cannot give us the speed of development we require'. Yet Japanese companies turn to acquisition only as a last resort, regarding it virtually as management failure. There are no prizes for guessing whose rate of growth is highest.

In fact, since the 1950s, Britain has had the highest rate of diversification amongst large companies in the leading industrial nations. As a result, Britain has the most concentrated economic structure and, coincidentally perhaps, the weakest small company sector. The process of diversification has been achieved through acquisitions and mergers at a rate far higher than in other countries. Even so, few British companies are dominant in their sectors at a world or even European level. Even in banking and financial services, Britain's dominant position has been lost.

Politicians have done little to control or limit acquisitions. Harold Wilson's government of the 1960s was particularly enthusiastic. The trend was such that the total value of company acquisitions in Britain rose from £501 million in 1964 to £1653 million in 1968 when 199 mergers were examined by the Board of Trade. One hundred companies now control nearly half of manufacturing production.

The hundred largest manufacturing firms' percentage share of net output, 1909–70

1909	15	1948	21
1919	17	1953	26
1924	21	1958	33
1930	26	1963	38
1935	23	1968	42
1939	23	1970	45

(Source: L Hannah, *The Rise of the Corporate Economy*, 1983)

Very few British companies have found that extensive diversification breeds success. Multiproduct companies like Hanson Trust and BTR, which have diversified continuously and successfully, remain exceptions in large part because acquisitions are expected to operate as if they were independent companies with active and profit-conscious shareholders.

In most cases, the initially impressive effects of diversification simply give an illusion of growth. It is not only that. A great deal of time, the expensive time of managers and professionals, has to be spent on each acquisition and on avoiding being acquired. In recent times we have witnessed the defiant stances of Pilkingtons against BTR and the brewers Matthew Brown against Scottish and Newcastle; costly and exhaustive exercises to preserve independence. Concentration is shifted from competitiveness to acquisition and merger, with finance which could be reinvested in the company finding its way elsewhere.

The onus on acquisition and merger may also explain much of the recent development in the financial sector. It is a process which demands a great deal of financial and legal expertise.

The car industry demonstrates the tendency towards amalgamation at

139

the cost of appropriate rationalisation. Car manufacturers became amongst Britain's largest, most top-heavy and unprofitable institutions. In 1920 there were ninety British private car makers; by 1929 there were a mere forty-one; in 1939 thirty-three and, by 1946, numbers had slipped to thirty-two with six companies really holding sway over the industry. The merger in 1952 of Nuffield and Austin into BMC reduced the number of major manufacturers to five – BMC, Ford, Vauxhall, Rootes and Standard. BMC was to evolve into British Leyland, perhaps the best chronicled story of industrial inflexibility. The company created a large centralised line and staff structure with a perpetual shuffling of personnel. It was a large, disparate organisation, but few attempts were made to bring the various parts of the company together under any corporate philosophy. The attempts, when they came, were cosmetic. At Jaguar, which produced BL's showpiece top-of-the-range product, attempts were made to submerge the company's much-valued identity. Sir William Lyons, the company founder, had the good sense to remove his portrait from the walls of the offices. He no longer wanted to be associated with the company. BL identified size with success and only the advent of Michael Edwardes as chief executive in 1978 brought rationalisation on a massive scale.

PRODUCTION PROCESSES

There are really two problems here. The first is lack of new manufacturing investment, which we discuss elsewhere in this book. The second is failure to understand that new equipment doesn't necessarily increase flexibility – the lessons of mass-production in the 1950s were that automation can all too easily deskill and reduce flexibility, undermining much of the expected productivity gains. The perceptive technology director can choose his new production systems to allow for fairly broad changes in markets, materials or other important variables. As is so often the case, his starting point has to be: how do we give customers what they want at a cost we can afford?

The situation in the UK in the past thirty years has been well summed up by the CBI's Vision 2010 report, published in 1986, which commented, 'British companies have been slower than our competitors to replace traditional dedicated production systems with flexible manufacturing systems and advanced process technologies which enable a fast product response.'

INFLEXIBLE SYSTEMS

Part of the nature of systems is that they tend to take on a life and purpose of their own as they are used. Either people adapt to doing things the system's way or they use the system to fulfil objectives for which it was not designed. If we are to believe what Japanese companies tell us about the manner in which they operate, there appears to be a fundamental difference between British and Japanese approaches to the use of systems. In Japan, systems are designed to help and to a greater or lesser extent designed by the person who has to operate them. He or she, therefore, has both an ownership of them and the understanding to adapt them to changing needs. In Britain, by contrast, systems tend to be owned by functional specialists who discourage interference by the people who have to use them. Just how real this apparent difference is has not, to our knowledge, been tested. It could make a fruitful area for future study. What we can say is that there is significant recognition that accounting systems, as designed and used in British and American companies, frequently work against the strategic and marketing interests of the organisation. Says Robert Kaplan of Harvard Business School, 'Existing cost accounting and management control practices are unlikely to provide useful indicators for managing the firm's manufacturing operations.'

Robert Sheridan of PA Management Consultants explains the problem in more detail in this extract from an article in *Issues* magazine:

In tomorrow's corporate culture, aims are defined in physical terms (quality, lead times and so on) rather than in cost terms. Blocking the achievement of those aims, however, is the dead hand of outworn accounting concepts, practised by accountants whose thinking is geared to short-term financial constraints and rules.

Accounting has to change so that its practitioners cannot merely cope with, but be partners in, the technological changes affecting manufacturing.

Manufacturing managements feel the constraints most in two accounting areas: costing and ROI [return on investment] calculations.

141

Today's costing systems have developed from the scientific management movements some three-quarters of a century ago and most standard textbooks on costing were printed in the 1930s. In the model 'T' Ford days, it was very effective in promoting the efficiency of mass production enterprises that made a few standard products with well-known characteristics, stable technology and a high labour content. Accountants could talk in terms of 'standard costs' and characterise production costs as direct, indirect, fixed and variable with overheads charged or direct labour, as the cornerstone of costing. Today's cost accounting still looks at these factors that used to be critical for success: direct labour efficiency through specialised work, usually on product-dedicated machines.

Now, however, it is neither labour cost nor machine cycles that make the difference, but service and markets. So it may well pay for a company to have an expensive machine and only use it once a week, if it removes a bottleneck that prevents speedy delivery, for example.

The return on investment concept is largely post-war, but it too concentrates on savings in labour, materials and overheads. Here the focus is on cash flow over time. Discounted cash flow (DCF) calculations ensure that the key time periods are no longer than medium term . . . In sum, ROI simply lacks the scope to reflect the information that top management needs if it is to make good strategic decisions.

What both Kaplan and Sheridan are saying in essence is that our accounting systems reduce companies' flexibility and therefore their ability to compete in international markets.

MANAGEMENT INFLEXIBILITY

The large corporation produces management systems and has, paradoxically, to encourage independence and leadership whilst extolling corporate identity and togetherness. Andrew Kakabadse in his book *The Politics of Management* states:

The professional will place marked emphasis on the quality of work he produces. He may see each new task as a challenge to his professional expertise. The task may have to be tackled in a slightly different way to all other previous tasks. Consequently the professional, whether engineer, doctor, lawyer, teacher or social worker, would probably attempt to tackle each job as he saw fit and not refer to the organisation for guidance.

The opportunity to tackle new problems with innovative methods is often difficult to achieve within a large company. At times the apron strings can feel like chains.

Responsiveness to change was seen by many of our observers as an essential attribute. The CBI's Vision 2010 Group observes, 'Companies must not regard change as something to resist until the last possible moment; rather they must embrace change willingly . . . The relative slowness of British industry to adapt new technologies and move into new markets must be attributable at least in part to management's failure to involve the workforce sufficiently.'

Part of this problem may be that a breakdown of the delegation of working tasks in a standard company could run like this: the chief executive delegates those bits of his job he can't or doesn't like to do to his senior executive colleagues. They do the same and the process goes all the way down the line to the person at the bottom who gets all the tasks no one wants to do. This, at least, is the common approach in most western companies. A more viable approach would be to design the bottom-level jobs around the customer's needs. This inevitably results in better, more interesting, more motivating jobs. It also means that the operators take over part of the responsibilities of the supervisor and so on up the chain, until one or more layers of the hierarchy disappears.

In practice, managers are often as tied down by particular disciplines as their employees. They may well believe themselves to be professional managers, but in practice they are more likely to be marketing, financial or production specialists. Management demarcation has been as much to the fore as worker demarcation.

The combination of horizontal (hierarchical) barriers and vertical (functional) barriers is the foundation of most bureaucracies. Observers are divided on whether it is a good thing for managers to stay with one organisation for most of their career. From the company's point of view, there are benefits to be gained from a constant infusion of new blood and ideas. But there are also penalties in the form of reduced loyalty to the organisation and less stability of corporate culture. Certainly, the rate of turnover at senior levels in Britain is less than in the United States.

143

In 1986 a Board of Directors study conducted by Korn-Ferry International showed that over half of the chief executives in Britain's largest companies had been with the same company for twenty years or more. Over a quarter had been with the same company for thirty years or more and eight out of ten had been promoted from within.

There are undoubtedly a great many professional, thrusting, ambitious young executives but it is still commonplace for managers to plateau in their late forties or fifties and accept that they have gone as far as they are going to go.

One oil company admitted in 1986 that some 40 per cent of its middle managers fell into this category. Many of these managers might have moved on to new jobs where they might have found greater challenges, but golden handcuffs, in the form of pension rights and accumulated benefits, often restrained them. While companies have been increasingly willing to buy these rights out, fear of the unknown or fear of future unemployment has prevented managers from moving on when it would have been for the good of their own careers and the good of the company.

Allied to this has been the fact that most managers increasingly specialise as their careers develop. When they eventually reach boardroom level, they find themselves in a completely different situation. Bob Garratt, a management consultant, argued in his book, *The Learning Organisation*, that companies need a strategy to develop the capabilities of their directors. Garratt points out that directors need to stop concentrating on their particular specialism and develop a broader appreciation of the organisation – no easy matter if you have spent thirty years developing specific skills. Successful companies tend to give people the opportunity to learn general management skills much earlier than unsuccessful companies – typically in the age range 25–35 compared with 40–50 in less successful firms.

The inflexibility of management structures has been exacerbated by constraints on management action set by government and unions. For example, managers in industries such as shipbuilding, which have been consistently bailed out by government, were almost forced into complacent and uncommercial attitudes because their freedom to take independent decisions had been mortgaged.

A few observers also point to the difficulties companies have had in abandoning commercial ventures that go wrong. In America there are relatively few barriers to laying off workers and closing plants. Similarly, in Japan flexible working practices permit plants to be closed and workers to be redeployed when necessary. In the face of overcapacity and other such problems, suggest our industrialists, British managers have often been prevented from adjusting manufacturing capacity and labour forces with the speed they require. Nevertheless, it has to be admitted that companies in other countries, particularly Benelux and Scandinavia, have coped relatively well with much stronger legislative requirements concerning dismissals and closure.

ON THE SHOP FLOOR

One of the best-chronicled examples of inflexibility is demarcation, the process of breaking down tasks into a variety of functions so that labour can be more easily directed and costed. Its predominance in some of Britain's traditional heavy industries, as well as many others, has been a millstone round the neck of progress, agree both industrialists and many trade union leaders.

Industries like steel and shipbuilding were strictly divided into a hierarchy of skills, wages and status. This anachronism was chiefly the result of the practice in the early twentieth century of breaking down skills so that managers could employ exactly the right amount of people every day. In the days when managers had a vast pool of willing labourers it was the easiest way of choosing who got the work. Training a person with a particular skill to develop another skill effectively put another person out of work. It was, therefore, discouraged.

The historical roots of demarcation may well go further back. Adam Smith's *The Wealth of Nations* pointed out that economies of time and operation could be achieved by dividing the production process into separate tasks.

The consequence was a complex and increasingly impractical division of labour. In the shipyards there were platers, riveters, caulkers, burners, drillers, shipwrights, blacksmiths, plumbers, joiners and carpenters. They brought with them anything up to twenty separate unions each of which demanded a say on behalf of its members.

With so many different voices, negotiations between management and unions were complicated and, at times, farcical. Even up to the late 1970s, negotiations tended to be on a national scale. Dr David Grieves, personnel

145

and social policy managing director at British Steel, comments, 'Increases in [labour] costs were mainly direct consequences of traditional negotiating policies involving regular annual increases in pay for union members negotiated at national level with no significant compensating improvements in productivity. These were negotiated nationally in a complex series of annual negotiations involving each group of unions on a separate basis.'

Given these complexities and the rigidity of demarcation, industrial disputes were inevitable. Shipbuilding suffered even during the Second World War and its troubles reached a head with the famous 1972 work-in on Clydeside led by Jimmy Reid. Industrial relations crises were combined with a fierce opposition to new technology. The equation that new technology meant job losses was easily accepted in such a claustrophobically rigid environment and formed the mainstay of arguments over the future 'leisure society'.

In allowing these attitudes and practices to develop, management was undoubtedly weak. The 1966 Geddes Report into shipbuilding revealed that management had short-term attitudes towards markets, men and money. Among the far-reaching effects Geddes associated with demarcation was a sense of lack of security among shipyard workers. The link between these practices and the lower productivity of the British yards is assumed rather than proven.

Demarcation was equally a result of management practice. Taylorism – the concept that work was most efficiently performed when broken down into small tasks that could readily be monitored – had been deep-rooted in British manufacturing since the early 1920s. It gave managers a sense of control over the little things, even if the major problems went unnoticed or ignored. The breaking up of tasks went furthest in much of the car industry where it had direct and generally disastrous effects on productivity and morale. A Ford motor worker, speaking in 1973, mused on the nature of his work in Huw Beynon's book *Working for Ford:* 'It's the most boring job in the world . . . Ford class you more as machines than men. They're on top of you all the time. They expect you to work every minute of the day.' Boredom, in no small part due to demarcation and lack of corporate identity, fuelled any potential friction.

Under these circumstances, rapid change to meet market needs became almost impossible and the savings from job specialisation rapidly became outpaced by the costs of inflexibility. Hence on Nissan's arrival in the northeast, Ford estimated that Nissan's production methods gave it a cost advantage of about £250 per car.

THE MOBILE WORKER

Says Sue Shortland, manager of the CBI's Employee Relocation Council, 'There is growing pressure on employers to boost their competitiveness – and this means using their manpower as efficiently as possible. However, there is increasing evidence that employers are wary of relocation, only considering it when it becomes crucial.'

British industrialists, in particular, are increasingly concerned at the costs and practicality of moving skilled employees or recruits to where the work is. The north-south divide, with affluence and work broadly being centred in the south, poverty and unemployment in the north, has accelerated in the eighties. Politically there is certainly a divide with the Labour Party prominent in the north, and dominating Scotland almost totally, and the Conservatives controlling the rest of the country. This process was highlighted in the 1987 General Election when traditional Labour areas of London chose to back the Conservatives.

The north, the traditional manufacturing centre, continues to be the most militant area in terms of days lost through strike action. The Department of Employment shows that the number of days lost through strikes in Britain was 89 per 1,000 employees in 1986. It was 216 in the north, 172 in the northwest, 165 in Scotland and 138 in Yorkshire and Humberside. The lowest figures were in East Anglia, with only 38 days.

The north has also been the area most drastically hit by the decline in manufacturing. But dramatic job losses in the inner cities have not been restricted to the north. In fact, between 1981 and 1987 Greater London lost 215,000 manufacturing and construction jobs. Only self-employment and 114,000 new service industry jobs have limited the decline. Two thirds of manufacturing jobs in London have been lost in the last thirty-five years.

Despite this, unemployment continues to be centred on the depressed north and economically devastated Northern Ireland. The regional breakdown at the end of 1986 is shown in the tables on page 148.

The decline in manufacturing has devastated northern industry. The employed labour force has also greatly decreased in most northern areas while growing in East Anglia, the southwest and southeast. The overall population has also declined in the north, Yorkshire and Humberside, the West Midlands, the northwest, Wales and Scotland.

Mrs Thatcher maintains, 'I don't think there is anything like the north-south divide that some people like to think.' However, economic growth

147

Percentage regional unemployment rates (December 1986)

Northern Ireland	18.8	Yorkshire & Humberside	12.9
North	15.9	East Midlands	10.8
Wales	13.4	Southwest	9.7
Northwest	13.6	East Anglia	8.6
Scotland	13.8	Southeast	8.2
West Midlands	13.2	United Kingdom	11.3

(Source: Department of Employment)

has been largely confined to the southeast which has the largest number of successful, fast-growing, small firms. In contrast, the north had the fewest and was the area where the largest numbers of small firms were taken over, according to Trends Business Research (July 1987).

Employment trends by region, 1976–86

	Employees employed in manufacturing (percentage change)	Employed labour force* (percentage change)
Southeast	−25	+2
East Anglia	−3	+13
Southwest	−15	+5
West Midlands	−29	−7
East Midlands	−18	—
Yorkshire and Humberside	−35	−6
Northwest	−35	−12
North	−35	−12
Wales	−34	−10
Scotland	−38	−8
Northern Ireland	−33	—

*Includes self-employed

(Source: Department of Employment)

Severe as the recession in the north may have been, it has not led to a migration south. Indeed, lack of mobility remains a major problem for British industry. An advertisement in the London underground sums up the problem: it features a picture of a northern road at 8.45 on a Monday morning and a picture of a tube train at the same time. The north is being sold on its slower lifestyle and its greater space. The attractions do not stop there. With property prices in London rising eight times faster than those in the north employers find it very expensive to encourage people to take up new jobs.

There is a concentration of wealth in the south. The Central Statistical Office's *Economic Trends* of 1987 showed that of the ten regions of the UK only the southeast and East Anglia enjoyed above average wealth. Whereas 30.4 per cent of Britain's population live in the southeast, they possess 35.7 per cent of the nation's wealth. On average, people in the southeast are 12.9 per cent richer than those in other parts of the country.

The north-south divide is seen even more clearly when relative house prices are considered. An October 1987 Halifax Building Society report on the housing market showed that a home buyer in Mansfield or Doncaster could buy five semis for the price of one in London. A semi-detached house in London cost an average of £105,950, against prices of £29,900 in Manchester, £31,900 in Newcastle or £38,500 in Glasgow. House prices are, in fact, rising faster in areas around London than in the city itself. Prices rose by 26.7 per cent between 1986 and 1987 in East Anglia while prices in the southeast increased by 23.5 per cent and 23.2 per cent in London. In contrast, in Scotland and the north prices rose by 6.6 per cent, less than the national average of 14.8 per cent.

With such differences, a move from the north to the south often means a substantial drop in living standards. The limitations on mobility apply at all levels. 'Most potential applicants for jobs are very restricted as to the geographical area in which they can seek work. Quite apart from the social costs of having to move home, the economic costs of moving house and the sheer difficulty of obtaining alternative accommodation may restrict "choice" of employment to the positions available in the local area,' noted *UK Society* (ed. Abrams and Brown, Weidenfeld, 1984).

The nature of the British housing market is also criticised by a number of our survey respondents. Says Philip Crowson, economic adviser to Rio Tinto Zinc, 'Important factors, such as the rigidity of the British housing market which greatly limits mobility of labour, tend to be completely ignored by all parties.' Sir Peter Walters, in a 1983 lecture to the Institute of Directors, also pointed to the problems: 'A genuine market for rented accommodation in the private sector could also make a substantial contribution both to increasing the mobility of labour, and to freeing young people from the immediate burden of large mortgage repayments so early on in their working lives.'

Competitive advantage for some companies depends on placing the right employees in the right job no matter what the location. Yet the CBI employee relocation council estimates that only about 250,000 people move house every year because of their job. A survey by the Institute of Manpower Studies at Sussex University in October 1987 showed that only 40 per cent of managers had moved during the previous decade. More significantly perhaps, of those who moved, only 40 per cent crossed the north-south divide.

John Atkinson, author of the IMs report, observes: 'Managers and other professional staff are certainly getting more resistant to mobility. There are obvious reasons for this, largely connected with regional variations in house prices. There are also less obvious reasons connected with their growing concern over quality of life. These people are not stick-in-the-muds. They are simply becoming more choosy about where they'll move and when they'll move.'

The survey was critical of relocation support from companies. It was said to be too complex and not informative enough. The costs both for companies and employees are large. The CBI has estimated that the cost of moving key individuals is often as high as £10,000 each.

The Institute of Manpower Studies has expressed concern that companies are taking the wrong approach to relocation. Says Atkinson, 'It is true that employers are increasingly concerned about the growing resistance of their staff to relocation, but instead of coming to grips with what is a very complex and many-sided difficulty they have gone in for knee-jerk responses, which consist of throwing more money into relocation packages and leaning on the Inland Revenue to subsidise them.'

To overcome this, according to Incomes Data Services, employers are increasingly trying to relocate employees within the same region, considering schemes to reduce house purchase costs and reexamining the many relocation packages on offer.

We searched for data to establish whether mobility had been a significant problem for companies in and after the immediate post-war years, but were unable to find any direct comparison. As far as we can tell, companies were less inclined to want to move people, not least because the reservoir of skills was more evenly spread. We found no evidence, therefore, that lack of geographical mobility was a significant contributory cause of industrial decline before the 1980s. However, comments from industrialists today suggest that it is a major cause for concern.

9

The Rise of Flexibility

'The pressures for change in working patterns and practices in the UK over the last decade have influenced attitudes. There is evidence since 1980 of a quickening in the rate of change and of the emergence of new trends which have helped companies become more competitive and respond more quickly to changes in market demands. These changes present opportunities to improve the UK's competitive position and to create more jobs.'
National Economic Development Council, 1985

'Flexibility can buy a shorter working week and a shorter working week can mean more jobs.'
Bill Jordan, president of the AUEW, 1987

'Today's intensely competitive environment has produced a different attitude towards business organisation. Organisationally, it has meant a move to greater decentralisation with a clearer focus on relating management decisions to individual profit centres. A physical manifestation of this is the demise of the large corporate head office and the growth of a more devolved structure.'
CBI, 1985

REACTION TIME

'Successful firms are notable for their ability to react rapidly to changed circumstances,' say Professor John Stopford and Dr Charles Baden-Fuller of London Business School. The link between expansion and flexibility is increasingly being emphasised, if not necessarily proven. 'In contrast to the management of reduction, the management of new growth is concerned with innovation, experimentation, freewheeling ideas, flexibility of response rather than a standardisation of systems,' says Andrew Kakabadse in *The Politics of Management*.

It is a message that is finding increasing favour and practical expression in British firms. Among the positive signs to be observed are the increasing decentralisation and federalisation of large companies and the breakdown of demarcation and increasing use of flexible working practices.

SMALL IS BEAUTIFUL

Although the acquisitions boom continues, British companies are rapidly decentralising operations to bring responsibility (and responsiveness) closer to the customers. Our earlier study conducted for *The Winning Streak* found that the most successful companies tend to:

●   Have small headquarter bureaucracies

●   Maintain the business as much as possible in small units, each with its own clear mission, tied into overall organisational goals

152

- Have relatively informal systems to ensure that the independent units worked with rather than against each other, while at the same time keeping inter-trade on a strictly commercial basis.

Some of Britain's largest companies have been, or are in the process of, significantly decentralising their operations. For example:

- Shell Chemicals has transferred its head office from London to purpose-built offices in Chester. Other small divisions within Shell, such as lubricants and bitumen, also operate in small self-contained units which, management believes, are more receptive to change.

- ICI carried out one of the most eyecatching decentralisation policies in the early 1980s under John Harvey-Jones. The changes were in response to ICI recording a loss in a quarter for the first time. The number of board directors was cut in half in 1983 and headquarters staff was cut from 1,500 to its present 550. Staff in ICI's fibres division has also been drastically reduced from 21,000 in the 1970s to around 7,000, who manage to maintain the same level of production. As a result, greater responsibilities are given to managers, directors and headquarters staff pushed into the field.

- BP decentralised in 1979 into a holding company with ten business streams each with a board of its own. The BP Group acts as a head office with the other companies only coming to it for major, normally financial, decisions.

- British Gas is decentralised into twelve separate regions each of which is totally responsible for all customer relations and services whilst targets and general policy are set by headquarters.

- BTR manages a turnover of £5 billion and 85,000 employees with a headquarters staff of a mere 130.

- Dalgety, the agricultural and food conglomerate, has similarly low levels of staffing at its headquarters with 80 staff overseeing 23,000 employees worldwide.

British Airways provides a notable example of how to make a large organisation more responsive. In 1983 BA reorganised its cargo unit into a separate business operation, giving it greater independence and flexibility. At the time BA Cargo was a demoralised, fragmented and under-resourced organisation, part of an airline whose main concern was passenger traffic, with limited capacity and based in Britain where the market was dormant. Colin Marshall, BA chief executive, told the company that its mission was to become 'the best cargo airline in the world'.

Five years later, BA was widely regarded as one of the leading and most innovative cargo airlines in the world. Cargo revenue had increased from £186.7 million to £265 million. The industry voted BA the world's best cargo airline in 1986.

Greater flexibility has been achieved by giving overseas managers day-to-day responsibility and authority. This has been supported by rigorous examination of the demand for the company's service, yields, and standards. BA Cargo has been able, as a more dynamic business unit, to develop a number of markets, like its 'Flying Pets Club' and 'Speedbird Express'. It has introduced a technical innovation with its 'V' scanner which measures cargo volume more accurately than the previous method – a tape measure.

THE DECLINE OF THE FEW

Part of the reason behind such decentralisation may well be that decline has had its most destructive effects in traditionally large-scale, labour-intensive industries such as steel and shipbuilding, where rationalisation and increased flexibility have occurred more or less simultaneously. According to a 3i report, *Britain in the 1980s: Enterprise Reborn*, 'There are some indications that the cessation and beginning of a reversal in the process of concentration reflect widespread changes in the structure of economic organisation and a welling-up of growth among medium-sized firms as well as increased numbers of small firms.'

Greater pragmatism and flexibility can already be seen in a number of companies. BP and ICI, two immense companies, have already set an example of strategic flexibility. It could even be seen as co-operation. Before 1982 both BP and ICI owned plants producing polyethylene and polyvinylchloride (PVC). They then traded their plants so that BP could make PVC and ICI polyethylene. As a result the plants were able to be rationalised on to one site.

International flexibility can also be of benefit. Cadbury Schweppes is involved in a joint venture with San Benedetto in Scorze, near Venice. The Italians have the largest soft drinks factory in the world. Says chief executive Dominic Cadbury, 'This is just one example of the many innovative partnerships we are initiating throughout the world. In every instance the basic goal is to make the company's brand assets work harder for our shareholders.' As a result, sales in Italy have increased from 9 million litres in 1983 to 26 million litres in 1987.

154

Another flexible practice of increasing importance is contracting out. The economic uncertainties of the 1970s and early 1980s have seemingly fuelled the trend. A *Financial Times* survey in 1986 showed that 35 per cent of companies had regularly contracted out work in recent years which they had previously carried out in-house. Not surprisingly, contracting out was more prevalent in larger companies. The number of companies contracting out was 2.5 times larger in those with over 1,000 employees than in those with less than 50.

FLEXIBILITY IN THE WORK PLACE

But what are the implications for employees? Ideas and definitions of the flexible organisation and the roles of employees differ dramatically. The Institute of Manpower Studies argued in 1985:

> The flexible firm consists of a 'core group' of employees, surrounded by peripheral groups of workers who may or may not be employees. The peripheral groups, with appropriate contracts and conditions of service, provide numerical flexibility. Functional flexibility is achieved in the core, supported by appropriate incentives and rewards, including the (implicit) guarantee of job security (or absence of the threat of insecurity), which is possible because the peripheral groups soak up numerical fluctuations in demand.

This view demands many readjustments to traditional means of organising and working. There is evidence that some of its criteria are now being instituted, particularly in the area of 'peripheral groups' with flexible working arrangements in terms of time or job specifications. On the other hand, a recent study by Warwick University failed to find much evidence that the theory was being applied.

There can be little doubt that the combination of international recession, high interest rates, exchange rate volatility and growing international competition has increased the rate of change in British working practices. Domestically, these international factors have been compounded by high levels of unemployment, the decline of manufacturing industry and the trend towards part-time working, an increased female workforce and self-employment. For many, merely having a job has increased in importance.

155

The enthusiasm and interest in the potential of flexible working is such that New Ways to Work, an information and advisory body researching into flexible working arrangements, receives over 2,000 enquiries every year. The Department of Employment estimated in 1985 that about a third of the British labour force is working flexibly – a 16 per cent increase since 1981.

The international trend is also towards flexibility of both working hours and practice. Large German companies like Messerschmitt-Bolkow-Blohm introduced flexitime as long ago as 1967. If there are entrenched attitudes in Britain, they are perhaps understandable – the unions regard flexibility as a sweetener in redundancy packages whilst managers may fear that flexibility will undermine their authority and the company hierarchy. A 1985 European Trade Union Institute report sums up the general union attitude.

> Flexibility is a slippery concept which covers a range of proposals. In some countries it has come to mean: cutting real wages; cutting lowest wages most; breaking up national negotiating procedures; abolishing employment protection legislation; making it easier to sack people; increasing job insecurity; attacking social security systems; and dismantling health and safety and environmental protection.

Even so, union willingness to seek flexible working agreements is on the increase. Moderate leaders identify flexible working with more jobs, a case which is not necessarily proven. The 1987 Trades Union Congress backed a motion from the EETPU and the UCATT construction workers which recognised that 'modern industry requires new working patterns, which a changing society is more prepared to accept'.

There are already some signs that pay settlements are now more likely to involve changes in working practices, hours and manning levels. A CBI report *Changes in Working Practices in British Manufacturing Industry in the 1980s*, by J Cahill and P Ingram in 1987, assessed around 9,000 pay settlements. It showed that over a third of pay settlements now include some agreed change in working practice rather than a straight acceptance of increased pay.

Changes in working practices have come in a wide variety of forms. At British Alcan they involve using short-term contract employees; at Findus there are three categories of manual workers (permanent, temporary and casual); and at Lyons Tetley there is a register of casual workers. Control Data uses a buffer of 'supplemental employees' on ten-month contracts. The advantages are generally that the company can tailor its employee

156

Changes in working practices agreed

Changes in working practices	Percentage of settlements 1979/80 to 1985/6 involving changes
Removal of restrictive practices	6.5
Introduction of shift working	3.9
Reduction in employees	7.0
Introduction of incentive payment schemes	5.7
Other productivity improvements	10.4

numbers to demand and that employees are prepared to be more flexible in meeting the company's requirements. This is backed by the 39 per cent increase in overtime payments since 1980. Central to these changes are a breaking down of demarcation.

BREAKING DEMARCATION

Changes in working hours do not necessarily affect demarcation. Nevertheless, even this aspect of inflexibility is being tackled aggressively and imaginatively in a number of its traditional strongholds. The most entrenched examples of demarcation are now being called into question. Cornerstones of industry like shipbuilding, steel and car production have radically reassessed their working practices at all levels.

Graham Day, then chairman of British Shipbuilding, secured a far-reaching productivity package early in 1984. The agreement allowed flexibility between trades so that, for example, a boilermaker could do an electrician's job in the bowels of the ship to save time. This step has been helped by the virtual disappearance of strikes. Yards such as Govan are now held up as shining examples of industrial progress.

The Harland and Wolff shipyard at Belfast has been particularly successful in eliminating outdated practices. By moving almost two-thirds of the

157

company's work indoors, instead of continuing with the traditional out-door construction methods, the workforce could be cut by 1200. This large-scale reduction in numbers was accompanied by an ambitious decentralisation of power and responsibility. New tiers in the management structure were introduced so that a project team headed by a single manager now supervises construction of an entire vessel with responsibility broken up into zones and modules with individual managers. The creation of vertical line management has been supported by excellent labour relations. Harland and Wolff now loses fewer than 1.5 per cent of man hours a year through strikes and stoppages. The degree of union support is such that when the company was tendering for a £70 million BP contract, the shipyard unions sent BP a message pledging support for the tight delivery schedule being offered.

Other stolidly traditional industries have also begun to adopt more flexible working practices. British Coal now has a training programme which turns out multi-skilled craftsmen. The programme, run with the Engineering Industry Training Board, greeted its first fifty-eight school leavers in December 1986.

The rationalisation of British Steel was one of the most dramatic stories in the challenge to old working practices. Demarcation lines were abandoned in favour of highly flexible methods of working. As a result, for example, production operators no longer require craftsmen to change shear blades for them and craftsmen drive cranes and undertake their own heavy lifting work. The savings in time and money were increased by contracting out work at peak periods to local companies. 'A frugal lifestyle was adopted in every respect,' says British Steel director, Dr David Grieves.

The main tenets of British Steel's restructuring were to reduce the number of management levels; broaden job specifications at all levels; increase mechanisation; use more contractors; have fewer shifts, a higher tempo of work and eliminate inessentials. Frugal indeed, but ultimately capable of saving the industry from extinction.

The Llanwern steel plant provides an example of the effects of British Steel's policy. In 1979 it employed 9,353 people. After three months of negotiations in 1980 this number was reduced to 4,899, a reduction of 52 per cent. The plant's commercial effectiveness was established. The seven man hours needed for every tonne of steel produced was reduced to 4.2 man hours in two years, a 40 per cent reduction. The employment cost per tonne decreased from £33.50 in 1977 to £25.60 in 1981–2, a 23 per cent decrease.

Even in industries most notorious for inflexibility, demarcation is being sidestepped as automation spreads. At the Land Rover plant in Solihull, 2,000 workers voted to extend their working day by two hours to 9.75 to meet demand and introduced a new four-day week. Massey Ferguson at Coventry now makes the same number of tractors as it did in 1977 – 80–90,000 – but with 2,500 workers as opposed to 6,500.

In 1985 Ford reached a two-year agreement with unions, which reduced the number of job demarcations from a massive 500 to 58. This meant shop floor operatives were expected to move around the plant and to take on jobs they would have previously ignored, like driving fork-lift trucks. Responsibilities now take in quality control, maintenance and general house-keeping.

Most companies in the motor industry have greatly reduced demarcation between skilled workers. Most now operate with two or three types of skilled craftsmen who are highly adaptable. This has run alongside attempts at harmonising conditions between blue and white collar workers which have so far met with less success.

Such harmonisation is an imposing challenge. Henley Management College's Centre for Employment Studies has observed that new working practices are more likely to be accepted when changes are also demanded of managers. It calls for managers to develop new techniques and skills to cope with the growth in part-time and sub-contracted staff as well as different working practices.

New demands on managers require different management techniques and skills. *The Times'* Kenneth Fleet has described the modern role of managers: 'A manager should no longer be judged by the number of people working for him but by his ability to manage change, usually inspired by advancing technology, within a corporate strategy he will have helped to formulate.'

TEMPS EXPLODE!

Amongst the challenges facing management is that of utilising staff time cost-effectively. There have been many developments in this area ranging from increased use of temporary workers to job-splitting schemes.

The explosive growth in temporary work is one of the many illustrations of massive changes in working practices. The Federation of Recruitment and Employment Services now estimates that agencies place 400,000 to 500,000 people every day. Some companies have boasted of 30 per cent increases in business every year since 1984. The dramatic expansion of the Blue Arrow Group graphically demonstrates the increased demand for temporary workers. More than 65 per cent of its profits come from temporary placements.

Though initially aimed at casual and semi-skilled workers, the temporary employment business is now broadening its appeal to professional and managerial temporary workers including accountants, managers and computer programmers.

PART-TIME WORKERS

The swelling ranks of temporary workers have been supplemented by growth in the numbers of part-time workers. In Britain, part-time workers now number more than a fifth of the total workforce, though this

Full and part-time workers, 1979–85

	1979–85 Growth		1985 Part-time workers as percentage of workforce
	Full-time	Part-time	
	per cent		
USA	+1.2	+2.4	17.4
Japan	+0.8	+2.1	16.5
West Germany	+1.1	+1.1	12.0
France	−0.6	+3.2	11.0
UK	−1.2	+5.0	21.2

(Source: OECD Economic Outlook, June 1987)

growth has been offset by a decrease of 1.2 per cent in the numbers of full-time workers. They are chiefly women working in the service sector, but increasing numbers of men and women are working part-time in a wide spectrum of sectors.

The growth in part-time workers has been an international one as the table on page 160 shows.

The OECD *Economic Outlook* shows that only the Scandinavian countries have similarly high levels of part-time workers. Britain has recorded the most dynamic growth in its part-time workforce over recent years – at over twice the American rate of increase. As the table below shows, the emphasis remains solidly on service industries.

Part-time work in Britain (thousands)

	Male	Female	Total	Part-time workers as percentage of workforce
All industries and services	797.1	3,939.4	4,736.5	22.2
Manufacturing	55.3	325.8	381.1	7
Services	683.8	3,513	4,196.8	30.2

(Source: *Financial Times*, 3.9.87)

JOB SHARING AND SPLITTING

As flexibility increases, possible working arrangements grow in number. In 1983 the government launched a job splitting scheme. This offered grants of £840 to encourage employers to split full-time posts into two part-time jobs. The scheme was not a great success with only about 500 full-time jobs being split. As a further effort in 1987, another job splitting scheme was launched offering a further £160. Unfortunately, the Civil Servants who launched the scheme were ignorant of the difference between job splitting and job sharing (the latter, as the

161

name implies, involves a genuine sharing and collaboration in the responsibilities of the job) and labelled it a job sharing scheme. The subsequent confusion inhibited both trends.

The Industrial Society believes that job sharing is increasing in importance. 'Job share arrangements are appealing to more and more employees and their employers,' it said in June 1987. The Employment Relations Research Centre at the Essex Institute of Higher Education has also claimed that job sharing and job splitting are more common than is generally thought. Its local research in Essex showed that up to 45 per cent of Essex enterprises may be operating some form of them. Even so, despite TUC backing, the system is still largely confined to public sector organisations. Some private companies, such as Thames Television, are considering its possibilities.

ANNUAL HOURS

In France, construction workers in the public sector will soon work a 1,770-hour flexible working year. The agreement stipulates that working time may drop to 32 hours per week during slack periods and vary between four, five and six days per week at different times of the year. The Industrial Society has supported similar developments in Britain. It believes that annual hours can not only increase productivity but increase job security, and give consistent earnings and increased leisure time. Companies can, through using annual hours, control production costs more tightly with overtime payments being restricted. Over fifty companies now operate an annual hours scheme, which organises working time not around the 39- or 40-hour week but around a working year. Companies with continuous production methods are clearly attracted to the scheme which now includes Dundee textile manufacturers Don and Low, lead smelters H J Enthoven, Pedigree Petfoods, and Blue Circle cement. The Industrial Society has estimated that over 500,000 people will soon be covered by annual hours agreements.

THE REMOULDED TYRE INDUSTRY

The British tyre industry, long set on the path of apparent decline, provides another notable example of change. Despite being reduced to one British-owned producer, Avon Rubber, the industry has fought back aggressively.

Says Joe Denton, manufacturing director of Pirelli's British operation, 'To compete we have to change. To change we have to have the trust of the workforce. To win that trust we have to maintain full employment. As soon as people are made redundant that trust goes.' As part of its efforts to introduce change Pirelli in Britain has introduced a work and production philosophy over a number of years. Its aim is to integrate previously isolated functions like design, sales, finance and production into a coherent whole.

On the shop floor, workers now join together in groups to tackle particular production problems such as quality control or the lay-out for new production lines. Responsibility for basic maintenance and quality control has been passed back to shop floor workers. Maintenance engineers now walk round looking for faults rather than being sent to examine them by supervisors and are, therefore, more responsive to problems and more efficient.

The company aims to eventually have just two categories of multi-skilled worker – electrician instrument controller and engineer machinist – rather than the traditional myriad of discrete skills. This is supported by heavy investment in retraining. Pirelli has built its own training centre costing £250,000 and all workers spend at least five days a year in training. As a result of these changes, Pirelli's British factories are now the most productive of its 117 plants throughout the world.

Pirelli's example has been followed elsewhere in the industry. Goodyear has now instituted continuous production at its Wolverhampton plant. This allows the plant to be in use for 342 days of the year rather than 232. The workforce has been reduced from 9,000 to 3,700, though Goodyear remains the biggest employer in Wolverhampton. With the full support of its four unions, Goodyear now has a weekend shift which provides 370 jobs, though there were 9,000 applications. This involves twelve-hour shifts on Saturday and Sunday and an occasional shift on Fridays.

The benefits and potential of flexible working stretch across all areas of industry. Crosslee, a Yorkshire tumble drier maker, has one of the most radical of a growing number of flexible working schemes. Based at Hipperholme, near Halifax, it now has a working week of thirty-two hours in the summer and forty-three hours in the winter. This allows it to respond more effectively to the fluctuating demand for its products. Whilst May accounts

163

for 3 per cent of annual sales; October brings in 12.7 per cent. Crosslee's 550 workers, supported by their unions the AEU and Tass, are now able to enjoy the summer months whilst working a little harder in the depths of the Yorkshire winter.

MOBILITY

On a national level there is little to suggest that British workers are now more mobile. Indeed, as we have seen, the rapid increases in southern house prices may well be widening the north-south divide. Says Social and Liberal Democrat party spokesman Malcolm Bruce, 'I despair of the London domination. We have to accept that it is possible to be a high flyer outside of the southeast. They opt in London for homes they wouldn't look at elsewhere, or they travel hours each day. Most are underperforming from the resulting stress. Yet we have examples like BP, which is moving 300 people from Aberdeen to the City, having moved them up several years before.'

Resistance to mobility remains a problem. A survey by Homequity, the world's largest relocation company, showed that north-south differentials are now a major obstacle to mobility. The survey featured 200 multinationals from all over Britain. When asked whether any of their employees had either expressed serious reservations about or even rejected relocation, two out of three said yes. The major reason cited in a staggering 85 per cent of the cases was north-south house differentials. Up to 60 per cent of the companies surveyed were having trouble getting staff to move from south to north because of fears that they wouldn't be able to afford to return to the south (the north-south divide works both ways, it seems). As many as 80 per cent of the survey's respondents expressed concern about stress and disruption affecting their families whilst others were concerned about loss of spouse's earnings, the lengthy process of house selling and the costs involved.

A report produced by Merrill Lynch Relocation Management in 1987 reflected similar attitudes. It covered 305 major British companies involved in relocation. Its conclusions highlight the limitations of both corporate support and employees' perspectives. The report noted 'the reluctance of employees to move from low to high cost areas continues to be a difficulty', 'large companies noted an increase in the resistance to move' and 'companies underestimate the cost of relocating'.

It is likely that very few British companies would be able to follow IBM's massive restructuring programme in West Germany. There it significantly changed the jobs of 5,000 of its 27,000 employees; around 1,000 were relocated. There were minimal problems in doing so.

The Institute of Manpower Studies has put forward a ten-point plan to increase the effectiveness of relocation:

1. Create clear managerial responsibility for policy and practice of staff mobility.

2. Conduct a five-year audit on mobility developments and patterns.

3. Keep the systematic mobility to a low level.

4. Bring corporate and employee expectations into line and detail them in contracts.

5. Reduce mobility through greater concentration on zonal and regional labour markets, moving staff when young and moving labour-intensive units out of areas of high cost.

6. Improve non-financial assistance for relocation and simplify regulations.

7. Review mobility incentives.

8. Have greater dialogue with staff.

9. Create a culture where mobility is accepted and regarded as a positive thing.

10. Review and improve financial assistance.

Resistance is offset in the upper echelons of business by the mobility of chief executives and an increased willingness to recruit chief executives from outside the company. It is estimated that more than 25 per cent of British companies used an executive search company for managing director appointments in 1985–7.

FUTURE FLEXIBILITY

So just how flexible have working practices in Britain become? The picture appears rather confused. In some areas, for example the use of temporary, part-time and other peripheral workers, the UK is clearly

165

much further down the path to flexibility than most of its competitors. The situation is, in some ways, similar to that in Japan where a vast array of young women and sub-contractors provide the flexible labour force that can be laid off in hard times.

In other areas, such as the ability of shop floor operators to manage several jobs, the UK appears to be far behind. This is, to a large extent, a matter of lack of training, but also an unwillingness on the part of management to create larger, more interesting jobs. Taylorism still lives.

Clearly, a great deal still needs to be done to make the British workforce as flexible as it needs to be to compete internationally. Most achievements so far seem to have been in adjusting the *times* that people spend at work. Part of the price has been the failure to create more full-time jobs. The real challenge lies in changing what people *do* when they are at work. It is here, we believe, that the battle of international competition will be won or lost.

10

The Decline of Research and Development

'The United Kingdom is now technologically obsolete. If we do not constantly inject technology into manufacturing products then we can only slide downmarket. We finish up competing with Third World countries and cease to compete at the top with the economically developed world.'
Lord Gregson, member of the House of Lords, Science and Technology Committee, 1986

'Whoever is generating new technology will conquer the market place. Technology is now the engine driving the world economy . . . A nation that does not accord the utmost importance to R & D has made a decision not to be in business in five to ten years.'
Dr Bruce Merrifield, US Department of Commerce, in The Times, *16 February, 1987*

'Britain's exclusion from the twenty-first century is already being mapped. The government has no policy for space. It hardly has a policy for science. It offers nothing to inspire and stimulate Britons who come of age in the next century.'
Leader in The Times, *September 1986*

'The current level of civil R & D in the UK is disastrous as far as the future of UK industry is concerned.'
Dr Rudge of the Association of Independent Research and Technology Organisations (House of Lords Select Committee Report on Research and Development, 1986)

FINANCING RESEARCH AND DEVELOPMENT

- In 1983, the UK spent £47 per head on civil R & D; Japan spent £60; West Germany £73; the United States £76.

- Total employment in R & D in the UK fell 5 per cent between 1981 and 1983, and by a further 7 per cent between 1983 and 1985. Most of these cuts were in support staff. The number of scientists employed actually rose 5 per cent between 1983 and 1985.

- British industry funded only 66 per cent of R & D from its own resources in 1985. By comparison, the United States funded 67 per cent, France 72 per cent (on latest available figures), Italy 76 per cent and West Germany 82 per cent. Comparative figures for Japan relate to 1986, when Japanese industry paid for 98 per cent of its own R & D.

- Between 1967 and 1981 the average annual growth in industry-financed R & D in the UK was 0.9 per cent – the lowest by far of any major Western European country. The comparative figures are: Belgium, 7.15 per cent; Ireland, 6.46 per cent; Sweden, 6.13 per cent; France, 5.93 per cent; West Germany, 5.88 per cent; Italy, 5.52 per cent; Denmark, 4.56 per cent; The Netherlands, 1.56 per cent; Switzerland, 1.21 per cent. Only the UK, The Netherlands and Switzerland failed to double their expenditure on R & D over this period.

- In 1963, the UK accounted for 26.3 per cent of European patents filed in the United States; West Germany accounted for 33.9 per cent. West Germany now accounts for 43 per cent. The UK's share has fallen to 15.4 per cent.

- Electronics is widely regarded as the key competitive sector for the next decade. Britain's R & D spending in this sector dropped 10 per cent between 1983 and 1985. By contrast, R & D on mechanical engineering rose 40 per cent over the same period.

- R & D as a proportion of UK Gross National Product showed only a small growth between 1968 and 1985, from 2.3 per cent to 2.6 per cent; Japan increased its proportion from 1.6 per cent to 2.6 per cent; the United States showed a decrease, from 3.1 per cent to 2.8 per cent.

- Another study, this time of Gross *Domestic* Product, shows Britain as the only major trading nation to have reduced its research and development spending as a percentage of GDP in the 1980s. The OECD Annual Review also showed that, in 1983, British civil expenditure on R & D, as a percentage of GDP, stood at 1.6 per cent. This figure was below that spent by France (1.7 per cent), West Germany (2.5 per cent), Japan (2.5 per cent) and the USA (1.9 per cent).

- The UK's share of European spending on R & D dropped from 27 per cent to 17 per cent between 1967 and 1982. The proportion of new to total investment rose 30 per cent on average in Japan, Sweden, West Germany and Belgium between 1970 and 1981, but stagnated in the UK.

A recent NEDC task force on innovation brings many of the issues into focus. Research and development for its own sake is of little value, it argues. The value comes from applying the results to new and existing products and then exploiting the potential of those products in national and international markets. This latter stage is primarily a matter of marketing. It is also a matter of having sufficient funding to exploit the product once it is developed, and to continue development as early imitators appear on the scene.

Management consultant Dr Gordon Edge, chief executive of Scientific Generics, claims that the inevitable influence of possible future applications on the nature and style of R & D is a plus point, not a minus, particularly where development is concerned. In practice, he observes, the more tightly drawn the specifications – to include not only functional requirements, but ease of manufacture, repair and maintenance, and price constraints – the easier it is to focus clearly on the required outcome. A side benefit is that research workers tend to be more motivated by the challenge to their ingenuity than would be the case in a vaguely defined project.

There is a strongly held belief, reflected by several of our interviewees, that Britain is brilliant at inventing but poor at exploiting. Just how true is that? One pointer is the share that we have in the world's annual patents. Whatever may have been the case in decades past, currently the UK is quite clearly not the invention powerhouse of the world. Indeed, its share of patents is steadily declining. To some extent, this is inevitable. As other countries increase the extent of their patenting activity in line with

169

increasing R & D expenditure, they can be expected to catch up. But some countries are already surpassing our performance in this critical area and West Germany, which was already filing more US patents than the UK in the early 1960s, has forged ahead to account for more than 40 per cent of all foreign patents registered in the US.

Much the same story holds true for citations. A report by the Science Policy Research Unit of Sussex University in November 1987 analysed British academic publications. Between 1978 and 1981 Britain's world share of publications fell by 2 per cent while Japan's share increased by 13 per cent. Between 1981 and 1984 Britain suffered a 4 per cent decline, to 8.1 per cent of the world total. During these three years, Japan's share grew by 8 per cent and Canada's by 4 per cent. The British decline affected all areas apart from biology and clinical medicine, whilst Japan advanced on all fronts. Since 1976, Britain's academic production in chemistry, engineering and physics has all declined. SPRU concluded: 'With companies in both traditional and new industrial sectors becoming increasingly dependent on the results of basic research for maintaining innovative activity and international competitiveness, the state of British science gives major cause for concern.'

How well, then, do we make use of our inventions? Most of the data here is anecdotal. Typical of many entrepreneurial companies is Auto Alloys, a Derbyshire company which sought help from the Department of Trade and Industry to commercialise a novel foundry process which the Steel Castings Research Association had developed in the laboratory. It took the DTI more than three years to award it £22,500, just over 6 per cent of the development costs, by which time it had already pushed ahead and proven the process itself. By contrast, Mitsubishi was banging on the door with a takeover offer four weeks after the results were announced. Yet it is not too difficult to duplicate such stories in our competitor countries, too. The inventor who cannot get home country backing for his idea is a familiar figure around the world and the possible reasons for his failure to do so are legion.

The NEDC has attempted to identify some of the reasons behind this.

Government support for industrial development is low in comparison with our European competitors. As well as developing it themselves, companies can license it from overseas, but there is evidence that this is less common practice in the UK than in any of our major competitors with the exception of the USA. Japanese and German industries have risen to leadership in many areas on the back of technology developed in other nations and are now consolidating that leadership by investing heavily themselves. Why do not more UK companies, once leaders in so many fields, do likewise?

The 1986 House of Lords Select Committee on Science and Technology asked similar questions and came to equally depressing conclusions:

> During the last five years . . . the general state of science and technology in the UK has not improved. In some areas it has even become worse. This is the unavoidable conclusion to be drawn from the evidence of nearly all witnesses outside government departments. In spite of the valiant efforts of individuals to make the present system work, and in spite of a few success stories in branches of science and technology, the overall picture conveys an impression of turmoil and frustration.

International comparisons made by the House of Lords Committee are also bleak. It points to the example of Australia where high unemployment, manufacturing decline and a worsening balance of payments were greeted by austerity measures and an *increase* in the resources allocated to R & D.

Other organisations have backed the committee's findings. The Science Policy Research Unit at Sussex University has reported, 'It is difficult to avoid the conclusion that the UK spends less on academic and academically related research than its two closest European competitors, France and Germany.' The 1984–5 Department of Trade and Industry Science and Technology Report observed, 'Of the five leading industrial nations, the UK now devotes the smallest share of its Gross Domestic Product to civil R & D. This disadvantage in quantity is not offset by any generally greater effectiveness of R & D in Britain.' As Britain's GDP is proportionately lower than the other major countries, the figures are significantly worse than they first appear.

There are several relevant issues to be considered. They include:

- The amount of spending on R & D by government and private sources
- R & D (by both government and industry)
- The status and rewards for scientists and engineers
- The diffusion of technology

R & D SPENDING

While Britain's R & D spending has effectively stagnated in the 1980s, the amount of cash spent as a proportion of GDP had been among the highest for many decades. While volume of spending must presumably have some impact on the innovation strength of an economy, it clearly is only part of

171

the picture. The same is true of companies. The companies with the largest and most expensive research facilities are not necessarily the companies with the best track record of innovation. Indeed, experience on both sides of the Atlantic suggests that, in electronics at least, innovations in development occur more readily in relatively small, entrepreneurial companies. (Fundamental advances, such as the invention of fibre optics, tend to come from very long-term, highly expensive projects in larger laboratories – but it is still often the smaller firm that exploits them first.) Hence the rush by large companies, especially in the United States, to acquire a stake in smaller ventures with R & D capability. A good example in the UK might be Rank Xerox's stake in Artificial Intelligence Ltd. Rank Xerox could certainly have carried out research in this area itself, and indeed its US parent company is doing so. But the company had the percipience to recognise that the chances of developing marketable products quickly were higher in the entrepreneurial environment.

The NEDC adds more fuel to the argument that spending on R & D on its own is an inadequate measure of performance.

In absolute terms R & D spending in the UK is substantially lower than in West Germany, Japan and the US and roughly comparable with that of France. This discrepancy is considerably greater if defence R & D is excluded . . . This does not automatically suggest a need for more R & D finance. In 1964, the UK had the highest absolute civil R & D spending in the world after the US. Despite this the UK's relative growth and trade performance have been poor.

In other words, what counts is not how much you spend on R & D, but how effectively you spend it. Nonetheless, there must be a lower point at which the level of spending in itself restricts the efficiency of the research effort, simply because essential resources are not available. This point, according to the Save British Science Campaign, has already been reached in many instances.

Britain's international standing in government-funded R & D compares unfavourably with our main European competitors as the table below shows:

Government R & D spending in European countries, 1985 (£ million)

West Germany	5564	Holland	911
France	5847	Belgium	373
Italy	2163	Britain	4582

Source: *The Times*, 26.11.87.

Britain's record is significantly altered if spending on defence R & D is deducted.

Government spending on R & D excluding defence (£ million)

West Germany	4900	Holland	883
France	4018	Belgium	372
Italy	1948	Britain	2203

Of equal concern is the low proportion of the UK's total R & D effort financed by industry itself: only 43 per cent. This compares with 80 per cent for Japan. Japan's situation is, of course, special, in that it has virtually no defence research spending. But its self-reliance is as much a matter of choice and philosophy as of government parsimony. Moreover, the proportion of Gross Domestic Product spent on R & D by Japan is still far higher than in the UK.

Other countries with a history of heavy government investment in R & D are steadily following Japan's example, as industry takes more and more responsibility for funding its own technological future. Western Europe is rapidly accelerating the proportion of industrial value added allocated to R & D, while in the United States industry-financed R & D increased from one third of the total in 1967 to one half in 1982.

Another useful comparison may therefore be the level of R & D spending by UK companies versus their international counterparts. Meaningful data is hard to come by, because many UK companies regard details of R & D expenditure as commercially sensitive information. But in almost every case where direct comparisons are possible, the UK companies turn out to be spending below the international market leaders.

As Professor William Gosling, technical director of Plessey, told *The Director*, 'If you look back ten years US electronics companies were typically spending 2 per cent to 3 per cent of their sales on research. In Britain, at the same time, it was 1 per cent.' Now it is closer to 6 per cent in both countries, but Japanese companies may spend twice as much.

In some sectors of the British economy, profits have been so low for so long that finding the finance to invest in R & D is difficult. But even in profitable sectors such as pharmaceuticals, the UK companies lag behind. For example, Beecham has increased the percentage of its turnover spent

173

on R & D from 7 per cent to an impressive 10 per cent over the past twenty-five years. But it has still failed to match its US competitors, some of whom spend 12 per cent or more. Until now, the British pharmaceutical companies have been able to compete through the effectiveness of their R & D. As their market becomes increasingly competitive, they may have to raise the volume of their spending as well.

DIRECTION OF FUNDING

One of the main concerns to observers of all parties is the proportion of *government*-funded R & D that is tied to defence objectives. At more than 50 per cent, it is considerably higher than in most competitor countries. Says *The Director* magazine, 'The vast bulk of government R & D spending, and practically all defence R & D, contributes nothing to wealth creation.' For the most part this research has no spin-off value other than export armaments sales, and even here the performance of British defence companies in world markets has not been sparkling. One of the main reasons has been that products developed to specifications for the British military have often not readily met the requirements of potential overseas buyers. Those UK defence companies that have shown the most impressive growth in the past decades have been those, such as Racal, which set out to sell to world markets first, and then the Ministry of Defence second.

Malcolm Bruce of the Social and Liberal Democrats expresses concern about the level of military R & D expenditure: 'A very high proportion of research in the UK is going into military equipment, from which the spin-off is low. The US dominates the defence industry, so we just pick up the crumbs. They can set standards that undermine the commercial applications of our research, even where we get better results,' he says.

The dilemma that has faced much of the UK defence industry is how to achieve the sales volumes necessary to provide an adequate return on the R & D investment. Derek Roberts, joint managing director (technical) of GEC pointed out to *The Director*: 'We must maximise the commercial benefit from the R & D we do. It is not uncommon for us to spend more than half of a product's subsequent production value on R & D in defence systems. We have to sell overseas as much as possible.'

The net result is that much of the defence industry has become heavily introspective. With only one major customer, the concept of market-oriented R & D became largely irrelevant. Only now are the major defence companies coming to grips with a less protected future, where keeping unit costs down by selling to a wider market is becoming an increasingly important factor in meeting Ministry of Defence requirements.

Witnesses to the House of Lords Science and Technology Committee were critical of R & D defence expenditure. Said the IBM representative: 'There is military/commercial overlap in the basic research area but this is not significant in applied research and development. The commercial benefit is certainly out of proportion to the extent to which British talent is concentrated in military R & D activities.' The Fellowship of Engineering took a historical view: 'If the post-war period from 1945 to the present is viewed as a whole, there is no doubt that defence and defence-related R & D has weakened civil research initiative, especially in industry, and that this has had a harmful effect on product innovation and industrial competitiveness.'

The NEDC report *Innovation in the UK* supports this view, declaring, 'The emphasis on defence R & D does not result in greater overall R & D, but fewer resources for civil purposes.'

The sharpest contrast, once again, lies with Japan. Without heavy funding from a defence establishment, it was inevitable that the bulk of R & D funds would come from the private sector. The proportion of private sector funding reached just under 78 per cent in 1983 and is steadily increasing. It is hardly surprising, then, that the popular image of Japanese technology as mainly imitative should be received with such scorn in Japan itself. A Japanese Government study in 1984 found that 76 per cent of companies felt they were on an equal or better technological level than their Western competitors; in telecommunications and electronics, no less than 90 per cent thought so.

Over the fourteen years between 1971 and 1984, Japan's balance of trade in know-how (measured as export value of intellectual property divided by import value) rose from a ratio of 0.136 to 0.314. By the early 1990s, the volume of Japanese R & D is predicted to raise the ratio to 0.863. This is expected to occur not from technological myopia, as appears to be the case in Britain, but because Japan is, quite clearly, aiming for international technological leadership in a wide spectrum of activities.

Another concern of many observers is the way in which research councils are organised and developed. There has been mounting criticism of the role of the Advisory Board for the Research Councils (ABRC). The

175

House of Lords Select Committee was told that the ABRC was 'a profoundly unsatisfactory body' and its increasingly high profile is viewed suspiciously as a step towards a single research council.

The manner in which the research councils divide their spending is also open to question. For example, only 9.8 per cent of research council funding goes into engineering, whereas 8.2 per cent goes into nuclear physics, 8.3 per cent into agriculture, and 20.6 per cent into medicine. The potential impact on industrial competitiveness can therefore be expected to be relatively low.

Of equal concern is the concentration of R & D resources on a relatively small number of macro-projects, which may or may not have extensive spin-offs. A research study for the Centre for European Policy Studies by Henry Ergas in 1986 divided the developed world into countries that focus their R & D efforts in this way (notably the UK, the United States and France) and countries such as Sweden and West Germany that are more concerned with creating a wide range of new technologies that will be applied to companies' products. Even though companies in these countries are smaller and therefore have less access to resources, says Ergas, they are 'diffusion orientated' and concentrate on issues such as achieving common standards, increasing awareness of technological developments, encouraging co-operative research and stimulating relevant skills education.

One attitude reflects belief in the power of breakthroughs; the other belief in the power of incremental improvements. While Ergas' study indicates that Japan uses a mixture of the two approaches as industrial policy, at the company level the emphasis is almost entirely on the incremental improvement. Breakthroughs come from industry associations or as the result of collaborations between firms. By contrast, British companies tend to have a strong belief in breakthroughs as a means of maintaining or regaining competitive position. We are not aware of any evidence that this faith is justified. Indeed, what evidence there is suggests that breakthroughs are far more difficult to implement and assimilate than incremental developments, not least because of the dislocation they cause.

What makes it worse is that British firms have traditionally been very reluctant to embark on the kind of collaborative ventures with competitors that spread the cost of achieving breakthroughs and pool the experience and skills available. Instead of working together with national competitors on breakthrough projects while competing through incremental improvements, they prefer to guard their secrets and ideas,

176

duplicating underfunded research activities. In terms of competing with multinational rivals or consortia of, say, Japanese companies in the same markets, both of which will have larger and more varied resources to bring to bear, their position is weak from the start.

In the area of space research, this outlook is particularly restrictive. Britain's space budget is on a par with India's and lags sadly behind France's and America, which spends £5,000 million. As a result of this lack of enthusiasm, Britain's HOTOL (horizontal take-off and landing) space plane project received minimal international backing. The decision in 1987 to freeze Britain's space budget at so basic a level does not bode well for future development. Though sufficient to cover a minimum involvement in the European Space Agency, it will not cover other joint space projects. HOTOL's champion, Roy Gibson, resigned as director of the British National Space Centre after his plans were rejected by government.

In theory, concentration on internally generated breakthroughs should result in very different products with unique features. In practice, what happens is exactly the opposite. Ergas' study concludes that British products are relatively less differentiated from those of diffusion-oriented countries. The fact is that radical improvements occur so infrequently that their total impact is relatively small; yet they eat up R & D cash that would have led to incremental improvements. Companies in the diffusion-oriented countries tend to establish distinct niches of technological excellence, simply by being very good in areas they see as important for product differentiation. The step-by-step approach allows each item of new technology to be assimilated, refined and mastered, with the result that new products tend to have a higher reliability. It is, in practice, the difference between the tortoise and the hare.

The dangers of relying on breakthroughs are illustrated by the experience of the US textile industry. Our case study of the British textile industry shows a picture of an industry under siege in the 1960s and 1970s. But the US textile industry was in far worse shape. Tracing the course of events in the Massachusetts Institute of Technology magazine *Technology Review*, Charles Sabel and his colleagues come to the following conclusion:

By the late 1960s, intense international competition in textiles led to rapid shifts in fabric production. Hence new kinds of textile machines were in demand. The European innovations became decisive. By the early 1980s most of the advanced products in the industry – sophisticated air-jet looms, highly automated and precise spinning equipment – was either unavailable from American producers or available only at prohibitive prices.

Why did the Americans fail to break free of the old mass-production system? Several apparently plausible answers turn out to be wrong. Money, for example, was not a problem. The firms were cash-rich, in part simply because they continued to earn good revenues from selling replacement parts and equipment. Nor was indifference to foreign achievements a problem. Thoughtful managers in the industry – and we spoke with many – had a clear sense of the technological threat they faced. In some cases firms even considered licensing designs that later took away a large portion of their business. For instance, Draper considered licensing the Sulzer air-driven shuttleless loom.

The American textile-machine industry was paralysed by the rigidities of the concentrated, vertically integrated mass-production system. Foreign competitors took the technological lead not in a single dramatic leap, but step by almost imperceptible step. Each isolated European refinement in machine design looked inconsequential by itself. Few innovations promised large increases in productivity, even in the unlikely case that they could be made by the largely unskilled workforce in the US textile-machine factories and used by the still less skilled mill workers. In a few cases innovation did promise productivity breakthroughs – for example, with the shuttleless loom. But American manufacturers thought that improvements based on their own design traditions would accomplish the same thing.

Decision by decision, the Americans' calculations are difficult to fault. Most of the potential breakthroughs could theoretically have been achieved by alternative means. But by systematically screening out refinements that would have taxed and thus developed engineering and manufacturing capacities, the US firms left their competition in unchallenged possession of a growing stock of new ideas. Some small fraction of these ideas were eventually incorporated into machine designs compatible with the around-the-clock operations and unskilled workforce of the US textile mills. Unfortunately, these were designs US machine makers could not match. (Reprinted with permission from *Technology Review*, copyright 1987.)

A similar story lies, at least in part, behind the collapse of so much of Britain's consumer electronics industry in the 1970s. The root cause appears to have been sheer lack of product development. While life cycles in consumer electronics declined from between ten and twenty years on average to between one and five, most British electronics companies behaved as if nothing had changed. Comparable Japanese companies retooled every couple of years to introduce new models that would keep them ahead or abreast of their rivals. This demanded a heavy and continuing investment not just in R & D but in capital equipment. By contrast, British companies, having invested in new equipment once, held back on new product development and model changes for as long as possible, in order to gain the maximum depreciation on their equipment. The contrast is one between accountant domination and marketing domination. The Japanese were smart enough to recognise that rapid equipment write-offs were a small price to pay for sustaining market dominance or increasing market share.

The shortening of product life cycles imposes great strains on the new product development process which many companies find difficult to cope with. Those that are competing successfully with the Japanese in maintaining the pace of new product development are by and large those that follow the same basic approach. Instead of the traditional sequential development process, in which marketing, R & D, design, production tooling et al. perform their part in sequence, they form project teams or task forces that ensure that all processes proceed as far as possible in parallel. Apart from speeding up development times – an essential competitive ingredient – this approach reduces the opportunities for errors and false trails, because all the people who need to be consulted are involved at all stages.

The overall picture that emerges from the past twenty-five years, however, is one of minimal purposeful direction of R & D by either government or industry itself. There has been little consensus on which technologies should be developed and who should pay for them. Sir Kenneth Durham, president of the British Association for the Advancement of Science, wrote to the leaders of all three political parties in 1987. The replies, he declares, lacked a recognition that 'the current economic revolution is science-led and other countries are doing something about it'. There was a strong feeling among many of the industrialists we surveyed that governments of all parties had little understanding of what the contribution of science should be and of the nature of the relationship between R & D and industrial productivity and profitability.

Hence the current confusion in the science-based university departments as to what role they are expected to play. As Beecham's group research director Keith Mansford told *The Director*, 'Universities are being asked to do more applied research, which they are not good at, at the

179

expense of basic research, which they are.' The problem is compounded by the relationship between research and teaching. Many university scientists feel that basic research activities are an essential part of teaching at post-graduate level.

Keith Durham is active among those trying to bring some semblance of coherence to this particular debate. He feels it would be sensible to split research from development. Basic research, he feels, should be government funded; development, however, should be funded by industry.

STATUS AND REWARDS

The brain drain is scarcely a new phenomenon and certainly not limited to the UK alone. But the intensity of the problem is illustrated by a 1987 survey by Incomes Data Services, which indicates that average salaries for technologists and scientists in the United States are almost three times higher than in Britain. Another light on the issue comes from a survey by the Royal Society, which found that scientists and engineers emigrating from Britain between 1975 and 1985 outnumbered those returning by about a third. In 1960, only 2.8 per cent of Royal Society members were living overseas; by 1986, the proportion had risen to more than 8 per cent. The problem is made worse, says the Royal Society, by the fact that so many of those leaving for the United States are leaders of research projects. Inevitably, they often attempt to take with them the best of their support staff, with the result that Britain loses not just an individual, but a complete team. Researchers such as Dr Abbas Ourmazd, reported by *The Times* to be earning five times as much working for AT&T as he did doing research at Oxford University, make a name for themselves in the United States and then come shopping for the brightest British talent to join them. Ourmazd contrasted for *The Times* the sophisticated laboratory facilities he enjoys in the United States and the financial strictures at Oxford, where, for example, telephone calls were rationed to afternoons only.

It is a theme echoed by many observers, among them former ICI chief executive Sir John Harvey-Jones. Threatening that ICI might have to pull its R & D out of Britain if the brain drain of scientists continued, he complained, 'If you look at the actual funding of labs in the UK, first of all it's all very short-term, and secondly, if you actually look at the amount of capital behind every scientist in the UK, it is pitiful compared to other countries.'

Rewards and status are difficult to separate, because society tends to reward best those it holds in greatest awe. Whatever the cause, there is in general still substantially greater competition for places on arts degree courses than on science courses. The shortage of high-calibre industrial research scientists may well become one of the most critical limitations on industrial expansion.

Even within companies, there is a status problem for scientists. Relatively few chief executives in the UK have a strong science or engineering background and even fewer since the collapse of Rolls-Royce, which was widely seen as caused by the lack of broad business perspective in engineer-dominated companies. But engineers do not have to be oblivious of commercial realities; nor can non-scientists and non-engineers in the chief executive chair afford to delegate the overseeing of innovation in their companies. There is now a growing body of evidence that unless top management constantly stresses the need for innovation and the directions in which it most wishes to see innovation take place, then very little will change. While it is commonplace for US corporations to have a group technology director, responsible for controlling the direction of research and its applications and keeping the board informed of technological threats and opportunities, relatively few British companies have evolved a similar function.

THE DIFFUSION OF TECHNOLOGY

Technology is only as good as the use you put it to. The difficulty is recognising when an advance in technology could improve a product, a process, or how it is delivered. From the standpoint of defence research, there seems widespread agreement that the transfer of technology to civil uses has been lamentably slow in Britain and that when such technology transfer does take place, it is other countries that reap the benefits. The flow of technology out of the annual £600 million paid to defence research establishments has been minimal. Yet there are many

181

technologies within the defence establishments that would make a significant competitive difference for British firms.

Quoted by the *Financial Times* as typical of the failure by the MoD to encourage commercial exploitation of its R & D work is the example of low-power liquid crystal displays. The Royal Signals and Radar Establishment did all the groundwork in the 1970s, then shelved its research. It was left to Japanese companies to complete the development work necessary to mass-produce the displays for use in calculators, digital watches and other consumer goods.

The problem often lies in companies not knowing how to take half-developed technology and turn it into significant commercial opportunities. This takes both time and a combination of technical and marketing expertise. It would make sense for defence scientists, who have worked on a new idea, to follow it into industry to participate in its exploitation. But, on the whole, scientists have been reluctant to do so and, to be fair, the system does not help them. There are few options for secondment and a permanent transfer between public and private sector employment involves complex issues of pension rights and job security.

Getting ideas out of the university laboratory and into industry is less of a problem, but still a far from satisfactory process. Says the Advisory Board for the Research Councils, 'There is a lack of purposeful direction, nationally, in the redeployment of university research effort, both between and within institutions.' While industrial liaison and funding of university research has increased substantially in recent years, it has traditionally been a minor source of development. Even now, with universities and polytechnics obliged by the government to carry out industrial work to fund basic research activities, the degree of collaboration between industrial and academic labs is limited. Of the £100 million spent each year on research by polytechnics, for example, only 40 per cent is externally funded.

This is a problem that even Japan is concerned about. Largely due to the stranglehold exerted on university research by the Ministry of Education, Science and Culture (Monbusho), and partially due to the strength of Japanese companies' internal resources for applied research, only 10 per cent of funding comes from industry. Of the total private sector R & D annual spending, universities receive less than 0.5 per cent. But Japanese companies tend to make up for the failings in their relationships with domestic universities by developing relationships with overseas universities and through extensive and thorough networks of technology intelligence.

182

Worried by the problem, Monbusho has started a number of schemes to improve relationships between industry and academia in research, among them a joint research programme which links university researchers and companies' own staff on specific projects. The company provides 80 per cent of the cost and the ministry provides the remainder.

In British civil research, too, technology transfer appears to have been a low priority. The chemicals industry is one where it might be expected that companies would have a good knowledge of new technology and how to exploit it. Not so, according to a survey by the Chemicals Economic Development Council into the awareness and usage of various sources of help. The survey concluded, 'There was a low level of use of external support by companies and either ignorance or dismissal of what was available.' Almost 80 per cent of companies had not heard of the British Technology Group or did not recognise how it could help them, 87 per cent were unaware or uninterested in the Department of Trade and Industry's Support for Innovation scheme, and 63 per cent responded similarly regarding Science and Engineering Research Council support.

Only one in four chemical companies had made any significant use of universities in keeping up to date, one in ten had used polytechnics, and only one in twenty-five had used other research establishments.

The lack of awareness among British companies of the potential of new technology to affect their competitive position is alarming. A 1984 survey of company policies on technology in five countries – Australia, Belgium, West Germany, Britain and the United States – found a high degree of complacency in the UK. When asked about the impact of new technology on their products and processes only 54 per cent of British companies rated it 'a great deal' and 50 per cent 'a fair amount' – far and away the lowest of all the countries surveyed.

There are bright spots in this gloomy picture. Some of them are referred to in the next chapter. And to place matters further in perspective, it must be said that most other Western economies share most of the same problems. Take the United States, for example. In a recent speech, Erich Bloch, director of the US National Science Foundation, propounded his fears that the United States' leadership in science and technology was under severe threat. While the United States had increased Federal R & D support from $33 billion in 1980 to $63 billion in 1987, this still wasn't enough to meet the competitive challenge from European and Japanese competitors, he claimed. His shopping list of remedial action is familiar. It includes:

- More federal support for basic research, even if that means cutting back on support for developmental research.

- A change in the status and rewards of science compared to 'better' careers such as the law.

- Increased emphasis on science subjects in school curricula.

- More effective transfer of technology from university to industry.

The point, of course, is that if this is what the world's largest technology-based economy is doing, then it represents the minimum that the UK needs to do just to stand still.

The last word on this contentious topic probably belongs to the NEDC:

This change in the UK's relative position, combined with continuing substantial defence commitments, poses a dilemma. Either the UK must devote a substantially *higher proportion* of its resources to R & D in order to compete fully with those abroad; or it must rely to a much greater degree on *licensing* technology from abroad, focusing its innovative input on the post-development stage which exploits the full commercial potential of the new technology; or it must put increasing effort into *linking* and *concentrating* its efforts to ensure that UK industry can match or better the competitiveness of others in certain areas.

11

The Rise of Research and Development

'In the long term most British companies, certainly of any size, and some small ones too, must spend perhaps a bigger proportion of their income on R & D than they have in the past if they are going to stay in the first league or, indeed, even not in the first league, with the rapid changes in technology that are going on all over the world.'
Secretary of State for Trade and Industry to the House of Lords Select Committee on Science and Technology, 1976

'The government have the responsibility of all governments, namely leadership. It must be seen to lead the country to new heights in science and technology.'
House of Lords Select Committee, 1986.

REVERSING DECLINE

The picture we painted of Britain's research and development in the previous chapter was almost universally gloomy. There seems little doubt among any one we interviewed that, in terms of applied technology, Britain has struck a bad patch. It was in 1971 that Lord Dainton warned that the post-war period of rapid R & D growth was coming to an end. Funding has remained at a virtually constant level since that time. But how reversible is this relative decline and what signs are there that a reversal is taking place? Let's look to begin with at the primary issues raised earlier.

THE LEVEL OF R & D SPENDING

Although the cause is partially a reduction of government investment in R & D in real terms, industry is slowly increasing its share of total (non-defence) R & D spending. It is planned to decrease defence R & D spending from 52 to 48 per cent of the government's R & D budget in 1989–90 (compared with a 3.5 per cent increase in civil R & D).

Two factors may help speed up the increase in the total R & D investment by industry. One is the growing profitability of many of the remaining manufacturing-based companies. The other is that, as competitive pressures become increasingly global rather than national, more companies will be forced to adopt international rather than local standards of R & D investment to stay in the race.

The United States introduced R & D tax incentives in the early 1980s. In Britain, however, the government has argued that this is incompatible with the British tax system and it opposes the existing large numbers of special tax reliefs. Again, the Australian government provides an example of what can be done. In an effort to create stronger links between research institutions and industry it has offered a 150 per cent tax incentive for expenditure on R & D carried out in Australia.

High levels of R & D expenditure have been behind one of Britain's most outstanding financial success stories – Glaxo, one of Britain's major companies whose name is not well known. The pharmaceutical company ascribes its success in large part to a refusal to cut back on R & D, whatever the circumstances. Indeed, in 1987 it increased its R & D spending from £123 million to £155 million.

Glaxo's dramatic growth from twenty-fifth to seventh in world rankings of pharmaceutical companies has been marked by a combination of large-scale R & D investment and innovative marketing. This has been supported by sales partnerships in the US and Japan which, though unusual in the pharmaceuticals business, have brought Glaxo an efficient international distribution network. This has played a part in reducing product development cycles so that Zantac, now the world's bestselling prescription drug, only took five years and four months from synthesis to launch in 1981. This compares with the twelve years it took Glaxo to introduce its Ventolin drug onto the American market in 1969.

Glaxo's future plans are for even further expansion in R & D investment. Since 1978 its development staff has doubled to over 3,000, and R & D accounted for almost 8 per cent of Glaxo's revenue of £1.4 billion in 1986. It plans to recruit another 1,500 R & D staff before 1992 as well as doubling its R & D expenditure.

Britain's pharmaceuticals industry is notably well-placed in the R & D race. Of the 48 major international R & D establishments with fundamental pharmaceutical research capacity, 31 per cent are in the UK, 13 per cent in West Germany and 6 per cent in France. While the UK has only 3.5 per cent of world pharmaceutical production, it accounts for 11.5 per cent of R & D expenditure. British research, it has been estimated, is responsible for over 17 per cent of the 100 leading products in world sales.

In the five years to 1985 the most outstanding relative increase in R & D spending was in the British motor industry, where it rose from £180.4 million to £371.6 million. This occurred despite the fact that none of the big car makers receives any government funds for R & D. Nearly a third of the motor industry's R & D spending is accounted for by Ford which has

3800 people at its Dunton research centre developing new models. Jaguar now has a similar centre with 1100 technical staff (compared with a mere 250 in 1982). It planned to spend £50 million on R & D in 1987, with the aim of matching Mercedes' performance of investing 4.5 per cent of total sales revenue in R & D.

DIRECTION OF FUNDING

The Conservative government's policy towards defence-related R & D has been to move away from open-ended, cost-plus contracts that result in products of interest only to the Ministry of Defence. Instead, it is looking increasingly to defence products that can be bought, in part at least, off the shelf. In practice, relatively little has been achieved. However, the disruption to the cosy relationship between the MoD and UK defence suppliers has been beneficial in the sense that it has stimulated the defence manufacturers to look much more seriously at developing products for international markets and to be much more aggressive in seeking alternative civil uses for defence-related research. There is still some way to go, however, before potential civil applications of technology are built into the structure of R & D from the beginning.

The House of Lords Science and Technology Committee received mixed reports on the split betweeen civil and military R & D. Sir John Kingman commented, 'The defence industry of this country will collapse, not necessarily for military reasons but for economic and political reasons.' Sir Robin Nicholson, however, pointed out that reducing spending on defence R & D does not necessarily lead to increased civil R & D expenditure. The Fellowship of Engineering disagreed. 'If the post-war period from 1945 to the present is viewed as a whole, there is no doubt that defence and defence-related R & D has weakened civil research initiative, especially in industry, and that this has had a harmful effect on product innovation and industrial competitiveness.'

There are positive signs in technology transfer from defence spending. These include the Royal Signals and Radar Establishment's programme, which allows industrial firms to second staff to RSRE, and a recently established operation called Defence Technology Enterprises. DTE tries, with MoD backing, to identify commercially exploitable aspects of defence research and to show companies how they could be further developed and exploited.

The flagship of government support for collaborative research has been the Alvey programme. Born of dismay at the decline in Britain's balance of payments in information technology, Alvey was formed to compete with Japan Inc., which had made clear its determination to achieve a collaborative breakthrough into the fifth generation of computers – intelligent machines that could duplicate some of the thinking processes of the human brain. Take-up of the £500 million made available was rapid and enthusiastic. Yet by the time the money ran out, there was very little to show in terms of commercially exploitable products.

However, the value of Alvey may rest more in its educative effect. Though research terms assembled during the time of the project have been broken up, the knowledge gained has been fairly widely diffused and the British computer industry is the stronger for it. The big question marks hang over whether we can keep up the research effort to the stage where we can gain direct benefit in terms of viable fifth generation computer products and how efficiently we can spread the technology already developed to companies not directly involved in producing computer hardware or advanced software.

Acost (Advisory Council for Science and Technology) reports to the Prime Minister and will decide which areas of science and technology should be supported by Government. However, there is considerable concern about its two main objectives: 'to identify areas of technology which British industry could exploit, and to identify areas where the Government could make substantial savings'. Hence the frustration of the British Association for the Advancement of Science and Technology, whose reaction to Government policy was aptly summed up by a past president, Lord Dainton: 'We like the restructuring, but where's the lolly?'

Positive developments may, perhaps, best be seen in the Link initiative which combines governmental and industry funding. Its first five advanced technology research collaborations were launched early in 1988. The aim is to spend £420 million over the next five years on Link collaborations between academia and companies of all sizes.

In terms of industry's own focus on R & D spending, the recognition that customers have a useful and significant input to make to product development, albeit slow in coming, has persuaded more and more companies to adopt market-oriented R & D. In some cases, this has led to remarkable degrees of customer research. The car manufacturer, Jaguar, for example,

189

having ignored customer complaints in the years of its decline, now actively solicits them as a means of improving both product and service. Computer systems company ICL learnt that making its systems truly 'user friendly' meant observing exactly how they used machines. It set up a laboratory where members of the public were given a manual and a computer terminal and were videoed as they wrestled with learning to operate the machine. Both the computers and their manuals underwent substantial changes to overcome the problems and frustrations revealed.

THE DIFFUSION OF TECHNOLOGY

It is in the diffusion of technology, perhaps most significant in its immediate effect on technological competitiveness, that the UK appears to be making most effort to catch up. The NEDC task force on innovation points to a number of positive steps in technology transfer, in particular the teaching company scheme, the Department of Education and Science's new regional technology centres, and private sector initiatives, such as NIMTECH.

The recently developed Centre for Exploitation of Science (CEST) may also provide a stepping stone towards greater co-operation between education institutions and industry. Headed by Sir Francis Tombs, CEST has raised £5 million from large science-based companies with an additional £1 million from the government.

CEST is expected to help in the development of new University Research Centres, thirty or forty of which are envisaged. The first URC will be at Cambridge University and will involve laboratories entirely concentrating on specific scientific opportunities exploitable within ten years.

Faced with government cuts, universities have been increasingly encouraged into seeking alternative means of funding. In 1984–5 the research income of all universities from industry was 78 per cent up on 1981–2, at £47 million. This growth has been backed at polytechnics by the 1985 Further Education Act, which allows them to sell their research and consultancy services on a commercial basis. The National Advisory Body for Public Sector Higher Education also now has a research fund though its finance of £2.5 million in 1985–6 fell dramatically short of the intended £20 million.

Nonetheless, NEDC believes the most effective method of transferring technology en masse is via 'sector-specific brokers' – industry associations or similar bodies, which take responsibility for making people in their sector of industry aware of the existence and potential of new technology, and which can advise on how to implement it. The task force's interim report does not discuss the other side of the coin – feeding back from companies within the sector information on the kinds of technology they would like to have available to achieve international competitive advantage. This is a more complex and demanding task, but would have a significant impact on the direction of R & D funding.

A good example of proactive attempts to raise the speed and quantity of meaningful technology transfer is the R & D Clearing House, set up in 1984 with NEDC help, as an initiative by the Chemical Economic Development Council. The Clearing House both transfers technology between members and also searches out new technologies among suppliers, customers and research institutions at home and abroad. In particular, it is looking for 'shelved' or aborted development projects which may be usefully licensed in part or whole to other British companies. Says the Clearing House

> Those of us who have been in the melancholy business of terminating developments will know that there is often only perfunctory attention paid to the possibility of retrieving some of the costs of development by looking for licensees. This is particularly true when the project is terminated when the development is incomplete . . . There is a considerable reservoir of potential products available, albeit often requiring some further development. Many of these are not available in technology transfer databases.

Frequently, the reason a project is abandoned is not that there is no market, nor that the product is inadequate, but simply that the company lacks one or more of the essential support elements to launch it successfully. For example, the company that has to invest heavily in new production equipment to exploit an innovation may calculate a lower return on investment than one that already has the right equipment written off its books.

The University of Surrey has helped pioneer a number of ways of increasing technology transfer from academia. The Surrey Network, for example, is a club that aims to link companies to relevant academics in the University. The network is structured around information and technology needs as defined by the companies, rather than on the organisation of the

191

University research departments. The University's Bureau of Industrial and External Liaison has also set up its own technology-based companies to exploit spin-offs from university research. Run by University research staff and financed by the bureau, some of these companies look set to make significant financial returns. Ownership of the majority of the equity and all intellectual property rights rests with the University, but the academics receive a share in the profits to invest back in their own research.

The picture that therefore emerges of the future state of British R & D is neither dark and stormy nor bright and sunny. Perhaps it can best be described, to continue the metaphor, as changeable, or sunny intervals. How it develops will depend upon a number of factors, among them:

- The willingness of the Government to show a technological leadership and concentrate resources in areas likely to lead to industrial competitive advantage.

- The willingness of companies themselves to commit resources to developing new products and processes and enhancing old ones; equally to improving the effectiveness of transferring ideas from the international marketplace to the development labs and from the labs to marketable products.

The Government's priority, say most of our respondents of all political shades, is to make up its mind what it wants to achieve from a science policy and get on with it. The House of Lords Select Committee called on the Government to examine further tax incentives to stimulate private R & D as well as making it a legal requirement for companies to disclose their R & D expenditure in annual accounts, and encouraging greater R & D spending in small firms.

The priority for companies is to increase technological awareness at all levels in the organisation, but particularly in the executive suite. No large or medium-sized company can afford not to have a clearly defined strategy for technology, because technology affects virtually every aspect of the business and, wisely used, can be a major instrument to achieve competitive advantage.

What, then, can companies do? The effective innovatory organisation in today's markets is essentially opportunistic. It may, if it is of the size of an IBM or a BP, finance a small amount of significant basic R & D in universities or its own labs. But it sees its R & D function as a strategic resource rather than a factory for new product ideas. As a result, it must aim to:

192

- Identify the technology which would have a strategic impact on its products and the way they are delivered or serviced, particularly technology that could alter the game in its chosen markets, as, for example, digital technology did in the watch industry.

- Gain a capability in as much as possible of this technology by effective monitoring internally and by strategic alliances externally. These alliances may consist simply of funding a university research project. Alternatively, they may involve minority shareholdings in small companies attempting to exploit new technologies, or joint ventures with other large firms.

- Be responsive to market changes and opportunities, so that identification of a market need automatically triggers a search for technology that would meet that need. This is perhaps the hardest part of all.

A good example of using technology as a strategic resource is the manner in which a number of companies have achieved lasting competitive edge by applying information technology where it will provide the greatest leverage. Avis, for example, has secured its market position by investment in a reservation system that provides an exceptional degree of customer service. The cost and time involved in setting it up have proved a considerable barrier to competitors wanting to follow suit. International Thomson enhanced its competitive position in the travel business by taking a lead through information technology. In the 1985 package holiday price war, Thomson was able to take bookings at an average of over two a second. Business was doubled in the year. Much of the credit is given by Thomsons to its TOP booking system which allowed its travel agents to book directly by computer rather than by telephone.

A study by Templeton College at Oxford looked at a hundred cases of companies which had achieved similar benefits from using information technology to improve customer service. The researcher, David Runge, concluded:

Companies which had successfully used IT as a strategic weapon . . . had two advantages over companies which failed to do so. The first was that their awareness of the potential of IT was much sharper. They found ways to make information more useful, more accurate and more available to their chosen marketplaces. They recognised where and how time windows and geographical constraints created an opportunity to use IT to enhance their competitive postures. By contrast, many firms look only within their operations for ways to put IT to use. The real strategic benefits of IT seem to come from looking outside.

193

The second advantage was the ability of the organisation to adapt and respond to the market opportunities presented by IT. They were able to align their business and their information systems strategy in a manner that allowed them to make use of their awareness of exploitable user needs.

Andrew Robertson of the Polytechnic of Central London outlines the three basic strategies that a company can adopt towards R & D. The first is 'offence' – aiming to become the technological leader and thereby steal a large market share before competitors catch up. The downside of this strategy is that, once you have proven a new product is feasible, competitors can follow suit without going down all the expensive side alleys that your R & D department had to follow. The offensive strategy also calls for a heavy investment in R & D as a proportion of sales and a very effective technology intelligence network, to take advantage of new ideas at the earliest possible moment.

The second strategy is what Robertson calls 'defensive striving' – keeping up with the leader while learning from his mistakes. Companies that adopt this strategy develop similar technology and aim to improve on the leader's product at lower cost. However, while the R & D costs are reduced, the technology information and monitoring costs are often higher.

Lastly comes the 'me-too' strategy – simply copying the leader as closely as possible, with the minimum possible level of R & D. This strategy often runs risks of patent infringement and can usually only work well if the company spends enough on R & D to gain an edge in design, quality control and production cost to be able to show significant advantages in terms of value for money and price.

In practice, most companies will attempt to mix all three strategies, if only because the cost of being first in the field across the board would be beyond their resources. But there has to be a conscious decision to adopt a particular strategy in each area of the business.

One of the great R & D success stories in recent times was Pilkington's float glass process. In essence, this success was less dependent on the quality or originality of the research than on the way the company chose to support and exploit it. Ironically, when Pilkington began to license its technology globally, it was criticised for selling off its greatest asset, particularly when the company's financial performance was lack-lustre. Yet the decision to license and the way in which the licensing was done is directly responsible for Pilkington's current position as the largest, most efficient and profitable glassmaker in the world. For a start, the flow of cash from licensing the product helped provide financial stability over the years and even now is worth some £40 million a year. Then, by insisting in the licensing agreement that, while all improvements in the technology would be passed on free to licensees, they must reciprocate in kind, Pilkington ensured that it remained the technological leader. Moreover, it became uneconomic for any other glass producer to invest the huge sums needed to produce a competing technology. At the same time, Pilkington's knowledge of close relationships with its competitors has made the acquisition path much easier in countries such as West Germany and the United States.

Not all work is best carried out independently and one of the roles that industry associations (and opportunistic private sector research companies) could carry out much more effectively than they do at present is to create research consortia – alliances of competing firms – to investigate potential applications of new technology. At present, most such alliances come about through EEC initiatives such as the European Research Co-ordinating Agency (EUREKA) in which Britain plays a substantial role. Indeed, the House of Lords Committee sees greater European co-operation as having 'made some important and confident strides'. It draws attention to programmes within the European Community such as ESPRIT, RACE and BRITE as well as those outside like the European Space Agency and European Science Foundation. The committee observed, 'The difficulties and disadvantages of collaboration are now better understood than they were, and there has also emerged a sounder sense of realism . . . it is companies, universities and laboratories which in the new climate are increasingly making the running.'

Again, examples from abroad may well hold important lessons for Britain. Co-operation in R & D is now common practice in Japan where strategic alliances play an increasingly important role – in 1986 there were over 3000 and one company, NTT, formed over 100 in the year. The alliances allow Japanese companies to acquire new technological know-how as quickly as possible. In the pharmaceutical industry it takes about ten years to develop a new drug so companies try to reduce the time scale by using external resources. When the Japanese government opened up pharmaceuticals to foreign competition a number of Japanese companies strengthened their R & D capabilities, globalised, diversified or acquired. The web of strategic alliances became so complex that co-operation and competition have occurred together in some cases. Genentech of the USA, for example, provides information on new anti-cancer drugs to both the

Toray/Daiichi alliance and the Kyowa Fermentation/Mitsubishi alliance. Both alliances are competing in development, manufacture and sales of the new drugs. The balance between companies with money and limited technology and those with the technology and limited finance can often prove mutually beneficial.

Increasing the *efficiency* of R & D in such ways is an essential part of our industrial future. The key is not how much companies spend on R & D, but on maximising the benefits from every piece of research. It is this philosophy, claims ICI, that has enabled it to match the performance of its main international pharmaceutical rivals in producing major new drugs on around half the research budget. By focusing resources onto selected, achievable targets, it is able to be realistic about the level of returns it expects to achieve.

In summary, it seems that much of the complacency that has led to the decline of British R & D is still with us. There is urgent need for all parties involved – government, industry, academia and commerce – to accept the need for meaningful strategies and the resources to implement them. There remains a strong science and engineering base on which we can build. But the longer we hesitate to provide resources that meet or exceed those of our main international rivals, the harder it will be to catch up.

12

The Decline of International Perspective

'We were a trading nation by the nature of things; our markets were captive not because we controlled them, but because we were the only people they knew. Other countries went to war because they wanted what we had. They have since systematically pushed into our markets because they had an international outlook and commercial aggression.'
Malcolm Bruce MP, Social and Liberal Democrats spokesman on Trade and Industry, 1987

'Throughout the country there are too many manufacturing firms – some of them quite large – who have an exportable product but don't do any thing like enough to promote their sales overseas.'
Sir James Cleminson, chairman of the British Overseas Trade Board, 1987

'Exporting is undervalued in Britain. Its managers are under-paid and, generally, have sparse budgets. The best brains are usually attracted to much higher salaries in other areas. Exporting creates jobs in Britain – we should invest heavily behind it.'
Stephen Perry, managing director of the London Export Corporation, 1987

GLOBAL BUSINESS

Business is now a truly international affair. But are British businesses and British business people truly international in outlook? Sir James Cleminson, chairman of the British Overseas Trade Board, put the international demands of business into perspective when addressing a CBI Council Meeting in September 1987: 'Today's market is global, competitive on a worldwide scale. The only way we as a nation can maintain what has already been achieved – and move ahead to improve our country's standard of living, our education system and our health and social services – is to accept the commitment and invest in success in that world market. This is the real challenge of business today.'

Robert Rosenfeld, Richard Whipp and Andrew Pettigrew of Warwick University published their research into Britain's international competitiveness in June 1987. They conclude, 'Internationalisation has been a central aspect of both strategic change and competitiveness in the 1970s and 1980s ... For British companies, the internationalisation of markets has had profound consequences for their competitive performance. It would appear that the conjunction of globally organised corporations with new technologies of co-ordination and production has led to truly worldwide competition.'

FAILURE TO DISCOVER AND DEVELOP
NEW MARKETS

The increased internationalism of trade, and so much else, has fuelled the widespread belief amongst economists that economic growth is most easily achieved when export-led. As a consequence, government policy has often encouraged companies to increase exports and replace imports with domestically produced goods. Tariffs, international trade agreements, export credit guarantee schemes, voluntarily accepted quotas on certain imports and Buy British campaigns have attempted to encourage this. British protectionism is inevitably countered by the vigorous attempts made by other countries to protect their own domestic markets.

Attempts at protection have not made a great deal of positive difference. The effects of greater competition, particularly from Japan, on the British share of international trade has been a major element in Britain's industrial decline. It has not affected Britain alone adversely. In 1950 Britain and the United States each had 26 per cent of the world's exports of manufactured goods. By 1986 Britain's share had been reduced to 8 per cent and the United States' to 14 per cent. In the same period, import penetration of the British domestic market rose from 5 per cent to 30 per cent.

The art of exporting has become shrouded in mystique. After all, Britain had a great deal of exporting expertise at the time of the Empire. The 1987 edition of *British Social Attitudes* confirms that people now believe that British exporting expertise is lower than that of our competitors – almost half the sample felt that Britain is worse than most of its international competitors at selling goods abroad, but better in inventing new products.

The fearsome international reputation of the Japanese contributes to the psychological block that the British seem to have towards conquering new markets. 'Japan's market still seems virtually impenetrable on any major scale,' reflected the Conservative Political Centre in August 1987. But it is not only in Japan that British industry seems frozen with fear. It has been estimated that more than £5 billion of sales in overseas markets is being missed by British companies because they overestimate the difficulties of exporting and do not appreciate the potential profits. Indeed, the trepidation is such that John Wilson, former director general of the Institute of Export, stated that, 'Many senior people in medium and small-sized firms either are afraid to get into the export business or feel that it is too much trouble.'

The British Overseas Trade Board is now encouraging smaller firms to take up export opportunities. It has carried out research with consultants Graham Bannock and Partners and produced a long list of reasons why companies don't fulfil their export potential.

Reasons for not exporting (percentage)

Satisfied with home market opportunities	13.1
Lack of confidence/experience in exporting	10.2
Exporting unprofitable	3.7
Cannot get suitable overseas distribution	4.1
Products unsuitable for export market	31.9
Lack of export demand	7.4
Lack of production capacity	2.6
Lack of management time	9.8
Lack of finance	4.4
Lack of market information	12.8

(Source: *Into Active Exporting*, British Overseas Trade Board)

This series of excuses may help explain the performance of British exporters when compared to those of France and West Germany.

Share of manufactured goods exported by OECD countries (percentage)

	1966	1979	1984
Britain	12	9	7
France	8	10	8
West Germany	18	19	17

(Source: OECD)

NATIONALISTIC ATTITUDE TOWARDS EXPORTS

'Direct investment overseas is sometimes seen as exporting domestic workers' jobs, and inward direct investment as allowing the domestic economy to become too dependent on foreign, possibly footloose, multinational enterprises,' says Arthur Francis of Imperial College London in *Internationalisation and Competitiveness* (June 1987). Caution has too often dictated that companies concentrate on their domestic market and turn a blind eye to export opportunities. A recent Loughborough University survey discovered that 87 per cent of the Japanese companies in the survey gave 'aggressive size growth' or 'market domination' as their goal. Only 20 per cent of British companies gave the same response.

In many companies, strategy is dictated by a peculiarly British insularity. Says Christopher Hogg of Courtaulds in *The New Elite*: 'We can't go about our business with one hand tied behind our backs. The maddening characteristic of this country is that it is so insular. It will not look outside and take its standards from the rest of the world. It leaves those of us who actually have to match up to overseas competition pretty darned exposed.'

As an example, Social and Liberal Democrat industry spokesman, Malcolm Bruce, provides an anecdote:

> John MacKintosh, the former Labour MP, used to tell the tale of two meetings he attended at the time of the referendum on British membership of the European Community. The meeting with European unionists took place in a magnificent penthouse office suite in the centre of Brussels, over an excellent lunch. He flew back to Glasgow to attend an evening meeting. This time the venue was a decayed building on Sauchiehall Street. After walking up four flights of stairs, he joined fellow unionists in a smoke-filled room with lino on the floor and was greeted immediately with, 'Afore ye start, John, we dinna want to be dragged down to the level of those Europeans.'

Former diplomat Sir Nicholas Henderson believes that our attitude towards the European Community is symptomatic of a limited international perspective: 'The half-heartedness of Britain's political commitment to Europe is reflected in a similar lack of total involvement by British industrialists in meeting the requirements of the highly competitive continental market,' he says in his *Channels and Tunnels*, published in 1987.

For some, failing to join the Community in the first place was a fundamentally short-sighted decision. Says APEX's Roy Grantham, 'Pre-1979 decline starts from the fact that we failed to join the EEC in 1949. We chose the slow-growing Commonwealth instead of fast growing Europe. It had a major impact on our ability to compete. France, Italy and other countries had to become more competitive to keep up with Germany. We assumed we had won the war when all we had done was survive it.' According to Grantham, when Britain joined the EEC it had already missed having a role in policy formulation. Britain was effectively left behind. 'By the time we got into the EEC we were past our prime. We had passed the peak of our ability to compete. We lost out on all fronts: on opportunities for industrial expansion; on moulding the Common Agricultural Policy to our needs; and on developing a market for services, which we still haven't achieved,' says Grantham. It is worthwhile noting that the CAP accounts for 70 per cent of the European Community's budget and was formed with the French and German farmers in mind rather than the British.

It has not only been a question of joining too late, but of failing to appreciate the Community's potential. 'Our attitude to the EEC is one of reluctant acceptance,' says Malcolm Bruce. 'If we were more enthusiastic about the cultural, political and trade exchanges there would be more interchange and we would assess their markets better.' Bruce believes that British perspectives of Europe as a distant foreign market are ludicrously misguided. 'To be a successful exporter you need a significant size of market. Companies should think of Europe as their domestic market. If they actually do think in those terms, recognition of the need for investment will follow.'

LACK OF PROPERLY TRAINED PERSONNEL

British myopia also affects its training of managers for international business. Global business requires global managers. Yet a survey by Ambrosetti Consulting Group in October 1987 of the top 200 British-owned companies showed that only 18 per cent of executive directors speak a foreign language fluently. Very few had any international business experience. In fact, nearly half the executive directors had no international experience at all, either through working abroad or directing international operations in their own companies. Almost one in ten of the companies questioned had no directors with international experience. John Wilson, formerly of the Institute of Export, observes, 'The major reason for companies' failure to export or to develop active exporting is, of course, the lack of knowledgeable personnel.'

Malcolm Bruce advocates a radical change in the way industrialists approach international training. 'Language fluency is important in training internationally orientated managers. If you have at least one other language, you can pursue part of your business studies abroad. Every senior manager should attend at least one course overseas in another language.'

It is not just the lack of foreign language speakers which has proved a handicap. Often, having identified possible export markets, British companies have adopted an amateurish approach. 'Top people in companies are very fond of going off to look at markets overseas but they are often the wrong people, going with no literature or photographs, no samples and without the time to carry out a proper study of the market,' Bill Sykes, an organisational development consultant, told the *BIM Report* (December 1986).

As a result, many British managers have found themselves burdened by long-term loss-making foreign subsidiaries. They have developed the habit of pioneering new foreign markets only to lose the advantage. Their attempts, at times, have been comically speculative. In 1925 Barclays Bank opened a branch in Rome in the hope of capturing the Vatican's bank account. It still hasn't achieved this ambitious aim.

13

The Rise of International Perspective

'Government policies have generated greater professionalism and aggression in exporting.'
Stephen Perry, managing director of the London Export Corporation, 1987

'UK-based manufacturers can compete successfully, selling seemingly mature products in a mass market against strong international competition.'
London Business School Centre for Business Strategy, 1987

'The only way to create the real long-term jobs Britain needs, the only way to achieve the higher wages everyone wants, the only way to earn the wealth so desperately needed for our educational and social programmes, is for British business to sell more and to sell better in the markets of the world.'
Sir David Nickson, president of the CBI at their 1986 conference

205

EXPORTING TRADITION

Despite the shortcomings of Britain's international perspective, Britain has always exported a higher percentage of its GDP than almost any other industrialised nation – steady at 25–30 per cent over the last decade compared to Japan at 12–15 per cent, USA at 7–10 per cent and Italy, West Germany and France at 20–30 per cent. Only West Germany now exports a higher proportion of GDP and it only gained the advantage in the late 1970s. In the early twentieth century British manufacturing industry exported nearly 40 per cent of its output. Some industries, like textiles, were almost entirely export-based.

The exporting statistics are supported by investment overseas. As a proportion of GDP, British investment overseas is the highest in the world. In 1976 of all direct investment abroad by the developed countries, Britain's amounted to 11.2 per cent, second only to America. In 1967, however, Britain had accounted for an impressive 16.6 per cent of direct investment abroad.

The geographical emphasis of British investment has also shifted from the Commonwealth to Europe and America. In 1962 only 36 per cent of British overseas stock was in Western Europe or North America; by 1981 it was 58 per cent.

Many British companies do indeed have international perspectives and are seeking competitive advantage on a global scale. John Wilson believes that, 'Our leading firms all have a global market view of their business.' There is an awareness among top companies that the UK is simply too small to be a viable market on its own and that true excellence only comes from competing on the world stage. Even in the retailing business, one demanding swift response to market change, top British companies carefully monitor foreign competitors. For example, Sainsbury's acquisition of a New England retailing chain was at least partially motivated by the desire to gain experience in new retailing techniques before transplanting them to the UK.

LONG-TERM INVESTMENT

Success abroad demands long-term investment and outlooks. It is an expensive business. British Aerospace, for example, secured a $200 million contract in China in 1985, after a lengthy period when the Chinese did not buy anything at all from any Western aerospace manufacturers. British Aerospace had the persistence to maintain an office in Beijing from 1974 onwards in the hope of obtaining an order which, when it came, was seen as part of a long-term relationship with and commitment to the Chinese.

Although not all companies have the financial strength to enter into such long-term commitments, there are a number of striking examples of British companies with truly international perspectives. Amersham International, which began by making radium dials for night-flying Spitfires during the war, now achieves nearly 90 per cent of its sales overseas. Yet all manufacturing of its radio isotopes is carried out in Britain. Despite these impressive figures, Amersham remains at risk from currency fluctuations. It has been hit, in recent years, by the declining dollar which has meant that American competitors could undercut its prices. GKN, the British motor components supplier and manufacturer, has suffered similarly. It is involved with all the major European car producers and has long-term exclusive contracts to supply Ford and Chrysler in America. In 1984, Britain accounted for half of GKN's sales but only a quarter of its profits. Even so, GKN's average profit growth of 30 per cent between 1976 and 1985 proves that British companies can successfully make money in overseas markets.

What British companies have failed to achieve in export performance, they have at least partially made up for in terms of investment overseas. As the table on page 208 illustrates, British investment overseas earned almost five times as much in 1984 as in 1979.

Overseas Investment (£ million)

	Accumulated balance	Investment income
1910	3351	170
1946	2329	110
1956	6–7000	660
1964	10000	800
1979	12500	1100
1984	70000	5000

(Source: *Empire to Welfare State*, T O Lloyd, Oxford University Press, 1986.)

AMERICAN EXPLOSION

British companies have become the most enthusiastic acquirers of American subsidiaries. In 1986 British companies made 108 acquisitions in the United States compared to 61 by Canada, 24 by Japan, 19 by Hong Kong and 18 by Sweden.

Between 1983 and 1986, British companies spent a massive $23 billion on acquiring American companies. Historically, this should come as no surprise. After all, as early as 1914 Courtaulds, Vickers and Dunlop had networks of overseas factories. In fact, before the 1950s, British companies had more foreign subsidiaries than their American competitors. British acquisition of American companies is growing apace. In 1987 a total of $29.2 billion was spent buying 314 companies. This record-breaking spending spree was achieved despite a sharp decrease in activity following the stock market crash in October 1987. The top takeovers, calculated by *Acquisitions Monthly*, are shown in the table on page 209.

The fascination with expansion through America applies throughout business. Habitat, for example, opened its first American store in 1977, using the name Conran's, and its American operation now brings in $60 million every year. Its only problem was the initial one of being seen as 'too English'. This has since been remedied and more stores may well be

Top American acquisitions by British companies in 1987

American company	Business	British bidder	Value ($ million)
Standard Oil	Oil	BP	7,600
Kidde	Conglomerate	Hanson Trust	1,700
Stauffer Chemicals	Agrichemicals	ICI	1,690
Newmont Mining	Mining	Cons Gold F	1,500
Manpower	Employment agency	Blue Arrow	1,340
Heublein	Wines and spirits	Grand Metropolitan	1,200
Hilton International	Hotels	Ladbroke	1,070
First Jersey National Bank	Banking	National Westminster Bank	820
ADT	Security equipment	Hawley Group	715
Rent-a-Center	Electrical rental	Thorn EMI	595

added to back up its twenty-eight in Europe, one each in Iceland, Singapore and Martinique and fourteen in Japan.

The American boom has grown despite a number of conspicuous failures by large British companies. For example, British American Tobacco had to sell off 40 per cent of its American retailing subsidiaries, including the famous Gimbel Brothers stores, and Midland Bank eventually had to sell its Crocker National Bank to Wells Fargo after a bitter seven-year struggle to make its massive investment pay off.

Amongst the most notable failures was the Imperial Group's purchase of the Howard Johnson chain of motels and restaurants for $630 million in 1980. Imperial seemed to have focused on the legal and financial implications of the deal rather than market or competitor analysis. The plain fact was that Howard Johnson was already past its prime. Eventually, in 1986, Imperial sold most of its holdings to the Marriott Corporation for a knockdown $314 million.

Two months after this sale, Imperial itself was taken over by the doyen of Anglo-American acquisitors, Hanson Trust. Its £2.7 billion takeover of Imperial in spring 1986 was followed by radical restructuring and the removal of virtually all of the top echelon of Imperial's marketing division. Imperial staff reported that as soon as the deal went through, accountants from Ernst and Whinney arrived to examine ways of cutting cash, overheads and making the assets work.

Within weeks Imperial was drastically reduced in size. Its 5,000 Courage pubs were sold to Elders and Trust House Forte took over the Anchor Hotel, Happy Eater and Welcome Break chains.

For Hanson Trust this sort of activity has become part and parcel of international success. It was only in 1973 that Hanson Industries was established as Hanson Trust's American arm. By 1986, through a rash of acquisitions, Hanson Industries was worth £3.7 billion. The companies acquired included Smith Corona, Interstate United, US Industries (for $532 million in 1984) and, in 1986, SCM. The bitterly-fought SCM purchase is typical of Hanson Trust's aggressive approach. Through sales of its assets, SCM has more than paid back the $930 million Hanson bought it for. Hanson Trust is left with SCM's highly profitable pigments business and another American subsidiary.

Hanson's strategy is to buy undervalued companies in basic industries such as food or building materials or low tech industries which will not need new capital. Unlike other British companies, Hanson Trust never overpays – a frequent criticism of other European acquisitors. On taking over a company, Hanson decentralises management to push responsibility down to the operating level. Rather than import British senior managers, it makes best use of local American managers. Hanson, started with Lord Hanson's share in the £3 million compensation paid when his father's haulage business was nationalised, is now Britain's fifth largest quoted company.

GOVERNMENT ASSISTANCE

There is a strong perception that, compared with say, Japan, the governmental assistance for British companies in overseas markets has been far from adequate. Embassy commercial staff have frequently been the target of criticism, albeit sometimes from vested interests. For example,

Stephen Perry of the London Export Corporation sums up the common view that the civil service structure for exporters has failed to move with the times, declaring, 'The civil service apparatus has not changed. It lacks any cohesive strategy or sense of priorities. As a result resources are poorly allocated.' His company is China's biggest trading partner in Europe, yet its unique expertise is never used by government. Perry advocates greater use of export consultants and closer relationships between academics, industry and government to provide coherent exporting assistance. He does, however, remain optimistic. 'The current weakness provides the opportunity for change,' he says.

THE EUROPEAN MARKET

Of immediate concern must be the creation of a single European market planned for 1992, the first stages of which – harmonising customs procedures – are already being implemented. Most British companies have only recently become aware that there are major opportunities to create truly European companies, capable of competing on equal terms with the United States with its 200 million domestic consumers and Japan with its 100 million. Europe as a unified market would contain 320 million people. Unfortunately most attempts at creating cross-border mergers have been dismal failures, Dunlop-Pirelli being among the most spectacular. Part of the problem here is that the two companies still did not see themselves as *European* and it is debatable whether any major company in any European country truly sees itself in this way. Those that have operations throughout Europe see themselves either as global companies (such as Philips) or national-based companies (such as Siemens of Germany). Very few can boast a truly European outlook. Anthony Bamford, JCB's chairman, believes that his company is an exception. 'JCB has sold its products throughout Europe for many years and in fact we look on it as our domestic market. We see great opportunities for us in Europe over the next five years,' he told *The Sunday Times* in January 1988.

The opportunities that await companies that do set out to be European, rather than British or French or German in their outlook, are considerable. Firstly, there are economies of scale, not just in sales terms but in research and development. Then there is the ability to develop truly

211

international managers by moving people about between operations in different countries.

The problem with creating massive European companies is that size has its disadvantages, too. European markets are not uniform, nor are they likely to be within the coming decades. The answer may lie in a federated system of operationally independent yet financially interlinked companies in each country. The underlying concept here would be partnership and alliance rather than ownership. British companies have the opportunity to lead such groupings; but there are few signs at the moment that they are seizing the initiative.

Sir David Nickson has drawn attention to Britain's unpreparedness. At the 1987 CBI conference, he complained that business people were still fearful of Europe and spoke of it as 'abroad'. 'We cannot even get our clocks to tell the same time yet,' he acerbically commented.

John Raisman, chairman of the CBI Europe committee, echoes the theme.

A couple of months ago one of the non-British EC Commissioners commented sadly to a small group in Strasbourg that whereas Britain deserves much of the credit for the conception and detailed planning for the completion of the internal market by 1992 and its acceptance by the Council of Ministers, it looked as if it would be the country least well equipped to benefit from it, judging from the apparent public apathy towards it at present. In France 4000 businessmen attended a recent conference to promote the interest of French industry in the subject – I doubt if we could attract 400 British businessmen to such an event today.

At the CBI's Brussels office, Neil Gibbs observes, 'A major effort to improve awareness is needed. British companies are lagging behind other European countries like France and Italy. 1992 has potentially huge implications, every aspect of some firms' operations may be affected, but there are still only a minority of British companies aware of the changes.' He points out that even taxi drivers in France have opinions on the internal market. Sir David Nickson has done his best to promote understanding of what will be involved in the changes. In December 1987 he told the Royal Institute of International Affairs, 'At the moment too few British companies are aware of the significance of 1992; one survey put business awareness as low as 5 per cent. In France, where it is claimed 80 per cent of companies know what 1992 means, the government has launched a television advertising campaign, presumably to get the other

20 per cent to wake up.' Britain's education programme only began to get underway in 1988.

As in other areas, British industry's response to 1992 will be, to some degree, a measure of how much industry has changed and of how willing it now is to accept far greater international involvement and commitment.

LANGUAGE CAPABILITY

Early in 1988 the newly appointed production director of a medium-sized engineering company was surprised to see a small language laboratory in his office. 'You'll be taking lessons in French, German and Italian,' he was told, 'and your language tutors call once a week.' The fact that he was so suprised is an indication of how far Britain has to go to achieve the true international perspective that characterises our most aggressive competitors. There was strong agreement among our survey respondents that knowledge of key foreign languages was lamentably low and that this was a major disadvantage in many overseas markets. The case for insisting that all senior managers and export salespeople have at least one other language seems to be strong. Yet there appears to be no significant pressure from either government or from companies themselves to insist that it happens. In practical terms, this is probably not an area where the government ought to become involved, other than by providing encouragement and/or incentives. The greatest impact can only come from industry itself, by tying promotion and reward in some measure to international experience and language ability. While a handful of UK-based multinationals do so, the vast majority of companies still have not tackled this important issue.

14

Decline Through Government Policy

'History will deal unkindly with both Labour and Conservative politicians for not creating better conditions for British business.'
Walter Goldsmith, The New Elite, *1987*

'We have been under weak political leadership for years. The Treasury has dominated the economy for too long.'
John Smith MP, Labour's Shadow Spokesman for Treasury and Economic Affairs, 1987

'Industry is too important to be regarded as a plaything of party dogma.'
Sir Francis Tombs, chairman of Rolls-Royce, 1987

'By the seventies, with pay, prices, dividends, capital and overseas investment all either heavily influenced or completely controlled by government, business leaders had lost confidence, authority and, to a large extent, executive autonomy.'
Institute of Directors, A New Agenda for Business, *1987*

GOVERNMENT AND INDUSTRY

With the end of the Second World War, Britain's industry, geared for the demands of war, was in the hands of government, which could dictate industrial development. The immediate result was the Distribution of Industry Act of 1945 which renamed the pre-war 'special' areas as development areas and gave the Board of Trade responsibility for the location of new production. The trend of governmental intervention was set. It was confirmed by the Town and Country Planning Act of 1947, which required planning permission to be granted for most new industrial buildings. The overall effect was an increased public sector and constrained industrial development along geographical as much as business criteria.

The governmental stranglehold over industry has hardly been released since wartime. In fact, governmental involvement in virtually all aspects of life has drastically increased. This can be seen in the proportion of GNP taken up by public expenditure. In 1914 it amounted to 14 per cent; by the mid 1970s it had risen dramatically to over 50 per cent. The public sector now accounts for nearly 40 per cent of the economy.

Given these figures it is not surprising that governmental enthusiasm to be involved in business has not, at times, been matched by adequate funding. Whilst our competitors were channelling money into industrial development after the war, Britain stood still. By 1961 the British government's spending on industry and employment still stood at less than one fifth of its spending on aid to agriculture.

STOP AND GO POLICIES

The effects of governmental intervention in industry are debatable. How much of industrial decline can be attributed to management or unions? The nature of politics means that successes are quickly claimed by politicians and failures deposited on the laps of others, however unsuspecting. Sir Christopher Hogg, chairman of Courtaulds, has observed that the intricacies of government and its democratic demands inevitably distance it from industrial reality.

> When ... one reflects on the size and complexity of modern governments, one should not be surprised at their inability to grasp instantly and coherently the business message, even assuming that it gets delivered without a background of noise that makes it inaudible. And when one further reflects that governments are accountable to electorates and not to shareholders, one should not be surprised that their focus is overwhelmingly a domestic one, not an international one; nor that their timescale is usually nearer to tomorrow's press than to the ten-year horizons which are now becoming necessary and fairly common in industry; nor that they find it very difficult to collaborate with other governments if it involves subordinating the interests of their own electorate to the good of all.

The question of whether governments should be able to interfere has increasingly been debated under Margaret Thatcher's Conservative Government, whose avowed aim is to be non-interventionist but which has, in the view of many of our commentators, continued the trend of greater government control in education, local government and other areas which have an indirect influence on business and commerce.

The Westland affair and, more recently, the furore over the Monopolies Commission's role in determining who should take over British Caledonian, have added fuel to the argument that, no matter how strongly a government *intends* not to intervene, it finds itself inevitably sucked in.

If some form of government involvement in industry is accepted as inevitable, what is perhaps of greater importance is the lack of consistency in government policies. Ministers change with regularity and opinions drift with the political wind, both industrialists and union officials comment. It remains remarkably easy for politicians to manipulate exchange rates, interest rates and taxes to suit the immediate economic and political environment rather than as part of a genuine industrial policy. The theory persists that governments should apply economic brakes when the economy shows signs of overheating and hit the accelerator when it slows down. The practice was demonstrated by the Wilson government, which preached the virtues of a high exchange rate but was then forced to devalue the pound in 1967 from $2.80 to $2.40.

Sir Francis Tombs, chairman of Rolls-Royce, says, 'Even in a single administration, quite major changes of emphasis take place with little warning when ministers are changed. The resulting uncertainty is damaging to industrial confidence and stems from the lack of coherent industrial strategy.' His criticism is backed by Sir Colin Corness, chairman of Redland, who points out that, 'There has been scant attention given to the maintenance of consistent policies.'

Government policy on the control of pay and prices illustrates the past vicissitudes. Controls were introduced in 1966 and came to a halt, temporarily, in 1970. Both were reintroduced in 1972, but pay control ended in 1974 and was then effectively reinstated in 1975.

Even under Margaret Thatcher's Conservative Government the Department of Trade and Industry, despite its importance, has been amongst the most unstable. Between 1979 and 1987 there were five Secretaries of State: Paul Channon, Cecil Parkinson, Leon Brittain, Norman Tebbit and Lord Young. They have each been surrounded with controversy. The Westland Affair claimed Brittain; Channon was caught up in the argument over selling British Leyland to America. All have faced the general run of disputes over job losses and cash shortages. Creating a genuine industrial policy under the circumstances would be a demanding task for anybody and, since 1945, say our survey respondents, the obstacles of political expediency and party dogma have generally proved insurmountable.

The need for a cohesive policy is supported by Sir Peter Carey of Dalgety (himself a former Permanent Secretary at the Department of Trade and Industry) who believes that all governments require an industrial policy in the same way that they have health or education policies. 'Any government needs to have at least a clear idea of what it wants out of industry in terms of national performance and should then test this out on industry's leaders,' Carey says.

Yet, even now, industrialists may not be consulted about important changes. Rises in electricity prices, for example, have wide-ranging effects on industry. The 15 per cent increase in electricity prices announced in November 1987 was symptomatic of the malaise. These increases went ahead despite the opinion of the CBI president, Sir David Nickson, that, 'Higher electricity prices must not be loaded on to business – full stop,' and warnings that the increases would cost industry £900 million over two years with bulk users, like chemicals, steel, artificial fibres and papers and board, being hit particularly hard.

The CBI expressed grave concern: 'The bulk users will be faced with the prospect of passing the increase on in higher prices – which could mean conceding business to their rivals – or holding prices and thus foregoing cash which is badly needed for their own investment.' In some chemical companies, electricity accounts for 25–33 per cent of production costs, yet government feels able to increase prices far ahead of our major competitors, including France, Italy and Belgium.

Governments abroad are, said the CBI, more supportive. In France, Atochem, a leading chlorine maker, has a ten-year contract for electricity at 1.3 pence per unit, for example, about half the most favourable price in Britain. John Banham, director general of the CBI, pointed out, 'French companies are able to buy electricity at a third less than in the UK. This gives them a cost advantage of at least 10 per cent. We want to see any rise in the electricity industry's earnings come from internal improvements. A lot of assets in that industry should be written down.'

Similar suggestions have been made about the gas industry. British gas prices exceed those of virtually every other gas utility in Europe.

The Monopolies and Mergers Commission began an investigation into British Gas' pricing policy in November 1987. The enquiry was prompted by British Gas' apparent unwillingness to quote a price for supplies on contract to industrial customers until they have gas- rather than oil-burning equipment. The businesses, therefore, find it difficult to judge the potential value of any investment. British Gas made it even more difficult for its industrial customers by offering contract prices only for a quarter or even shorter periods. Companies have a great deal of difficulty in estimating future costs when this is the case.

PARTY POLITICS

It could be argued that the gas and electricity organisations are simply applying commercial thinking, but they play a great role in dictating the costs (and competitiveness) of industry in general. Their importance can at times be not so much industrial, as political. The 1987 electricity price increases, for example, were suspected of being designed to fatten the industry for privatisation. Government denials did not appear to change the widespread suspicion among the industrialists we surveyed that this was true – political issues again trespassing on to commercial territory.

The two-party system is also called into question by some of our observers. David Owen's book *Face The Future* begins, 'Let us face the facts: The British nation has been ill served by its political parties over the last quarter of a century.' From the leader of a minority party such a view may not be altogether surprising. But the two-party system means in practice that it is assumed that if one party is elected it will promptly reverse the other's policies. Indeed, at the 1987 election the Labour Party was committed to renationalising the companies privatised during the previous Conservative administration. At the extremes, the confrontationalist two-party system can produce the high farce of the 1940s and 1950s when some of the country's major industries swung between public and private ownership. Steel, for example, was nationalised in 1949, denationalised in 1953 and was renationalised in 1967. The results can clearly be destabilising and demotivating.

One of the reasons behind this may well be that political points have, in many ways, been scored for the wrong ends. Discussion and policy formulation has centred on the ownership of industry rather than its organisation, operation and management. In a newly created welfare state it was perhaps inevitable that the central issues should be the distribution of industrially created wealth rather than how effectively or competitively it is created.

This is, in the eyes of many, exacerbated by the inflexibility of the British parliamentary system. 'Our parliamentary system and procedures are outdated and require radical overhaul,' says Dalgety's Peter Carey. Industry, according to many industrialists, is too important to be subject to the whims of government policy. 'Our confrontational and divergent approach between the two main parties is not shared by our competitors and lies at the root of many of our economic and social difficulties,' says Sir Francis Tombs.

The effects of partisan politics dominating, rather than industrial logic, have played a part in Britain's industrial relations too. Union-related legislation, for example, has generally been identifiably pro- or anti-union, or has at least been regarded as such. No government has successfully framed its industrial relations policy around bringing both sides together for the common purpose of building up a successful industrial base.

The wisdom of politicians formulating industrial policy can itself be questioned. Former Prime Minister Sir Alec Douglas-Home once commented: 'There are two problems in my life. The political ones are insoluble, and the economic ones are incomprehensible.' Few MPs have direct industrial experience. In Britain anyone moving from senior levels of industry to politics would be an exceptional case, though it is more common for former politicians to graduate to the higher levels of industry. In the past, the reverse has been true. The 1895 Parliament, for example, contained 31 of the estimated 200 millionaires in Britain. Some of the country's most successful businessmen were politically involved: Brunner and Mond represented Cheshire constituencies; Spencer Charrington was an MP for Mile End, Stepney; and Harland and Wolff represented Belfast North and East respectively.

Now, MPs are generally limited in their involvement with industry to directorships or consultancies. David Shaw, Conservative MP for Dover, has a total of thirteen directorships whilst his colleague Ian Taylor, MP for Esher, has six. Companies such as Glaxo, the Channel Tunnel Group, Yorkshire Television, Hanson and Ready Mixed Concrete all employ MPs as consultants.

Sir Francis Tombs is pessimistic about the level of industrial expertise amongst the high echelons of politics. Says Tombs, 'I see little hope of securing amongst the Cabinet Ministers or senior civil servants sufficient experience of industry's problems to make their intervention constructive.'

There is also an argument that the British two-party system encourages governments which are simply too strong – any party with a comfortable majority can usually see its policies transformed into the law of the land. Roy Grantham, general secretary of APEX, points out the advantages of weaker government. 'One advantage the French and Italians had was that for thirty years they were run by civil servants who knew what they were doing. Minority governments were a boon, because they left the civil servants in charge. People from the Grandes Ecoles were able to move freely between industry and the civil service. Germany was able to do well without this because it had an industrial culture already.'

The nature of the British government's influence on industry is also questioned by our survey respondents. The tiers of government, and the red tape created by them, have caused problems. 'In industry we live in a society dominated at the top by Treasury administrators and at lower levels by government administrators. Their all-pervading dead hand of influence leaves little scope for management activity or, to put it into today's words, enterprise,' said Bill Miller of Prestwick Holdings at the 1986 CBI conference.

One serious net effect of all this is that decentralisation of political power would be virtually impossible even if the political will were there. Explains Labour's John Smith, 'Germany has devolved its government. The regional governments are very strong and very helpful to industry. Financial and other institutions are also dispersed. You don't have to go to Bonn to raise capital – you raise it where you are. The British government is very centralising.'

INDUSTRIAL POLICY

As in so many other areas, Japan leads the way in government industrial policy. Its Ministry of International Trade and Industry (MITI) is a working example of a government body wielding great influence over industrial development and priorities. It does so not through statutory power, but primarily by involving industry in the policy formulation process. MITI continually collects commercial information which it uses to develop policy whilst sharing it with industrialists. It acts, in a variety of ways, as an advice and information centre for industry. MITI offers guidance on tax and finance as well as administrative, marketing and technological matters.

MITI also formulates long-range visions of industry through a large number of advisory committees which include academics, trade unionists and industrialists and journalists. Yet MITI only spends 650.6 billion yen a year – less than 2 per cent of Japan's national budget. It attracts the best talent to its staff of 12,600. Because it is a genuine authority, it is listened to by industry in a way that our own NEDC is not.

In Britain, governmental attempts to formulate industrial policy have, virtually without exception, floundered. Most have been short-lived.

Harold Wilson's Labour Government of the 1960s created the National Plan and set up the doomed Department of Economic Affairs and the Industrial Reorganisation Corporation (IRC). The latter came to the conclusion that units of production were in many cases too small to compete effectively. Consequently it encouraged the eventually disastrous trend of mergers. Chaired by Sir Frank Kearton, its brief was 'to promote industrial efficiency and profitability'. With £150 million to be used as a revolving credit, the IRC brought about the GEC and BL mergers and gave support to Rolls-Royce and Cammell Laird when they hit trouble. It was abolished in 1971 after the Heath government declared it 'out of control', but the idea was speedily reborn in the shape of the Industrial Development Executive created in 1972. This was soon to be supplanted by the National Enterprise Board in 1975.

The Department of Economic Affairs under George Brown suffered from a typical case of political needs overriding long-term industrial requirements. Its optimistic initial expansionism was soon to be followed by deflationary measures and closure. It was the Ministry of Economic Affairs which was responsible for one of government's most energetic attempts at economic intervention, the Prices and Incomes Plan. Its planning was, at times, foolishly optimistic. In the mid-1960s a target of expanding national income by 25 per cent by 1970 was set. This required an extra 200,000 more workers than were available.

The longest-running agency to attempt to formulate an industrial policy for the government has been the NEDC. Formed by the Conservative Government in 1961, it is a tripartite body with representatives of capital, labour and government. In 1962, at its first meeting, its tasks were defined as: 'To examine the economic performance of the nation with particular concern for plans for the future in both the private and public sectors of industry; to consider together what are the obstacles to quicker growth, what can be done to improve efficiency, and whether the best use is being made of resources; to seek agreement upon ways of improving economic performance, competitive power and efficiency, in other words, to increase the rate of sound growth.' It suggested that an economic growth rate of 4 per cent per year should be the aim. Labour and Conservative politicians concurred.

Formulating policy, however, has been easier than applying it. Whilst the Japanese have managed to implement a consistent, not to say singleminded, policy the NEDC itself has observed that, 'The instruments of [Japanese] policy have in general been no different in kind from those employed in many western economies. The unique features are the way

223

in which policy is formulated and implemented, and its strong element of selectivity.'

Political critics of the British system include Shirley Williams, who outlined her objections in *Politics Is For People*. 'Government policies of both parties have tended to reinforce the momentum towards concentration, creating a dialogue of a limited and sterile kind between the proponents of private concentration and those of public concentration.'

But the nature of the political system means that governments cannot be told what to do. The taking of advice is at times arbitrary. The work of months can be dismissed in minutes if it does not measure up to the political objectives of the moment. A week may be a long time in politics, but industry more often requires years and decades of development.

As recently as 1985 the Government's industrial policies were severely criticised by the House of Lords Select Committee on Overseas Trade. It accused the Government of failing manufacturing industry by not protecting it from the consequences of the high exchange rate of sterling between 1979 and 1981. The Government responded by suggesting that the report was facile and interventionist.

At the same time, in the opinion of some industrialists, mutual misunderstanding between government and industry is caused, in some ways, by the industrialists themselves. Sir Christopher Hogg has observed:

Businessmen are notoriously unsympathetic to government. From their cushioned positions of power in their semi-dictatorships (usually pocket-sized) they love to blame governments for everything. In doing so, they tend to switch off entirely whatever shrewdness, realism and perspective they bring to the government of their own affairs, even though they understand better than most the difficulties of effecting change on any scale.

ASSISTING THE SICK

Whilst the question of government intervention has been raised continually since 1945, the issue has usually been which industry the government should be helping; not whether the government should be helping at all. As early as 1947, Sir Frederick Leggett told the British

Institute of Management, 'The impression made by my experience was that the tendency of management is to regard the government as something that should be used only to protect their interests and to save them from taking what may be great trouble to reach an understanding with their employees.' Leggett went on to encourage management to include employees in production planning and to use line supervisors as consultants. In effect, he was advocating the modern idea of quality circles.

The tendency to call on the government for help persists. Rolls-Royce, Chrysler and British Leyland are notorious examples. It is significant that the financial sector has maintained a distance from any long-term industrial policy.

The areas and merits of government protection have, however, been increasingly questioned. In *British Economic Policy*, edited by F T Blackaby, the ideal and proper role of government is described as 'limited to a peripheral role of tidying up at the edges, rather than providing any central thrust to alter and improve industry's performance and that of the economy as a whole'. The Conservative Party aims to follow Abraham Lincoln's much quoted advice: 'Do not ask the Government to do for people what they could and should do for themselves.' Yet Charles Baden-Fuller, an expert on competitiveness at London Business School, points out that all post-war British governments have consistently supported ailing industries, such as shipbuilding, at the expense of expanding ones: 'People have underestimated the importance of firms and overestimated the importance of the macro economy.'

The propping up of ailing industry did much to undermine Edward Heath's government. The threat of a shipbuilding collapse on Clydeside prompted the chief constable to ring Downing Street to say that he would find it impossible to guarantee order if the yards closed. The Heath government was forced to compromise even though it was theoretically opposed to government support for dying industries. John Davies, Heath's first Secretary of State for Trade and Industry, had told the 1970 Party conference, 'We shall not prop up lame ducks.' Unfortunately, governments since the war have been forced to compromise on this issue. The spending on such support has been immense. In 1975, the National Enterprise Board spent £500 million (of its £600 million budget) on supporting British Leyland, Rolls-Royce, Ferranti and Alfred Herbert. This hardly fulfilled the objective of supporting enterprise.

225

PROVIDING THE MOTOR

Perhaps the most infamous example of government intervention is the car industry. It is a story with a good deal of glamour, drama and political intrigue, from the excesses of DeLorean to the propping up of British Leyland and the attempts by Tony Benn to save Chrysler.

The car industry unhappily demonstrates the cyclical nature of government's industrial policy since 1945. Immediately after the war, the fledgling car industry was encouraged actively to develop in the northern manufacturing areas. Car plants emerged at places like Speke and Halewood in Liverpool and Linwood in Scotland. The result was a geographically decentralised industry. Almost predictably, the next swing was towards integration and amalgamation. This was equally unsuccessful. The Austin Rover merger in 1952 was the first step towards the creation of the British Motor Corporation and, eventually, the merger in 1967 of BMC with British Leyland. This brought around fifty sections of the car industry under one company. Commercially it made little sense and Leyland cars such as the Marina and Allegro competed against each other in the 1970s. The next step was towards rationalisation under Michael Edwardes as chief executive (1977–82). The number of models was cut, ten assembly plants were closed, production was concentrated and 70,000 car workers lost their jobs. Still, British Leyland lost £28 million in 1978, a figure which increased until a £293 million loss was recorded in 1982.

Government's responsibility for this can easily be exaggerated. It was not managing the industries itself, but saving them from extinction. But the 'stop-go' policy on tax and hire purchase in the 1950s and 1960s created fluctuations in demand which produced inevitable planning difficulties. This continues, with calls for the government to stop the special car tax and other measures which depress the market and mean that British consumers pay up to £2,550 more per family car than their counterparts in West Germany, the European Community's cheapest 'open market'.

The vacillating nature of government policy can be seen in the fact that on eighteen occasions between April 1960 and December 1973 there were changes in the hire purchase terms and/or purchase tax or VAT or car tax. In 1967 alone there were three changes in hire purchase terms. This instability still continues to some extent. In July 1982 the government suddenly abolished hire purchase controls, laying the basis for the revival of consumer spending.

The DeLorean example demonstrates the potentially disastrous cocktail of short-term political objectives, government money and commercial opportunism built on optimism rather than rationality. The DeLorean car company carried the advertising slogan 'live the dream'. The aim of selling 20,000 to 30,000 cars a year in America was itself little more than a dream. The attraction to the Government of creating jobs in economically stagnant Northern Ireland was irresistible, no matter what the potential risks. The Government's enthusiasm was such that negotiations only lasted forty-six days. In August 1978 Roy Mason, Secretary of State for Northern Ireland, was able to announce a 'tremendous breakthrough'. A new plant in Dunmurry, West Belfast, created essential jobs. Government subsidies eventually totalled $119 million. By 1982 the plant was on a three-day week and, on its closure, unresolved debts of $64 million remained. The plant was auctioned in 1983, leaving MP Nicholas Winterton to comment, 'There are a lot of questions to be asked about the naivety of the ministers involved.'

Within the car industry in general the blame cannot be singularly attached to government; a great deal of blame must rest with management. Government was, after all, often reacting to what the industry said it wanted in terms of assistance. Harvard academic Dr Michael Porter pinpoints the DeLorean affair as a strategic failure. There are, he believes, only two viable long-term strategies for success in consumer manufacturing. One is to do one thing extremely well – for example, produce luxury cars as Jaguar has so successfully done in recent years; the other is to make products on a large scale at low, highly competitive prices. British Leyland, in particular, tried to do both at once. As a result, it either had no strategy at all, or two competing strategies. Either path led inevitably to disaster.

TEXTILES

Adventures such as DeLorean's inevitably devalue sound commercial advice when it does emanate from government. In some industries, the government has taken a lead only to be rebuffed by industrialists. In the textile industry, the government was recommending rationalisation and modernisation as early as the 1950s. The 1959 Cotton Industries Act involved a scheme for eliminating redundant capacity by offering grants for re-equipping. There was little response – the industry continued to believe that an upturn would come. For the next twenty years Britain suffered from a problem of overcapacity, which is only now being redressed. Even today, most of the British textile industry's equipment is obsolete. Three quarters of all spinning and weaving machinery is more than ten years old compared with 50 per cent and 44 per cent respectively for the Italian textile industry.

Yet government policy has also provided the textile industry with some degree of protection in the form of the Multi-Fibre Agreement which has now been in place for twenty-five years. The agreement fixes quotas for the imports of clothing from the developing countries and is able to check their growth. Having achieved some measure of control in this market, governments have made little impression or effort elsewhere in industry. The suspicion is strong that the agreement's primary effect has been to slow down the rate of re-equipment and rationalisation – and therefore *reduce* competitiveness. Courtaulds' Christopher Hogg has firm opinions about government involvement in the textile industry. In a 1985 speech he claimed, 'International trade in textiles has for decades been distorted by government intervention in various forms.'

AEROSPACE

In the aircraft industry, historically relatively free of severe industrial relations complications, government has had full-scale commitment since the war. In the years immediately after the war, governments encouraged and backed a great deal of uncommercial activity, which meant that the industry became too thinly spread with too many projects and too many firms. The emphasis was on manufacturing and designing rather than marketing. Poor costing of development made matters worse. The TSR2 project in the 1960s was originally estimated to cost £90 million but expenditure rose to £750 million before Harold Wilson brought a halt to it. As a result, 5,000 people were made redundant and Sir George Edwards, Chairman of British Aircraft Corporation, commented, 'Hours of work and dedication over the years were carelessly being thrown away by some chap making a speech in the Commons.'

THE IDEA OF EUROPE

The role of the European Community as a whole also needs to be examined. The Community, despite its much vaunted aims, has conspicuously failed to provide uniformity. A fully free internal market is envisaged by 1992, but generally the Community has failed to utilise its potential market power. It has continued to be preoccupied with consumption rather than investment. As a result industry has been made to bear the brunt as public finances have got out of control. The level of industrial co-operation, promised in the Treaty of Rome, has not materialised. Instead, European markets for the most part remain fragmented. The continuation of inward investment in the Community has meant that European companies have often negated each other's efforts. Parochial and nationalistic attitudes persist.

Again, Britain's indecision about joining the European Community has undermined her position and may well have affected Community morale. Even during the 1979 and 1983 elections, the Labour Party was committed to taking Britain out of the Community. The nationalistic nature of British politics has clearly been a strong influence. 'Nowhere as much as in Britain has prevailing economic thinking been so unquestionably nationalistic. Both for purposes of economic analysis and economic policy it has been the national economy which has been the central unit of consideration,' the Conservative MP David Howell told *The Times* during the 1987 election campaign.

All of this suggests (and here we are, indeed, drawing our own conclusions) not simply that government industrial policy has always been poor or misdirected but that there has never actually been a unified policy at all. Instead, we have had a multitude of different policies. It is like a company in which each director creates policies and strategies for his own function without reference to any overall guiding strategy. In a company it would (and does) cause chaos; in a national economy it can do no less.

15

Rise Through Government Policy

'Government involvement in industry is now inescapable. Whether as owner, tax-collector, legislator, supplier or purchaser, the State is a huge direct influence on industry and on the climate in which it works.'
Geoffrey Chandler, former director general of NEDC, 1983

'We have to develop a strong entrepreneurial base. The Government can't restore the econony by taking macro economic decisions.'
Lord Young, Secretary of State for Trade and Industry, 1987

'The Government has done much to encourage and free business over the past few years.'
Sir David Nickson, president of the CBI, 1987

INTERFERENCE OR SUPPORT?

Criticism of government industrial policy has to be set against the constant claim by industrialists that they are the people who have the power to change things. The CBI, the Institute of Directors and the British Institute of Management all regard the businessman as the prime mover in the development of a more prosperous nation.

'The greatest contribution which a future government can make to British industry is freedom from unnecessary intervention and distractions,' said Sir James Blyth, chairman of Plessey. Denys Henderson, chairman of ICI, has also spoken on this theme. 'Government cannot legislate to make us internationally competitive. That task is for us.'

Indeed, governments in the past may well have been pressed into industrial involvement due to the banks' lack of enthusiasm for industrial restructuring. The 1970 Wilson Committee recorded that banks in the 1950s and 1960s were not generally prepared to lend money for more than two years for buying capital equipment. Businesses were forced to rely on their own savings, the stock market and, when necessary, the coffers of government.

Mrs Thatcher's Conservative Government has made much of its lack of interference with industry and its belief that, left alone, the best businesses will prosper. It is basically a belief in the survival of the fittest. Says Lord Young, 'If you over-regulate society, it slows down. My fear is that Europe could go down as Spain did after the Armada. We have no *right* to be among the wealthiest nations in the world.'

John Gardiner, chief executive of the Laird group, has reflected on Mrs Thatcher's effect on business in the *Financial Times*: 'Her big contribution has been to burn up the controls and release us all. The thing she has changed is the view that the State has to solve all our problems.' He also

232

refers to the period of 1950 to 1980 as 'thirty years of state corporatism'.

The stability of government since 1979 has also led to more consistent policies. Sir Charles Villiers has applauded the Conservative Government's consistency: 'The current recovery in the UK economy is enormously welcome, and it is largely due to consistent government policies (although much more could have been done).'

INTERVENTION OR NON-INTERVENTION?

Despite the withdrawal of government from many areas of industry, it has become clear that governmental interference is, in many respects, unavoidable.

To J N Clarke, chairman of Johnson Matthey, government has a definite role in creating the right climate: 'Government can establish the framework in which longer-term programmes can be developed, for example in education and training, and perhaps most in encouraging social change, which permits a consensus rather than a divisive approach. Government can also, by fiscal and monetary policy, influence changes in the financing of longer-term investments for industry, and in the funding and direction of fundamental and applied research and development.'

The perceptions of the public clearly make the link between government involvement and job creation. According to the *British Social Attitudes* 1987, edited by Gower, 59 per cent of people in the survey believed that government's failure to create jobs was an important factor in Britain's economic decline.

If government involvement is inevitable, the questions of how much and where have to be answered. Some, like Alistair Graham of The Industrial Society, see government as stepping in when industry is seen to be failing in some way. Graham comments on training in industry: 'The various reports on training in Britain raise the question of whether voluntarism will succeed. I'm against industrial training boards. But I do think that something like the French system might become a necessity if industry isn't seen to be doing enough training.'

Labour's John Smith takes a similar view, believing that government must select likely areas for growth and invest in training people in these fields. Smith says, 'Companies left to their own devices don't do R & D or training. There's a danger of losing our technological base. We have to get ahead in certain fields, picking areas for the future.' The boundaries between helpful support and intervention are not easily defined.

The most sensible and balanced view may again come from Japan. Shinji Fukukawa of MITI has said, 'To foster the dynamic growth of today's industrial society we must combine Adam Smith's "invisible hand" of market forces with the "visible hand" of policy foresight, sharp analysis and reasonable thinking.' John Smith agrees on the fundamental role which government should play. 'I'd like to see the Department of Trade and Industry as the powerhouse of government, taking a leading role. We need to plan investment, much as MITI does,' he says.

At the 1987 CBI conference, Sir Trevor Holdsworth, CBI deputy president and chairman of GKN, called upon government to appreciate more fully the ramifications of industrial decisions. 'Government should demonstrate that its policies take full account of the effect that decisions have on the national wealth-creating capability – not just for small firms, but for all,' he said.

Nevertheless, complaints continue. Sir John Banham of the CBI commented in *The Sunday Times* in January 1988:

> Corporation tax, rates and employers' national insurance contributions have increased by £10 billion in real terms since 1983. Lower taxes, competitive interest and exchange rates, and rolling back the threat of increased electricity prices, business rates and other costs must be a top priority for government if British business is to be internationally competitive.

The Department of Trade and Industry has set about creating the framework for an industrial policy, though stopping short of putting pen to paper and producing a five-year plan. Lord Young has sought to emphasise that the department's job is wealth creation. 'It is government policy to see that wealth creation is respected and grows,' he says. To this end he has called for less emphasis on supporting big business and increased support for people and enterprise. Lord Young's main aims are to create more competitive markets free of restrictive practices like cartels or monopolies. Even so, the DTI's 1987 budget involved direct cash subsidies to aerospace, shipbuilding and steel totalling £182 million.

Government policy may well now be framed on an increasingly commercial and pragmatic rationale. Whilst cutting subsidies to development agencies, the government has maintained its commitment to the

Scottish Development Agency which has been seen to be making strides in a recession-hit area. The SDA has become 'the acceptable face of intervention', providing industrial renewal and job creation. Iain Robertson, the SDA's Chief Executive, claims that the agency will still have work to do in 2000.

It is not only that the Conservative Government has developed a more pragmatic attitude to regional aid and no longer waves a cheque book without considering long-term aims. Companies themselves have developed more realistic attitudes. ICI, for example, has refused government assistance. Others, such as Jaguar, have thrived when released from the shackles of government financing and involvement.

Efforts are underway to develop the level of understanding between industry and government. The Industry and Parliamentary Trust was established in 1977 with this express purpose. Under the Trust, MPs have to agree to devote twenty-five days a year to going into a company to learn what makes it tick. On the other side, the CBI-run Linkman scheme involves CBI members keeping their local MP briefed on matters of concern to their industry.

To most of the industrialists we interviewed, the future role of government, if it is to be effective, must be based on a stable administration committed to long-term policy goals rather than short-term political ends. Most doubt that government can do a great deal to help resolve their short-term problems. A 1986 Sussex University survey on future employment issues, for example, showed that government policy would have only a minor influence on future employment planning in both the private sector and in local government. Nearly half of the companies in the survey said that they were pursuing their manpower goals 'quite independently' of government.

But governments can create the industrial climate. Says Sir Colin Corness, chairman of Redland, 'It is manifestly the job of government to set the right climate for a reversal of the downward trends of British industry.' If government policy is properly framed, the efficient companies will thrive and the weak be driven to follow their example. 'What must be done is to ease the path for the businesses and industries which are in the ascendancy so that they can flourish and for those in decline to be redeployed with all speed and efficiency,' Sir Gordon White, chairman of Hanson Trust, said in *The Times* in 1986. Malcolm Bruce of the Liberal Party believes that the importance of government in framing industrial policy is clear: 'Government has a pivotal role – working closely with industry to ensure that their objectives harmonise.'

235

CONCLUSION

The argument about government intervention or non-intervention may well be, to a large extent, irrelevant. The questions facing government are straightforward:

- What can it do directly to help industry?
- What can it do to indirectly help industry?

To answer these questions requires a fundamental attribute – vision. In company terms, it is essential to have a vision, or mission, to point everyone in the right direction. The same applies to industry as a whole. Mrs Thatcher undoubtedly has a vision, but it is shared by less than 40 per cent of the population. There is a desperate need to focus upon a vision that will motivate and direct the efforts of all those involved in British industry.

16

The Decline of Rewards, Status and Incentives

'British managers were paid nothing. In the 1970s you had people behaving like capitalists but living like paupers. You couldn't pay them more because tax rates were so high they didn't keep it.'
Sir John Egan, chairman and chief executive of Jaguar Cars, 1987

'In too many cases, reward has been based on a salary determined as much by seniority and by comparability with what is being paid elsewhere as any other factors – often with the help of complicated formulae devised by consultants.'
Sir Alex Jarratt, chairman of Smiths Industries, 1987

'Industry appears restrictive, in the sense that career options narrow rather than widen; it does not pay particularly well; and it does not hold the prospect of much fun. Other than that it has a great deal going for it.'
John Banham, director general of the CBI, 1987

'All errors in finance and taxation which obstruct the improvement of the people in wealth and morals tend also, if of sufficiently serious amount, positively to impoverish and demoralise them.'
J S Mill in Representative Government, *1865*

PAYING MORE; PRODUCING LESS

The battle cry of the 1980s has been that we are paying ourselves too much for doing too little. 'You can't avoid the consequences of your own action,' Mrs Thatcher has said. 'If you pay yourselves more for producing less, there *will* be more unemployment.' Paradoxically, this equation of performance and pay has been complicated by the argument that senior managers are not adequately rewarded for the responsibility they carry. Equally confusingly, while the CBI has generally endorsed Mrs Thatcher's view, the Institute of Directors has championed the view that low pay equals low performance.

Pay increases, accelerated by high inflation, outstripped increases in productivity and performance during the 1970s in particular. Yet during this period the salaries of British executives fell behind those of their international competitors, while many observers claim they were subject to 'punitive' taxation. The picture that emerges from our survey is that poor rewards eradicated the major incentive to succeed in a capitalist society. Business people became attuned to disappointment and failure rather than success. Says Sir John Hoskyns, 'Businessmen were deeply programmed to expect failure. The penalties for failure were severe, the rewards for success were low.'

Without suitable incentives, the desire to take on responsibilities was lessened. One of our survey respondents observed, 'Given that most rewards arrangements were to do with maintenance of equity and status quo, rather than enterprise and reward for change, then they contributed to industrial decline. But I do not feel that rewards and incentives were causal – rather they were symptomatic.' The problem stretched right down the line. Lack of motivation is infectious. Says Labour's John Smith:

It's a British weakness to want to put our children into respectable middle-class professions. It's astonishing the low levels of salary of the average works manager. He is in the front line, dealing with problems of industrial relations; he has a complex and aggravating working life. No government forced companies to treat them in that way. It arises because of a tendency to compare their salaries with shop floor wages rather than other management jobs.

Middle management was caught in a hierarchical battle between shop floor unions that went over their heads and top management who were themselves demotivated and rudderless.

The entire question of paying managers more for their increased responsibility was, in the main, avoided. Unions regarded it as greed while managers could see little point in making a fuss, because any increase would be heavily taxed. The case for higher executive salaries has been put by Sir Ralph Halpern, Burton's chairman: 'What's the point of taking all these risks as businessmen? What's the point of making all these decisions and getting them right? If we're not going to be rewarded we'll go back to the situation where no one bothers: where they all go and play golf.'

According to many industrialists, the chief reason for lack of interest in creating wealth was the income tax system. In the late 1970s, income tax was set at an unprecedentedly high rate. By the 1975–6 tax year income tax receipts accounted for 53.5 per cent of central government's taxation; in 1969–70 the figure had been 33.2 per cent. In the 1970s the highest rate of income tax of 83 per cent was exceeded only by Algeria, Egypt, Tanzania and Portugal. The top tax rate on investment, a startling 98 per cent, was only matched by two other countries. The results were an exodus of professional high earners and the cold shouldering of business people into a kind of sub-professional class. The tax disincentives stretched down the pay scale. Britain's lowest tax rate in the 1970s was higher than anywhere else in the world.

The perceptions of the importance of business and the value of the people running it were drastically altered. Amazingly, Lord McGowan, the chairman of ICI in 1937, earned almost the same amount of money, £65,410, as his successor did in 1972.

The importance of business was neglected in no small part because British education is traditionally geared to targeting talent elsewhere. Says Nuala Swords-Isherwood in *Technical Innovation*, 'The problem in Britain lies mainly in the anachronistic conflict between educational and industrial aims, and in a culture that is anti-industrial. Our system probably provides more channels than many other countries for able candidates from the shop floor to reach management levels. It does not, however, ensure a supply of the most able people from the best or most prestigious educational institutions for management roles.'

Tesco's Ian MacLaurin is particularly critical of the anti-business environment, which persisted in Britain:

> A fixation with the economic aspects of the 'British Disease' has tended to disguise the cultural environment in which the economy operates – an environment in which the educational prejudice against the business community insidiously colours the attitudes of those entering the civil service, the professions and, more especially, the academic world so that the prejudice is again recycled . . . This curriculum of elitism has had malign consequences as much for the establishment's appreciation of economic reality, as for the businessman's sense of alienation from the centres of economic power.

This alienation may well have been accentuated by the taxation system. As John Hoskyns points out, 'If you have an environment, as was the case in Britain after the war, where inherited wealth was not taxed but earned wealth was, inevitably that produces a limping economy.'

In summary, one way or another, the rewards for Britain's industrial managers became smaller and smaller in comparative terms over the thirty-five years after the Second World War. Along with the decline in rewards, say our industrialists, came a decline in self-esteem, in entrepreneurial spirit and in status: scarcely the stuff of which industrial renaissance is made.

17

The Rise of Rewards, Status and Incentives

'It is government policy to see that wealth creation is respected and grows.'
Lord Young, 1987

'A lot of people who were going to sell up in 1979 decided to keep going when the tax ceiling came down.'
Sir John Hoskyns, 1987

'The basic need is for all parts of our society to recognise that wealth creation is an essential part of the country's life. Wealth creation should be applauded rather than denigrated or thought second class.'
Peter Holmes, chairman of Shell, 1987

THE MORALITY OF WEALTH

In the 1980s a harder, almost ascetic, perception of industry's true role in society has arisen. 'Our role is wealth, not job creation,' said one executive. Sir John Harvey-Jones, former ICI Chairman, has also argued that 'the major role for manufacturing industry is to create wealth'. Another executive said of his workforce, 'They enjoy doing a good job, they enjoy working for a successful company. They enjoy the rewards they get.'

The emphasis in Britain seems to have changed, say our industrialists. Said one executive, 'Leading companies and their chief executives have a much higher profile. Problem areas (in the public and private sector) have been pushed off the front page. There is more focus on success.' Success by itself is justifiable. Uneconomic monsters, such as British Steel or British Shipbuilding, have been crudely but effectively rationalised.

Mrs Thatcher's view was probably most clearly expressed in 1980 when £675,000 was paid to Lazard Freres to obtain Ian MacGregor's services at British Steel: 'What sort of country is it which says we can pay enormous sums to footballers, but not to get the best person here to Britain to get a steel industry, which is in trouble, thriving and flourishing again?' The carrot is success and profitability. 'We need to create a mood where it is everywhere thought morally right for as many people as possible to acquire capital,' Mrs Thatcher told *The Economist* in October 1985.

TOP PAY

With the intention of creating a meritocracy, the salaries of chief executives have effectively doubled since 1980. The gulf between directors' pay and shop floor wages is widening.

Rise in chief executives' earnings

Company	1979–80	1985–6	Percentage increase
Grand Metropolitan	50,380	176,289	349.92
Marks & Spencers	64,077	217,016	338.68
Tesco	42,407	118,461	279.34
Imperial	68,000	171,368	252.01
ICI	124,380	312,991	251.64
BAT	94,726	226,830	239.45
GEC	75,000	177,000	236.00
RTZ	66,000	145,993	221.20
BP	120,385	260,972	216.78
Courtaulds	65,620	126,288	192.45
GKN	82,342	145,000	176.09
British Leyland	54,200	98,367	171.97

Source: *The Times* 25.3.87.

A survey of executive salaries in October 1987 by management consultants Inbucon, showed that executive salaries are continuing to grow at a far faster rate than inflation. In the 1986–7 period, managing directors saw their pay and bonus systems rise by an average of 10.7 per cent; inflation rose by 2 per cent to 4.4 per cent in the same period.

The Central Statistical Office provides more evidence of these changes.

Its economic trends statistics show that the top 10 per cent of money-earners increased their share of personal income from 26.1 per cent in 1978–9, the last tax year under Labour, to 29.5 per cent in 1984–5. This concentration of income has been intensified by incentive schemes introduced after decreases in the highest levels of tax. Almost the first act of the new Conservative Government in 1979 was to reduce the highest tax rate from 83 per cent to 60 per cent with the aim of reducing the minimum level to 25 per cent. The trend towards increased rewards at the top has also encompassed a rise in the availability and variety of perks to middle and top management.

The Inbucon survey highlighted the increased number of perks and bonuses now available. Company cars are routinely accepted – 98 per cent of directors have them. Share option and bonus schemes now form an integral part of executive salaries with 77 per cent of the 7,080 company executives in the survey receiving one or both. The number of executives offered share options has more than doubled since 1982. The stockbroker, Hoare Govett, estimates that the market value of options held by directors of quoted public companies is £4.5 billion. The Inbucon survey estimated that fringe benefits (pensions, company cars, share options etc.) vary in value between 80 per cent and 110 per cent of basic executive salaries. However, there is a suspicion that such high levels of benefits may encourage an interest in short-term profits rather than long-term investment.

Profit-sharing agreements provide lucrative additions to the salaries of a growing number of executives. Britain's second-highest-paid director in 1986, Michael Slade of Helical Bar, the property development company, earned £1,106,000. This was due in a large part to the terms of his profit-sharing agreement, established when Helical Bar was not making any money. In 1986 the company made £6.7 million in pre-tax profits and Slade reaped the benefit. Lord Hanson, chairman of Hanson, has also benefited from a performance-related bonus. Between 1986 and 1987 his pay rose from £327,000 to £1,263,000 to make him one of the highest-paid executives in Britain. Of this amount, £295,000 came by way of performance-related bonuses. His was not an exceptional case in Hanson. Between 1986 and 1987 its pay to board members doubled from £3 million to £6 million.

The rise of executive benefits has also been charted by Hay Management Consultants. Its 1987 survey into boardroom earnings showed that a director on a salary of £100,000 collects an average of 45 per cent extra in benefits.

Executive incentives

Typical director salary	Value of benefits as a percentage of base salary			
	Pension	Car	Share options	Other benefits
£33,000	27	16	4	4
£75,000	28	12	7	3
£110,000	32	9	9	3
£160,000	28	6	9	1

Source: *The Boardroom Remuneration Guide*, 1987.

More cynical observers may question the motivational value of such benefits and ask whether a period of relative prosperity – for those in work – has just happened to coincide with a stream of new incentive schemes. Says Stephen Turley, personnel manager at Burmah Oil: 'The increased incidence of so-called incentive schemes has coincided with a major improvement in UK business performance. There is a likely connection but it is a brave (or foolish) individual who claims incentives have improved performance, as opposed to performance producing appropriate rewards.' The Mecca Leisure Group's personnel manager, P J Hunt, is equally scathing: 'Too many executive schemes have not reflected effort but have produced millionaires on the back of windfalls or booming stock markets. This is the experience both in the US and UK.'

With the decrease of inflation, salary increases have levelled off during the 1980s. However, perks, particularly for managers, have expanded. Though many companies have incentive schemes of various sorts, only around 500 have profit-sharing schemes involving everyone in the company. In contrast, over half of Britain's directors now have some performance-related pay element in their salary. At Burtons, for example, an incentive scheme was introduced in 1980. The company chairman, Sir Ralph Halpern, whose salary was then in excess of £1 million, told shareholders – a minority of whom were openly hostile: 'The aim of the whole incentive scheme is to clarify individual accountability and to relate individual performance to the achievement of overall profit figures.'

A continental trend which may also find a place in Britain is that of

245

'interim management' where top managers hire themselves out on lucrative contracts for three or four years. Headhunters already see it as a likely and highly profitable development for senior managers.

Despite these handsome increases and the much-voiced argument that we have to pay the best managers the best wages, the British executive is still paid less than his counterparts in most countries of the developed world. Figures for 1987 in *Employment Conditions Abroad* show that, in gross pay terms, amongst the developed countries only the Australians, Greeks and South Africans are worse off than British executives. The greatest purchasing power of executives lies in Switzerland and the USA with West Germany and France close behind. The gulf can be seen in comparisons with US companies. In 1987 Michel David-Weill of Lazard Freres took home £75 million; Lee Iacocca of Chrysler £11 million in 1986 and Paul Fireman of running-shoe company, Reebok, over £7 million. The best-paid British chief executives scarcely reach the bottom of this extravagant pay scale.

When it comes to taxation the position is reversed. France now has the highest taxes of the Group of Five leading industrial countries. Taxes account for 45 per cent of its gross domestic product, compared to less than 40 per cent in Britain and West Germany and less than 30 per cent in the USA and Japan. Sir David Nickson, the CBI president, has expressed continuing concern about the complexities of the taxation system and its effect on industry: 'For small and medium-sized firms as well as for individuals, the burden of our complex system is both costly and distorting.'

The Institute of Directors is also calling for a simplification of the taxation system. It suggests that workers at the lowest end of the scale should not have to pay tax and that the higher rate of tax should also be abolished. Its manifesto, *A New Agenda for Government*, argues: 'The tax system would be more efficient – simpler to administer, cheaper to collect and less prone to avoidance – if tax were levied proportionately across all income bands above the tax-exempt thresholds.' It believes that revenue would be generated as people no longer would take action to avoid paying higher rates of tax. Changing taxation levels does not alter the way people think overnight, as Sir John Hoskyns points out: 'Even if you reduce tax tomorrow it doesn't make people more economically active. Change in economic status always happens at the margin – you tip people over the edge into doing it on their own.'

However, the link between performance and pay is being developed and clarified at all levels in British industry. The worrying part of the trend is that differentials are increasing between top and middle management and incentives are still seen as something for management rather than employees. Very few companies have attempted to overcome this. The confectionery company, Mars, provides a good example of one that has. It has a single status environment in which everybody has to clock on. As a result everyone is eligible for a good timekeeping bonus. Similarly, everyone at the company is on a personal pay progression scheme – a merit pay scheme based on measurements of performance against potential assessed and agreed annually.

Perhaps the most interesting development in this area has been the innovative scheme announced by Rank Xerox, which is tying senior managers' pay to what customers have to say about the products and services they have received. The company believes the scheme will focus managers' attention firmly on the prime goal of customer satisfaction.

PENSIONS

Allied to the growth of incentive schemes has been the dramatic growth in company pension schemes. Both in terms of numbers included and pension benefits offered, there has been a sizeable increase. The numbers involved in company pension schemes expanded from 2.6 million in 1936 to over 12 million in 1967 and now, according to Professor Peter Moore of the London Business School, to around 11 million, or half of the working population. Moore has also drawn attention to the huge amounts of money in pension schemes. He says, 'Pensions have now become a major factor in total labour costs in most large manufacturing and service industries.' He calculates that the average cost of pension schemes in the 1980s is around 15 per cent of a company's annual wage bill, and in some cases as high as 20 per cent. Pension schemes in Britain held funds of over £140 billion in 1985. This growth has been fuelled by increased legislative protection of pension rights. From the 1973 Social Security Act, which obliged schemes to preserve pensions after five years of service, to the 1985 Act, which introduced compulsory inflation-proofing for deferred pension benefits, employees' rights have been enhanced. Perhaps as a result, the 1980 Wilson Committee projected that pension scheme membership would reach 13.7 million by the year 2000.

With choice between personal and company pension schemes (SERPS) the conflict between employer and employee interests has been highlighted. Some observers believe that pensions provide a level of security which can act against commercial considerations. Says Moore: 'For many companies their pension provision is seen as a burden and is not always appreciated by employees as much as employers believe that it should be. With the greater flexibility now available, a fresh look at how best employers' and employees' aspirations can be met seems highly desirable.'

THE STATUS OF BUSINESS

A number of our industrialists believe that the role of wealth creation is now more socially acceptable and ascribe much of the credit personally to Mrs Thatcher. However, as Malcolm Bruce comments, 'Management is respected in Japan; but managers in that country respect their workforces. Status is something you have to win. In Germany, scientists and researchers are more respected than managers. In the US, it's entrepreneurs. Training and retraining of managers can give them more status.' Perhaps it is not so much a question of training, but of communicating the manager's role in the company and economy as a whole.

The 1987 edition of the survey *British Social Attitudes* indicates that business has not, as yet, been able to convince the public that successful industry creates a successful society. The belief persists that British business is operated in a fundamentally unfair manner. In the survey, 65 per cent agreed that ordinary working people do not get a fair share of the nation's wealth. Industry seemed to be regarded as exploitive rather than caring, some 59 per cent of respondents agreeing that there is one law for the rich and another for the poor, and 54 per cent believing that big business benefits at the expense of its employees. Paradoxically, the British view profits as a good thing and two thirds felt that the less profitable industry is, the less money Britain will have to spend on things like education and health. The report showed that more than half the population feel that profits should be spent on investment in machinery, training and research.

A number of organisations are already bridging the gap between management and the rest of society. There is now a Graduate Industrial

Society which aims to improve the effectiveness of graduates in industry and commerce. An English Graduate Enterprise programme also offers six weeks' full-time business school teaching to graduates while Durham University Business School heads a consortium of colleges running a Graduates Into Enterprise programme. This aims to help graduates to start their own firms.

Similar programmes, intended to create a more industrially aware education system are undoubtedly on the increase. The MSC's Graduate Gateway programme, aimed at graduates with degrees which are not popular in industry, places graduates with firms for ten weeks to give them experience. Shell also has a Technology Enterprise programme which takes students to work in industry during their summer vacations.

The CBI has also joined the bandwagon to bring professional status to industrial management. Its campaign, launched in October 1987, calls for a national approach to recruitment and training of managers. The CBI wants academic and government bodies as well as large companies to become closely involved in management training. It calls for more university and polytechnic places for management studies; increased on-the-job training and systematic career planning and post-entry modular management education programmes. Says John Banham, 'For relatively small sums of money – £2 million to £3 million a year, perhaps – concentrated in the right places, it should be possible to turn the present entrenched and out-of-date attitudes around.'

There are, perhaps, a few signs of changing attitudes. In the 3i report *Britain in the 1980s*, David Bannock comments, 'It used to be a very unfashionable thing in Britain to start up in one's own business, a route taken predominantly by the untrained and uneducated. Now it is all the rage. Large numbers of graduates of bodies in higher education now express a desire to have their own firm and many start one straight away.' Bannock quotes a letter from a Fellow of Balliol College to *The Observer* bemoaning the departure of intelligent minds from academia: 'There is the siphoning of newly trained brain-power out of academia. Smart graduates look for brilliant careers elsewhere. Graduate scientists take (often non-scientific) jobs in industry and commerce. Many of the best and brightest go into the City.'

The latter trend is perhaps of greatest significance. Little is likely to be achieved to change the relative levels of rewards, status and incentives while there still exist major differences in actual and potential earnings between, say, manufacturing managers and financial managers. Indeed, the 1987 stock market crash found industrial managers cheering at the ringside in hope of blood. The output of top business schools, such as the London Business School, have tended to go not to industrial positions, where salaries and status are relatively low, but to more lucrative options in, say, merchant banking or management consultancy.

All this is slowly changing as the rewards of management in manufacturing increase and those of financial management begin to plateau. To achieve a substantial revolution a number of things must occur, among them:

- The public perception of the value of real wealth creation (of making things profitably) must continue to rise.

- Managers must become more competent, more qualified. This, in turn, will lead to greater self-worth and confidence.

- Companies must be prepared to provide compensation packages that reward all success and initiative well and exceptional success and initiative exceptionally well.

18

The Decline of Quality

'We have to live by our own efforts in this country, and Japan has to live. Our stuff is better than Japan's. Let us go on selling it.'
Air Vice-Marshall Bouchier of the Federation of British Industries, in The Director, *April 1950*

'By the 1970s the label "Made in Britain" frequently meant poor quality and an excessive price, and consumers again and again voted with their purses for imported goods which earlier they would have despised as thoroughly inferior.'
Dr Charles Hanson of Newcastle University at the Institute of Economic Affairs Conference, October 1987

'Some degree of poor performance, both in serving customers and in the service received from suppliers, appears in many cases to be considered inevitable and hence even acceptable.'
Anthony Ovenden of the British Institute of Management in his Competitiveness in UK Manufacturing Industry, *1987*

CHEAP AND INFERIOR?

As the quotation from Air Vice-Marshall Bouchier shows, Britain in the immediate post-war years had a certain confidence and complacency about the quality of its industrial products. It was a confidence that was to prove disastrously misplaced. It was assumed that people would buy British no matter what. The belief that Made in Britain meant that a product was superior created an almost cavalier attitude towards quality.

An American survey, reported in *The Director* in March 1967, showed that neither Americans nor Europeans associated quality with British products. Only 15 per cent of Europeans and 12 per cent of Americans feel that 'Made in the UK' is a mark of quality. Of the major European economies, only products made in Italy are rated lower than those made in the UK.

The reasons for the relative decline of British quality, seen through the eyes of both our survey respondents and quality experts such as Dr Steve Smith of PA management consultants, can be summarised as follows:

- Failure to recognise the significance of the Japanese approach to quality.

- Reliance on correcting errors rather than preventing them.

- A lack of top management commitment to quality as a strategic weapon.

- Half-hearted adoption of new management ideas, which then fail.

- Forgetting that the customer is king.

Our touchstone for quality of products and services over the past ten years has increasingly been the Japanese. Indeed, the reputation of the Far East as a source of cheap goods of inferior quality has been virtually reversed. To a large extent, say both industrialists and trade union leaders, Britain was left behind. Quality was, to others, a matter of national pride rather than fact. Take, for instance, this comment from Sir Basil Feldman, chairman of Better Made in Britain, quoted in *The Director*, December 1987: 'If we are going to bring more business back to Britain, our manufacturers have got to design better, improve quality and marketing strategy, and have the confidence to get in there and bat like Botham on a good day.'

The cost of low standards of quality and failures in quality has been immense. In 1978 the Department of Trade and Industry estimated that the cost of quality failures in Britain amounted to £10 billion, or 10 per cent of GNP. Quality-related costs can range from five to 25 per cent of a company's turnover.

The reasons behind Japan's great leap forward in quality and Britain's neglect of quality have been much discussed. Whatever the reasons, torpor and indifference, mixed with chuckling, were the reactions when Dr W Edwards Deming, an American statistician, proclaimed: 'I told the Japanese that they would capture markets the world over in five years.' This was after the end of the war which saw the Japanese suffer ignominious and catastrophic defeat.

Deming was ignored in America and scarcely mentioned in Britain. After preaching the gospel of quality in the 1950s alongside another American academic, Joseph M Juran, Deming was eventually proved right in the 1960s. Quality now pervades Japanese industry, simply but spectacularly. 'Quality means quality of person as well as product. So the basic idea is to improve our own ability,' says a Sony executive.

The results of imposing high quality levels can be stunning. The Japanese retail chain, Seibu, has a mere 700 items returned each year; it sells 78 million and most of the faults are caused by customer handling. The influence of high Japanese quality standards on worldwide markets has been immense. The scale and breadth of the change is demonstrated by the following figures quoted in PA's management guide, *How to Take Part in the Quality Revolution*:

- The Japanese share of the British watch market grew from nine to 29 per cent between 1976 and 1985.

- Japanese manufacturers accounted for over 93 per cent of motorcycles sold in Britain. In 1970 they accounted for around a third of the market.

- Japanese imports numbered less that 0.5 per cent of cars sold in Britain in 1970. They now account for 11 per cent.

- Japan's share of world markets exceeds 50 per cent in shipbuilding, hi-fi, robotics, microwave ovens and plain paper copiers.

Interviewed in *International Management* in August 1986, Juran put the Japanese quality drive into perspective. 'The example has been pretty much set by the Japanese. They discovered that in order to be an industrial society, they were going to have to make their products compete in the world market. They developed ways to do that. They broke with Western tradition quite a bit to do that. The top people personally took charge of the quality function. That was unprecedented.'

Deming and Juran recognised that top management must make the pursuit of quality a corporate goal. Inspection of products when they have been completed is regarded as wasteful; the emphasis, instead, should be on preventing errors and using statistical process control to produce quality goods. Quality, therefore, has to go hand in hand with training.

Japanese quality management revolves around straightforward ideas and organisation. They demand company-wide quality control and a quality control audit. This is backed and encouraged by education and training which promotes total quality control. It starts with directors and works down through the company.

Quality circles, first established in 1962, operate in a huge number of Japanese companies. By 1984 the Japanese Union of Scientists and Engineers alone had 192,101 quality circles with 1.6 million members. The circles are groups of eight to twelve employees doing similar work who have been trained in statistical control procedures.

Nissan UK's personnel director, Peter Wickens, in his book *The Road to Nissan*, 1988, points out the British tendency to introduce aspects of a quality approach in isolation rather than as a corporate philosophy. Says Wickens:

> To believe that Quality Control Circles (QCCs) can simply be introduced into the UK, and be successful, without fundamental changes in attitude, is a delusion. It is not insignificant that those British companies which have had most success with QCCs, e.g. Wedgwood, Black and Decker, Mullard (Hazel Grove) and IBM (Havant), are those whose whole management style accentuates both quality and participation. Equally, some of the most celebrated failures have been where management has decreed that QCCs will be introduced and little else is changed.

The Japanese figures are impressive: Nippon KK steelworks has 1,320 quality circles submitting 112,000 suggestions every year of which about 103,000 have been adopted – four improvements per worker per year. 'In a very real sense, our people treat each other as customers,' runs a Mazda advertisement. 'Only work that reaches Mazda standards is allowed to pass from one person to the next.'

In contrast, criticism of British quality awareness and implementation of quality practices is widespread. Peter Wickens has pointed out the British tendency to introduce quality initiatives in isolation and without full management support. In his book, Wickens observes: 'You cannot achieve quality by sending people on courses and most of all you cannot mouth platitudes and then do everything to demonstrate that you do not mean what you say. To achieve real quality everyone at every level in the organisation has to genuinely believe in it and act on that belief. Management must mean what it says.'

The quality problems faced by British companies are exemplified by the electric oven manufacturers, Belling. Its production director, Neal Steeper, has identified the problems faced by the company as an 'autocratic and inconsistent management style' which made quality control difficult. Steeper told The Industrial Society: 'There were no management guidelines, little employee consultation and the documentation system was inadequate. As a result quality was controlled by a vast array of inspectors and only at the end of the line.' He recalled that supervisors spent most of their time chasing after materials and little time on the shop floor motivating and monitoring operators. Support from senior management was weak. Neal Steeper observed, 'They were the classic meat in the sandwich.' Since that time Belling has redressed its quality problems, with radical benefits.

19

The Rise of Quality

'Higher quality is associated with gains in market share and profitability.'
Dr Charles Baden-Fuller and Professor John Stopford, London Business School,
June 1986

'From a minor, obscure activity, usually relegated to the lowest levels of
organisation, it [quality control] has emerged as a major industrial function which
increasingly commands the attention of leaders of the national economy.'
J M Juran, Quality Control Handbook, *McGraw-Hill, 1951*

'Over the last decade there has been a quality revolution. Some firms have taken
advantage of this and some have not. But I think that one of the most damaging
myths that has pervaded industry since the 1920s is that good quality costs more
than bad. Nothing could be further from the truth.'
Dr Armand V Feigenbaum, in International Management, *January 1984*

NATIONAL QUALITY

It is not often that governmental initiative comes in for praise from all sides. But our industrialists, trade unionists and academics broadly agree that the National Quality Campaign has been both timely and relatively effective in raising awareness among companies of the importance of quality as part of the competitive armoury. The campaign has been strongly backed by the CBI and other influential bodies, motivated in large part by the impact of higher quality competition on markets which are lost or embattled.

The National Quality Campaign launched in 1983 and the British Quality Awards introduced in 1984 have encouraged the trend away from competing on price towards competing on quality of products and services. Already 50,000 companies are involved in the National Quality Campaign. The DTI intends eventually to involve 80,000. The National Society of Quality Circles, formed by 22 companies in 1983, now boasts 210 active sites in Britain and more every month. Even so, this is well behind the Japanese level and not particularly impressive by comparison with some of our European competitors.

Paul Channon, when Secretary of State for Trade and Industry, expressed the concern in this way: 'Competitiveness in the present world trading climate depends on very much more than just low prices. It is also increasingly dependent on a whole range of non-price factors, including good design, technological innovation, reliability, delivery on time and after-sales service – in short, on quality.'

The result, claims the CBI, is that most executives of medium or large firms at least recognise the need constantly to raise the quality of their products. A large portion of them have also accepted the need for continuous improvement in quality of service, too. PA's Dr Steve Smith has written of the need for improving existing standards:

258

What might have been acceptable fifteen, five or even one year ago, may no longer be acceptable to today's customer and risible to tomorrow's. Increasingly, customers are expecting high standards in the products they buy and raising those standards as new products and services create norms. Those norms apply not just to the product itself, but to the whole package of services and presentation associated with it. In most cases, where an established product has faded from the market, it has not done so because it was a poor product, but because customers' expectations had been raised by a product that fulfilled their needs better.

Smith goes on to point out that people are generally prepared to pay more for quality. A Gallup poll in the US showed that people would pay 135 per cent more for a pair of shoes, 66 per cent for a television and 36 per cent more for a car if it were seen as a quality product.

In almost every case where companies have managed to implement a successful programme of total quality management, top management has put its muscles behind the programme. (The quality gurus estimate that 80 per cent or more of all quality problems are caused by managers, so it is perhaps not surprising that it takes a strong commitment from management to make programmes work.) This is one issue where the responsibility for creating and maintaining positive change lies entirely in management's hands.

The trade unions have also espoused the cause. As early as 1981 Moss Evans of the Transport and General Workers' Union told the *Financial Times*: 'We accept wholeheartedly and would co-operate to the maximum with efforts to improve the quality of products.' On quality circles, the TUC takes a less encouraging stance. Said a 1981 policy paper, 'Quality circles are a belated recognition of employees' expertise and knowledge and the need to put them to use.'

Quantitative data on the improvement in quality of British industrial output is difficult to obtain. Certainly, there are examples of companies such as Nissan which have been pleasantly surprised to see quality levels in their British operations meet and even exceed levels at home. And many sectors of industry, such as car or electronic components manufacturers, have had to reduce defect levels radically to survive. Inter-firm or international comparisons, however, are few and far between. So for our purposes we intend to rely upon a number of examples of companies which have learnt how to compete successfully through the strategic use of quality. We do not claim that these firms are typical; merely that they illustrate what can be achieved.

259

IN PURSUIT OF PERFECTION: JAGUAR CARS

Perhaps the best known example of total quality at work in British industry is at Jaguar. 'Our cars had luxury, style, performance – and poor quality,' Sir John Egan, the Jaguar chairman, has commented. The quest for quality under the slogan 'In pursuit of perfection' has played a radical part in altering the organisation and performance of Jaguar. A loss of £52 million in 1980 has been transformed into annual profits of over £100 million in 1986 and £97 million in 1987.

The change of fortunes at the company has been immense. In 1980, 10,500 workers made 13,800 cars. In 1982, 8,000 workers made 28,041 cars and in 1986, 11,000 made 41,437. Productivity has continued to rise since then with workers now averaging 3.8 cars per man every year against 1.3 in 1980. 'Better quality, less manufacturing time and lower production costs are the way to beat the competition,' says Arnold Bolton, manager of Jaguar's corporate affairs. Jaguar's competitors have most clearly suffered in the American market where Jaguar's sales have increased from 15,815 in 1983 to 24,464 in 1986.

Jaguar set about achieving this by an intense concentration on the quality of its cars. It identified 150 faults – of which 60 per cent were caused by outside suppliers – by analysing customer warranty claims and the performance of its competitors as well as conducting lengthy interviews with Jaguar owners. Jaguar then assigned each problem to teams within the company and even brought suppliers in to join them. The twelve worst problems were left to the board of directors. All were eventually solved. In order to maintain its new standards, Jaguar now has an extensive quality auditing system which takes cars randomly from the production line. A system of demerit points, awarded according to the seriousness of the fault, provides a weekly quality index figure. By using this to isolate and identify problems, Jaguar has slashed the number of faults per car by over 60 per cent and achieved reliability often better than its competitors.

Outside the factories, the company makes vigorous attempts to follow up on the gripes and plaudits of Jaguar owners. Hundreds are interviewed after they have had their cars for thirty days, nine months and eighteen months. Any trends or common complaints are then followed up. Some Mercedes and BMW owners are also consulted to keep up with the competition.

Similarly, Jaguar dealers and suppliers have not been allowed to rest on their laurels following the initial quality drive. Under normal warranty agreements suppliers have to replace all rejected components. Jaguar, however, has led the way by introducing a stringent threshold clause which stipulates that over a 1.5 per cent failure rate, the supplier also pays all labour and handling charges. So far very few suppliers have had to meet that condition. Jaguar believes its example will become more widely adopted and that quality at every level will be increased.

Dealers are also included in the quality programme – after all, they are the people with the most direct contact with Jaguar customers. 'As far as Jaguar is concerned the customer is the most important person in our business and our dealers are very often our only point of personal contact with them,' says Roger Putnam of Jaguar sales and marketing. 'Any dealer who fails to provide a good standard of customer service will not be a long-term prospect.' As a result of this policy, some dealers have left the Jaguar network, though most have responded to the need for higher standards. To continue this development, Jaguar now gathers its overseas service representatives together every three months for three days to pre-empt problems which arise in individual markets.

Jaguar has found the shop floor workforce as keen on producing quality cars as the managers. The company now has over sixty quality circles which deal with all aspects of Jaguar's activities. They come up with new ideas for practical matters like welding and painting as well as organisational proposals. All this is backed up by a 'right first time' policy, which aims to eliminate time wasted on repeating work. 'You have to impose the highest standards on yourself,' says Arnold Bolton. 'In the luxury car market an obsession with quality is commonsense.'

COPYING SUCCESS

The quality message arrived in Britain by way of Japan and America. American companies in Britain have, to a large extent, set the example for British companies to follow. In 1974 Xerox had 90 per cent of the world photocopier market; by 1980, with increased competition, its share was down to 35 per cent. It had failed to respond effectively to a receding market share as the market expanded in size. Having enjoyed a near monopoly for thirty years, Xerox's initial response was the standard one of pruning costs and making redundancies, reducing its worldwide workforce from 120,000 in 1980 to just over 100,000, including 8,000 in the UK. Its next steps, however, were aimed at developing quality at all levels in the organisation, its products and service. The example of its Japanese subsidiary, Fuji Xerox, was closely examined and the company set about developing a system of 'competitive benchmarking'. This basically sets standards at Xerox at the level of the highest standards found in its competitors or the highest standards found in any relevant industry. 'The entire management and workforce of the plant has been dedicated to achieving the objectives of excellence and customer satisfaction through its quality strategy,' a Xerox spokesman explains. 'Every key function of the operation must at least match or improve upon the performance achieved by any other organisation.'

Competitive benchmarking even involves Xerox in close relations with its competitors – to the point of exchanging information on quality costs. It is, however, only a part of Xerox's quality drive. It now questions 30,000 customers each month and has set up quality circles and teamwork groups. Standards are reviewed three times a year at quality meetings, which also deal with any new quality problems that arise.

These steps were combined with a great deal of thinking about what sort of company people wanted Xerox to be. Its policy statement sets the tone for everything in the company. 'Xerox is a quality company. Quality is the basic business principle for Xerox. Quality means providing our external and internal customers with innovative products and services that fully satisfy their requirements. Quality improvement is the job of every Xerox employee.'

By February 1988 all employees in Xerox's British subsidiary Rank-Xerox had undergone at least five and a half days of formal training and follow-up activity in total quality management. Around fifty employees have full-time quality management responsibilities. As a result the company has won two Quality Association awards, the number of contract cancellations is lessening and customer satisfaction ratings have increased.

APPRECIATING QUALITY

Whether a company is in the manufacturing or services sector, its first step in total quality management is, typically, to attempt to rid people of the idea that defects are acceptable. It then attempts to measure exactly what happens in each task to create defects. Once the extent of a problem is known, the company can bring an array of resources – including the know-how and creativity of its operators – to bear in devising and testing solutions.

Industrially depressed Sheffield is not an obvious place to look for companies which have used quality management to achieve international competitiveness. Yet the cutlery company Richardsons, for example, has such confidence in its product that its Laser series knife carries a 25-year money back guarantee. The company manufactures 800,000 fine steel blades each week and exports over 60 per cent of its products to 70 countries.

Says managing director Bryan Upton, 'We have three very basic rules in this company – they are that all correspondence is answered the same day, that if anyone asks for a sample they get it that day and that the telex (which put 25 per cent on our business) is answered instantly.' In developing concentration on quality, Richardsons got rid of bonuses and piece work and now pays 20 per cent above the base rates.

To encourage higher quality standards some companies have taken the paradoxical step of reducing the number of quality controllers on the grounds that each employee should provide the quality control in his or her own work. Black and Decker introduced a policy of preventative quality assurance in 1981 which did just that, reducing the amount of inspection and increasing the responsibility of operators. Initially this led to quality problems and loss of productivity. Gradually, however, the reject rate was reduced from 12 per cent in 1982 to five per cent in 1984. The current target is to reduce it to 0.5 per cent.

The Black and Decker quality philosophy is to exceed the customer's expectations through excellence in all aspects of its business. In researching, designing, producing, selling, delivering and servicing, the customer comes first. As at Jaguar, this also applies to the company's suppliers. Operatives from Black and Decker's container supplier have been encouraged to visit Black and Decker factories to see the end result of their work. Consequently, errors decreased. The company motto, 'we are only as good as yesterday's deliveries', runs true. Increasingly it is realised that quality is continuous and embraces all aspects of industrial life.

Corporate quality policy statements are now more common. Some have the aura of the Japanese quality philosophy. Mullard of Manchester, for example, states of quality circles, 'A quality circle should be aimed at improving the lives of all people . . . Circle members strive to create an environment in which women and men can move in the direction of the realisation of human worth and dignity.' For many companies, survival and future prosperity may well depend on such encouragement of quality awareness.

263

THE RISE OF CUSTOMER CARE

'If we want to compete here in the world market it's all about looking after the customer's needs,' says Frances Sacker of The Industrial Society. 'Too often we try to sell what *we* want rather than identifying what the customer really wants. We've got to look at both the product and the sort of service *they* want.'

The breadth of interest in customer care is immense. Coutts Bank, Glasgow City Council, a number of health authorities and even the London Underground have instituted customer care programmes. Their examples are a reminder of W. Edwards Deming's claim that quality is important in every type of business. 'In the service industry, most workers do not think they have a product. They think they just have a job. They do have a product – service,' he declares.

Adds Frances Sacker, 'The best companies have now realised that effective customer care is a crucial part of commercial success. The key is for managers to treat staff as they would hope staff would treat customers,' she says. 'Customer care is not just about service industries. It commits everyone to the job they're doing and is central to the success of any business.'

It was Marks and Spencer's Lord Sieff who said, 'There's a worldwide demand for goods of high quality and value and there's no reason why they should not be made in Britain.' The story of how Marks and Spencer uses quality as the cornerstone of its corporate philosophy has been told elsewhere too many times to justify repetition here. Yet it is significant that it has only been in the 1980s that large numbers of British companies have seen M & S as an example to follow.

QUALITY A MILE HIGH

British Airways, the world's largest international airline, is one that does admit a debt to the M & S example. It has launched a massive drive to improve the quality of its service. 'Customer service was seen as the critical factor that could give a competitive edge but could not be easily duplicated,' says Michael Bruce, senior development projects manager. Chief executive Colin Marshall sees service as another means of providing value for money. 'A lot of customers are interested in price, of course,' he told *Marketing* when the idea was getting off the ground in 1985. 'But what they are really concerned about is value. They will pay for better service.' With this in mind, Marshall has a monitor giving details of departures on his desk. A glance tells him which planes are late; a phone call discovers why.

British Airways was also following the example of Scandinavian Airline System (SAS). Having lost $8 million in 1981, SAS appointed a new chief executive, Jan Carlzon. His outlook changed the company's fortunes. On taking office he proclaimed, 'From now on we shall stop looking on our assets as 60 airplanes and start considering our one million satisfied customers.' Within two years SAS had made a profit of $71 million.

British Airways recognised that the roots of its problems lay in a failure to view airlines as a service industry. Instead the emphasis had remained on the operational rather than commercial needs. Consequently it didn't recruit managers with service industry experience and carried out very limited market research. Inevitably, it grew out of touch with what its customers wanted. Safety and punctuality were dogma whilst commercial considerations played second fiddle.

Attitudes have changed and Bruce now simply states that 'being obsessively concerned with what customers want is the key for success'. To achieve this BA has launched 'Putting People First' and 'Managing People First' programmes as well as quality circles involving everyone in the company. Colin Marshall believes that the increased emphasis on quality has brought dividends and points to a 20 per cent increase in passengers carried.

The onus, however, remains on management. They set the standards. 'The values and norms of the organisation are set by the management group,' says Bruce. With this in mind BA now has a performance appraisal system for managers and has set up performance-linked pay. Under this system, managers receive a lump-sum bonus payment of up to 20 per cent of their basic salary. It is half determined by what the manager achieves and half by the manner in which he or she achieves it.

BA has even set up an entire department to examine the performance of its competitors so that it can match their standards. In fact, every act of BA employees is now subject to quality standards. 'Each branch has set and agreed a list of action points for pursuing straight away . . . from simple things like aiming to answer every telephone call faster or greeting every single passenger with a smile, to expenditure needs for refurbishing travel shops or executive lounges,' reported *BA News* in November 1986.

THE NOVELTY OF QUALITY

The means by which British companies have striven to improve quality in recent years are encouragingly diverse. The tyre-fitting company, Kwik-Fit, aims to improve customer care through the total involvement of all its staff. It promises '100 per cent customer satisfaction'. As a result, every member of the management team spends a week a year working in one of the depots and, to increase involvement and motivation, Kwik-Fit employees are used in its extensive TV advertising. This ties in with the company's customer policy which, though corny, seems to work in terms of focusing employee and customer expectations: 'I am your customer, satisfy my wants – add personal attention and a friendly touch – and I will become a walking advertisement for your products and services. Ignore my wants, show carelessness, inattention and poor manners and I will simply cease to exist – as far as you are concerned.'

Kwik-Fit's philosophy has enabled the company to grow dramatically from being a small tyre and exhaust business based in Scotland to being Europe's largest independent operator with 350 depots in Britain, Belgium and Holland. Kwik-Fit's investment of £8 million per year on advertising means that 92 per cent of motorists are reputed to know the company name. The combination of competitive pricing and efficient and reliable service helped Kwik-Fit's profits rise by 50 per cent in the first half of 1987 to £8.03 million.

Not all quality programmes need to be as extrovert as Kwik-Fit's, though the greater the customer contact, the more hard-hitting the programmes tend to be. For others, the drive for quality can take the form of an internal programme. At Honeywell monthly quality meetings are held in its employees' own time. Attendances are regularly high. At Philips Business Systems a monthly team briefing process has been instituted with six-monthly 'focus days' to feed back progress in the quality improvement programme to its 850 staff. This is supported by visible performance measurements in all departments and monthly newsletters. Emphasis has been placed on communication skills training, which is now regarded as an essential part of staff development. For the managing director the effects have been wide-ranging: 'Two years ago Philips Business Systems was arrogant, autocratic and deaf to its dealers' needs', he says. 'PBS is now seen as a caring, listening, business partner.'

FUTURE QUALITY COMPETITIVENESS

Earlier we said that the decline in quality of British goods was relative. What has happened, by and large, is that the expectations of customers in both overseas and domestic markets have been raised by improvements in service and product from elsewhere. While British companies have continued to invest time, effort and money in quality improvements since the 1950s, the *rate* of quality improvement has not risen as rapidly as in our most successful competitors. For Britain to catch up with where its strongest competitors are now in quality terms may take a decade. But those competitors (notably Japan, but increasingly the United States) are still accelerating their rate of quality improvement. Unless Britain is able to make a concerted, national effort to catch up and overtake these competitors, it will find itself even further behind in ten years' time.

The danger in the medium term is perhaps even greater. Some of the newly industrialised countries, such as South Korea, are starting quality-based industries virtually from scratch. Europe could swiftly become a quality backwater, while North America, Japan, and Southeast Asia turn the growing economies of the Third World into virtual private trading fiefdoms.

For example, many senior managers still fail to appreciate the link between quality and growth, which is expressed by the Strategic Planning Institute's Bradley Gale in *The Quality Review:*

> Quality is also tied to growth, because the customer always seeks better value. A customer who gets superior quality at a low price gets better value. And, obviously, a customer who gets inferior quality at a high price gets worse value. In a competitive marketplace the customer's choices determine which products are winners or losers. Quality becomes whatever the customer says it is, and the quality of a particular product or service is whatever the customer perceives it to be.

Some senior managers still find it difficult to accept that quality can be accurately and commercially measured. Middle managers sometimes suspect that a quality programme is merely aimed at apportioning blame for faults. On the shop floor, total quality management may still be perceived as a means of increasing productivity or decreasing manning levels. All employees need to realise the *necessity* of a total quality focus before a company can achieve international competitiveness on quality.

As more companies develop quality initiatives, others may become

267

convinced that such initiatives are necessary. The worldwide Profit Improvement of Market Strategy (PIMS) data base has concluded that the most significant factor associated with long-term high financial performance is 'relative product quality'.

PA's Steve Smith provides a list of the benefits of quality orientation which should prove irresistible to companies which have yet to develop quality awareness. It includes:

- Improved company image
- Improved productivity
- Cost reductions
- Improved certainty in operations
- Improved morale
- Improved management
- Committed customers

Just how uncompetitive quality levels remain in some industries is illustrated by a recent study by the National Institute of Economic and Social Research into kitchen furniture manufacture. The NIESR report compares the British kitchen furniture industry with that of West Germany. It found that the British were outgunned on virtually every quality issue:

- British companies work in cramped conditions with large stocks awaiting the next stage of production.
- British companies are geared towards mass production whilst their German competitors organise production around small batches to minimise stock levels and be more responsive to their customers.
- German companies maintain regular contact with customers whilst British companies generally do not.
- German production is matched to the needs of customers with computers used to sequence production lines. In Britain, production is geared towards increasing stock.

The lack of quality awareness and practice is compounded by the lack of training in British kitchen furniture companies and lower productivity levels – West German productivity is 66 per cent higher than in Britain.

The kitchen furniture industry accounts for a mere 1.9 per cent of manufacturing employment in Britain. While its attitudes and practices are not necessarily typical – inflexible manufacturing techniques, lack of quality control, limited technical expertise and lack of responsiveness to customer requirements – they demonstrate the scale of the problem to be overcome.

An equally depressing picture (hotly disputed by many of the British companies concerned) emerges from a recent study of Japanese companies' purchasing practices in the UK. Conducted by Coopers and Lybrand on behalf of the Government, the study was part of a broad project to identify ways of increasing the local content of products made by UK subsidiaries of Japanese companies. In some areas, such as switches, resistors, capacitors and discrete semiconductors, the Japanese sourced all or virtually all of their supplies from outside the UK. On the other hand, 55 per cent of the printed circuit boards they used were made in Britain.

The criticisms expressed by the Japanese companies in Britain focused mainly on price and quality. In many companies, they complained, quality management programmes 'tended to be somewhat superficial and not effectively implemented down to shop-floor level'. Other frequent, quality-related problems included late deliveries (even though the quoted delivery times were longer than those from companies in Japan), inefficient management and poor response times to customer enquiries.

Amongst the changes which were suggested by people we talked to were the following:

- The creation of a British quality training body along the lines of the Japanese Union of Scientists and Engineers and the American Society for Quality Control.

- Greater management-led quality initiatives.

- As in the American example, absorbing quality practices via a Japanese operating subsidiary. To date, few British companies have followed this path.

- Greater monitoring of corporate quality standards against the standards of competitors.

- Integration of the marketing-design-testing-production process to create an overall quality outlook.

- More stringent control of suppliers to ensure that quality exists right through the company.

- Wider employee participation and training to cultivate a quality philosophy.

Once again, the verdict must be a good start, but a long way to go.

20

The Decline of the Entrepreneur

'The small firm sector is in a state of long-term decline, both in size and in its share of economic activity.'
The Bolton Report, 1971

'In the post-war boom of the 1950s and 1960s, when the number of small firms and their share of output and employment was declining in most countries, it became the accepted wisdom that this was a good, and indeed an inevitable, thing.'
David Bannock, The Director, *October 1987*

BIG BUSINESS AND SMALL MEN

'This is not the age of the small man,' J K Galbraith has observed. He might have added that this is also not the age of the small business. The trend since 1945 has been towards conglomerates. They have commanded the attention and resources of government. The Bolton Report in 1971 showed that the numbers of small businesses and their share of output and employment had declined steadily in Britain since before the Second World War. Whereas there were 93,400 manufacturing businesses with ten employees or under in 1930, there were only 32,900 in 1963. The share of small businesses in manufacturing employment also fell during this period. In 1935 around 38 per cent of the total labour force in manufacturing industry was employed in small enterprises; by 1958 this figure was 24 per cent and, by 1963, under 20 per cent. The report gloomily reflected, 'In manufacturing, the share of small firms in employment and output has fallen substantially and almost continuously since the mid-1920s.' The Bolton Report identified the prime cause: 'The decline of the small firm should be seen in the context of a more general process of concentration that is going on.'

Despite eulogies on its importance and value, the small firms sector is traditionally weak in Britain in comparison to our competitors. Even so, the industrial sector most closely associated with innovation and flexibility is small business. The Bolton Report, despite its general discontent, believed that 'the qualities of vigour, enterprise and ambition' were generally prevalent in small businesses. International comparisons show that these qualities, no matter how laudable, have failed to allow small businesses in Britain to keep pace with foreign competition. In West Germany the small family-owned firm has always played a major part in the economy. Small and medium-sized businesses account for around half of West Germany's gross national product, employ two-thirds of the workforce, make over 40 per cent of investment and train over 80 per cent of apprentices. There are nearly two million small and medium-sized businesses. They have access to a variety of loan facilities at preferential rates to finance expansion, modernisation and innovation.

In America, the Small Business Administration estimated that there was a 23 per cent growth in small businesses between 1978 and 1988. As a result, 47 per cent of the private sector workforce is employed in small businesses generating 38 per cent of gross national product. Traditionally, increases in employment in America have centred on small businesses.

In Britain there are 2.7 million self-employed people and 1.6 million small companies employing up to 200 people making up a sizeable, though sometimes ignored, part of the business world.

CREATING THE CLIMATE

While there has been a platform of government-backed aid schemes for small businesses, the Employment Institute claims it has been by and large poorly directed. 'Much of the assistance currently given to small firms is headed for the pockets of entrepreneurs rather than the creation of new jobs,' it said, in pressing for more money for established businesses rather than for starting up new businesses.

Criticism of government's role has gone on for a number of years. The Smaller Businesses Association, in its submission to the 1971 Bolton Report, claimed: 'For businesses to flourish, one of the essentials is confidence. There are, of course, many factors which affect this, but in the UK since the war, the factor with the most widespread and continued effect has been government action. Attempts at influencing businessmen by legislation have often seemed to businessmen to be threats to the continuance of their enterprises.'

Small businesses have also been criticised for not making use of the money available to them. Says Professor Allan Gibb of Durham University in his *A Guide to Small Firms Assistance in Europe*, 'The typical small business is frequently not aware of assistance resources, nor yet inclined to use them.'

There is ignorance of potential resources and of the detail of administration and tax which weigh down any business. The 1980 Wilson Committee observed that 'compared to large firms, small firms are at a considerable disadvantage in financial markets'. The traditional problem of cash flow persists. It has been estimated that as much as £57 billion is owed to small businesses and a 1985 CBI survey of owner managers showed that 81 per cent had late payments problems.

A MORI poll for the British Venture Capital Association in October 1987 showed some of the problems there are in starting a business. Top of the list were lack of personal and external finance. These were followed by problems as diverse as fear of the stigma of failure (larger in America than in Britain), having to take a salary cut, concern about loss of pension, lack of a suitable management team and family opposition.

In the opinion of some observers, the attitude of the City towards small businesses and entrepreneurs leaves a lot to be desired. The minister responsible for small firms, David Trippier, has condemned the perform-ance of pension funds and insurance companies in supporting small business as a 'national disgrace'. He points out that around 1 per cent of their huge multi-billion pound resources are used to support small com-panies not quoted on the stock exchange. Trippier has suggested that doubling this investment would create another 10,000 jobs every year. Says Trippier, 'How will the ever-increasing population who will have to rely on these funds fare if the custodians of their future do not invest in young companies which will grow to become the employers and wealth creators of the future?'

Not only is the prospective entrepreneur up against a lot of start-up problems, but recent statistics are far from encouraging for small busi-nesses. One study estimated that 90 per cent of start-ups fail in the first five years. Trends Business Research has also reported that most small firms employed fewer people in 1986 than they did in 1983. It is, perhaps, a question of attitudes and environment. Sir John Hoskyns comments, 'The general intellectual culture is set by academics and other commen-tators who have never had the desire to make a fortune, have security of tenure and work that is reasonably interesting and has perks in the form of such things as travel, that are denied to the toiling masses.' Hoskyns believes that the British still tend to see entrepreneurial activity as a means of making money and retiring to spend it. 'We still have a small small-business sector. It's still the thing to do to sell up and go and live in Jersey,' he says.

21

The Rise of the Entrepreneur

'We're lucky we're getting more small businesses and more self-employed because that's where the new jobs are going to come from.'
Margaret Thatcher, Prime Minister, 19 November, 1986

'Being civilised costs money. What we really want in the UK is twenty-five years of blatant vulgarity. Just as when there was a war you found the most unlikely people doing what was necessary, so you need lots of people now who may not be particularly delightful to touch.'
Sir John Hoskyns, 1987

'It is many years since the business climate for enterprise and opportunity in this country has been better.'
Sir David Nickson, president of the CBI, at its conference in 1987

THE ENTREPRENEURIAL CLIMATE

Ironically, after the 1971 Bolton Report came out reporting the decline of small British businesses, the numbers began to grow. In fact the number of new company registrations has risen in every year since 1968 except during the oil crisis of 1973–4. Small business and the entrepreneur are now firmly on the business agenda of government and large companies alike. The so-called 'enterprise culture' has been fuelled by the greater availability of venture capital, tax incentives (like the Business Expansion and Enterprise Allowance Schemes) and lower income tax rates. The role of Margaret Thatcher, as a figurehead at least, has been thought significant by many entrepreneurs. In a recent book on Britain's entrepreneurs, Clive Rassam observes:

> By the spring of 1979, when Acorn computers was set up by Hermann Hauser and Chris Curry, who had earlier worked with Clive Sinclair, the entrepreneurial revolution was almost complete. What this revolution needed was a voice that would acknowledge and recognise what had happened and enable it to flower further. They found that voice, imperfect as it was, in the shape of the soon-to-be-elected Thatcher Government, which in opposition seemed to personify their aspirations.

The Conservative Government has indeed ceaselessly preached the enterprise philosophy. In particular, its programme of privatisations has provided an opportunity to involve more of the population in share ownership. In 1987 an editorial in *The Director* magazine reflected on the far-reaching changes which have been brought about since the advent of Mrs Thatcher: 'Eight years on, the man on the Clapham omnibus knows what the "enterprise culture" means, may well be part of it and almost certainly wants his children to be.'

The new seriousness and respectability with which the entrepreneurial world is seen is reflected in the appointment of six professors of the subject (at the time of writing) as well as increased government involvement and support for their development. A Small Firms Division was set up at the Department of Trade and Industry in 1971 and the Department of Employment was eventually granted a Small Business Minister. The government's Small Firms Service now has thirteen regional offices and there are 328 Local Enterprise Agencies. The EEC also created a small and medium-sized enterprises task force in 1986 which sought to identify the problems facing these businesses.

IMPROVED FUNDING

There has been a radical increase in the sources and availability of venture finance for new and established small and medium-sized businesses. The stock exchange, for example, now has an Unlisted Securities Market, a market for shares in small companies, launched in 1980 and, more recently, a Third Market for even smaller companies. The success of the USM can be seen in the number of companies obtaining listings.

The USM's success (with 567 companies admitted by June 1987) provided an incentive for the introduction of yet a third market, which will deal primarily in the shares of even smaller companies. The Business Expansion Scheme has provided an additional form of venture finance for small and medium-sized companies and another investment opportunity for people who may previously have ventured no further than unit trusts.

At the same time, the number of venture capital organisations has increased from 20 in 1979 to 120 in 1986. More importantly, perhaps, the amount invested by British venture capital organisations has mushroomed from £195 million in 1981 to £671 million in 1986.

The growth of Britain's venture capital industry is illustrated by the activities of Britain's largest provider of funds, Investors in Industry (3i). It has invested £1.5 billion between 1981 and 1987 – three times as much as in the thirty-six years between 1981 and its foundation in 1945. As a result of this unprecedented growth, the number of independent venture-fund managers has increased tenfold. They have persuaded institutions such as pension funds and individuals to spend £1.35 billion between

277

Number of companies obtaining full listings and USM quotations on the stock exchange

	Official list	USM	Third Market
1973	96		
1974	14		
1975	19		
1976	18		
1977	24		
1978	35		
1979	48		
1980	35	23	
1981	61	61	
1982	59	60	
1983	79	85	
1984	87	101	
1985	80	98	
1986	169	94	
1987	189	75	35

Source: Stock Exchange.

1982 and 1987. It has been estimated that there is a venture capital pool of £4.5 billion which has been or is ready to be invested. This has been backed up by the Business Expansion Scheme which has invested around £170 million since 1981 through its package of tax incentives for financing approved projects.

The sources of backing for small businesses are now encouragingly diverse, as the table opposite demonstrates.

According to Sir John Hoskyns, the outlook is good: 'There is more happening below the surface entrepreneurially than people recognise.' Lord Young is equally enthusiastic: 'Now we see a resurgence of entrepreneurs,' he says. 'The heroes of the stock exchange today are people like John Ashworth, the chief executive of Coloroll. That man's school wanted him to go into law; his father wanted him to work in a bank.'

Sources of funds to smaller businesses (excluding traditional bank lending)

	Year	Investments in £000 per company			Total per annum in £m
		Minimum	Maximum	Median	
USM	1984	600	3,200	1,600	262
OTC*	1983/4	240	3,200	1,300	39
Business Scheme: Direct	1983/4	5	150	40	66
Business Expansion Scheme: Approved Funds	1983/4	50	500	200	39
Venture Capital	1984	250	750	400	228
3i	1984/5	10	500	90	270
Loan Guarantee Scheme	1984	1	75	33	75
Local Enterprise Boards	1985	100	750	350	18

* Over the counter market (a less controlled market for share placings).
Source: CBI City/Industry Task Force, 1987.

In terms of statistics, enterprise is thriving. Figures for new company registrations and liquidations in Britain demonstrate the size of the growth.

A greatly increased range of financial services is now available to small companies. It is estimated that the four major clearing banks have about £20 billion of outstanding loans and overdrafts to businesses with a turnover of less than £1 million. NatWest claims that it now has £7 billion invested in small firms.

The Government's Loan Guarantee Scheme enables banks to lend money for projects which would otherwise go unfunded. Its effectiveness has been severely questioned and it has yet to match similar schemes abroad. In Japan small businessmen can borrow at a rate of 2.5 per cent if they have attended a business course. The West German Loan Guarantee Scheme is eight times the size of its British counterpart. The British LGS

279

New company registrations and liquidations in Britain, 1970–86

	New registrations	Liquidations
1970	30,262	8,782
1971	39,445	8,412
1972	54,456	8,215
1973	67,349	7,240
1974	42,496	7,885
1975	45,678	9,795
1976	56,085	10,640
1977	52,214	9,974
1978	63,566	9,205
1979	66,472	9,019
1980	69,374	11,481
1981	72,416	12,920
1982	87,166	16,731
1983	96,188	17,978
1984	97,908	18,250
1985	104,581	19,614
1986	114,831	Not known

Source: Department of Trade and Industry, *Companies in 1986.*

also brings with it a burden of paperwork under the Consumer Credit Act of 1985. Tentative investors may also be dissuaded by a requirement to pledge personal assets under the scheme.

REDUCING THE LEGISLATIVE BURDEN

A whole range of legislative and taxation incentives for small business has been introduced during the 1980s. The rate of corporation tax has been reduced to 25 per cent for small businesses. However, the Association for

Independent Businesses does not believe this is enough of a reduction, calling for a 'complete reform of the business tax regime'.

Legislation has provided minor improvements. Statutory sickness payments have been altered to remove disadvantages against small firms. The smallest firms are now exempt from provisions of the Employment Protection Act. Much could be done, however, and the Association for Independent Businesses calls for 100 per cent capital allowances on the first £50,000 of investment. This, it believes, should be backed up by lower interest rates, easier access to low-cost capital, the reform of local business rates, a ceiling on employers' national insurance contributions and a further lowering of corporation tax. It also says that small businesses require greater commitment from the British Overseas Trade Board and the Export Credit Guarantee Department. It points out that full British membership of the European Monetary System would enhance export potential.

The Small Business Research Trust has demonstrated the continuing financial problems afflicting small business. Its quarterly survey of over 1,000 British small businesses showed that, in the third quarter of 1987, the chief problems encountered by small businesses remained finance and interest rates. The other difficulties were equally familiar – tax burden, low turnover, lack of skilled workers, competition from big business, government paperwork and shortages of supplies and materials. Interestingly, inflation and high rates of pay were relegated to the position of least pressing problems.

The CBI City/Industry Task Force also concluded that the major problems still facing small businesses when raising capital were: 'high fixed costs when raising small amounts of equity, a lack of sound professional advice to companies preparing investment proposals and the inability of potential investors to weigh up risks in a start-up.' Nevertheless, in general, companies are able to meet their financing needs. A 1986 NEDC study of 176 small and medium-sized firms in the electronics sector concluded: '80 per cent of fundraising attempts reached a successful conclusion. Around 90 per cent of companies seeking either loan or equity capital received offers, and 90 per cent of the offers of both forms of finance were accepted. It was concluded from this that there was no evidence of a large-scale failure by sample firms to meet their financing needs.'

The Small Business Research Trust had more optimistic news on other fronts in 1987. It believed that employment amongst small firms was on the increase. In fact employment was up over 22 per cent on 1986's figures with, not surprisingly, the most buoyant areas being the prosperous Southeast and East Anglia. The growth in employment was stimulated, according to the SBRT, by an average 44.7 per cent increase in sales since 1984 amongst the companies covered.

CREATING JOBS FROM SMALL BUSINESSES

Politically, one of the most controversial aspects of the role of the entrepreneur is his or her capacity to create jobs. The belief that entrepreneurs and small businesses create employment has been enthusiastically championed by both the Government and the Labour Opposition. The Government has a positive view. Says Lord Young: 'Out of every 100 people who go into self-employment, 61 per cent survive three years. For each 100 that survive after that, there are 99 more jobs created. After five years, 1000 small firm starts fall to between 500 and 600. Of these, 45–50 may grow well. One or two employ more than 1000 people.' Labour's John Smith concurs: 'I'm more interested in small businesses than in medium-sized ones of 500 or so people.'

The politicians have also sought to establish a causal link between small businesses and flexible working practices, but this remains unproven. Indeed, the record of small businesses in this context has been criticised. A European Community report (*Small and Medium-Sized Enterprises and Employment Creation in the EEC Countries*, 1987) found that small firms employed a relatively high proportion of female and part-time workers who were paid lower wages and offered inferior conditions. The report goes on to question whether small businesses are one of the solutions to unemployment. Its conclusion was entirely negative: 'Low-paid, unstable part-time jobs, or skilled manual jobs are unlikely to be attractive to the unskilled and semi-skilled males who dominate the unemployment registers.'

The Employment Institute adds fuel to these flames, declaring: 'Small business growth is certainly not the "answer" to the problem of high unemployment, and it is seriously misleading to suggest that this could ever be the case.' A study between 1982 and 1984 by the Institute concluded that, 'The emphasis on the role in increasing employment is difficult to understand, for although there are more of them [small businesses] their contribution to total employment is small, according to official data for manufacturing and distribution.' The tendency remains for small businesses to reach a threshold of employing twenty people before slowing down or stopping recruitment.

The growth in small businesses remains a difficult thing to evaluate. When it comes to statistics, entrepreneurs are not the most informative of people and the high risk nature of entrepreneurial activity means that failures and the reasons for them may not be recorded. In fact, though the number of small businesses has increased, especially since 1980, the number of liquidations has risen at a faster rate. Allied to these statistics is the poor flow of graduates into self-employment. Only 0.33 per cent of British graduates start their own business; in the United States 2 per cent do so. With the redesign of the Graduate Enterprise Programme it is hoped that more graduates will become entrepreneurs. It is now hoped that the scheme will have enough places each year to turn 450 graduates each year into entrepreneurs. At present, only 150 are given help through the Manpower Services Commission.

The conclusion must be that though the future role of small businesses is potentially large, there are still many obstacles to overcome before we create a truly entrepreneurial culture.

22

The Decline of Design

'It may be a relic of puritanical Britain that connected design with art, art with pleasure and pleasure with something that must on no account be enjoyed.'
David Maroni, chairman, Olivetti, 1987

'Many people feel that industry is throwing away key areas of competitive advantage by neglecting design.'
Professor Peter Doyle of Warwick University at the 1987 CBI Conference

---

THE BRITISH ATTITUDE

In his annual address to the Confederation of Art and Design Associations in October 1986, Sir Hugh Casson came to the controversial conclusion that the English (not the British) were 'artistically insensitive, politically lazy, suspicious of foreigners, wary of rhetoric in speech or buildings, snobbish, hypocritical . . . but basically decent'.

In the opinion of some of our observers, Casson's remarks are borne out by British indifference to design and its role within industry. A recent Design Council survey of managers revealed that over two thirds thought that Britain was 'insufficiently design conscious'. Nevertheless, 76 per cent confidently claimed that their own company stood apart from this distressing trend and did in fact 'pay sufficient attention to design'.

Managers – let alone the public in general – frequently have little idea of the scope of design nor of how it can profitably be applied to their businesses. Their problem is emphasised by the range of definitions of design. J C Jones' *Design Methods* provides an example of how far views on what design actually is differ considerably. Among the suggested definitions were:

- 'A goal-directed problem-solving activity.'
- 'The imaginative jump from present facts to future possibilities.'
- 'The conditioning factor for those parts of the product which come into contact with people.'

Historically, little has been done in Britain to develop design standards and awareness in industry. Indeed, as early as 1867 a government committee observed, 'A great deal more could be done for design.' A great deal more has been done in many respects, yet fundamental attitudes have taken a

286

long time to change. The separation of 'industrial' and 'engineering' design remains a point of argument. Mark Oakley, teacher of design management at the University of Aston's Management Centre has observed:

> These two disciplines of design arise from different roots and different educational systems, but there is much common ground between them and in many countries the relative absence of demarcation is accompanied by a high level of commercial benefit. British industry and education have been slow to recognise the damaging effects caused by these divisions. Industrial design and engineering design are still taught and practised as separate disciplines, and the distinction between them is still reinforced by organisations such as the Design Council, the Engineering Council and the engineering institutions.

Inevitably, all the confusion about what constitutes design and the designer's role in the company means that few managers may have an idea of what makes good or bad design. This is the view of Sir Simon Hornby, chairman of the Design Council and W H Smith, who has told the CBI that there is a lack of understanding in Britain of all the elements of design as product development. Said Hornby at a 1987 CBI Conference, 'The design element in a manufacturing company will be successful only if it is clearly understood and managed.' Hornby called on chief executives to answer six key questions about design in their companies and their own attitude towards it:

1. Were they personally committed to design management?

2. Were their companies imbued with a code of practice which made the customer pre-eminent?

3. Were their companies making the products that their customers really wanted?

4. Were they satisfied that there was a correct and universally understood definition of design in their companies?

5. Were they satisfied that they were carrying out the best practice of design management?

6. Were they giving regular training in design and design management?

The multi-dimensional nature of design means that different specialists view it from their own perspectives – engineers think of technical performance, industrial designers of ergonomics and appearance, customers of value for money.

Though many managers undoubtedly accept the importance of and need for designers, design education has long been neglected and produces a mere 5,000 graduates and fewer HNDs annually. The teaching has been unresponsive to the demands of industry and, say many industrialists, the design student has remained isolated. Christopher Lorenz, author of *The Design Dimension*, has written that, 'The educational system in most countries remains "bookish and wordy". The designer, trained to coordinate words, hands and visual imagery, is still very much the exception.'

Since the early 1920s when General Electric established a committee for what it called 'product styling', many companies have struggled to find a place for design in the workplace. Difficult to categorise, it crosses many of the traditional barriers of organisation within companies. It is neither marketing nor production and has not normally been regarded as a career, at least within the normal chain of manufacturing command. The many skills of the designer cannot be fitted into the usual hierarchy of craft specifications or business specialisation. Allied to this is the designer's need to be involved in a production 'team', rather than to be an individual manager ploughing his own narrow furrow. The refusal of many companies to break up into smaller operating units meant that designers became lost in an amorphous organisation.

Merrick Taylor, managing director of Motor Panels and a Design Council member, believes that the problem is that the onus has been on financial expertise. 'It is not a problem of fitting designers into organisations but one of the increasing domination by the financial disciplines,' he says. For Taylor, the commercial force of design is unquestionable. 'Design uses creativity and the logic of control to produce a finished product,' he states. In his opinion the forces of control have held too great a sway over the creative powers of the designer. The result has been a compartmentalising of design, which ultimately blunts its creative edge. Effective design means that Motor Panels uses a third of the floorspace to produce the same number of vehicle bodies as its Japanese competitors.

The problem for many companies may well be the difficulty in proving the link between good design and profitability. It is fundamentally difficult to provide statistics which back up a correlation between design and competitiveness. Significantly, there are a number of Education & Science

Research Council (ESRC) projects currently seeking to establish such a relationship.

The 1979 Cornfield report for the National Economic Development Council strongly argued the case for linking design and profitability. It claimed that 'Better product design would make a significant contribution to improving economic performance.' NEDC working parties have also claimed that the UK's loss of market share has owed much to the inappropriateness of British products to market requirements. A Design Council report, *Design and the Economy*, 1983, prepared by a group of economists, concluded that poor design and a failure to innovate were major causes of Britain's loss of home and foreign markets. The report claimed that penetration into British domestic markets was, in part, due to the persistent failure to compete in non-price areas such as design and quality. The case was illustrated in the report by the example of Ford and British Leyland. Whilst Ford achieved long-term success through its Cortina ranges over twenty years, BL struggled with its Allegro models. One of the differences, identified by the report, was that Ford closely analysed customer requirements and designed the Cortina to fit in with those needs. The BL car, though technically advanced, failed to follow suit. Aston University's Mark Oakley states:

> The evidence of weakness is considerable and the case for action to improve design performance seems strong . . . While it is less clear the extent to which Britain's overall industrial performance relative to that of other countries is a consequence of a widespread lack of concern about design, there is considerable evidence Britain does indeed pay less attention to design and design strategy than foreign competitors.

With no conclusive evidence to back their case designers were forced to play their part in essentially short-term management. Design, after all, demands long-term commitment and a long-term strategy as well as high levels of investment. Warwick University's Professor Peter Doyle has pointed out the conflict between the potential long-term benefits of effective design and the short-term need to make money. A Warwick University survey of 400 companies, produced by Doyle, showed that most concentrate on gaining return on investment through cost cutting, improved efficiency and cash flow. The alternative strategy of defining target markets, designing appropriate products and evolving strategies suitable for the particular market are, in his opinion, neglected in Britain. At the 1987 CBI Conference, Doyle claimed, 'This improvement in efficiency has worked, but the long-run effects are apparent in many areas in weak marketing performance.' According to Doyle, the British design weakness is centred on manufacturing. He points out that Britain is a world leader in certain areas of design, such as education, consulting, retailing and fashion. In manufacturing, however, the UK continues to lag behind. Whether this is being, or can be, redressed is discussed in the next section.

23

The Rise of Design

'Design pervades our lives. Today most of us in the developed world live most of the time in urban society where man-made things predominate over the natural; and all of these man-made things have been designed.'
Sir Peter Parker, president of the Design and Industries Association, 1987

'We need a design culture in which all citizens, both as producers and as consumers, are aware of good design and will not accept second-best.'
Kenneth Baker, Minister for Education, 1987

'There are many routes to improving industrial performance, but I believe that it is hard to find any that will bring greater benefits than improving standards of product design.'
Simon Hornby, chairman, W H Smith and the Design Council, 1987

'Design is a long-term strategic business weapon. The design of a product, service or company represents the very core of its identity and values. It plays a vital role in leading or reflecting a chosen strategy.'
Jan Hall of Coley Porter Bell, design consultants, at a 1987 CBI conference

CHANGING ATTITUDES

A conference held in 1987 at the CBI's Centre Point headquarters attracted numerous chief executives, many of them from the largest companies in the land. Hardly surprising, except that the topic was design in industry. A few years before, stressed the organisers, it would have been hard to get a single chief executive to attend.

In a range of interviews with people concerned with the application of design in manufacturing we have detected a remarkable surge of optimism, tinged, to be fair, with concern as to whether this new-found boardroom awareness of the value of design will last. It seems that, finally, design is being regarded by some leading companies at least as a strong part of the driving force behind product innovation and behind the maintenance and growth of market share. The design consultancy, Crighton, declares, 'We believe that design can order change, anticipate it, even inspire and make it exciting.'

Several things have happened to stimulate this change in attitude and approach. One is a growing sense among companies of what design involves. It is now commonly seen to encompass all the development work which goes into an individual product or series of products from the initial tests to the laboratory work, calculations and drawings. We are moving towards the idea of 'product design and development'. Consequently, design's role and contribution in the workplace and organisation are easier to identify.

Companies' awareness has been raised partly by pressure from overseas competitors and partly by a determination on the part of both employers' organisations and the Government that design should play a stronger role in British industry. The Prime Minister, Margaret Thatcher, has said that 'good design is first among the reasons for profits and success'. She emphasises the need to provide sophisticated products for increasingly visually aware and sophisticated customers. 'People will not give a second look at a product unless the design attracts them immediately. But products must be designed with commerce in mind. Buyers are increasingly discerning and products must be designed functionally and price-effectively.'

This pressure has led to the second stimulus for change – a rapid growth and reorientation of design education. The craft, design and technology courses now taught in many schools, aim to make use of teachers with industrial experience. Department of Education reports show that there has been an 80 per cent increase in applications to teach the subject, though teaching numbers still remain low. In higher education, the London Business School, for example, has had design as part of its MBA curriculum since 1976. In 1982, it established a Design Management Unit under Peter Gorb which teaches, researches and preaches design to the unconverted.

The Design and Industries Association claimed in its 1987 handbook:

Young designers are perceptive and inventive, and try to meet the needs they see around them. Manufacturers, on the other hand, seem to be unimaginative and unadventurous; no longer willing to invest resources in developing products, opening new markets, looking to the future. Until they're prepared to change, the outlook for British manufacturing must remain bleak. Devotion to design could bring new life, new hope, and a better world for both industry and its customers.

Sir Simon Hornby of W H Smith and the Design Council calls for increased management awareness and education: 'All managers of whatever discipline should have training to develop an understanding of design, marketing and product development.' Awareness of design may well have been increased by the broader range of design work now on offer. Design is no longer consigned to the obvious packaged goods of the supermarket shelves, but is casting its net far wider than ever before. With the product maturity of many of the goods we now take for granted, like hi-fis or typewriters, new ways have been found to make them more attractive and adaptable to demand. The splintering of markets into increasingly specific niches has meant that design has to be tailored to far more accurate criteria.

THE DECLINE AND RISE OF BRITISH INDUSTRY

THE ROLE OF THE DESIGN COUNCIL

The true potential of the Design Council has only recently started to be exploited. Its 'Support for Design' programme is probably its most successful since the Council's inception in 1944. The programme was launched in 1982 and has since been used by over 6,000 British companies. The programme offers a subsidised design consultancy to small and medium-sized companies for product packaging, promotional literature, interior design and ergonomics, amongst others. From those who have taken part so far it is estimated that 93 per cent have had a successful conclusion to their consultancy.

The successes, in some cases, have been dramatic. For example, design assistance enabled the Hydrovane Compressor company to cut manufacturing costs by 54 per cent and reduce the list price of its product from £740 to £428 whilst increasing its gross profit margin. New designer boots raised another company's sales by nearly 400 per cent in two years whilst the Clarence Clothing Company doubled its workforce from forty-five to ninety after introducing a new designer trouser range.

DESIGNING FOR BRITAIN

Camillo Olivetti, launching his first typewriter in 1911, commented, 'The aesthetic side of the machine has to be carefully studied. A typewriter . . . should have an appearance that is elegant and serious at the same time.' The ordinary can be made extraordinary.

Richardsons of Sheffield, already mentioned in the chapter on quality, shows how design of a product as apparently simple as a kitchen knife can improve its commercial impact. 'It's a fashion business,' said managing director Bryan Upton in a case study by the London Business School. 'We were the first knife manufacturers to bring out coloured handles. We'll give the customer knives with any colour of handles he wants. We regularly revamp the packaging. The packaging must be professional and attractive. It's got to appeal to the customer and capture his attention. We change our retail displays every year – no one else in the business does that. It's new items and new images all the time.' Backed by an awareness and use of design, Richardsons increased sales at an average annual rate of 29% between 1974 and 1986.

Bringing about such changes is now reaping British designers the financial rewards they once missed. They are gaining international reputations. The Italian company, Reggiani, for example, has recently taken on the Conran Design Group to design a major new product, the Eton lighting range – a sign that British designers may be emerging from the shadow of Italians.

Elsewhere, there has been an expansion in design consultancy with growth in this area estimated at 30 to 40 per cent a year. The design consultancy market in 1986 was estimated to be worth £220 million with £30 million being taken up with print and graphics (including corporate identity); £40 million on products (including furniture); £30 million on offices and interior design and a massive £120 million on retail, travel and leisure. If engineering and architectural design were included the total design bill for Britain would be around £1 billion.

The spread of design can be seen on the high street of any British town. The retail boom has meant that it is not only the large multiple stores which engage in design, but also out-of-town DIY and furniture chains as well as banks and building societies. Shopping is no longer a simple business. Designers have endeavoured ambitiously to turn it into 'a leisure experience'. The most ambitious have aspirations to turn shopping into theatre.

Design has clearly benefited a great number of retail outlets. Next, for example, has created a more permanent image, a design which outlasts the ephemeral trends of youth culture. Its example has been followed by Dolcis, the shoe chain; W H Smith, which has pruned its operation down to ten clearly distinguished departments; and even the once dull Woolworth group, which has trimmed down its product range to six key areas and considerably brightened its stores, its appeal and its profitability. In 1987 alone, three out of the four major clearing banks launched redesigns and the last intends to join them.

THE COMPANY AND DESIGN

The role of the designer in the management team is also becoming clearer. The broad combination of skills the designer needs can be used efficiently. Philips is one company which has used designers successfully. Its performance and profitability have recovered sharply since the early 1980s when it was savaged by Japanese competitors. Since 1982 the power within the company has shifted away from Philips' subsidiaries towards the central product divisions, their constituent business units and the smaller product groups responsible for individual product lines. The 'Design for Market' programmes run by Philips have succeeded in furthering the role of design within the company. The seminars, which started in 1985, concentrated on co-ordinating the management of manufacturing, marketing, industrial design and development within the company. Each session has around twelve specialists, from three different product groups, whose interests may be as diverse as in-car entertainment and dishwashers.

CONCLUSION

The mistake of the past was to treat design as something different, an exception in the management process. Wally Olins, chairman of design group Wolff Olins, comments, 'Design is a corporate resource like any other.' Often, design is regarded as the answer to everything, a cure-all, says David Maroni of Olivetti, who adds 'Design thrives where management is efficient. It can't reverse bad management. It is not a panacea for all management ills.'

Yet the changes achieved by design are all around us. Design can change the way we look at things. Simple plastic was once regarded as being cheap and cheerful, a harmless lurid replacement for natural materials. Design developments mean that plastic goods are now regarded as durable, clean and colourful.

The need for investment in design and increased understanding remains. An Open University report states that: 'Competitiveness is gained from increased investment, not just in more productive plant and equipment, but in the human resources needed for the effective management and practice of product design and innovation.'

Wally Olins is optimistic that design will continue to increase in importance. He told *Marketing*, 'The design business may have stumbled as it was running but its momentum and pace will continue.' He acknowledges the changes that have already occurred: 'Ten years ago, few people recognised that the design business existed.' But how many more years will it be before the true value and importance of design is fully reflected across the spectrum of British industry?

296

24

The Decline of Marketing

'The lessons from successful international competitors have not been learned and firms are still talking of manufacturing costs and prices as the only critical influences in world markets.'
Tony McBurnie, director general of the Institute of Marketing, 1987

'The best brains have not been attracted to the vital job of selling.'
Sir John Harvey-Jones, BBC Dimbleby Lecture, 1987

MARKETING FAILINGS

Criticism of British companies' interest and expertise in marketing was widespread amongst industrialists in our survey. Their criticisms are backed up by academics and the Institute of Marketing itself.

The most commonly highlighted deficiencies were seen as:

- The lack of a marketing strategy in many companies.
- Defensive marketing reactions to aggressive foreign competition.
- Poor market intelligence systems making an effective corporate marketing response difficult to achieve.
- A poor division of marketing functions within companies.
- Excessive emphasis on price and cost competitiveness.

These criticisms were backed by a 1986 survey reported in *Chief Executive* which concluded that 'the general standard of salesmanship in this country is mediocre'. It attached the blame to 'the way sales forces are recruited, trained, motivated, supported, and above all, used'.

These problems were further highlighted in a 1987 report by the School of Industrial and Business Studies at the University of Warwick. The report studied forty-five British, American and Japanese companies competing in four markets: hi-fi, machine tools, household electrical goods and office equipment. It concluded: 'Most British companies lacked any coherent marketing strategy. They lacked ambition and commitment to market share, and reacted defensively to the Japanese penetration of their markets . . . Often their products had no competitive advantages and they were left with the lower-priced, down-market segments.'

The American companies were also criticised in the Warwick report, though their marketing inadequacies were generally less than the British companies'. For example, it was shown that 47 per cent of British, 40 per cent of American and 13 per cent of the Japanese companies were unclear about the main types of customers in the market and what their needs were.

Considering the importance of market segmentation and positioning in modern marketing strategies, the comments of British managers in the survey make depressing reading. One observed: 'I don't know if we segment the market or how we really position ourselves against the competition, but I expect our advertising agency knows . . . I think we are probably up-market because we advertise in some very posh magazines.' Another said, 'We have not broken the customers down. We have always held the opinion that the market is wide . . . and the product has wide appeal, therefore why break the market down at all?'

Criticism of Britain's marketing expertise has frequently been expressed. A British Commission in the 1880s drew unfavourable comparisons with Germany. Germany, it said, showed a 'knowledge of markets, desire to meet the tastes of consumers, determination and tenacity' and was 'gaining ground on British business', while UK companies continued to aim for large existing markets rather than seeking out new ones.

In 1951 the shortcomings of basic British marketing in the United States were covered in the magazine *Marketing*. The critic observed: 'I am afraid that we think about packaging in a functional kind of way, which gives the American consumer the illusion that our goods are dowdy or old fashioned. While we pursue the elegantly functional idea and the Americans go for flashy luxury, I can't see our stuff getting a place on the sales counter.' The journal also featured a claim that the British 'had been too timid and too reluctant to preach salesmanship as the foundation of success, and so it was that many looked upon it as some unpleasant growth of modern civilisation'. Another crystal-ball gazer noted: 'With the rebirth of Japan and Germany as world manufacturing powers, and the remarkable growth of new ones like India, to cite only one, we with the nation's goods to sell have a job before us which is going to be steadily tougher and tougher.'

Tony McBurnie, director general of the Institute of Marketing, provides further damning and more up-to-date evidence of Britain's marketing myopia. He points to what he calls 'the two-thirds syndrome':

● Two thirds of British companies admit they are not good at marketing.

299

- Two thirds of British companies do not use market research, do not carry out planned design and development of new products and do not train their sales force.

- Two thirds of British managing directors have no marketing or sales experience.

McBurnie illustrates the situation by pointing to Britain's sixteenth place in the international marketing league. He declares:

> There is no longer any doubt that marketing performance is the Achilles heel of many UK companies . . . After six years of productivity and manufacturing efficiency gains, many UK companies improved their cost competitiveness quite dramatically. But this did not produce the expected improvement in sales volume and market share, and with increasing costs, particularly on labour, hard-earned competitiveness is now being dissipated and profits are falling. Plant closures, labour shedding, product range reductions and all the other rationalisation moves are back again on many board agendas, as they move into another downward spiral of the vicious circle.
>
> The reason in many cases is a lack of awareness of how the market environment has changed, with new, high value-added products, aggressive competitors, and enhanced customer expectations. Tired, obsolescent products and inadequately trained and motivated sales forces do not satisfy such expectations.

The chairman of the British Overseas Trade Board, Sir James Cleminson, has also claimed that the chief complaint about UK exporters is that their marketing efforts are neither as consistent nor as persistent as our competitors. Companies, he has said, do not visit foreign markets often enough and, when they do, fail to send senior enough executives.

Of major concern must be the state and status of industrial marketing which the Institute of Marketing (IM) has referred to as a 'Cinderella in the world of marketing'. Said one of its reports, 'all the evidence suggests that the industrial manufacturing sector in general neither fully understands the markets in which it competes nor appreciates the role that effective marketing can play in generating strong, internationally competitive business.'

The marketing limitations of manufacturing industry were blamed on:

- Large sections of manufacturing being dominated by small companies which simply cannot afford large marketing departments.

- The tendency of manufacturing companies to have relatively small numbers of customers and thus assume that they had a good knowledge of them.

- The general decline of manufacturing industry.

- The high costs involved in changing the infrastructure of manufacturing companies so that their products could be tailored to customer requirements.

The commonly held belief that British innovatory expertise is not matched by marketing skills is backed by anecdotal evidence. Examples abound of marketing failures. Clive Sinclair's electrical car is a famous case. Though the technology behind the machine was advanced, the car was launched in the middle of a British winter when even the most hardened driver would have been unenthusiastic about braving the elements in its open design. Sinclair wrapped up and took to the nation's roads, but suffered the consequences of trying to sell a product the market simply did not want.

A British software company also had a similar experience when taking a domestically successful product to the US. It received a favourable response from the American trade press, but sales were low. The reason was that the company had failed to look into the market – it did not realise that American distributors insist on standardised packaging which its product did not have.

Comparisons with Japanese companies reveal how much ground needs to be made up by British companies. The University of Warwick's survey demonstrated some of the advantages held by Japanese companies. It showed that Japanese marketing in Britain involved:

- A more long-term outlook than British firms.

- Fast market adaptation.

- Greater aggression.

- A clear view of their customers.

- Fast product development.

Japanese companies, such as the watch company Citizen, have clearly-defined marketing aims. Citizen's two key goals are 'to become number one in all it does, and to increase market share in all its products.' The British motorcycle market provides a demonstration of how the Japanese approach has worked. Initially they aimed at the low-cost end of the market. Once they had gained a reputation for reliability and innovation, they expanded to large luxury bikes. The British motorcycle industry has, as a result, been all but wiped out.

The Japanese also afford greater importance and status to the skill of salesmanship than the British do. Pauline Moylan of the Institute of Sales and Marketing Management recently observed, 'The public does not view the sales person as a skilled negotiator and communicator, and selling does not enjoy the same status in the UK as it does in Japan or the United States, or even West Germany.'

This view is supported by remuneration statistics. A British Institute of Management survey of salaries in 1987 showed that marketing and sales managers received the lowest pay rises of any management group.

25

The Rise of Marketing

'We all need to learn more about achieving greater market share, sales and profits. I believe the single most important way to do this is by understanding and using marketing. That means researching into what customers want, focusing precisely on what they need, understanding markets, developing business objectives, and positioning strategies in line with your resources, to meet those needs.'
Sir Ralph Halpern, chief executive, Burton Group, CBI Conference, 1986

'If UK business is to take full advantage of an improved economic climate, it will be necessary for management to reconsider and re-evaluate the traditional components of marketing effectiveness and to refashion them in the light of the needs of the mid-1980s and beyond.'
Marketing in the UK, a report by the Institute of Marketing, 1984

MARKETING A PRIORITY

Management guru Peter Drucker regards marketing and innovation as the sole functions of business. Indeed, in a growing number of agile and dynamic companies, such as Casio or Britain's Amstrad, manufacturing has become largely subcontractual.

The drive to compete in international markets has elevated marketing in many companies from a role of pure promotional support to one of central strategic importance. The Institute of Marketing's Tony McBurnie sees marketing as a top priority: 'Most organisations have solved the problems of poor industrial relations, manufacturing inefficiency and overmanning which dogged their profitability prior to 1979. Now they realise that the only route left for profit improvement and growth is through an increased share of existing markets or the exploration of new ones. They are therefore looking to marketing people to take the lead in achieving this.'

The belief in the effectiveness of combining quick responses to market changes with long-term strategies may well be spreading. Says Dennis Urquart, marketing director of Bass, 'You have to think in the long term, rather than of the quick buck, to create a steady flow in profit growth. You have to have a clear idea of where your company's strengths are relative to your competitors'. Our field intelligence means that we can respond. We have the skills to evaluate and research changes in the industry. After all, you can't sell anything without market research.'

Some successful companies have, in fact, altered the orientation of their strategy completely to make more effective use of marketing. Tootal, the British textile group, is one such company. After struggling throughout the 1970s, Tootal was forced to close factories and sell off loss-making subsidiaries. Recovery was delayed as the company fought off the attentions of the Australian textiles group, Entrad, in 1985. The arrival of Geoffrey Maddrell, formerly of Bowater-Scott, as managing director provided a complete shift in emphasis. Maddrell, a business school strategist in the mould of Courtaulds' Christopher Hogg, gave Tootal a new mission statement. This sets the scene for 'a worldwide marketing organisation built upon providing excellent design, service and distribution skills'.

Achieving such a change in emphasis and direction was a considerable challenge in an organisation the size of Tootal which had fifty operating companies. The first step was a complete reorganisation of senior management. A group and management board were established so that group decisions could be made whilst the day-to-day decisions remained with the operational heads of the divisions. This was backed by a large training programme – the companies spent £500,000 in 1987 on management training alone. The Tootal plan is to diversify into industries which require similar marketing and distribution skills as its own traditional textile base. It has already acquired Sandhurst Marketing, a stationery and office equipment supplier, and plans to continue to develop its marketing expertise.

The rebirth of the Woolworth retail chain in Britain has also been marketing-led, with the company's emphasis changing from variety to specialisation. As part of the company's recovery, a marketing department was established for the first time with each individual unit having a clearly defined marketing strategy.

Despite such efforts calls for changes in the way we perceive and use marketing strategically continue. Loughborough University of Technology has called for a four-point improvement in British marketing:

1. **Professional marketing.** Good quality products are insufficient for success in today's highly competitive markets. Many American and British companies had these but lacked the information and professional marketing skills to exploit them through forceful segmentation and positioning strategies. Performance declined as predictable trends in market segments, competitive strategies and product developments were missed because managers lacked the knowledge base.

2. **Decisive entry strategies.** Successful companies enter markets or use new technology early because they identify clear opportunities. Many British companies tend to be sucked in reluctantly in a vain attempt to defend their businesses. American companies have their own problems, says Loughborough – they frequently wake up to global

opportunities only after their own home market shows signs of saturation.

3. **Commitment to market share.** All the successful businesses in the sample had ambitious market share objectives. They developed broad product ranges and marketing policies to achieve these goals over the longer run. Companies whose top management focused too closely on short-term profits invariably lost market position to more aggressive competitors. This was especially marked in higher growth markets.

4. **Organisational commitment.** The top management of successful companies exhibited greater professionalism and commitment. This appeared to be the result of structuring the organisation around individual products and geographic entities, of a belief in group involvement in strategy formulation, and of continuous, informal monitoring of progress in the market.

To bring about changes Tony McBurnie calls on action from all quarters:

More chief executives need to change their own and their companies' thinking towards the market place, and to the preparation of aggressive, carefully thought through marketing strategies.

More government investment in marketing support is needed to strengthen medium-sized and small companies, with the inevitable payback in jobs from increased manufacturing output needed to meet increased sales volume.

More executives need to be trained in the fundamentals of marketing and how to improve their performance in the market-place.

More emphasis is needed on developing the marketing strategies and effective organisations to match the needs of a fast-changing market environment and less on ad hoc use of marketing tools, tactics and jargon.

More effort is needed to communicate the critical impact of marketing performance on economic prosperity, employment and company profitability, to Parliament, business, the City, academia, the media and public at large.

More thought needs to be given to attracting bright young people into the excitement and satisfaction of a career in marketing.

The Institute points to many companies where marketing has proved a foundation for success. JCB, Europe's leading construction engineering company, is one such company. It has managed to hold off its larger

American and Japanese rivals by learning as much as possible about their products, plans, strengths and weaknesses. Competing products are examined and dismantled so that they can be better understood and their standards exceeded.

The Coventry engineering company, AE, has also recorded healthy profits as a result of a close attention to marketing. It has a comprehensive five-year plan for existing and potential markets which is updated by monthly reviews gathered from extensive market research.

There are other more generally positive signs that marketing is assuming a more substantial role in British companies. Budgets allotted to marketing departments have risen – in 1986 *Marketing* reported that 81 per cent of marketing managers had bigger budgets than the previous year. There is, perhaps, also increased optimism amongst marketing professionals. Initiatives to encourage marketing have been widespread – the Institute of Marketing now has a register of marketing consultants and the 1985 CBI Conference saw the launch of a joint initiative with the IM to promote marketing excellence and raise awareness among chief executives.

A 1987 Institute of Marketing survey of chief executives in The Times top 1,000 companies made optimistic reading. Of the executives:

- 64 per cent spent more time on marketing and selling aspects of their business than on any other activity;

- 46 per cent were seeking to expand into new markets in the next five years, twice the figure for the past five years;

- 57 per cent had experience in marketing, again almost twice the level of seven years ago.

The examples of marketing-led success may well accelerate marketing awareness. Companies like 3M, Black and Decker, Johnson and Johnson, Beecham, Clark's and Rowntree spend a great deal of time and money in analysing market needs and their competitive environment. The approaches differ – 3M emphasises market-linked R & D; Black and Decker identifies market opportunities and tailors its products to take advantage of them – but the level of marketing awareness and sensitivity in all functions is often a common bond between successful organisations.

These improvements are supported by Professor Michael Baker, former chairman of the Institute of Marketing, who has observed: 'More and more young people are now receiving formal marketing education at

307

universities, polytechnics and colleges and this will help raise the professional standard of marketing in the longer term.' Professor Bernard Taylor, editor of *Long Range Planning*, has also perceived a change in attitude, while lamenting the time it has taken: 'It seems incredible after twenty years of lip-service that at last marketing seems to be catching on.'

Even so, some of the negative aspects apparent in British marketing were again brought up by executives we talked to. It was thought market research could be put to better use and there was an over-reliance on internally generated market data rather than primary external information. Specialist advice, particularly that of market research agencies, was not fully utilised.

Tailoring corporate culture and creativity for marketing ends, as well as developing commitment to marketing needs, remains a demanding task. In a previous book, *The Marketing Edge*, we identified the common denominators of companies with a successful track record of marketing as:

- Chief executive commitment
- Clearly defined objectives
- Understanding the market environment
- Assessing assets
- Market segmentation
- Knowing the competition
- Competitive advantage
- Open-minded perspectives
- Marketing personnel
- Dedication

Assessing these characteristics in relation to British companies is virtually impossible, but it is likely that a fairly small number actually have all of them.

The message in marketing must be the same as in design and quality – but growing awareness of the possible advantages of marketing has not, as yet, translated itself into increased marketing expertise at the level needed for British companies to be internationally competitive, especially in manufacturing industry.

In his commentary on a 1984 IM survey of marketing executives, marketing consultant and author Aubrey Wilson presented an overview of how marketing has, in some respects, finished up where it began:

Once the marketing concept penetrated the conscience of management, particularly top management, and once the realisation had occurred that selling is not marketing, then the rush to get marketing-orientated was on. Marketing was trumpeted from the prayer towers of industry as the only true faith; it was offered from the shrines of business as the miraculous cure for all ills; it was propounded in rhetorical, if Delphic, terms as the arbiter of fates of corporations. And when all the words and all the actions had been sifted and analysed, management could be seen sitting in precisely the same posture as they had been before the thought of marketing struck them.

To keep the wheels of the marketing revolution turning requires, says the IM, 'a major task of education'.

26

The Decline of the City

'London's preoccupation is one for returns rather than for maintaining capital. Still less is the City concerned with sustaining British industry.'
Ralf Dahrendorf, On Britain, 1982

'For years, established institutions largely sheltered from the effects of Britain's loss of power, influence and wealth have oozed cosy analyses of the reasons for our industrial decline. Their collective views on the subject have been lent an air of credibility through constant repetition, but in reality they have helped to accelerate the rate of economic decline rather than stem it.'
Merrick Taylor, managing director, Motor Panels, 1987

'We now have a financial system that has almost stopped serving the industrial interests of our nation.'
Neil Kinnock, Leader of the Opposition, during the 1987 General Election campaign

THE CITY: PROBLEM OR SOLUTION?

The markets, financial institutions and professional services offered by the City of London have variously been described as one of the chief perpetrators of economic decline and, as they have burgeoned in recent years, the nation's saviour. The question rarely answered is whether the City is part of the problem or the possible solution.

Criticism of the role played by the City is based on a number of perceptions:

- The City is preoccupied with short-term financial success to the detriment of long-term industrial prosperity.

- Takeovers, fuelled by City enthusiasm, are not the best way for industry to expand successfully.

- The City fails to provide adequate support for small and medium-sized businesses.

- Industry and the City are irreversibly separated and are unable to communicate their aspirations and requirements to each other.

SHORT-TERMISM

For once there is cross-party agreement. All of the major political parties have been critical of what they see as the short-term perspectives of the City in recent times. The City's case has not been helped by the increased news coverage of its activities after the Guinness scandal, which has provoked far greater scrutiny of the way in which the City deals with industrialists. The voices of industrialists and politicians are increasingly to be heard.

The Labour Party's *Making the City Safe* (March 1987) observed:

Many industrial companies find it [the City] values their shares by present profits rather than future prospects, and that those who fail this test are vulnerable to takeover. The perverse result is to inhibit management from investment in research and development which will only show a return in the long term, for fear that the necessary reduction in distributed profits will reduce share prices in the short term. Thus the short-term perspectives which the City adopts in share dealing obliges industry to manage on the same short-term horizon.

Equally critical of short-term perspectives was the Liberal Party's *Investing in our Future: Tackling Short-termism in the British Economy* (September 1986). It claimed: 'The City has a short-term approach . . . Such attitudes from the investment community act as a real deterrent to company managements from the taking of the long view. The new growth is often pruned rather than the dead wood. What Harold Macmillan, fifty years ago, called "casino capitalism" is not serving British industry well.'

Even the Chancellor of the Exchequer, Nigel Lawson, has drawn attention to limited City views. In June 1986, he said, 'Quite apart from the positive benefits of individual share ownership, the big institutional investors nowadays increasingly react to short-term pressure on investment performance. As a consequence many British industrial managers complain that their institutional shareholders are unwilling to countenance long-term investment or sufficient expenditure on research and development.'

Criticism also comes from industrialists. Sir Colin Corness, chairman of Redland, attributes some of the blame for Britain's relative industrial decline to the prevailing attitudes in the City. He identifies 'a lack of a sense of urgency within the City' as a significant factor and adds, 'This neglect can be partly attributed to complacency arising from historical factors such as the Industrial Revolution and the wealth generated out of the former British Empire; but it must also be seen in the context of the way in which our financial systems favour short-term returns rather than long-term investment, as in Japan and West Germany.'

Sir Alex Jarratt, chairman of Smiths Industries, also supports this view. Says Jarratt:

A weakness that has contributed to the problems of manufacturing industry in this country is that of our length of vision. I acknowledge immediately that external circumstances have often not helped here – the era of rapidly rising inflation; the more recent period of acute volatility in currencies and interest rates; major changes in government policies, certainly as between the major political parties, but also by government during their periods of office.

It has increasingly shown itself in financial markets and has done so in two ways. First, the importance attached to short-term performance by stock-brokers' analysts, the business columns of the press and institutional fund managers – each being fuelled in turn by a public, including the trustees of our own company pension funds, seeking the maximum return in the shortest possible time. Secondly, we now have the phenomenon of financial flows crossing the world at the speed of a micro-chip, seeking the marginally higher returns that may be available, and far outweighing in value and importance – in terms of their effects on currencies and interest rates – the flow of physical goods in world trade.

None of this encourages long-term thinking and planning, sometimes the very reverse.

Malcolm Bruce of the Social and Liberal Democrats is damning when asked about the City. Says Bruce:

I regard the City as a necessary evil. Its workings are erratic and it is divorced from industry. They mix in different circles, even in terms of social contacts. They live in a hothouse environment, making judgements often based on short-term results and fashion rather than long-term paybacks. Industry loses out because it has not been sufficiently fashionable. It is far too concentrated in one tiny corner of the country, with the result that it doesn't know how people elsewhere live or what makes them tick.

Roy Grantham of APEX points to the different requirements of the City and industry. Says Grantham: 'The gap between industry's need to plough back and the City's need for dividends is difficult to bridge, especially now that companies can't differentiate between distributed and undistributed profits. Now if they need investment cash they have to borrow.'

Economic, social and geographical isolation, even elitism, were common complaints of the City amongst those we talked to. Merrick Taylor, managing director of Motor Panels, recounts one of many anecdotes displaying the gulf in understanding which often seems to exist between industry and the City:

At a recent dinner attended by eminent representatives of the major political, financial and educational institutions I posed a simple industrial problem.

A medium-sized engineering firm wants to borrow £500,000 for an investment for which there is no collateral yet which has the unanimous support of its management and board. The payback is estimated to be six or seven years. It cannot be guaranteed – and there is a less risky short-term alternative.

Industrialists apart, my dinner companions guffawed at the absurdity of the proposal, until I said that the aim of the project was training. At that stage, a thoughtful silence fell in the room.

'But we all know that funding training is an impossible equation, which is why government should step in,' I was told.

Now it was the turn of the industrialists to laugh. For them, training was just one of at least ten 'impossible equations' facing the average wealth-creating industrialist every day.

Age-old grievances, such as the problems of short-term investment, unreasonable demands for high returns, an obsession with bottom line results, and the need for the finance sector to do more to help industry, were repeatedly voiced by our industrialists. The prevailing view was that firms do not get a fair deal from the City.

Even though the fundamental changes in the financial sector highlighted by the 'Big Bang' have served to provide a focus for dialogue between industry and the City, the divide between the two sectors is as great as ever. British companies clearly continue to claim the City does not do enough to help them; the City continues to retort that industry still fails to market itself properly and that many problems arise because it has a poor grasp of the mechanisms of the financial sector. Only one thing is clear – the two sectors disagree about the nature of their responsibilities and misunderstand the economic and financial considerations governing their actions.

EXAMPLES OF LACK OF CITY SUPPORT

For some companies short-term City perspectives have affected their ability to raise much-needed capital. Tom Lloyd of the *Financial Weekly* was involved in a management buy-out of the magazine. It turned to a Swedish company for

315

finance; support was simply not available in Britain. As Lloyd says, 'We tried to get venture capital in the UK. Although I knew some of the venture capital guys quite well, I was very disappointed. I don't think they realised what wonderful operational gearing there is in publishing once you pass break even. Most of them moaned about our being a one-product company.'

The trade union bank, Unity Trust, has attempted to fill the breach left by lack of City enthusiasm for some projects. Its Employee Share Ownership Programmes (ESOPs) are discussed in the chapter on Industrial Relations. They have already provided an alternative means of funding for a number of companies after attempts at wooing City institutions failed.

At City Vehicle Engineering, a company being established in Shildon, County Durham, to make minibuses, a Unity Trust ESOP covered a shortfall in equity needs of £3 million. This not only solved the funding problem, but created a constant incentive for future employees.

At the former British Rail Engineering subsidiary, Doncaster Wagon Works, Unity Trust also emerged to provide financial support. A management consortium of four, led by site manager Steve Hinton, found little joy when approaching City institutions to finance a buy-out. The fact that all were long-term employees of the company and had a wealth of experience counted for little. Said Hinton: 'There was a very definite attitude that as managers in a nationalised concern such as BR we did not possess enough experience or skill to run a commercial enterprise.' With support from Unity Trust and Yorkshire Enterprise, the buy-out eventually went ahead and over 600 jobs were secured in one of the nation's most depressed areas.

A dramatic example of the City's apparent lack of industrial acumen was provided by the demise of Stone Platt Industries in 1982. The company, formerly one of Britain's major textile machinery operations, was placed in the hands of the receiver after the City withdrew its support. This came at a time when, in the opinion of many, the company had a realistic chance of returning to profitability in the near future.

Stone Platt's chairman, Leslie Pincott, observed at the time of the company's collapse, 'I am worried about the fact that the system cannot help an engineering company with technology and hard-working people.' He later was to conclude: 'Something is deeply wrong with the system.'

The case of Amstrad demonstrates the fickleness of some City analysts. When Amstrad's chief executive, Alan Sugar, warned that the company's monumental growth would not continue at the same rate the company's share price fell and has never recovered its previous high price. Sugar, however, was not being pessimistic, but simply pointing out that extraordinary levels of success cannot carry on indefinitely. Amstrad's share price remains at 65 per cent of the market average, at the time of writing.

MERGER MANIA?

The emphasis on so-called 'merger mania' is something which undoubtedly has a double edge. The City can hardly be criticised for widening its services, but the feeling among a number of our respondents was that time and money spent on mergers would be better spent elsewhere.

According to Roy Grantham, we are paying the price of the City's success. Says Grantham: 'Our industrial culture suffers from the most successful City in the world. If your company is successful, it will take over or be taken over by someone else. If it is unsuccessful, you will get taken over. This isn't true, by and large, in Germany or Japan. Companies that grow in those countries are the ones that plough back the money.'

In the United States and the UK, a growing number of mergers and acquisitions have run alongside a bull market in shares, rising profits and the assumption of debt to finance acquisitions. The mergers and acquisitions have often taken place under a climate of bitter and highly expensive antipathy, with companies jealously attempting to preserve their independence. This is, perhaps, demonstrated by the fact that of the record number of mergers referred to the Monopolies and Mergers Commission in 1986, a mere four received approval.

The CBI's City/Industry Task Force in 1987 had deep reservations about the acquisitive trend. Its report observed, 'There remain real concerns among CBI members at the power of the market, the uncertainty of long-term commitment, and the effective disregard of the other stakeholders in a business when decisions affecting a company's future are being determined.'

Attention has also been focused on the growing costs of mergers, which reached £500 million in 1985 alone. Says one business observer: 'The

317

investment institutions and the various professionals in the City benefit enormously from the underwriting costs and fees of a merger. Naturally, they don't welcome any disruption to the smooth running of the goldmine.' Indeed, fees for merger and acquisition activity have begun to play an increasingly important part in the earnings of both merchant banks and stockbrokers in recent years.

This is hardly surprising – Guinness' £2.4 billion bid for Distillers, for example, cost £110 million. Most of these expenses are generated by professional fees, printing offer documents and underwriting costs. Alarmingly, the cost of defending against a takeover bid is also escalating rapidly. Woolworth, for example, spent almost £16 million chasing off Dixons, which ironically only spent £11.7 million on the takeover. 'Unfortunately, in many cases, the takeover has such a traumatic effect on companies that they will agree to pay any price to rid themselves of a predator,' says a merchant banker.

The Governor of the Bank of England, Robin Leigh-Pemberton, has also expressed concern. Addressing an Industrial Society seminar in June 1987, he observed: 'I have been concerned when predators have sought to use a minority shareholding to unsettle a perfectly well-managed company and to create an atmosphere in which a bid becomes daily expected. Such activity can amount to a thoroughly irresponsible exercise of shareholder power.'

The City attitude can be double-edged. Hanson Trust has, for example, criticised the City for under-valuing its shares and Lonrho had a poor relationship with the City for a number of years. The bigger companies become, the less, it seems, the City is prepared to make allowances. Growing by way of acquisition is all very well, but suitable companies may not be available at the right time. Large companies like GEC can become, in the eyes of the City, lethargic cash monsters lacking the dynamism required to achieve short-term profits.

Not all the criticism is directed towards the City. The wisdom of successive governments' merger policies is being widely questioned because it is seen to ignore the implications for the competitiveness of British companies overseas. The length of time investigations by the Monopolies and Mergers Commission take has also been criticised.

It can be argued that the growth in takeovers is, in itself, encouraging the taking of short-term perspectives. Companies, shareholders and City institutions become obsessed with short-term performance of dividends and share prices, effectively prohibiting companies from making long-term investment in R & D. Management time is taken up fighting off takeover attempts. It means that effort is focused on defence rather than on making the business grow.

318

27

The Rise of the City

'Behind the changes of the Big Bang, the internationalisation of capital markets, privatisation and the bull market itself, there are solid achievements being made in the provision of finance for growing companies.'
Graham Bannock, in the 3i report, Enterprise reborn?, 1987

'The Task Force found no evidence to link attitudes of the City directly to the long-run decline of the nation's manufacturing sector – nor to its resurgence in recent years.'
CBI City/Industry Task Force, 1987

THE EXPANDING CITY

As manufacturing industry has declined, the City institutions have rapidly expanded. Banking, finance and insurance now account for 10 per cent of total employment in Britain. This is compared to 7.1 per cent in 1979 and ignores the employment created by spin-off activities.

Despite this eyecatching growth and profusion of new services and activities, favourable remarks about the City from our survey respondents were hard won. One commentator recently said of the City: 'It is thriving much as a drug company thrives in an epidemic.' Opinions of industrialists were generally along the lines of 'it's about time it changed and started listening to us'. Says Sir Francis Tombs: 'Even the City is gradually becoming more adaptive to the needs of industry and more aware of its problems.'

The Wilson Committee on the Role of Financial Institutions in 1980 discovered that widely held preconceptions of the City are often more important than the reality. The report claimed that contrary to expectations there was no shortage of capital available to companies. Industry's dissatisfaction with the City's performance had more to do with the entrenched and inaccurate attitudes of businesses themselves than with economic reality.

A more recent survey by the National Economic Development Council about the availability of capital for businesses revealed that similar misconceptions still exist. A section of the survey examined why some companies had chosen not to seek additional finance, even though this meant limiting their growth. These companies believed that approaching the City for finance would be a costly, lengthy procedure, which would probably entail at least a partial loss of control. While there may be some truth in these fears, the survey concluded that this view is exaggerated.

The CBI's City/Industry Task Force attempted to debunk some of the common misconceptions of the City. It was widely castigated for its final report, which refused to apportion blame for Britain's relative industrial decline to the City alone. One of the chief perceptions debunked by the CBI report was the idea that the threat to morale or security posed by merger-mania was all-pervasive in industry. A CBI survey of chief executives in 1987 showed that few are intimidated by the threat of takeover. The table below shows its results:

Constraints on long-term investment

Percentage of respondents mentioning:	Of major significance	Significant	Not significant
Shortage of capital	5	10	85
Cost of capital and/or fears of an inadequate rate of return	24	53	23
Exchange rate uncertainties	2	26	72
A lack of confidence in market prospects	9	39	52
Weakness in your share price or rating	7	34	59
Fear of takeover	0	12	88
Pressure from financial institutions/ analysts	4	19	77

The lack of perceived concern about takeover threats has been supported by research by Deloitte Haskins and Sells conducted in April 1987. Its survey showed that a minority of companies believe that the City inhibits industry. Mergers, takeovers and asset stripping were also seen as the least potent of the five reasons put forward as causes for deferring investment.

The CBI report argues that the amount of money spent on mergers and acquisitions (£13.5 billion in 1986) has to be compared with money spent on fixed investment in R & D and training (£25 billion in 1986). It also points out that City institutions are prone to support incumbent management rather than invaders. Between 1983 and 1986, it estimated that only a third of contested bids succeeded. The report provides a reminder that the threat of takeover can actually improve business performance and concludes, 'The view that it is the financial system in the UK that has caused companies to focus on the short term, rather than on investment for the longer term, is not substantiated by the evidence.'

The conclusions of the CBI Task Force were:

● Many British companies have given insufficient weight to long-term development but this does not arise primarily from City pressures. It arises mainly from underlying economic and political factors, including inadequate profitability.

● Most financial institutions (which own around 60 per cent of UK equities) are long-term investors, not surprisingly in view of the long-term nature of their obligations. Moreover, the shareholders' average holding period is not the critical issue; it is company time horizons, and their readiness to invest for the longer term, that matter.

● There is no general shortage of funds for good small or high-risk ventures, though financing costs are sometimes high.

● The cost of City facilities has fallen since the Big Bang, as competitive pressures have had their effect.

● Managers of companies under threat of takeover do not defer investments to enhance their current earnings. Indeed, the threat can be a spur to management performance. However, acquisitions are not necessarily the best way of improving management; they can be expensive and are also risky for predators.

To solve some of these difficulties, the Task Force highlighted the need for effective communications. It suggested that solutions could be achieved by:

● Companies making more effort themselves to keep the market informed about their longer-term strategic intentions and in particular about spending on research and development, as well as training and other aspects of innovation. A voluntary approach is far preferable to statutory intervention which will introduce unwarranted inflexibility and legal complexity.

● Financial analysts being better trained in the skills necessary to provide a strategic assessment of a company's prospects, particularly at the more senior level. At present, the quality of analysts can appear very uneven.

● Independent non-executive directors comprising at least a sizeable minority on all but the smallest public company boards, adding to the range of skills and experience available to the company. There may even be exceptional circumstances when it is desirable for a non-executive director to play a role in communicating shareholders' concerns about management performance to the chairman and/or chief executive.

- Discussion between company managements and the trustees of their pension funds on the ways in which the funds fulfil their responsibilities as shareholders, in addition to their responsibilities to members and pensioners.

- Institutional links between the City and Industry being strengthened. The CBI plans to enhance its own ability to contribute to and follow up the debate on City and Industry relations.

The CBI report followed on from a more critical study carried out for the Committee on Finance for Industry and the Electronics Economic Development Council in September 1986. It examined the issue of availability of finance for medium-sized firms in high growth sectors. On the whole, the report found that there was considerable scope for financial institutions and businesses to help each other function better, mainly through the former supplying more information and the latter having a better grasp of the equity market and forms of negotiating.

Although almost all of the companies succeeded in gaining either loan or equity capital, a disturbingly high proportion were dissatisfied with the treatment they received. Many businesses felt the terms offered were unfairly weighted in the favour of the investor. The report found, however, that companies were often ignorant of the way their investors calculated the equity base. Also, their bargaining position was weakened because they had approached only one source of finance, so they were unable to assess the competitiveness of the offer they received. In many cases, companies applied for the wrong type of finance, frequently underestimating the advantage of relinquishing equity.

A large number of companies felt that their situation and needs had not been understood by the source of finance. They were also inclined to expect greater assistance and support than investors were willing to provide. They felt that many of the institutions regarded the investment as nothing more than a commodity.

As the COFFIE report reflects, the differing expectations of the services that the City should provide to industry are a major bone of contention. Many financial organisations feel that they are caught in a cleft stick; on the one hand, companies expect hand-holding, especially if they lack expertise in such crucial areas as marketing or financial planning. On the other hand, businesses are often overly sensitive to the amount of involvement from an investing organisation, and accuse it of interfering.

Although the issue is still fiercely controversial, it is slowly becoming accepted that it is justifiable to expect the City to provide non-financial

323

support as well as cash. Sir Monty Finniston comments: 'Investment is not just a question of financial resources. Small and medium-sized companies frequently lack specialist skills. The City can do all sorts of things to improve industry's performance by providing help, advice and better monitoring of business' need and difficulties.'

Although the COFFIE report focuses solely on the experiences and perceptions of businesses, it makes a number of recommendations to both the City and industry.

To firms seeking medium-term finance, it recommends that:

● Growth-orientated firms plan their financial requirements ahead and research into different forms of external finance at an early stage.

● Firms ensure they accept the most appropriate and competitive packages by approaching several institutions.

● Firms hire professional advice.

To the financial institutions, it recommends that:

● They should communicate their investment criteria at the earliest possible stage, what kind of detailed data should be included in a proposal and the range of terms open to a company.

● They should publicise more widely the range of financing options available.

● They should recognise the importance of rapidly processing applications and speed up negotiations.

● They should clarify their agreement with the company in which they invest and explain the basis on which the structure of the offer is arrived at.

● They should outline why they refuse to give finance to a company.

Calls for change are widespread but, despite criticism of the role and organisation of the City, the system, with its shortcomings, remains. David Walker of the Bank of England struck a suitably realistic note at the 1986 CBI Conference when he observed:

I regret the polarisation between City and industry often found in discussion on this subject. Relationships between finance and industry are complex, and to say that there are no easy solutions to problems that arise is neither to duck the issue nor to be complacent. It is just realistic. Equally, whatever attraction some have seen in the past in other systems, such as the universal banks in Germany, we have to work with the capital market-based system that we have in this country and, if we are not satisfied with it, make it work better.

Achieving longer-term perspectives within City institutions is, in the opinion of many industrialists, absolutely essential. Merrick Taylor spells out the equation:

Investing in boom . . . is highly inflationary, as companies suck in labour to meet a rise in market demand. When the boom is over, they are left with hefty overhead costs financing capacity far in excess of that they require, and cash flow problems as the banks draw in their loans. They are also left with an out-of-date product ill-placed in a sharply competitive market, which results in declining sales.

But this philosophy has been imposed by British financial institutions with unswerving dedication for over three decades. It has played havoc with industry's cost and labour relations, and regularly leaves the economists marvelling because the prescription has failed to cure the disease.

We cannot continue to blame yesterday's symptoms for our industrial decline, as long as eminent institutions exercise control devoid of creativity.

A first step towards greater understanding would be better and more effective communications between the City and industry. Sir David Plastow, chairman of Vickers, has forcefully expressed this point: 'I would like to see a commitment to communication between the City and industry – then perhaps we can dispense with such nonsense as short-termism and talk of divisions between City and business.'

The entire argument is put into industrial perspective by Sir Hector Laing of United Biscuits:

Success for any enterprise requires that all concerned with it should have a clearly defined common objective. Most people who work in industry now seem to recognise the interdependence of management and employees but I think we have to question whether the difference of perspective between managers of a company and its institutional owners is not detrimental to national economic progress. Where the owners of an enterprise are those who manage it, the goal and means of achieving it do not come into conflict. For a publicly quoted company, however, with proprietary control in the hands of a relatively small number of institutional fund managers, there is a danger of divergent

325

goals, or at least of different timescales. Because the fund manager's performance appears to be measured in a short time-scale, he may have little choice but to focus on short-term gain which is incompatible with sound industrial management and can be positively harmful.

The responsibility of investment managers is of course to obtain the best possible performance out of the monies under their control as required by their client who could well be a company pension fund. Thirty-three per cent of shareholdings in UK quoted companies are owned by pension funds and it may be that fund managers have not been asked to view their responsibility as being to both the working members of the companies in which they have a stake and to pension fund members, especially the same people. It is time to rethink the balance of responsibilities between those who manage companies and those who own them.

Industrial managements, as investors in respect of their own pension funds, expect to see those funds performing well, without considering whether or not that means the fund managers operating short-term. As industrial managers, however, they expect their institutional share-holders, in essence those same fund managers, to take a long-term view with regard to the company's profit performance. Industrial manage-ments as pension fund trustees should perhaps take a lead in helping to set new ground rules by being more explicit about the philosophy they want followed where investment policy is concerned.

The first priority for a business is to establish a long-term profitability level which satisfies the needs of the business and its shareholders. Adequate profitability alone can provide for the risks, growth needs and jobs of tomorrow. These needs are all long-term and what is certain about commitments to the future, which are a necessity for industrial companies but not to the same extent for the financial sector, is that long-term profits are not achieved by piling up short-term gains.

Whilst earnings per share growth must be a very important criterion by which a company's performance is judged, at least as important is the underlying long-term strength and competitiveness of the business on which those earnings depend.

If a company's first concern is to keep its earnings per share growing at the fastest possible rate, it is likely to be failing to invest enough in the future security of the business – its technology, its market share and its people. More recognition thus needs to be given by fund managers to the prospective rewards to be gained from ongoing investment in state-of-the-art technology and in developing world market share. These yardsticks should always be applied alongside earnings per share to provide a balanced picture of a company's strength.

State-of-the-art technology is not a luxury – its effective assimilation is the stuff of long-term survival, and embracing relevant technology has to be a continuous and dynamic process, part of the corporate way of life. In an increasingly harsh competitive environment in the world market, companies which do not embrace new technology as part of their way of life will not remain competitive for long.

It is not difficult for a manufacturing business to maximise short-term profitability and boost earnings per share for reasons of expedience by compromising standards of quality and service and by under-investing. The price, however, is inevitable decline. As is engraved on the tombstone of many a defunct business, 'They sacrificed the long term for the short term and long term finally arrived.'

The main justification for the capitalist system is that it provides the best climate for innovation and risk-taking, but if the managers of a business are discouraged from taking risks, from undertaking research or from investment in innovation and in increasing market share, capitalism itself is put at risk.

If the managements of even our best manufacturing companies feel the need to operate their businesses to meet short-term stockmarket expectations, particularly when these are heightened by bid fever, they are unlikely to risk the financial commitment required for the technological quantum leaps which are vital to long-term competitive success.

In such circumstances, Britain will continue to lose ground against countries like Germany and Japan where the shareholders' identification with their company seems to be closer and where the Damoclean sword of opposed takeovers is still virtually unknown.

I am not calling for a radical change in our capital system or state involvement in capital management; neither am I 'laying blame'. Rather I am seeking to encourage a change in the climate of opinion in which the owners of British companies accept the responsibility of 'ownership' and take a rational, informed and reasonably long-term view of the assets which belong to them.

28

The Rise of British Industry?

'There is no room for complacency. We have built a platform for growth; now we can and must use it – by investing in the technology, infrastructure, plants and people that we will need to be competitive in [the year] 2000.'
John Banham, director general, Confederation of British Industry, 1987

'UK manufacturing is certainly leaner, fitter and more efficient than in 1979, but it is also much smaller.'
Weekly economic survey by Barclays de Zoete Wedd, July 1987

'British industry is in good shape and providing that we do not talk our way into difficulties, it is well placed to ride out the upheavals on the financial markets.'
David Wigglesworth, chairman of the CBI's economic situation committee at the CBI conference, 1987

'Manufacturing industry in the UK has come a long way since the low point we reached eight years ago. It has been a remarkable transformation and I believe it is a permanent one. The question now is, how do we sustain this momentum of growth?'
Sir Trevor Holdsworth, chairman of GKN, in the Sunday Times, *1988*

'Profitability is very low by international standards even though it has recovered strongly in recent years.'
Confederation of British Industry, 1987

THE RISE OF INDUSTRY?

● The rate of return on investment in the UK in 1965 was 11.3 per cent, compared with 23 per cent in the United States. In 1986 it was still way behind, at 8.9 per cent compared with 20 per cent in both the United States and Japan.

● The Treasury's Economic Progress Reports have shown that the average annual increase in output per head (productivity) of the employed labour force in UK manufacturing was 3.8 per cent from 1964 to 1973; 0.7 per cent in the recessionary years 1973–9; and 3.5 per cent between 1979 and 1986. By contrast the productivity growth rate for the economy as a whole during the latter period was only 1.9 per cent. While Britain's rate of growth of manufacturing productivity was the lowest by far compared with the United States, Japan, West Germany, France, Italy and Canada (which averaged 3.2 per cent) during the period 1973 to 1979, it was the highest from 1979 to 1986 (when the others averaged only 2.5 per cent).

● According to a paper by Warwick University's industrial relations unit, labour productivity in the United States was 2.67 times higher than in the UK in 1986 – a marginally smaller gap than in 1980. However, the productivity gap between Britain and Japan fell from 1.96 to 1.76 over the same period, reported the *Financial Times* (4 April, 1988).

● Britain's manufacturing output rose 5.5 per cent in 1987, the highest rate since 1973.

● At the time of writing (February 1988) manufacturing output in Britain had only just returned to the levels of 1979. Given that most other developed countries steadily increased their output between 1975 and 1983, while Britain's output fell 3 per cent over the same period, the return to 1979 levels can be seen only as an early step towards recovery.

- The UK's share of world manufacturing trade in 1979 was just under 12 per cent. Since then, it has hovered below the 10 per cent mark, only breaking above it in 1986.

- In 1979, companies in the Venture Capital Association lent £20 million to new and developing enterprises. In 1986, they lent £384 million, 22.4 per cent of it to start-ups.

- Britain's investment gap continues. In manufacturing industry, Britain invests less than £2,000 per worker in fixed capital. In comparison, West Germany spends £2,650, the United States £2,800 and France £3,200.

MAKING UP GROUND

Measured from the nadir of 1981, Britain has made up a significant amount of the ground lost to its major international competitors. Britain's 1987 economic growth rate of 4 per cent exceeded those of Japan (3.9 per cent), the US (2.7 per cent), Germany (1.5 per cent) and France (1.8 per cent) according to the Nomura Research Institute. CBI surveys regularly record increased confidence among manufacturers, while consumer spending and retail sales have shown record growth. But we still have a long way to go and, measured from the mid-seventies, we have still only reached the first rungs of the ladder of competitiveness.

The length of time required to achieve industrial regeneration has been underestimated by many. Sir John Hoskyns of the Institute of Directors believes that many people's conceptions of time are misguided: 'People are incredibly unrealistic about time. The good things happening now are only the result of decisions taken in 1979–80. Mrs Thatcher was told it would take ten years to get the economy headed in the right direction. Attitude and culture change is a slow business.'

The two-yearly report from NEDC, published in October 1987, while describing Britain's improvement in economic performance as 'encouraging', gives few grounds for complacency. It points to the value of sterling against other European currencies, the rising levels of both productivity and profitability and control of inflation as key helping factors. But it also points out that investment in capital equipment and R & D are still low by comparison with our competitors; that Britain has created fewer jobs than its main competitors, all of whom have

331

increased the number of people in full-time employment, while the UK is still struggling to reach pre-1979 levels; that wages are still rising faster than in West Germany, Japan and the United States; and that Britain is still way behind in the numbers of people taking higher education.

Hoare Govett's financial breakdown of Britain's industrial performance offers an interesting outlook. It takes historic and projected financial data on 160 major quoted companies. Together they constitute 70 per cent of the London equity market in terms of capitalisation. Under the title of 'Quoted UK plc', it gives an illuminating insight into the state of industry.

Hoare Govett's results for the first half of 1987 showed that in 160 companies, pre-tax profits increased by an average figure of 27 per cent to £26 billion. Earnings per share went up by 19 per cent. Forecasts for 1988 were optimistic, as the table below shows.

Quoted UK plc consolidated profit and loss account (£ billion)

	1986	1987	1988
Turnover	424.4	475.5	538.3
Pre-tax profit	45.7	56.9	65.2
After-tax profit	29.9	36.6	41.5
Earnings per share (indexed)	100	117	133

(Source: Quoted UK plc)

In 1984, the pre-tax profits of Quoted UK plc were £40.1 billion. The report concludes: 'Continued double-digit profit, earnings and dividend growth in each of the next five years is now a realistic target.'

Cautious optimism linked with concern about levels of investment and productivity are features of other economic surveys, too. The London Business School forecasts that manufacturing output will increase more rapidly than the economy as a whole. Warwick University's Institute for Employment Research predicts slow but steady economic growth over the next few years. However, it expects manufacturing employment to continue to fall by about 1 per cent a year. This would amount to a loss of 500,000 jobs in manufacturing by 1995.

The National Institute of Economic and Social Research also offers little hope for a decrease in unemployment. It estimates unemployment will remain at 2.8 million in 1989. On other fronts it points to a slowdown in growth with manufacturing output increasing by 1.3 per cent in 1989 and GDP by 1.5 per cent.

A recent 3i survey of the northwest found that, compared with the low point of 1982, profits in local businesses were up more than 700 per cent and the ratio of profits to sales by just over 200 per cent. But these figures disguise the decline of manufacturing in the region since 1979. Manufacturing employment fell from 971,000 to 638,000 – more than one third – and manufacturing's share of regional gross domestic product fell from 42 per cent in 1975 to 37 per cent in 1985. In Britain as a whole manufacturing as a proportion of GDP fell from 36 per cent to 31 per cent during those ten years. Nonetheless, 3i displays a great deal of confidence in the region's industrial future, claiming that those industries remaining are stronger, more broadly based and generally more secure in their markets.

Another 3i survey, *Britain in the 1980s: Enterprise Reborn?*, published in September 1987, provides a cautiously optimistic outlook. It points out that real GDP in 1986 was still only 10.5 per cent above the 1979 level and manufacturing production remained a disappointing 4.5 per cent below 1979 levels. Even so, Britain's annual growth rate now exceeds OECD averages.

Average annual percentage growth rates in real GDP of the OECD and Britain

	1950–70	1970–80	1980–6	1986
Total OECD	4.5	3.1	2.2	2.5
Britain	2.8	1.9	2.0	2.7

(Source: 3i report *Britain in the 1980s: Enterprise Reborn?*)

Despite this, the 3i report observes that Britain's rise, like its decline, is a relative matter: 'Although the recent indicators mostly point to continuing growth and some features of the economy are worse or better than expected (the balance of payments and the rate of inflation, for example) there is little really convincing evidence in the macro-economy that we are experiencing anything other than a prolonged recovery from a severe recession.'

333

The national situation can be illustrated by some of the major industries, upon which so much of the UK economy has traditionally depended. There is much to quarrel with in the concept of sunrise and sunset industries, but for our purposes here it provides a useful means of distinguishing between the manufacturing-based industries so severely damaged during and before the recession, and the higher value-added industries upon which so much hope has been pinned for the future.

SUNSET INDUSTRIES

Steel

The story of steel's decline and rise is well told by chairman Bob Scholey himself, in a speech to the Institute of Purchasing and Supply in November 1986:

> The strategy developed by the corporation in the early 1980s, implementation of which was made possible by recognition on the part of both management and work people after the three-month strike that radical change was indeed essential, comprised five major elements, all involving substantial change:
>
> 1. Closure of uneconomic steelmaking and concentrating production on modern technology (involving, inter alia, no open-hearth steel furnaces by 1980).
> 2. Slimming of manpower to improve productivity in ongoing plants.
> 3. Decentralising pay negotiations and generally reducing central control and associated managerial overheads.
> 4. Improving direct communications with the workforce.
> 5. Employing an active social policy contribution to mitigate the effects of inevitable change and to create a climate where these changes could become more acceptable.
>
> These elements in the strategy interacted to achieve major restructuring over a short period. The effects upon the business

and therefore upon the security of employment for the remaining employees have been highly beneficial. The process is not yet complete, but it is clear that the really major objectives of the strategy have been successfully achieved.'

This rationalisation policy has turned round British Steel in a quite dramatic manner. Losses of nearly £700 million in 1980–1 have been turned into profits of £200 million in 1986–7. Bob Scholey commented: 'British Steel has carried through a step-by-step strategy which has transformed the industry and placed us today in the first rank of steel-makers. Now production is up. Productivity is up – dramatically. Quality standards are up. So are profits. Indeed, we are now one of the very few integrated steel companies in the world to be in profit and self-financing.' Britain is now a net exporter of steel and British Steel's exports are worth almost £1 billion, accounting for 40 per cent of its production. Confidence is such that privatisation is envisaged in 1989.

Tradition and success

In some of Britain's other traditionally strong industries there have been encouraging signs. Since 1980, Britain's textile firms have increased productivity by 40 per cent and raised export levels by more than 25 per cent. Harry Leach, president of the British Textile Confederation, claimed in 1986, 'Textiles has been one of the star performers in the British economic scene.'

Though the adage 'Britain's bread hangs by Lancashire's thread' is no longer true, the textile industry still employs nearly 500,000 people in Britain. Rationalisation has not affected the paradoxical nature of the industry with the two largest textile groups in Europe, Courtaulds and Coats Viyella, existing alongside a myriad of small workshops.

Despite productivity improvements and a slight increase in exports in recent years, the textile industry remains under threat. With imports rising quickly (up by 19 per cent in the third quarter of 1987) and companies still loath to invest in new capacity, the prospects for dynamic change are limited. The *Financial Times*' Alice Rawsthorn put the textile industry's situation into perspective in January 1988: 'The British industry may still lag behind its chief European competitors, in Italy and West Germany, in the level of modernisation but it has made great advances . . . it will be far less exposed should economic conditions become less clement.'

The traditional metal-bashing industries have also undergone something of a revival. Exports have almost doubled in value terms since 1980 and productivity has more than doubled. In the machine tools industry, 1987's growth in output of £519 million was the highest of any of the major machine building nations. Whilst British orders increased in 1986 those of Japan and West Germany actually fell and large European companies like Oerlikon and Georg Fischer have had financial troubles.

As a result, a number of companies are already reaping the benefits. The former TI machine tool plant has the biggest order book in its history (worth £40 million) whilst Beaver is building a new factory to make lathes, the kind of development which would have been unthinkable a few years ago. In the paper-making machinery industry there are similar signs of success. Beloit Walmsley has a full to overflowing order book; Holders is expanding and Black Clawson is rebuilding successfully.

But the good news is limited. The British machine tool and textile machinery sectors still lag behind their foreign competitors. Britain now has very few companies which are big enough to compete internationally for large projects like factory systems, integrated spinning and weaving mills or complete printing plants. The major machinery battles of the near future will involve the Swiss, Germans and Japanese rather than the British. In fact, the output of the British machine tool industry has yet to return to its 1979 level. West Germany still manages to produce six times as much with less than three times the British workforce. The Swiss manage to produce a third more than Britain with half the workforce. In Italy well over 50 per cent of machine tool output is exported and a balance of payments surplus is maintained. The Italians now hold around 20 per cent of the world market for machinery and equipment. The recently opened Yamazaki machine tool plant at Worcester may provide an insight to the future. It employs less than 200 workers. All the design and technological development is carried out in Japan.

Shipbuilding

The shake-out in shipbuilding has been a long-drawn-out process.

Some yards have returned to profitability through sheer pragmatism and determination. Others, such as Scott Lithgow, whose workforce has declined by two-thirds since 1982, have simply not been able to come to terms with today's working environments or markets in sufficient time.

Even if the shakeout has not yet finished (and it continues in other European countries, too) there are clear survivors with the potential for significant growth. In particular VSEL, made up of the former Vickers and Cammel Laird yards in Barrow and Birkenhead, has begun to thrive. It was subject to a buy-out in March 1986 and has since captured orders for two Trident submarines. Freed from the control of the nationalised British Shipbuilders it has quickly shown itself to be innovative and forward thinking. Its chief executive, Dr Rodney Leach, claims: 'We have been breaking down old demarcations without the change being forced by crisis.' Its 15,000 employees are all shareholders and the company is making strides towards breaking down traditional management-worker divides. VSEL is also heavily committed to training, with around 300 to 350 new apprentices arriving each year. Training accounts for 1.5 per cent of its turnover and VSEL has links with University College, London, and Salford University. VSEL has enough work to last until the year 2000.

Ceramics

Since 1979, employment in the UK's £1.5 billion ceramics manufacturing industry has been reduced by nearly one third as imports of table and kitchenware more than doubled to between 15 per cent and 20 per cent of the market. Exports have held relatively steady, falling slightly in some areas but increasing slightly in others. Since 1986, however, employment in the industry has been steadily rising, and the benefits of massive investment in productivity, design and quality have begun to pay off.

The *Financial Times* quotes the example of one of the smaller companies in the heart of the Potteries, Arthur Wood and Sons, where 'manpower was cut from the highpoint of 515 in 1977 to 350 in 1982 but has now climbed back to 420. Productivity, however, is much higher than a decade ago. Production runs are much longer and the company is able to respond quickly to fashion changes'.

337

Strides forward have also been made at Britain's best-known ceramics company, Wedgwood. Its hotel-ware division was faced with increasing foreign competition and responded by beginning a major investment programme rather than cost-cutting. Its £5 million investment in a new production flow system expanded its theoretical capacity by three times. Output is now 50 per cent higher and 150 more staff have been recruited.

Cars

The British car industry is, in the opinion of some of our observers, a shining example of an industry transformed since the 1970s. Industry minister, John Butcher, has talked optimistically of an 'economic miracle of the type achieved in West Germany in the 1960s'. New car sales in Britain have expanded from just over 1.5 million units in 1980 to a record two million in 1987. Car imports have fallen to less than half of total new car sales and in exports too a steady long-term decline has been reversed. The 1987 statistics of 235,000 units exported mark a 25 per cent increase from the previous year.

Even so, car imports remain at more than four times the export volume. With demand for new cars increasing the car industry's external trade deficit has significantly worsened, rising to £3.09 billion in the first nine months of 1987, up £74 million on the same period in 1986.

Nevertheless, with increased demand so strikingly in evidence, British car production has risen dramatically. Sam Toy, former chairman of Ford in Britain, has predicted that British car production could reach 1.5 million units a year by 1990. This figure can be compared with the 880,000 cars made in 1982 and around 1.2 million in 1987.

Confidence can be seen in Ford's expenditure of £300 million a year on improving its British facilities and its plans to increase output from 380,000 in 1986 to 450,000 in 1988–89, while increasing capacity by 20 per cent. Ford is also encouraging its West German suppliers, hit by the rise in the mark, to relocate in Britain where costs are lower.

Vauxhall has similar long-term plans with a £100 million investment in modernising plant to increase capacity from 220,000 to 300,000. It has gone a step further than Ford and has switched the purchase of £100 million components from the Continent to Britain. Its sister company Opel also plans to increase its British components purchasing by £100 million.

Similarly, Peugeot-Talbot aims to increase production by as much as 50 per cent at its Ryton plant. The Nissan plant in Sunderland is also continuing to expand, with a new £216 million investment announced late in 1987.

Against these impressive figures it should be remembered that:

● Most market share successes have been accounted for by foreign companies such as Ford and General Motors.

● The fall in imports is offset by counting Nissan's output at Sunderland as 'British-made' (a total of 29,000 cars were made there in 1987).

● The only British-owned volume car producer, Austin-Rover, actually lost market share in 1987.

● Other British companies like Jaguar and Land Rover are export-orientated and remain susceptible to currency fluctuations.

● The increasing number of older foreign cars on Britain's roads has also led to an increase in the number of imported components, which were worth £2,790 million in the first nine months of 1987.

SUNRISE INDUSTRIES

Pharmaceuticals

Pharmaceuticals have recently outperformed almost every other industrial sector, particularly in the levels of innovation and productivity. Eight of the fifty bestselling drugs in 1986 were British, well below the United States, which had twenty-three, but ahead of Switzerland, West Germany and Japan, all of which have large and very aggressive pharmaceuticals industries.

Dr John Cantwell of Reading University, a specialist in the industry, has few reservations about the industry's improvements in the last decade. Says Cantwell, 'Britain has made a spectacular recovery since the early 1970s,' and he goes on to cite our European market share which has increased from 14.8 per cent in 1970 to 19.2 per cent in 1980, close to the 20.2 per cent averaged in the 1960s.

339

Britain's drugs business includes some of its most successful companies like Boots, ICI, Glaxo, Wellcome, Beecham, Fisons, and Smith and Nephew. Drugs account for around £5 billion per year of the chemical industry's turnover of around £20 billion. The overall pharmaceuticals business has increased sales by 26 per cent between 1980 and 1985. Of the thirty-two major pharmaceutical producers, Britain now has four against the two in France, three in Switzerland and four in West Germany.

Electronics

Output in virtually every area of electronics has increased since 1980. Data processing output has increased from £1,013 million in 1980 to £2,899 million in 1986; consumer electronics from £505 million in 1980 to £831 million in 1986; telecommunications from £908 million in 1980 to £1,617 million in 1986. However, the increases have been based on successful advances in market niches in relatively tranquil, protected domestic markets like defence and communications. Even large British companies like Ferranti and Plessey direct their energies at fairly narrow markets. Moreover, many areas of the electronics industry, like television and video equipment, have been entirely surrendered to foreign competition. The trade imbalance in the electronics industry amounted to £2 billion in 1986. West Germany, by contrast, had an electronics trade surplus of £1.7 billion in that year.

Part of the problem is that British electronics companies, too long content with domestic markets, are simply too small to compete on tomorrow's world scene. Plessey's acquisition of Ferranti's semiconductor business in November 1987 may help in reducing fragmentation. Plessey also expressed interest in Inmos, a Thorn EMI subsidiary, and in GEC's semiconductor operations.

It should also be noted that foreign-owned companies are heavily involved in the British electronics industry. Over 50 per cent of British semiconductor production is from foreign-owned companies.

Computers

In the rapidly expanding computer field (increasing by 10 to 15 per cent a year) Britain only has one large-scale competitor, ICL, which has limited overseas interests and only 20 per cent of the large mainframes market.

British world market share in data processing, telecommunications and computing remains at only 5 per cent. ICL has sales which are less than 4 per cent of those of IBM, the dominant company.

The National Economic Development Council has also claimed that British information technology companies are suffering from a lack of resources. A 1988 NEDC report pointed to the £1.2 billion trade deficit in the leading information technology product sectors in 1985 and called for more co-operative projects within Europe.

The experiences of these companies illustrates that there is in reality no such thing as a mature industry and that 'sunset' or 'sunrise' are pretty meaningless in terms of identifying profitable long-term manufacturing opportunities. Indeed, the 'sunrise' industries are frequently among the most risky, because of the level of investment needed to secure a market lead and because of the short tenure of that lead as new technology changes competitive positions. As Sir Alex Jarratt expresses it:

A lot of emphasis, in fact too much emphasis, has been placed on the distinction between 'sunset' and 'sunrise' industries. I admit that there are some industries where the sun has gone down so far that it is highly unlikely to come up again. But there are many mature businesses meeting well-established demands that can too easily be written off into the sunset but which are perfectly capable of survival, and surviving well, if they have a bit of sunrise, by which I mean new technology, new design, new marketing, pumped into them. Life is still about cardboard boxes as well as computers, and we should not forget that.

A small example from my own company, which had a subsidiary with some experience in moulding plastic for, amongst other things, artificial eyes and teeth. Thanks to the inventiveness of the man who led it, and the confidence of the then chief executive of Smiths Industries in backing him, that business today is one of the world leaders in single-use plastic devices in anaesthesia, respiratory care and thoracic surgery, exporting 70 per cent of its product to over 90 countries, with Japan as its biggest market.'

PROBLEMS NOT RESOLVED

Low investment

Investing in the future still does not seem to be a strong point of British industry. As the *Financial Times* summarised it in April 1987:

British business is still a long way short of an economic miracle. Managers' self-confidence has not yet been translated into bold new expansion plans. The level of capital investment in plant and machinery remains disappointingly low, and there is clear evidence that companies have used the opportunities presented by falling input costs to push up profit margins rather than to expand sales volumes. Few British groups have emerged as major new players on the world scene: they have become a lot more efficient at what they do, but have not by and large established strong positions in growth industries.'

The manufacturing union, TASS, puts it more strongly in its analysis of the economy in recent years:

Looking at total investment, that is including housebuilding, as a proportion of GDP, the UK has in every year since 1979 performed worse than its major competitors, although part of this may be the UK's lower spending on housebuilding. In 1985, the latest year for which complete figures are available, investment in the UK economy accounted for 17.2 per cent of total output. This compares with 19.5 per cent in West Germany, 18.9 per cent in France, and 18.2 per cent in Italy. In Japan, 27.5 per cent of output was invested for the future . . . relatively low investment for the future has been a problem in the UK economy for decades.

On manufacturing on its own, TASS claims that: 'Investment in new capital equipment for use in manufacturing industry in 1986 was a startling 19.2 per cent lower than in 1979. This means investment in manufacturing has fallen much more steeply than manufacturing output, down by 4.9 per cent over the same period. Indeed . . . far from adding new assets, British manufacturing industry has been running down its capital base since 1979.'

Much the same message comes from the CBI: 'The reinvestment rate in manufacturing has been very low by international standards (in 1985 it was only 10 per cent of manufacturing output compared with 14 per cent in Japan, for instance); and, as a result, much British plant and equipment is not world-competitive.'

The CBI's Director-General, John Banham, has warned of the dangers of ignoring manufacturing industry's importance and potential. In a speech to the Policy Studies Institute in January 1988, he criticised Mrs Thatcher's emphasis on the growth potential of the service sector, commenting, 'We have built a platform for growth; now we must use it – by investing in the technology, infrastructure, plants and people that will need to be competitive in the year 2000.'

Dr Charles Hanson of Newcastle University believes that a great deal of improvement is required before Britain can become internationally competitive. 'A future significant increase in quality and productivity in manufacturing industry is still necessary before the UK can match the international competition, let alone beat it,' he observed at the IEA Conference in October 1987.

The Institute of Directors issues a similar warning note in its *A New Agenda for Government*: 'It would be foolish . . . to believe that no further radical action is necessary. The British economy may, at this moment, be growing faster than its European competitors, but it is still fragile and growing from a low base. Unemployment remains high. We are still far behind the best of our competitors abroad and they will not mark time while Britain tries to catch up.'

Congratulations on achieving greater efficiency by *reducing* output are premature. That, after all, is the easy bit. Much more difficult is identifying where to reinvest and gaining commitment to making reinvestment work. In our studies of British and European companies that have achieved turnarounds since 1982, one of the clear lessons is that success belongs to those companies that simultaneously cut back on the loss-making or low-margin activities and invest the savings (plus a lot more that may have to be borrowed) into growth opportunities. One of the prime reasons for the demise of many companies during the recession was not that they failed to make cuts, but that they failed to use cost-cutting as a means of *strengthening* their operations. As Denys Boyle of the Service Management Consultancy Group expresses it: 'The key is making reductions a means to an end – a better business – rather than an end in themselves. Like any other [management] tool, cost-cutting must be strategically guided.' The companies that failed typically reduced product quality or service – on which customer loyalty depended. Wise companies cut only where the negative impact upon customers would be negligible or nil and put additional resources into *increasing* customer loyalty.

The problem has been exacerbated by the way in which large companies have tended to use their investment resources. As we have observed earlier, a large proportion has gone not into organic growth as is typical in major Japanese or West German competitors, but into acquisition, particularly overseas. On the one hand, increased acquisition of overseas capital resources is an investment in future income. On the other, it represents a net reduction in the amount available for regenerating and expanding domestic industry. Lord Young points out that in 1974, the net worth of the UK's investments overseas was £2.5 billion. By 1979 it had risen to £8 billion. By 1986, it had climbed to a staggering £80 billion. 'The only country with greater overseas investment than Britain is Japan. We have more investment in the United States than the United States has in Britain,' he declares.

Labour costs

While UK labour costs rose only by 1 per cent in 1986 – much lower than France or West Germany – both Japan and the United States *reduced* labour costs.

Skills shortages

As we have seen in the chapter on education, skills shortages continue to afflict a great many industries and companies. Traditional trades are apparently as prone to the problem as newer skills. In the booming building industry, shortages are particularly acute. Bricklayers are in the shortest supply with carpenters and plasterers close after. Employers in some areas are now prepared to pay up to four times the negotiated minimum rates for skilled workers. In London, the Building Employers' Confederation reports that 90 per cent of builders have difficulties finding skilled trades people.

Oil income falling

The Damocles' sword of trade deficit continues to hang close. Without the income from North Sea oil in the late 1970s and early 1980s, Britain would have run a massive trade deficit. But oil output has peaked.

344

According to TASS, 'The Department of Energy forecasts that by 1990 oil production from the North Sea will be down to 85 to 115 million tonnes, compared with 127 million in 1985. Estimates from the National Institute of Economic and Social Research suggest it could fall further to 80 million tonnes by the year 2000.'

Quality levels

The Department of Trade and Industry suspects that the cost of quality failures remains close to the 1978 figure of £10 billion.

Government consumption as a percentage of gross domestic product

Whereas in 1914, government only took up 14 per cent of gross domestic product, the public sector now accounts for nearly 40 per cent of the economy.

Balance of payments

According to the OECD Economic Outlook of June 1987, 'Slow growth, unemployment and large payment imbalances are likely to persist.' In the first quarter of 1988 the balance of payments deficit was £2,776 million.

PROBLEMS PARTIALLY RESOLVED

Sterling values and inflation

Sir John Hoskyns observed in *The Director* in October 1987, 'The people who run Britain's businesses still can't quite believe the new sense of relative stability. And they would certainly be most unwise to take it for granted.'

The high value of the pound was a contributor to the collapse of British manufacturing in the early 1980s. The pound rose to 4.2 Deutschmarks in

1982 against 3.15 in early 1988. Paradoxically, the cause of its overvaluing was our good fortune in discovering and exploiting North Sea oil. The knowledge that oil would act as an economic float buoyed up the value of sterling even while industry was falling apart. Michael Edwardes was reported as saying at the time: 'If we had known what would happen, we'd have been better off leaving the stuff at sea.' High exchange rates forced Edwardes to close otherwise rescuable plants such as Abingdon. Claims Roy Grantham of APEX, 'He never intended to shut it, but in the circumstances he couldn't keep it going.'

The pound is probably still overvalued, says Grantham, who now explains: 'We are barely out of overvaluation of sterling. In 1981, according to the best estimates, we were 40 per cent overvalued. The fall is almost right, but we need to drop another 15 per cent against the German mark to allow for the difference in inflation rates since then'.

Even so, exchange rates need not be an impenetrable barrier to trade expansion. Indeed, they can represent an excellent opportunity to raise productivity (by buying the most modern capital equipment cheaply) and hence achieving a competitive advantage when sterling values fall. Unfortunately, this is not how we used the opportunity. High yen depression, or *endakafukyo*, has not affected Japan greatly, in part because the shakeout of manufacturing employment coincided with a massive expansion in the private service sector. Another reason, however, was that the relentless drive for greater productivity and cost reduction has enabled Japanese companies to maintain prices and hence market share, often without losing margins.

Industrial relations

As we discussed in Chapter 3, it is clear that a new, more positive industrial relations climate has emerged within the past few years. The question remains: how effectively can we build upon it in the rest of the twentieth century?

Low productivity

In the early 1970s Henry Ford II swore never to invest again in Britain. The reason he gave was that productivity and industrial relations were appalling. In 1987 Ford Motor Co. had nothing but praise for the productivity of its

British plants and planned to invest £1.5 billion in the UK during the following five years. The twin advantages of low labour costs (in part a result of currency devaluations) and internationally competitive levels of productivity have impressed Ford. How far Ford's resolve continues in the face of its clash with the unions over its now defunct Dundee plant remains to be seen.

Nonetheless, the productivity gap remains. Reports from subsidiaries of Japanese companies in Britain are mixed. Whilst Japanese investment in Britain has increased rapidly – from $1,933 million in 1980–1 to $4,125 million in 1986–7 – reservations over British skill levels continue. NEC Technologies' video recorder plant in Shropshire, for example, only uses local firms to build the chassis of the product. It complains over the performance, pricing and delivery from local firms. Mitsubishi's Scottish television factory has also encountered some difficulties in changing working habits. Its British general manager has remarked, 'British workers' utilisation of their working day, or their attention to detail, is not as good as their counterparts' in Japan.'

So why the productivity problem? In large part, it is the result of low investment in capital equipment and training. But there are apparently other factors, too, if a recent comparative study of four Japanese, US and British manufacturing companies is to be believed. The study, carried out by researchers at the London School of Economics and San Jose State University found that, contrary to expectation, the two Japanese companies did not achieve their significantly higher productivity through better employee relations. On the contrary, the Japanese companies studied proved to have high productivity in spite of relatively poor labour relations and job satisfaction. The US company had high job satisfaction but only moderate productivity, while the British company had only moderate levels of job satisfaction and the lowest level of productivity. What *did* make a clear contribution to productivity in Japanese firms, claim the researchers, is the intense focus they placed on the management of production and operations. Work disciplines were tighter; work measurement, quality and cost control were enforced; and everyone from engineers to assembly workers contributed to error and cost reduction. The researchers describe it as 'the single-minded pursuit of performance improvement, technological adjustments, method analysis, work study and work incentives, linked to strategically important goals'. In other words, a sheer dedication to production efficiency and excellence. None of this is alien to our own manufacturing philosophy; the difference lies in the intensity of conviction on management's part that it really matters.

347

It is also important to place the productivity increases that have taken place into context. Productivity is a measure of the number of people employed and the output of the factory in which they work. It is perfectly possible (and so it often occurred) to reduce output but maintain productivity simply by cutting the number of people faster. The difficult part is to increase productivity by increasing output – and that, in many cases, we are still learning to do.

Quality of management

As we observed in the chapter on the rise of leadership, there are signs that the typical manager of the 1990s will have more to offer than his or her counterpart of the 1970s. It is not that the people are intrinsically any different, merely that they are likely to be better trained, more broadly experienced, more conditioned to entrepreneurial roles. David Plaistow of Vickers is quoted as saying: 'At the end of the 1970s it would not have been possible to run a business like this. You couldn't ask managers to bust a gut for the business, because you couldn't offer them meaningful incentives to do so. Now we can and do and they can and do.'

The roles that all partners in industry need to play in achieving a real and lasting turnaround in all of these problem areas are examined in Appendix 1. These recommendations are distilled from the comments and advice of the wide range of people we have surveyed in preparing this book. Most important, the recommendations are forward-looking, not because we wish to ignore the lessons of the past, but because no one ever won a formula one race by watching the rear-view mirror.

We will content ourselves here with reviewing a few of the most critical changes of attitude that are required of everybody. These can be summed up as five key points:

1. *There is no such thing as a mature industry*

In virtually every devastated sector we have examined, there have been shining examples of companies which have outperformed not only their sector, but the average of companies in all sectors. The reason is simple: companies, like people, are only as old as they feel. In practice, any

348

industry is open to radical change through new technology, new distribution methods, better service systems or any of a dozen other variables.

On the other side of the coin, many 'sunrise' industries have already peaked. Much of what remains of the electronics equipment industry, for example, consists purely of assembly of bought-in components. The technology is fairly well established. What product innovation there is occurs largely in the components, most of which are the result of R & D carried out abroad.

The trick is to innovate in *all* sectors all the time.

2. *Take exporting seriously*

Says Lord Young: 'We still export more than Japan. If we can beat the best of the world here, we can do so elsewhere.'

3. *Invest in people*

Many of the companies which wrote in their annual reports 'people are our most important asset' during the early 1970s, had shed a third or more of that asset by the early 1980s. It has taken, or perhaps more accurately is taking, a considerable time to rebuild that asset. Companies must steer a careful course between allowing themselves to become too fat again and demanding too much of an overstretched workforce. The key is to develop every direct and indirect employee to his or her maximum ability – to train them continuously, not just for the work they do now but for the work they could do in the future. Unless British companies grow their own skilled, adaptive workforces they will find themselves at an increasing competitive disadvantage.

4. *Take the long-term view*

Government, industry and trade unions must all learn to think beyond the next general election, the next dividend, the next union election. They must learn to plan together, for thirty years ahead. There is no evidence to suggest that any of the three institutions yet have the capacity to look that far ahead, or even ten years ahead, within their own boundaries, let alone within a common vision.

Observers on all sides of industry agree upon the need for a tripartite consensus. Says Sir Colin Corness, chairman of Redland: 'Strategic planning is needed to establish which goods and services Britain is best positioned to supply to world markets. These targets then need to be reflected in the entire educational process and in our national investment priorities, both public and private. Then there needs to be steadfast, disciplined and consistent adherence to these objectives without political interference.'

This, to a large extent, was what NEDC was intended to do. Few people, including NEDC itself, consider that it has achieved any real form of lasting consensus on direction or policy. One reason was that the various participants have been unwilling or unable to deliver. The exception was when the trade unions agreed in the late 1970s to an industrial strategy, which accommodated two or three years of wage restraint, in expectation of an improvement in the economy and price restraint. In this case, the Labour Government, caught in an international spiral of inflation and depression, was unable to deliver its side of the bargain.

Whatever the rights and wrongs of this period, there does seem at last to be a genuine willingness among many industrialists and many trade unionists to plan together for the long term within an appropriate forum. The missing partner is Government. Whether NEDC goes or stays, some form of long-term consensus planning body is probably an essential element in a national industrial renaissance. But it will not be effective unless there is strong Government commitment.

5. *Restore the will to win*

'There seems to be a real change in people's values and attitudes,' observed Ralph Dahrendorf in October 1987. Quinn Mills, a professor at Harvard, tells the tale of a group of managers at a training session who were told to write on a piece of paper the name of the person with whom they would most like to pair up for the rest of the day's course. The purpose of the course was to help establish why the company kept losing out to the competition. The managers were told to put the note in their pockets, then to find and stand by the person they had named. After a couple of minutes of confusion, everyone was paired off. Then the instructor asked to see the notes. Several managers had paired off with a different person than they had named.

'Why didn't you go to that person?'

'Someone else was already there.'

'Did anyone tell you you couldn't muscle in?'

'No.'

'So, why didn't you?'

After some to-ing and fro-ing the managers admitted that it was because they were afraid of being rejected, of failing. 'That,' said the instructor, 'is what is wrong with your company.'

That story probably held true for a good 50 per cent of British companies in 1981. But there seems little doubt in the minds of most of the industrialists who responded to our survey that something positive has emerged out of adversity. Declaring that he sees 'signs of the background conditions shifting nearer to those which favoured the Industrial Revolution', Sir Adrian Cadbury maintains that, 'The new mood favours enterprise and change, because the prospects of a future which is a continuation of the present is unacceptable . . . The country's rate of economic growth is primarily dependent upon the energies and enterprise of its citizens. There is no reason to suppose that people in Britain now are different from what they were at the time of the Industrial Revolution.'

SUMMARY

If this vision of Britain's manufacturing future is filled with uncertainties and maybes, then so be it. That is the nature of the business and economic environment into which we and our competitor nations are hurtling. Clearly, Britain has little option but to continue to be a trading nation and to do all it can to hold onto its markets for manufactured goods. As Arthur Francis of Imperial College has noted:

> Fears of a fundamental lack of competitiveness of British industry seem largely unfounded. In particular, wild talk based on Britain's declining share of world trade, which seems to equate the national economy with a down-at-heel department store looking out to brash new multiples, ignores the fundamental economic principle of comparative advantage. On that principle it will always be rational for national economies to trade with each other, even if one economy is more poorly endowed than all the others in every respect.

To increase competitiveness, British companies have to evaluate their own strengths and weaknesses by international standards and create viable competitive strategies based on the best they observe elsewhere.

While there is little room for euphoria and even less for self-congratulation, it is clear that the shakeout in British manufacturing could as equally be the beginnings of an industrial renaissance as the short-lived second childhood of a senile economy. The choice is very much up to the key players – industrial leaders, financial institutions, government, academia and trade unions.

The Institute of Directors paints an optimistic picture (whilst warning against complacency) in its *A New Agenda for Business*: 'Today, British business operates in an environment changed beyond recognition from that of ten years ago. As the political and economic scene has started to change, so have the attitudes of business. With steady growth, healthier profits, stronger balance sheets and exchange control freedom, British business is beginning to think long-term and more deeply about the world in which it operates.'

Long-term perspectives may well be emerging but many changes need to be made to secure long-term prosperity. The current industrial situation requires commercial realism and vision. It is perhaps appropriate that an industrialist should provide the most cogent description of our current status in manufacturing. Says Sir Alex Jarratt, chairman of Smiths Industries.

It is true that the volume of our manufacturing output has declined absolutely in comparison with our main competitors. But it is also true that there is still an enormous market for manufactured goods, both in this country and overseas, to be satisfied now and one that will grow over the years as the world's still largely unsatisfied needs are gradually fulfilled.

Even as things stand now, British-based companies make and supply two thirds of the manufactured goods we buy in this country. Our manufactured goods' exports are greater by one quarter than our earnings from oil, banking and insurance combined. In total, we export per capita one third more than the Japanese. We undoubtedly need to do more . . . in our home market, too, where the amount of foreign competition sometimes makes it feel like the biggest export market of the lot.

If, as we speculated in the foreword to this book, the cycle of empire and entrepreneurism is an accurate reflection of economic development, then the experience of previous centuries tells us that the full thrust of change takes a while to come about. In a large company, with extensive training resources and a hands-on management committed to making people do things in new ways, it takes anything from three to ten years to realise significant changes in culture. How much longer then must it take to turn round the industrial culture of a whole country? It took many years after the loss of the colonies before there were radical changes to behaviour and attitudes of industrialists, workers and politicians. In the last gasps of the twentieth century we have far greater resources with which to effect change than we had two hundred years ago but also far more baggage to hinder our progress.

We have deliberately not set out to judge the policies – either individually or severally – of the Conservative administration and the Opposition parties. In large part this is because it is still too early to tell. The enthusiasm now being felt among many industrialists is a reflection not of having made it back to the front ranks of international competitiveness, but of recognition that there are opportunities and that we are able to pursue them, if we dare. Whether the price we have had to pay to reach this position has been worthwhile depends primarily upon how well we seize the opportunities.

Appendix 1

AN ACTION LIST FOR INDUSTRY, THE FINANCIAL SECTOR, THE EDUCATION SECTOR, GOVERNMENT AND TRADE UNIONS

The following checklists are not exhaustive. But they do represent the very minimum that each of these key players should be doing now if the 1990s are to be a period of continuous improvement of industrial competitiveness.

Industry must

1.   Recognise that it is now in a global market; that Europe is part of its domestic market; and that global players need a different set of attitudes, behaviours and resources.

2.   Invest continuously in all key resources and particularly in people, technology and advanced equipment. Any manufacturing company not investing at least 10 per cent of sales turnover in training, equipment and product development is unlikely to be investing sufficiently seriously in its future.

3.   Place quality high on the daily agenda, from top management down to the lowliest operator.

4.   Constantly seek ways to increase involvement by employees at all levels.

5.   Plan for the long term.

6.   Become truly sensitive and responsive to customers' needs and potential needs.

7. Promote the cause of industry to schools, government, trade union members and the public at large.

8. Never forget you are in business to win.

Government must

1. Recognise that a hands-off approach means exactly that; that volume of legislation, including reforming legislation, is an inhibitor to industrial growth.

2. Accept its roles as guide and adviser; as provider of resources, standards and incentives; as facilitator of trade; and as builder of industrial consensus.

3. Set an example in terms of taking a long-term planning perspective.

4. Recognise that establishing global businesses may require a re-examination of monopolies and merger legislation.

Trade unions must

1. Accept that they, too, have a role to play in wealth creation.

2. Acknowledge that they have an important role in the training and career development of their members.

3. Develop levels of professional expertise equivalent to or better than those of the businesses they negotiate with.

4. Fulfil their role as stakeholders through constant pressure on employers to maintain international levels of competitiveness; drawing on the expertise of members elsewhere to facilitate changes that will improve both the health of the company and the employment security of their members.

Appendix 2

THE VIEWS OF INDUSTRY – responses from our leadership survey

Ian Butler, Cookson Group
Sir Alan Dalton, English China Clays
R W Adam, London and Scottish Marine Oil
Lord Rothermere, Mail Newspapers
Sir Ronald Dearing, The Post Office
Nicholas Horsley, Northern Foods
Brian Budd, Monsanto
Sir Simon Hornby, W H Smith
P L F Crowson, Rio Tinto Zinc
J N Clarke, Johnson Matthey
Michael Peacock, Nurdin and Peacock
Peter Holmes, Shell
Viscount Sandon, Dowty Group
Sir Colin Corness, Redland
Bob Scholey, British Steel
Sir Alex Jarratt, Smiths Industries

IAN BUTLER, CHAIRMAN, COOKSON GROUP

You seek the prime reasons for 'Britain's industrial decline'. A major factor was international and did not only affect Britain. The artificiality of inflation had allowed many lax attitudes to develop but many of them were compensated by the steady world growth which had taken place since 1945 but which was halted or reversed by the oil price rises and the energy price cartel operated in this country. In Britain the industries which declined or died were primarily those that believed that they could operate with indifference to world competition and that their own attempted suicide would always be prevented, or at least delayed, by government action. In those cases management, unions and government, through its subsidy policy, bear blame but so, indeed, do many individual workers who had belief in this artificial utopia.

It ought to be recognised that many well run industries in this country have been flourishing over the past two to three years and that their only initial period of setback was due to restructuring that had to be done rapidly in 1979/81 for international reasons mentioned in the above paragraph. They have only got to set about producing the right products with good service and ensuring that their price structure makes them internationally competitive. This in itself does not call for action by industry as a totality, by government, by the educational system, by the trade unions or by any other organisation except, possibly, for the communication of this message. Certainly there could be a reduction in the adverse activities of some of these and this, in itself, might have some positive action.

I am wary of the expression 'a long-term programme of recovery', particularly if it involves some implication of a national programme or a national plan and I find little benefit from trying to apportion responsibility to any party or body for something which I hope will not occur. One would most seek that there would be no interference particularly from government other than that it provides a sound economy based on a balanced budget or a surplus, that there is a proper legal structure which probably means legislation repeal rather than new legislation and that their balanced budget be achieved by much more substantial reductions in government expenditure than have been sought hitherto. A balanced budget would assist the required trend towards stable currency. Government has an enormous task to reverse two generations of socialism, a task which would also necessitate radical tax reform and the abolition of a mass of grants and the stupidity of centrally determined regional policy.

The one area where constructive action – indeed it might be described as interference by many – is needed is in the education system. The good schools must be allowed to prosper with their staff being well remunerated by results. The bad schools should die rapidly and this would best be achieved by the freedom of parents to choose schools, perhaps by the use of a voucher system and should encourage new 'private' grant schools to compete with those run by the so-called Education Authorities. Any nation such as ours, which allowed one of the best educational systems – namely the grammar school – to be killed off must take some drastic action but it will certainly not be achieved by elimination of fee-paying schools or the steady reduction of our educational system to the lowest common denominator, which could only have the effect of us approaching 100 per cent illiteracy before the end of the century. There is also room for considerable improvement in tertiary education. There is little incentive for performance when both sides are effectively paid by the taxpayer. There seems nothing wrong with the system used elsewhere of 'working through college' or of loans instead of grants. With loans, at least the students would demand more constructive courses from the academics so that they would be ready on completion of their course to perform a useful job attracting the sort of remuneration that could repay the loan.

SIR ALAN DALTON, CHAIRMAN, ENGLISH CHINA CLAYS

Prime reasons for Britain's industrial decline

The post-war belief that the world owed us a living and the rapid advance of welfarism led too early to the conclusion that exertion in the nation's interests was a thing of the past. In the laissez-faire environment of that era power was handed over to trade unions in a vacuum created by industrial management, the 'divide' became deeper, suspicion about means and motives reached corrosive and destructive levels. Leadership lost its followers as standards evaporated and there was too much evidence of self-interest.

Major remedial actions

Less interference by the state, which we are beginning to see under the present government. The changes in legislation, particularly those which have brought trade unions into a more thoughtful and responsible frame of mind, have been helpful. There is still much room for deregulating in the 'planning' arena. The objectives of 'lifting the burden' are admirable but achievement by the Deregulation Unit is dismal.

The education system is not producing the skills needed by industry and leaving the liaison between the two to the meagre and essentially voluntary resources of bodies like UBI is absurd. Industry can and should do more in its own interests, but is frustrated by incessant fiddling by bureaucrats and examiners which is leading to lower and lower standards being regarded as acceptable in order, apparently, not to be unkind to the low performers. School/industry liaison is too important to be left to the muddling of the multiplicity of bodies involved in that field.

What is involved in a long-term recovery

The creation of an environment in which enterprise and profits are encouraged; in which self-respect and self-reliance are reasserted as desirable targets; in which government's role is more clearly defined as an enabling, rather than a preventive body, retaining responsibility only for that which is undelegable. To achieve a government which is concerned more about the public good than party gain has to be a priority and some reform in the mechanics of elections, with, perhaps, the US system as a model, should be undertaken. Responsibility for recovery thereafter can more readily and fairly be allocated to citizens in all walks of life, on the principle that 'if we all swept our own doorsteps, the whole village would be clean'. Too many bucks are constantly being passed, and I am personally fed up with the partisan flavour of much of current and recent experience.

R W ADAM, CHAIRMAN, LONDON AND SCOTTISH MARINE OIL

In the post-war period the UK still had access to substantial traditional markets – the old empire. It took a number of years before other countries, due to war damage or lack of skills, were able to penetrate these markets. This bred a certain amount of complacency in the minds of British management who were slow to adapt to changing circumstances.

There were a number of family or private companies in existence in the UK in the early post-war period. The proprietors were able, in general, to make a comfortable living and the rewards for risk-taking due mainly to high taxation and bureaucracy did not encourage expansion into new fields.

Trade unions, under a Labour government, had no regard to the economic realities and the changes that were going on in the world; restrictive practices abounded and strikes proliferated.

Management and the City must have regard to those industries in which we can compete worldwide, either through technical skills, research or natural resources.

We are not alone in having suffered the loss of heavy industry. Most European countries are in the same situation and will be joined in due course by Japan.

We must use to the full and best advantage our natural resources in the shape of oil and coal, recognising that they must compete with other sources in the world and cannot be subsidised. Subsidies would only lead to an uncompetitive position.

The government must ensure that as far as possible free enterprise is allowed to flourish, that tax rates are not excessive and that grants are not made in a fashion which leads to long-term economic nonsense (development grants encouraging capital investment in depressed areas have much to do with the present economic situation. They should have been given to encourage employment and not to finance, for example, chemical plants and refineries in the 'wrong' parts of the country.)

Trade union leaders must recognise that Britain cannot opt out of the economic scene and that productivity and wage rates must be as good as those of our competitors.

There is a crying need for an improvement in educational standards and this improvement must be a joint operation between government, unions and parents.

LORD ROTHERMERE, CHAIRMAN OF MAIL NEWSPAPERS

What are the prime reasons for Britain's industrial decline?

It seems to me that this may have begun in the 1860s, or 1870s, when the British iron industry allowed the Bessemer process to go to Germany. I think that management has been primarily to blame throughout the decline of British industry and that an unfair portion of the blame has been given to the trade unions.

361

The trade unions really only became sufficiently powerful to affect the economy in the last forty years, since the Second World War. They effectively formed industrial cartels and, like cartels, forced up the price of their product, i.e. labour, until the market broke. Socialist legislation, which increased their powers, only hastened their end. Of course, unions have not ended and are rapidly recovering and one can only hope that this part of history will not repeat itself.

What major actions could be taken now to bring about the rise of British industry?

I think the government must provide legislation which prevents unions from being able to impose industrial cartels and ruin industries. This should be accompanied by education on the responsibilities of trade unions. Personally, I am very much in favour of trade unions and support them. I think they have a very necessary job to do.

What would a long-term programme of recovery involve?

I think it must involve the regeneration of British management and this must be accompanied by legislation enabling incentives to be offered, which has, to some extent, already been accomplished. Management attitudes are inevitably a product of the society from which management comes and the climate of this society can be best changed by the education system. If we are to have a capitalist society, then students should be taught how to develop it for the best results to themselves and society in general. It is obviously foolish to educate students to despise the system upon which the country is going to depend.

SIR RONALD DEARING, CHAIRMAN OF THE POST OFFICE

Industrial regeneration can only be led by managers and the responsibility lies clearly with them to energise their enterprises, bringing their unions with them, change the attitudes of society towards the key role of management and to win the support of local and national government to the cause of industrial regrowth.

But if I had to pick one small group outside management as central to regeneration, it is the trade union leadership where the key issue is that instead of defending the past, it should be challenging management for any want of drive, vision and courage to make the change industry needs and within that framework ensure that society affords sufficient protection for those who are displaced by change and to ensure that its members who remain in employment are competitively rewarded in relation to the value of what they do. Some unions are of course moving that way, but we need to see change.

NICHOLAS HORSLEY, DEPUTY CHAIRMAN NORTHERN FOODS

I think there are three prime reasons for Britain's industrial decline:

- Lack of investment,
- Too much power in the trade unions, and
- An unwillingness to innovate.

I think to some extent all these problems are being dealt with. Certainly the unions' powers have been drastically curbed.

In general terms I feel that better and closer relationships between government and industry is important, and also feel that the relationships between education establishments and industry have been appalling and need to improve drastically.

BRIAN BUDD, CHAIRMAN, MONSANTO

When Britain became the workshop of the world in the nineteenth century, we had a captive market in the British Empire and a powerful merchant navy. Trade followed the flag. There was dramatic growth in manufacturing and in banking and other commercial services. But competition was limited and complacency set in. This monopolistic position led to:

- Insufficient attention to product design and technical development.
- Limited selling and marketing skills.
- Lack of incentive to reduce costs by manufacturing efficiency.
- Laissez-faire and amateur management.

Competitors who started later had (like Avis) to try harder and were less hampered than the British by social divisions.

Our original success was based on native pragmatic inventiveness, much of it at the artisan level. The landed gentry despised 'trade' but were not averse to taking its money. The public school system was designed to develop colonial administrators, officers and gentlemen. The newly rich industrial barons sought social acceptability for their children by sending them to public schools and to the ancient universities of Oxford and Cambridge. The reverence for the classics and the contempt for science and technology at these institutions persisted well into the twentieth century. This gulf between Board School and Eton, Mechanics Institute and Oxbridge does not seem to have been mirrored elsewhere, certainly not in America, Germany or Japan. Social snobbery therefore directed our better brains and the strong personalities into law, medicine and the Church and into the services both civil and military. Politics and banking were also acceptable.

This social contempt for industry and neglect of science and technology encouraged absentee management and a generally amateur attitude. The Battle of Waterloo may indeed have been won on the playing fields of Eton but the battle for world market share may also have been lost there.

Then there is the attitude of the 'working class'. I daresay that exploitation was endemic in all industrialised societies but it started earlier in Great Britain and the resentment may be more deep-seated. And there is a pig-headed, obstinate, pragmatic bravery and resistance to change inherent in the British character. This served us well in war but has been a major factor in our failure to adapt quickly enough to the realities of a hard competitive world and the loss of our imperial power.

Younger industries have sometimes fared better. My own experience is in chemicals, which has a high proportion of 'redbrick' graduates. It demands a relatively high level of competence at shop floor level and lends itself to constructive communication between workers and management. But it is not so long ago that our flagship ICI was riddled with class distinction and conspicuously weak in marketing skills, having relied heavily on cartels and monopoly positions. It is a salutary thought that it took the inspiration and personality of a non-establishment maverick, John Harvey-Jones, to restore the competitive edge and profitability to our premier chemical company.

You ask where the blame is to be allocated. In my view it must lie with the leaders of our society in the period up to World War I and to some extent beyond. Their social and educational values did not equip them to provide industrial leadership in an increasingly competitive world market. Their attitudes, coupled with the stubborn British character, encouraged the stifling grip of the trade unions. But I strongly believe that management gets the unions it deserves.

Action needed

We have to create a climate in which talented people at all levels *want* to work in industry for the job satisfaction and material success it offers. But so long as our society remains so deeply divided, I am not hopeful. The lead has to come from the top and the ceaseless bickering of politicians does not help to create a constructive climate. Social snobbery on the one hand and socialist dogma on the other maintain a cultural divide which seems unbridgeable. There is a widespread ignorance of the simple fact that we have to generate wealth from industry and commerce in order to achieve socially desirable objectives such as better schools, houses, hospitals and pensions. In short – caring capitalism.

The Sunday Times of March 1st contains an extract from Michael Heseltine's book, *Where There's a Will*. The extract is aptly entitled 'How to cure the ills of British Industry'. He pleads for a strengthened role for the Department of Trade and Industry. If this would enhance leadership and create a more favourable climate in which *private* industry can flourish, then I would support him.

It would not come amiss if our honours system gave more recognition to industrialists. We favour politicians, civil servants, service people, actors, sportsmen and philanthropists, but rarely people from industry.

On the other side of the coin industrialists have got to speak up more – we need more leaders and spokesmen of the calibre of Sir John Harvey-Jones. At the level of the enterprise such strong leadership will:

365

- Eliminate social distinctions (e.g. hourly, weekly, monthly paid) in the workplace as well as restrictive practices.
- Foster excellent communication on the objectives and results of the enterprise and make training and *total* quality an integral part of *every* job.
- Create a better image of industry in schools and higher education.

In the longer term we can only complete our industrial renaissance by an unusual level of competence, dedication and determination. This implies political consensus, more demanding educational standards and excellence in science and technology, allied to entrepreneurial skills to turn scientific discoveries into profitable products.

SIR SIMON HORNBY, CHAIRMAN, W H SMITH

I believe that the industrial decline started at the end of the nineteenth century when the owners, having made a lot of money out of their businesses, went away to spend their money and left the businesses to be run by untrained managers. In a nutshell, it was absentee ownership. It is worth examining this thesis carefully because I believe it was pervasive through the first half of the twentieth century. There was a complacency and apathy in many companies' owners or major shareholders.

There was, of course, little training. Managers had no formal business training. There was no formal planning in business and, as a result of this, investment was not made when it should have been. The absentee ownership led to the growth of trade unions and, of course, the trade unions are one of the prime reasons for Britain's industrial decline. It was not originally their fault and it would not have happened had the directors of companies worked with the unions to develop an understanding of what was best for the employees and the employers. There was no training at all of the work force. The industry I know best is, of course, the newspaper industry and nowhere can this be better seen than rich owners, bad managers and powerful unions, which became more and more powerful as the owners bought peace at any price.

Another reason for Britain's industrial decline is that we continue to prop up declining industries rather than letting them go and investing in new industries much more quickly. A good example of this is the textile industry. We should have consolidated textiles, investing in a few but not propping up the many where much cheaper textiles could be produced in developing countries.

What major actions could be taken now?

Since Mrs Thatcher's Government came into power, a great deal has already been done. One reason for the decline which I did not give was very high taxation. A reduction in the top level of taxation, which should be further reduced, will undoubtedly be an incentive to better management. There should be even more encouragement to share options and share ownership so that management and staff can benefit from the success of the business in which they work. We need to invest much more in research and development and design. Product development and design has been an area in which Britain has lagged (and so, incidentally, has America). Skilled training has been poor at all levels, from top management through to the shop floor. Children need to be taught at school about business, about elementary accounting, about design. Action is already being taken to improve the educational system and there are already good examples in some of the universities of research projects and company teaching schemes which are improving industrial performance.

I don't believe that government can have an entirely laissez faire attitude because our competitors in other countries are having partnerships of government and industry working together. I believe this to be essential. It is necessary for government to reduce company legislation so as to cut out a lot of bureaucracy, but it is also necessary for government to plan with businesses how best they can work in partnership to develop export markets. The government has already taken a lot of action over trade union legislation and I believe that the relationship between management and unions has changed fundamentally for the better. It is essential that this change is maintained and that management works with the unions to make certain that there are always good communications between the two sides. The greatest threat to the future is protectionism and great efforts should be made by governments to avoid this.

If I was to say in a nutshell what a long-term programme of recovery should involve, I would say that the government must reduce controls and taxation and improve education. Industry must improve its rewards, its training and, above all, it must be concerned with good design because design is what has given both Germany and Japan their leadership in world markets.

P L F CROWSON, ECONOMIC ADVISER TO RIO TINTO ZINC

There have been complaints about Britain's industrial decline for well over a hundred years, which suggests that it is firmly rooted in the UK's institutional structure. Yet we must recognise that for much of the period any decline has been relative rather than absolute. Any leader will inevitably experience increased competition as other countries develop, catch up, and overtake with the benefit of more advanced capital and the preceding examples. Britain's problems seem to lie in its adversarial political system, and in an educational and governmental system whose prime object for over a century was to turn out good administrators. This meant that technical and business skills were not as highly regarded as they have been in mainland Europe and Japan. When the educational system is combined with an extremely efficient financial system which has always been designed for servicing trade rather than industry, the mixture becomes fairly predictable. The failure to establish an appropriate exchange rate for much of the post-war period, even during the early 1980s, has been a further factor. Whilst it is conventional to blame the tax system, the strength of trade unions, and an ultra-rigid system of wage determination, these seem more in the nature of symptoms rather than causes.

Many studies have shown that British management can be highly effective overseas in a different institutional framework. The answers to Britain's problems seem to be to tackle the educational system and the system of government in a coordinated fashion. Here the trouble is that there have been many attempts to reform both over the post-war period. There is a tendency to give insufficient time for any reform to become established, and also to limit the funds available below those needed to secure success. In the face of the failure of many initiatives perhaps the best response is for the government merely to establish an appropriate exchange rate, and a compatible monetary and fiscal regime. Going beyond that, the apparent success of the Airbus suggests that governmental support for industry can be beneficial. The problem seems to be that governments become seduced by the large projects, such as Concorde, rather than more cost effective, but less exciting, smaller ventures. The response of Britain's farmers to monetary incentives shows that British industry could respond if given the chance.

Governments from all parties seem to spend far too much time concentrating on broadly irrelevant issues, whether it is nationalisation by the Labour Party, or privatisation by the Conservatives. Some of the more important factors, such as the rigidity of the British housing market, which greatly limits mobility of labour, tend to be completely ignored by all parties.

J N CLARKE, CHAIRMAN, JOHNSON MATTHEY

The description 'the decline of British Industry' is in itself too simple. Decline reflects a combination of many factors including the mature economy of the UK, the industrialisation of the NDCs and LDCs, political change affecting trade patterns and changes in levels of employment reflecting improvements in manufacturing technology.

In terms of the prime reasons I would identify:

- Education
- Training
- Structural and social rigidities stemming not least from the inadequate use of our housing stock
- The financing structure of UK industry by comparison with two major competitors, Japan and West Germany

In terms of the major actions I advocate:

- Reform of the education system and immediate improvement, which requires co-operation between unions and management, in apprenticeships and training.
- Improvement in competitive ability which must include:

- (i) Research and development. There could be improvement in government/industry funding and targetting
- (ii) Design and quality
- (iii) Market development and service.

Two specific examples which may be relevant are Johnson Matthey's development of catalysts for the world automobile industry and, in the case of my other main responsibility, our subsidiary Anderson Strathclyde which over a period of five years before receiving a material order, established a basis of selling high technology coalmining equipment to the Chinese market, which has established it as a long-term supplier.

Government can establish the framework in which longer-term programmes can be developed, for example in education and training, and perhaps most in encouraging social change which permits a consensus rather than divisive approach. Government can also by fiscal and monetary policy influence changes in the financing of longer-term investments for industry, and in the funding and direction of fundamental and applied research and development.

For the remainder the prime responsibility probably rests with management.

MICHAEL PEACOCK, CHAIRMAN, NURDIN AND PEACOCK

From personal observation in my own industry of wholesale grocery, I believe a large part of the reason for Britain's industrial decline has been a lack of commitment by management. Regrettably, even in the present competitive climate, many in management positions do not seem to be interested in giving good service. For instance I am still hearing complaints about non-delivery by suppliers, particularly in the field of home produced non-foods, and a lack of interest in the problems caused.

This same lack of commitment has I believe in the past left a vacuum which was filled by troublemakers so that in more recent days even good management has had to struggle hard to restore good relationships with workforces. Unfortunately this has been beyond many, hence the demise of so many businesses – and industries.

Even with good management it is possible for a clever troublemaker to lead a workforce astray and it is essential that their leaders are elected frequently by supervised, secret ballots. I advocated this in correspondence and in an interview with Mr Prior in 1978 before the Conservatives came into power and am only sorry it has taken so long to bring it about. It is impossible to overstate the fear element that the bully boys can bring to bear in an open meeting, let alone the other techniques they use.

Looking to the future, I believe more commitment is required of management and also a more genuine interest in their workforce, otherwise, if and when we return to full employment, we will pay the price. We hear many stories of employers exploiting the present unemployment when we are interviewing for staff.

It must be right to bring industry closer to education so that young people know more about it before making their choice of career. There are a number of voluntary organisations involved in this field and they should be encouraged. Profit sharing *for all levels* should also continue to receive encouragement.

Finally, I do believe that the imbalance of trade with the Far East needs to be addressed by recognising two factors:

- That the work ethic, for whatever reason, appears to be far stronger there than in the English-speaking world and we need time to adjust, otherwise they will dominate one industry after another.

- The Japanese, particularly, are considerably more patriotic in terms of buying home-produced goods than we are.

PETER HOLMES, CHAIRMAN, SHELL

During the First Industrial Revolution (roughly the last two quarters of the eighteenth century and the first quarter of the nineteenth century) the creation of wealth was an acceptable aim for Britain's active middle classes. The Yorkshire factory owner was very happy to see his son succeed him as a factory owner.

During mainly the second quarter of the nineteenth century there was a dramatic change of direction. A need had arisen to educate a large number of middle class sons for service in the colonies. To meet this need a large number of secondary public schools were created in the middle years of the nineteenth century. The ethos of the teaching of these schools was essentially that the supreme aim in life should be to serve. These schools admirably suited their purpose and created many thousands of fine district officers for the empire, but they totally stifled the impetus for wealth creation. It was no longer proper to create wealth; it was only proper to possess wealth.

It can be argued that these values were a continuation of the much older values held by the aristocracy and certain elements of the middle classes broke free of these stifling values and created the First Industrial Revolution. It may be that Britain was too successful in this First Industrial Revolution in that so much wealth was created that the country lost its wealth-creating impetus. The result was that Britain did not participate in the Second and Third Industrial Revolutions which followed in the second half of the nineteenth century and which were led by Germany.

The prime reason [for Britain's industrial decline] is the shift of educational direction in the second quarter of the last century. (Indeed the 1851 Great Exhibition was the high-water mark of Britain's industrial supremacy and the seeds had already been sown for decline.) A force for Britain's industrial good at this time was Prince Albert and his premature death may have contributed to the decline.

The basic need is for all parts of our society to recognise that wealth creation is an essential part of the country's life. Wealth creation should be applauded rather than denigrated or thought second class. Until quite recently it was all right to have money but never to talk about it or to create it. (The contrast with the United States' attitude has always been very marked; theirs has been a wealth-creating economy par excellence at most times in the past century.) No long-term recovery will be possible unless there is a complete change of attitude towards wealth creation in every part of our society.

Such a change *is* possible and the example of Japan in the 1960s, which did almost precisely the opposite to what Britain did, is instructive.

VISCOUNT SANDON, CHAIRMAN, DOWTY GROUP

The private sector of British industry and some of the public sector is in much better shape than it was, and this is evidenced by the leadership Britain has in the EEC growth rate. This doesn't mean, of course, that it is adequate in relation to America or Japan. However, a great deal of 'fat' has been taken out of the economy during this period – a painful exercise which we had to get right before we can absorb our surplus human assets. The one fault we are still committing, which will ultimately cost us dear if we don't curb it, is paying ourselves more than our competitors do in relation to the real growth in productivity. As to the rest of the public sector, they will ultimately have to learn the same hard lessons and suffer the same penalties in doing so. If we are really to come out on top it is worth adding that this improvement is nothing in economic terms to do with the oil bonanza. There is perhaps one other point worth making in this paragraph, and that is that we ought to stop talking about dying industries. After the cut-backs – some of them severe – what is left of the so-called dying industries have a market, are essential and are thriving. For instance steel, without Ravenscraig, would be one of the most efficient and profitable in the world. Of our decimated textile industry the residue can compete anywhere right across the whole range of products, not just at the top end of the market. It is just possible that shipbuilding, once it has trimmed its capacity to demand, might do the same, especially if governments learn not to order or authorise ships which aren't needed.

There are two specific points I would like to make which require deeper government attention. Firstly, it is essential that playing-fields are even throughout the world. Two examples of this are financial services, where regulatory provisions must not fall more heavily on protagonists in one country than another, and a further example might be in the tax treatment (incentives) of R & D right throughout the whole field from pure research to development. The second point urgently needing government attention is the shortage of skills – and there are two subdivisions of this. Firstly, there is a lack of mobility, particularly because of regional differentials in house prices, and partly because of shortage of rentable accommodation. If ever a piece of legislation achieved exactly the opposite effect to what was intended, it was the 1916 Rent Act, copied throughout many parts of the world and disastrous in its consequences. The subsequent legislation has ensured that entering into the private sector business of rented accommodation is just not worthwhile economically – quite apart from the hassle. The second aspect is training and re-training. The golden opportunity of the early eighties was missed, but it is not too late to start out now on a new tack. If unemployment benefits are equal to two-fifths of the average industrial wage, why cannot the grant of that amount of money be dependent for, say, people under the age of forty-five, on undergoing an up-grading course for those two

373

days a week? I do not accept the common belief that most unskilled people are incapable of absorbing a skill. War-time service taught me exactly the opposite. Given mobility and the will, any skilled man or woman can find a worthwhile and productive job.

SIR COLIN CORNESS, CHAIRMAN, REDLAND

My experience during thirty years in industry has been almost wholly gained within the construction industry and is not likely, therefore, to be typical or generally representative. I say this because the construction industry is essentially a service industry reflecting the needs of other sectors of the economy and not, of itself, an object (rather it is a consequence) of government policies.

Subject to that important proviso, I offer the following personal opinions of the main factors contributing to Britain's relative industrial decline in a world context.

- Failure by governments (at least since the end of the Second World War but probably from earlier times) to adopt and maintain any consistent strategy towards industry. This can be explained, perhaps, by our adversarial style of politics and by the short-term perspective of most politicians but it has to be noted also that, even within the life of any one government, there has been scant attention given to the maintenance of consistent policies, e.g. as to the tax treatment of industrial investment.

- A lack of a sense of urgency within the City and within industry itself about the need to invest in new and improved technology even where that technology was invented or developed in Britain. This neglect can be partly attributed to complacency arising from historical factors such as the Industrial Revolution and the wealth generated out of the former British Empire; but it must also be seen in the context of the way in which our financial systems favour short-term returns rather than long-term investment, as in Japan and West Germany.

- Resistance to change among both managements and trade unions, matched by inadequate reeducation and training programmes designed to make such change easier and more acceptable to those involved.

- Confiscatory taxation regimes which have blunted the willingness of investors to take risks in the hope of achieving worthwhile rewards.

374

- The culture in our educational system, particularly in the private sector, that esteems employment in the professions and in service sectors as preferable to industry.

Having put forward these general observations, I must say at once that the construction industry does not suffer to any greatly apparent extent from these negative influences. Indeed, it is remarkable how our industry has flourished throughout the world in spite of (maybe it is because of!) the severe limitations imposed upon it within the British economy. Hence, there has been an enormous increase in the construction industry's contribution to the British balance of payments by virtue of direct investment overseas and the undertaking of international contracts by British construction companies. I mention this to demonstrate that adverse conditions in the home market can often create the right climate for a more venturesome attitude towards international business.

It is manifestly the job of governments to set the right climate for a reversal of the downward trends of British industry. Strategic planning is needed to establish which goods and services Britain is best positioned to supply to world markets. These targets then need to be reflected in the entire educational process and in our national investment priorities, both public and private. There then needs to be steadfast, disciplined and consistent adherence to these objectives without political interference. It has to be considered whether such a result could not best be brought about by way of the adoption of a new election process based upon proportional representation. As to the other major actions required, they are essentially the converse of the negative factors summarised above.

Some specific additional measures could include a shift in the balance of taxation to favour long-term wealth creation at the expense of short-term speculative gains, an enhancement of the status of the education profession and a genuine enlargement of the principle of industrial co-ownership designed to secure long-term integration of our society.

BOB SCHOLEY, CHAIRMAN, BRITISH STEEL

In our own industry it is evident that the technical leadership and market preeminence of Britain in steel in the middle of the last century has been progressively eroded as others – some countries with better raw material

375

resources and some with bigger domestic markets – developed their production. This process accelerated after the Second World War when the Japanese expansion coincided with the development of oxygen steel-making which they installed on a large scale, whilst the slightly earlier UK post-war steel development effort had been based on the open-hearth process which rapidly became obsolescent.

The crunch time came for us, as for many industries, in the late seventies and early eighties. First we experienced a substantial increase in imports from other European Community countries shortly before and immediately following UK entry. Then the two oil price crises in 1974 and 1979 gravely affected demand throughout the industrial world. In the UK, steel consumption fell by 25 per cent between the years 1979 and 1982 alone. This scene confronted us with the need for drastic restructuring for survival. This included the requirement radically to tackle excess capacity compared with foreseeable demand, a string of technically uncompetitive plants, and over-manning by international standards even in the more modern and technically good plants.

SIR ALEX JARRATT, CHAIRMAN, SMITHS INDUSTRIES (FROM THE 1986 HENRY FORD LECTURE)

The first weakness I would identify is our apparent inability to manage and motivate people as effectively as the best of our competitors appear to do. In some ways I find this paradoxical. As an industrialist, for example, I have never been obliged to bring foreign management into a British-based business to sort it out, but I have had to do the reverse on several occasions. I have marvelled – as perhaps you have – at the response that work people can make in a crisis, whether at the level of a troubled domestic business or nationally as we witnessed during the Falklands war.

Perhaps some of the words I have used give a clue to the paradox – 'sorting out', 'response' and 'crisis' – all indicative of that oft-remarked British trait of reacting well when our 'backs are against the wall'. This is admirable, but when your back is against the wall there is nowhere else to go – the options are closed off. It is leading people forward and away from walls that management and motivation need to be about in a fast changing world, where your options are many and flexibility is at a premium.

What have been the causes of this apparent inertia until we are forced to act because of the lack of other viable alternatives? First, I think we have the attitudinal problem of not liking change, an attitude that can be found as much in the boardroom as on the shop floor. Change implies thinking through alternative business strategies and inevitably taking risks – matters I want to return to later – but as far as people are concerned it means explaining, educating, persuading and leading them in directions which disturb the comfort and reliability of their status quo. You have got to be convinced yourself to do this; you have got to have the arguments that will convince others; and you have got to have the will and the means with which to do it. Clear thinking at the top and clear communication through to the bottom: neither have been strong suits.

Secondly, we have too often built inertia into our business structures. I spent half my working life in the Civil Service so I know something about bureaucracy. Too much of our business has been bureaucratised. We have too often been over-managed and undermanaged. One of the beneficial aspects of recession is that it has caused most of us to look critically and act promptly on our overheads – and it is sad to have to say that because again it sounds like a reaction rather than an initiative. In particular it has encouraged us to seek slimmer, more decentralised, more personally accountable management structures than we had previously. In the earlier post-war years we allowed shop floor control to pass from first-line supervision to the shop stewards, and as time went on and the going remained good, we burdened operating management as a whole with the weight of top-heavy superstructures. Here, as I have said, one can see changes taking place. Even in the case of some recent mega-mergers, which would appear to be going in the opposite direction, the argument has often been the need to drive the constituent parts more effectively than was the case under previous management.

The third weakness in the management and motivation of people has, of course, been the adversarial nature of our industrial relations. This has been the weakness most commented on by people outside this country. It has acted as a major constraint on change. It has diverted management attention too often from forward thinking to immediate fire-fighting and, I suspect in some cases, given management an excuse for such diversion: 'we can't do such-and-such because the men or the union won't wear it' has sometimes been a useful alibi for inaction.

It is easy to lay the blame for a long record of industrial disruption at the door of the trade unions. In part, it is justified. For too long they appeared to be more concerned with their survival as individual institutions than with playing a constructive role in strengthening the manufacturing businesses in which their members gained employment. For too long, they sought to bring their prime influence to bear at the political rather than the industrial level at which the main interests of their members really belonged. And for too long, they were able to operate within a framework of law which gradually increased their immunities until they were virtually immune from all legal redress to an extent not shared by any other institution.

But management has its share of the blame. Too many top executives thought that a friendly relationship with the general secretary was synonymous with, or a passport to, good industrial relations. Too few boards took sufficient interest – if they took interest at all – in the employee relations in their own companies. Too few negotiators had an adequate brief on what their company or industry required as distinct from instructions on how to respond to what the unions demanded, often only to be withdrawn or watered down when trouble began to brew. And too few managements showed enough interest, enough trust, enough initiative, to encourage their work people to see themselves as their employees rather than the unions' members.

Much of this has now changed, some of it dramatically. But importantly, the mechanisms of change have, at least initially, been exerted from outside, namely, changes in the law and changes in the level of employment. The truly constructive mechanisms have still to be fully developed and herein lies one of our greatest opportunities that I will be returning to later.

One reason underlying our relatively poor performance in managing and motivating people constitutes the second weakness I would point to in British manufacturing industry. We have lacked the professionalism, the dedication to training and development, the rigorous pursuit of high performance in management that typifies the best of our competitors. I am talking here not only of people skills, but those that maximise the use of all the resources that are brought into the production and selling process.

In part, again, the problem has been attitudinal. Perhaps still a touch of the old-fashioned prejudice in favour of the gifted amateur rather than the work-tempered professional. A belief in the virtues of 'working by Nellie' compared with learning from books or from courses. A belief that managers emerge by some generalised process of experience rather than being created by a constructive process of development which certainly includes experience in his own environment, but which will expose him to other environments, as well as enhance his skills through training in a wider variety of ideas, concepts and techniques. . .

We have been slow in coming to terms with this much more rigorous professionalism. It shows itself in the lesser importance we have attached to management education, including in some companies almost a distrust of post-graduate degrees in business on the grounds that they are too academically based, produce people who are 'too clever by half' and who, consequently, take themselves off to pastures where their enhanced skills are more readily appreciated and rewarded.

It shows itself in the lack, in many organisations, of structured programmes of management appraisal, training and development. I have come across this repeatedly in my personal experience, but I am also pleased to say that more recently I have been witnessing, both in business and in my contacts with several management schools, a recognition of the urgent need to get such programmes in place.

Finally it has shown itself in our system of rewards. In too many cases, reward has been based on a salary determined as much by seniority and by comparability with what is being paid elsewhere as any other factors – often with the help of complicated formulae devised by consultants – a satisfactory pension, and a selection of fringe benefits that appeal to one's sense of status and, hopefully, do not appeal to the Inland Revenue. Performance-related reward, unless you are a pieceworker or a salesman, has been the exception rather than the rule. The company whose name is associated with this lecture is a notable exception, as has often been pointed out to me by its managers!

But here again things are changing. In the last two or three years I have witnessed a marked increase in the use of performance-related payments to management, including the executive directors of boards. I cannot say that all the systems adopted will necessarily produce the results they were designed to achieve; there is a lot of experimentation going on. The important thing, however, is that the need to link pay and performance at the highest levels in a company is now being recognised.

A third area of weakness that has contributed to the problems of manufacturing industry in this country is that of our length of vision. I acknowledge immediately that external circumstances have often not helped here – the era of rapidly rising inflation; the more recent period of acute volatility in currencies and interest rates; major changes in government policies, certainly as between the major political parties, but also by governments during their periods of office.

379

It has increasingly shown itself in financial markets and has done so in two ways. First, the importance attached to short-term performance by stockbrokers' analysts, the business columns of the press and institutional fund managers – each being fuelled in turn by a public, including the trustees of our own company pension funds, seeking the maximum return in the shortest possible time. Secondly, we now have the phenomenon of financial flows crossing the world at the speed of a micro-chip, seeking the marginally higher returns that may be available, and far outweighing in value and importance – in terms of their effects on currencies and interest rates – the flow of physical goods in world trade.

None of this encourages long-term thinking and planning, sometimes the very reverse.

At the end of the day it is the problems and opportunities of coping with change that lie at the heart of the future for British manufacturing industry. There is no inherent reason why we should not be successful, no major impediments in terms of resources or geography or even political stability. The key lies within ourselves, and particularly those who work in manufacturing now and will do so in the future.

Appendix 3

LEADERSHIP SURVEY

When asked if there was a decline in industrial leadership between 1950 and 1980, the respondents replied:

	per cent		per cent
Yes	79	No	21

Asked to identify the chief contributory factors in the decline of leadership over this period, the response was:

	per cent
Lack of vision and imagination	40
Remoteness	21
Poor technical competence (including financial)	19
Lack of dedication	11
Lack of honesty and integrity	9

When asked if there has been a revival of industrial leadership in recent years the response was:

	per cent		per cent
Yes	81	No	19

Identifying the prime factors behind the perceived rise in leadership the following were identified as improved elements:

	per cent
Vision and imagination	26
Visibility	21
Technical and financial competence	21
Courage	16
Dedication	9
Honesty and integrity	6

Bibliography

Abernathy, William; Clark, Kim and Kantrow, Alan, *Industrial Renaissance*, Basic Books, 1983

Anderson, Perry *et al.*, *Towards Socialism*, Ithaca Cornell University Press, 1966

Barnes, Dennis and Reid, Eileen, *Government and Trade Unions*, Gower, 1980

Barnett, Correlli, *The Audit of War*, Macmillan, 1986

Batstone *et al.*, *New Technology and the Process of Labour Regulation*, Clarendon Press, 1987

Beynon, Huw, *Working For Ford*, Penguin, 1973

Blackaby, F T (ed.), *British Economic Policy*, Cambridge University Press, 1978

Cahill, J and Ingram, P, *Changes In Working Practices in British Manufacturing Industry in the 1980s*, Confederation of British Industry, 1987

Chatterton, Allan and Leonard, Ray, *How to Avoid the British Disease*, Northgate Publishing, 1979

Crosland, Anthony, *Socialism Now*, Jonathan Cape, 1974

Dahrendorf, Ralf, *On Britain*, BBC Books, 1982

Dicey, A V, *Law and Public Opinion in England 1914*, Transaction Books, 1981.

Dicken, P, *Global Shift*, Harper & Row, 1986

European Economic Community, *Small and Medium-Sized Enterprises and Employment Creation in the EEC*, 1987

Francis, Arthur, *Internationalisation and Competitiveness*, Imperial College, London, 1987

Galbraith, J K, *The New Industrial Estate*, Penguin, 1967

Garratt, Bob, *The Learning Organisation*, Fontana, 1987

Goldsmith, Walter and Berry, Ritchie, *The New Elite*, Weidenfeld & Nicolson, 1987

Granick, David, *The European Executive*, Ayer Co. Publications, 1962

Hannah, L, *The Rise of the Corporate Economy*, Methuen, 1983

Handy, Charles, *The Making of Managers*, NEDO Books, 1987

Harrigan, Kathryn Rudie, *Strategies For Declining Businesses*, Lexington Books, 1980

Heller, Robert, *The State of Industry*, BBC Books, 1987

Henderson, Sir Nicholas, *Channels and Tunnels*, Weidenfeld and Nicolson, 1987

Institute of Economic Affairs, *New patterns of Work*, 1987

Jenkins, Clive and Sherman, Barrie, *The Collapse of Work*, Eyre Methuen, 1979

Johnson, R W, *The Politics of Recession*, Macmillan, 1985

Juran, J M, *Quality Control Handbook*, McGraw-Hill, 1951

Kakabadse, Andrew, *The Politics of Management*, Gower, 1983

Lloyd, T O, *Empire to Welfare State*, Oxford University Press, 1986

Lorenz, Christopher, *The Design Dimension*, Blackwell, 1986

MacInnes, Dr John, *The Question of Flexibility*, Department of Social Economic Research, University of Glasgow, 1987

Mill, J S, *Principles of Political Economy*, 1865 edition

Nairn, Tom, *The Break Up of Britain*, Verso Editions, 1982

Nelson, R and Clutterbuck, D, *Turnaround*, Mercury Books (WH Allen), 1988.

Ovenden, Anthony, *Competitiveness in UK Manufacturing Industry*, BIM, 1986

Pearson, Richard; Hunt, Rosemary and Parsons, David, *Education, Training and Employment*, Gower, 1984

Peters, Tom and Austin, Nancy, *A Passion for Excellence*, Collins, 1985

Porter, Michael, *Competitive Advantage*, Collier Macmillan, 1985

Routh, G G C, *Occupation and Pay 1900–79*, Macmillan, 1980

Sampson, Anthony, *The Changing Anatomy of Britain*, Hodder and Stoughton, 1982

Seaman, L C B, *A New History of England*, B & N Imports, 1982

Smith, Adam, *The Wealth of Nations*, 1776

Walker, W B et al., *Technical Innovation and British Economic performance*, Macmillan, 1980

Wiener, Martin, *English Culture and the Decline of the Industrial Spirit 1850–1980*, Cambridge University Press 1981

Williams, Shirley, *Politics Is For People*, Penguin, 1981

Index

385